A SURVEY OF LINGUISTIC SCIENCE

A SURVEY OF
LINGUISTIC SCIENCE

Edited By William Orr Dingwall

 GREYLOCK PUBLISHERS

Stamford, Connecticut

Printed in the United States of America.
Library of Congress Catalog Card Number: 78-60709.
ISBN: 0-89223-014-2 (hard cover).
ISBN: 0-89223-015-0 (soft cover).

For My Mother

CONTENTS

Preface

LINGUISTIC THEORY

1 *Generative Phonology*   1
   THEODORE M. LIGHTNER

2 *Historical Linguistics*   33
   PAUL KIPARSKY

3 *Linguistic Metatheory*   63
   BARBARA HALL PARTEE

4 *Mathematical Linguistics*   83
   ROBERT E. WALL

5 *Computational Linguistics*   97
   CHARLES J. RIEGER

TRANSITION

6 *Towards a Reconstruction of the*
     Methodology of Experimental Linguistics   135
   WILLIAM ORR DINGWALL

EXPERIMENTAL LINGUISTICS

7 *Experimental Phonetics*   159
   CHIN-WU KIM

8 *Neurolinguistics*   207
   WILLIAM ORR DINGWALL AND HARRY A. WHITAKER

9 *Experimental Psycholinguistics*   247
   PHILIP B. GOUGH AND RANDY L. DIEHL

10 *Developmental Psycholinguistics*   267
   DAN I. SLOBIN

11 *Second-Language Acquisition* 317
    STEPHEN KRASHEN

12 *Sociolinguistics* 339
    WILLIAM LABOV

13 *Evolution of Speech and Language* 377
    PHILIP LIEBERMAN

TOPIC INDEX 397

Contributors

DINGWALL, William Orr
Linguistics Program
University of Maryland
College Park, Md. 20742

GOUGH, Philip B./
   DIEHL, Randy L.
Dept. of Psychology
University of Texas
Austin, Texas 78712

KIM, Chin-Wu
Dept. of Linguistics
University of Illinois
Urbana, Illinois 61801

KIPARSKY, Paul
Dept. of Linguistics
Massachusetts Institute of
   Technology
Cambridge, Mass. 02139

KRASHEN, Stephen
Dept. of Linguistics
University of Southern
   California
Los Angeles, Cal. 90007

LABOV, William
Dept. of Linguistics
University of Pennsylvania
Philadelphia, Penn. 19174

LIEBERMAN, Philip
Dept. of Linguistics
Brown University
Providence, R.I. 02912

LIGHTNER, Theodore M.
Dept. of Linguistics
University of Texas
Austin, Texas 78712

PARTEE, Barbara Hall
Dept. of Linguistics
University of Massachusetts
Amherst, Mass. 01002

RIEGER, Charles J.
Dept. of Computer Science
University of Maryland
College Park, Md. 20742

SLOBIN, Dan I.
Dept. of Psychology
University of California
Berkeley, Cal. 94720

WALL, Robert E.
Dept. of Linguistics
University of Texas
Austin, Texas 78712

WHITAKER, H. A.
Dept. of Psychology
University of Rochester
Rochester, N.Y. 14627

PREFACE TO THE FIRST EDITION

Linguists are often asked by students and prospective students, by colleagues in psychology, speech and hearing, English, education and other related areas as well as by interested laymen to suggest some source which will provide them with an overview of linguistic science today—the areas in which the majority of research is being done, various trends within these areas, how these areas interrelate to one another, and the direction in which the science as a whole is moving. Unfortunately, no really adequate source of such information is currently available. By general agreement, there is no introductory text of the breadth and depth of coverage displayed in the classics of Bloomfield [1933. Language. New York: H. Holt & Co.] and Hockett [1958. A course in modern linguistics. New York: The Macmillan Co.] which are now in large part outdated. Collections of readings, of which a number have been published recently, are generally confined to one area and often do not reflect views which are current. Finally, such surveys of the field as are available are either outdated due to lags in the submission of papers and their publication or hopelessly superficial in content. [Two important exceptions to this general statement have happily come into being since this *Survey* was planned: (1) John Lyons (ed.). 1970. New horizons in linguistics. Baltimore: Penguin Books, Inc. and (2) Richard O'Brien (ed.) . 1971. 22nd annual round table. Linguistics: Developments of the sixties— viewpoints for the seventies. Washington, D.C.: Georgetown U. Press.] There is no review (annual or otherwise) of the field of linguistics such as exists in anthropology, psychology, biology, etc. It is hoped that this *Survey* will, at least in part, fill the lacunae discussed above by providing an up-to-date and comprehensive appraisal of linguistic science and that it may establish a tradition of periodic reviews of the field in the future.

The following ten areas have been chosen for review:
(1) EXPERIMENTAL PHONETICS
(2) NEUROLINGUISTICS
(3) EXPERIMENTAL PSYCHOLINGUISTICS
(4) DEVELOPMENTAL PSYCHOLINGUISTICS
(5) METHODOLOGY
(6) GENERATIVE PHONOLOGY
(7) HISTORICAL LINGUISTICS
(8) LINGUISTIC METATHEORY
(9) MATHEMATICAL LINGUISTICS
(10) COMPUTATIONAL LINGUISTICS

These areas constitute in the opinion of the editor and a number of his colleagues the foci of major research interest in linguistics today. Still, it is inevitable, in a field as vast as linguistics has become, that many important topics have been neglected. Perhaps by varying the selection of subdisciplines to be dealt with in future surveys, as is presently done, e.g., in the *Annual review of psychology*, this necessary evil can be overcome.

Preliminary drafts of the reviews contained in this volume were presented at a conference at the University of Maryland on the 8th and 9th of May, 1971. An edited version of the discussion which took place at this conference is included in the belief that such an exchange of views often provides an extremely helpful and revealing elucidation of the issues touched upon. In these discussions as well as elsewhere throughout the *Survey*, an attempt has been made to provide as extensive and explicit bibliographical coverage as possible as an aid to the reader who wishes to undertake further research.

In selecting reviewers, three basic criteria were employed: (1) recognized scholarship in the subdiscipline involved, (2) the degree of *distance* needed to provide a reasonably objective review and (3) lucidity of prose style. Each reviewer was asked to present, in as unbiased a manner as possible, his opinions on the current state of the subdiscipline assigned to him and the direction in which he believes future progress will lie. No strict limits were placed on the length of the written presentations.

Considering the great diversity in interests and training manifested among the reviewers, it might have been expected that there would be little consensus in their judgments of the current state of linguistics and its future prospects; at least there should have been a noticeable divergence in views between those engaged in the more empirical undertakings represented by areas (1) through (5) above as opposed to those whose interests lay in the more theoretical realms represented by (6) through (10). Although the latter cleavage at times was evident, there was a surprising degree of unanimity among the participants on such points as the following:

[1] that work within the Chomskyan paradigm has resulted in a general increase in our knowledge of the nature of language;

[2] that the "standard theory" of transformational grammar fails to account for many important aspects of natural language;

[3] that the "standard theory" exceeds the generative capacity necessary to describe natural language;

[4] that many current proposals for revising the theory are *ad hoc* in nature and serve to expand rather than limit the power of the theory;

[5] that within a theoretical framework with rules of the power of transformations, there is no way to decide

among alternative hypotheses;

[6] that one way of constraining the theory is by expanding the range of data for which it is held accountable by taking into regard the results of allied disciplines such as psychology, experimental phonetics, neurology, sociology, etc.;

[7] that formalization should not be (but often is) confused with explanation in linguistics;

[8] that increased reliance on experimental method is desirable.

Although many, alas most, aspects of language remain as obscure as ever, agreement on such points surely offers some hope that one day linguists in company with other scholars working within the "human" sciences will at last discover the essence of this most distinctive characteristic of man.

Finally, acknowledgment should be accorded the Office of Education of the U.S. Department of Health, Education and Welfare [Contract No. OEC-0-71-2412 (823)] and the University of Maryland for providing partial financial support for this undertaking. In addition, I wish to personally express my gratitude to Norma J. Raymond for an excellent job of typing what was a most difficult and variform manuscript, to my former student, Donald E. Crook, and my Mother for assuming the arduous task of proofreading with me the final camera-ready version and to the faculty and staff of the Computer Science Center of the University of Maryland, in particular Richard G. Oden, for their assistance in ways too numerous to mention.

W. O. D.

Bethesda, Maryland
August 1971

PREFACE TO THE SECOND EDITION

Although the first edition of the *Survey of Linguistic Science* has been out of print for several years, it continues to be widely cited and demand for copies from institutions and individuals continues to be high. For these reasons, it was decided to reissue the *Survey* in a revised and expanded version. The original contributors were given the option of either revising their papers if they felt up-dating was necessary or leaving them substantially unchanged if they did not. Professors Lightner *(Generative Phonology)*, Partee *(Linguistic Metatheory)*, Gough and Diehl *(Experimental Psycholinguistics)* and Labov *(Sociolinguistics)* have all revised their original contributions in various ways. The papers by Professors Kiparsky *(Historical Linguistics)*, Wall *(Mathematical Linguistics)*, Kim *(Experimental Phonetics)* and Slobin *(Developmental Psycholinguistics)* are reprinted here in their original form. Joyce Friedman decided to withdraw her paper on computational linguistics because of insufficient time for carrying out the revisions she felt were warranted. In addition, a number of new papers has been added. Three of these replace contributions on roughly the same topic in the first edition, viz., Charles Rieger *(Computational Linguistics)*, W.O. Dingwall *(Methodology)* and W.O. Dingwall and H.A. Whitaker *(Neurolinguistics)*. This latter paper is a slightly revised version of a chapter with the same title in the Annual Review of Anthropology, Vol. 3 and is reprinted here with the permission of the publisher. Two new topics have been added to the original list, viz., *Second-Language Acquisition* and *Evolution of Speech and Language* which are discussed by Stephen Krashen and Philip Lieberman respectively.

Finally, the volume has been reorganized so that the reader is first introduced to various aspects of linguistic theory. Next, in a transitional paper, it is shown how such a theory can be integrated into an experimental framework for the investigation of data. Then, in the final section, some of the fruits of such an approach are surveyed under the rubric of experimental linguistics. It is in the realization of this feedback relationship between theory and experimentation that hope for substantial progress in linguistic science surely lies.

W.O.D.

Bethesda, Maryland
February 1977

Chapter One

Generative Phonology

Theodore M. Lightner

In this paper I shall try to outline as briefly as possible (Section 1) the position taken by Chomsky, Halle, and their adherents in the early 1960's, and then (Section 2) to present a few of the revisions that have been proposed for this theory. Next (Section 3) I give a sample of some current problems in phonology. I have chosen topics that particularly interest me, and there are numerous omissions (for example, I do not discuss many types of notational conventions, markedness, "linking" rules, etc.). A complex problem in morphophonology is given next (Section 4), leading to the conclusion (Section 5).

1. The Position of the Early 1960's.

The phonological component of a grammar was considered to consist of two (or perhaps three) types of re-writing rules:

(i) *Morpheme-structure rules.* In English, for example, it was claimed that there is a rule that when a morpheme begins with two obstruents, the first of these is *s* (as in *stick, spot, school, sphere,* and so on).[1]

(ii) *Phonological rules.* These rules account for alternations that occur in the phonetic representation of morphemes that are joined together to form words (and in a few cases larger units such as *NP, VP, S*).[2] Thus, for example, in the pair *electric* ∿ *electricity*, one finds stress alternation and *k* ∿ *s* alternation.

(iii) *Late phonetic rules.* For example, in English the [g] of *goose* is articulated at a point farther back in the oral tract the [ǵ] of *geese*. Again, word-initial voiced consonants in English begin with voiceless onset. Again, there are some "lazy velum" dialects of English in which words like *ample* and *apple* are minimal pairs, distinguished solely by the fact that the first vowel in *ample* is more fully nasalized than the first vowel in *apple*. Fine phonetic detail of this type[3] was rarely mentioned in phonological discussions of the early 1960's. The rules accounting for this detail were not explicity considered to be at a distinct level of phonology, but one can observe, as in the examples given above, that one is here often forced to extend the purely binary feature specifications to *n*-ary specifications.

Phonetic representations are considered to be segmentable into discrete units. These segments are defined as bundles of features, the features being for the most part given previously by Roman Jakobson and revised slightly in Jakobson, Fant, and Halle—features like ±*nasal,* ±*voiced,* ±*grave,* ±*compact,* ±*vocalic,* etc.

A precise format for writing phonological rules in given:

(1) $A \rightarrow B \; / \; X[\underset{C}{\underline{\quad\quad}}]Y$

where the arrow is to be interpreted as *is specified* and the slash (/) as *in the environment.*

Thus, for example, if one wants to write a rule to drop post- consonantal word-final liquids in verbs, the rule may be written roughly as follows:

(2) $\begin{bmatrix} + \text{vocal} \\ + \text{cons} \end{bmatrix} \rightarrow \varnothing \; / \; C\begin{bmatrix} \underline{\quad\quad} \\ +\text{VERB} \end{bmatrix}\#,$

where $\varnothing$ represents   *zero*[4]   and   #   represents *word-boundary.*

Such a rule is required in Modern Russian, for example, where the representation *mog* + 1 = l is realized as *mog* 'he was able', but the representations *krug* + 1 = l and *rubl'* are realized as *krugl* 'round' and *rubl'* 'rouble', respectively (details in Lightner 1972, henceforth *PTP*, and 1973a).

The rules are considered to be partially (or perhaps fully) ordered. In Slavic, for example, velars shift to the corresponding palatals before front vowels, and *ē* in position after a palatal shifts to *ā*. The rules are as given below and must apply in the order shown:

(3) $\{k, g, x\} \rightarrow \{\check{c}, \check{3}, \check{s}\} \; / \; \underline{\quad\quad\quad}\ddot{V}$
(4) $\bar{e} \rightarrow \bar{a} \; / \; \{\check{c}, \check{3}, \check{s}\} \; \underline{\quad\quad\quad}$

As a somewhat more complex example, consider the following three rules of Tübatulabal: a rule of alternate lengthening, a rule of secondary shortening, and a rule of word-final devoicing. The rules must apply in that order. The rule of alternate lengthening lengthens every other vowel, starting with the beginning of the world, but the provision that a vowel next to an underlying long vowel may not be lengthened; the rule of secondary shortening shortens a vowel before a voiceless segment; and the word-final devoicing rule devoices word-final obstruents. A sample derivation is given below (for specific forms and details on the rules, see Swadesh and Voegelin 1939):

underlying representation	t V p V b V g V k V l V k V p V d V g V b
alternate lengthening:	V̄　　　V̄　　　　　　　　　　V̄　　　V̄
secondary shortening:	V　　　　　　　V
final devoicing:	p
phonetic representation:	t V p V b V̄ g V k V l V k V p V d V g V̄ b

There was really nothing new in all this; all the devices mentioned so far could be found, for example, in some of the works of Bloomfield or Sapir. Descriptions formulated in this framework had a superficial novelty because of their extreme explicitness and also, of course, because most of the work in phonology at this time avowed allegiance to a theory of phonemics, a level of representation whose existence was explicitly denied by Chomsky and Halle.[5]

Nor was there anything new in the *evaluation criterion* (discussed briefly a few paragraphs below). All linguists had an intuitive feeling that one description of a set of data might be more highly valued than another description of the same set of data. In many cases—if the descriptions were very close, for example—linguists might not agree on which of the two descriptions should be more highly valued; but in extreme cases, linguists would agree. The novelty of the Chomsky-Halle evaluation criterion is that it was precise: it permitted (or it seemed as if it would permit) one to evaluate two very similar descriptions.

What was new in the framework of the early 1960's was the overall view of grammar. It was considered to be composed of three components: syntax, semantics, and phonology. The *syntactic component* was subdivided into a *phrase-structure grammar* and a *transformational grammar*. Transformations did not change meaning (Katz & Postal, 1964), so that the *semantic component* operated on the output of the phrase-structure grammar. The *phonological component* operated on the output of the transformational grammar:

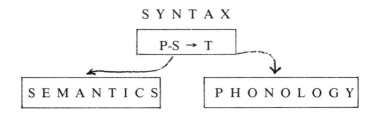

Fig. 1. The relation between sound and meaning in the early 1960's.

The syntactic component was thus the central device of the grammar; the phonological component and the semantic component were ancillary, interpretive techniques which linked sound and meaning.

One might add also that a precise way of handling exceptions was proposed: one marked exceptions in the lexicon as not undergoing certain rules. Thus, for example, one finds in Russian the following three rules: the shift of velars to palatals before front vowels (mentioned above), the palatalization of consonants before front vowels, and the shift of short *e* to *o* before non-palatalized consonants. With velar stems, one has, typically, derivations of the following type:

underlying representation: pek + u   ped + e + t

$$
\begin{aligned}
&(K \rightarrow \check{C})\text{:} \quad \underline{\hspace{2cm}} \quad \check{c} \\
&(C \rightarrow C')\text{:} \quad p' \qquad\quad p'e\check{c}' + e + t \\
&(e \rightarrow o)\text{:} \quad\; o \qquad\quad\;\; o
\end{aligned}
$$

phonetic representation: p'oku   p'eč'ot

There is, however, an exception: one finds 1 sg *tku* parallel to *p'oku*, but not 3 sg **tč'ot* parallel to *p'eč'ot*. The 3 sg of this verb is *tk'ot*, with the velar intact. The root is marked as an idiosyncratic exception to rule $(K \rightarrow \check{C})$; from underlying *tk + e + t* the other two rules apply to derive the correct phonetic representation *tk'ot*.

Finally, a device for handling assimilation and dissimilation was proposed: the *alpha-convention*. Greek letters are used as variables ranging over the values of + (plus) and − (minus). Suppose, for example, that one wants to write a rule which assimilates the voicing of an obstruent to that of a following obstruent. The rule is written as follows:

$$
(5) \quad [+\text{obstr}] \rightarrow [\alpha\text{voice}] \quad / \quad \underline{\hspace{2cm}} \begin{bmatrix} +\text{obstr} \\ \alpha\text{voice} \end{bmatrix}
$$

In concluding these brief remarks on the theory of the early 1960's, let us return to the evaluation criterion and give a couple of examples to show how it works. The criterion is simple: for any two descriptions cast in the same theoretical framework and covering the same amount of data, one simply counts the number of feature-specifications in each description. The description with less feature-specifications is the more highly valued description. This is sometimes called the "simplicity criterion."

Consider, for example, a language in which word-final obstruents are always realized as voiceless. If a word-final obstruent is voiceless in underlying representation, then, of course, no change occurs; a change occurs only in those obstruents which are voiced in underlying representation. One might, therefore, propose the following rule:

$$(6) \quad \begin{bmatrix} + \text{obstr} \\ + \text{voice} \end{bmatrix} \rightarrow [-\text{voice}] \; / \; \underline{\hspace{1cm}} \; \#$$

But if the *+ voice* specification to the left of the arrow is suppressed, then the same phonetic representations are derived; the difference is that in this second description, given below in (7), the rule applies vacuously to the representation of a word ending in a voiceless obstruent.

$$(7) \quad [+\text{obstr}] \rightarrow [-\text{voice}] \; / \; \underline{\hspace{1cm}} \; \#$$

Since rule (7) contains one feature-specification less than rule (6), rule (7) is more highly valued than rule (6).

A more complicated example is found in Sanskrit, where underlying *s* is retroflected if preceded by *u, i, k,* or *r.* One's instinct—my instinct, at least—is to write the rule with three separate environments.

$$(8) \quad s \rightarrow \d{s} \; / \quad \left\{ \begin{array}{l} \{u, i\} \; \underline{\hspace{1.5cm}} \\ k \; \underline{\hspace{1.5cm}} \\ r \; \underline{\hspace{1.5cm}} \end{array} \right.$$

Actually, the situation is not quite this bad because *l* never appears before *s,* so that one can replace *r* by *L* (= any liquid), and before *s* the only velar or palatal that occurs is *k,* so that one can replace *k* by the archisegment characterizing any palatal or velar. Using the features of the early 1960's, the rule can therefore be written along the following lines:

$$(9) \quad s \rightarrow \d{s} \; / \quad \left\{ \begin{array}{l} \begin{bmatrix} + \text{vocal} \\ - \text{cons} \\ - \text{comp} \end{bmatrix} \underline{\hspace{1cm}} \\[6pt] \begin{bmatrix} + \text{vocal} \\ + \text{cons} \end{bmatrix} \underline{\hspace{1cm}} \\[6pt] \begin{bmatrix} - \text{vocal} \\ + \text{comp} \end{bmatrix} \underline{\hspace{1cm}} \end{array} \right.$$

The evaluation criterion, however, excludes (9) as a possible description because there exists another description which contains less feature specifications, namely the one given below (from Zwicky 1964):

$$(10) \quad s \rightarrow \d{s} \; / \quad \begin{bmatrix} \alpha\text{vocal} \\ - \alpha\text{comp} \end{bmatrix} \underline{\hspace{1cm}}$$

In other words, the theory forces one to consider *i, u, r, k* before *s* as a natural class in Sanskrit. If one does not like this description, not much can be done: the theory required this description, and one could either accept the description or provide a new theory. Since new theories are hard to come by, most accepted the description of (10). Many, in fact, pointed out that situations like this gave confirmation to the correctness of the theory, in that the theory could give a straightforward account of well-attested phenomena like the retroflection of *s* in Sanskrit.

2. Refinements of the Early 1960's Theory.

2.1 Consider first the proposal of Emmon Bach (1968). We return to the case of velars in English. Bach observed that it was not only before front vowels (*keep, geese*) that velars were fronted but also after front vowels (*leak, league* vs. *Luke, fugue*); he calls this *statement I*. Within the early 1960's framework, one had to write a rule something like the following:

$$(11) \quad [+\text{comp}] \rightarrow [\alpha\text{grave}] \; / \; \left\{ \begin{array}{l} \begin{bmatrix} -\text{cons} \\ \alpha\text{grave} \end{bmatrix} \underline{\hspace{2cm}} \\[1em] \underline{\hspace{2cm}} \begin{bmatrix} -\text{cons} \\ \alpha\text{grave} \end{bmatrix} \end{array} \right.$$

Bach writes "It is apparent that we have here another Case of the Missing Generalization. For the simplicity metric, making use of current abbreviatory devices, would evaluate the above rule in exactly the same way as a rule we might write to express the following hypothetical statement: *II*—a velar stop varies in graveness according to the graveness of a preceding vowel or the voicing of a following stop...I think it is obvious that *I* is a more general statement than *II*. Hence, we should be able to express *I* in a form that is evaluated more highly (given a lower measure by counting feature specifications) than *II*. My first proposal is, then, a new abbreviatory notation which can be applied in the first instance but not the second to express the greater generality of the first example and to capture the obvious fact that the same class of segments is specified in both parts of rule (11). A rule like (11) will be abbreviated by eliminating the environment dash: *a → b /c*. Let us call the convention the 'neighborhood convention'." (from p. 129).

With the introduction of the *neighborhood convention*, rule (11) can be written as follows:

$$(12) \quad [+\text{comp}] \rightarrow [\alpha\text{grave}] \; / \begin{bmatrix} -\text{cons} \\ \alpha\text{grave} \end{bmatrix}$$

As another example, consider obstruent devoicing in Tübatulabal: the devoicing is not only of word-final obstruents but also of word-initial obstruents. One finds, for example, some phonetic representations with word-initial $t-$, $p-$ etc., with related reduplicated forms in $Vd-$, $Vb-$ etc. (V represents the reduplicated vowel). The underlying representations of such forms are in $d-$ and $b-$; if these segments appear in word-initial position they are devoiced to $t-$ and $p-$; but if a vowel precedes due to reduplication, then the underlying voiced quality remains intact. Using the neighborhood convention, the rule is simply:

$$(13) \quad [+\text{obstr}] \rightarrow [-\text{voice}] \ / \ \#$$

2.2   Consider now a slightly more radical proposal for revision. Lloyd Anderson (1967) discusses two rules of Finnish:

$$(\text{GRAD-}\ \text{ATION}) \quad \left\{ \begin{array}{l} \text{tt} \rightarrow \text{t} \\ \text{kk} \rightarrow \text{k} \\ \text{t} \rightarrow \text{d} \\ \cdot \\ \cdot \\ \cdot \end{array} \right\} / \underline{\hspace{1cm}} \text{V (i) C} \left\{ \begin{array}{l} \# \\ \text{C} \end{array} \right\}$$

$$(\text{DELETION}) \quad \text{t} \rightarrow \emptyset \ / \ \text{V} \underline{\hspace{1cm}} \text{V}$$

For example, the gradation rule applies twice to underlying *ohtakkeh*, resulting in phonetic *ohdakeh* 'thistle'. To underlying *talota* the deletion rule applies to give phonetic *taloa* 'house (part. sg.)'. The question is: in what order do the two rules apply? Examples like *ammatin* 'profession (gen. sg.)', from underlying *ammattin*, suggest that the order must be (DELE) and then (GRAD); the reverse order of application would result in **ammain*.

But underlying *harakkatin* is realized as *harakkain* 'magpie (coll. gen. pl.)', and it is evident that the order (DELE) and then (GRAD) results in **harakain*. In fact, the correct phonetic representation cannot be derived even by reversing the order of application of the two rules, for (GRAD) and then (DELE) applied to underlying *harakkatin* results not in *harakkain* but in **harakkadin*. Evidently the following rule ordering is required:

(GRAD)   to the left of a particular vowel.
(DELE)   to the right of that vowel.
(GRAD)   to the right of that vowel.

The reader can check for himself that this set of rules results in the correct phonetic representations for all the forms presented. But it has the undesirable quality of repeating an entire rule. Anderson proposes that instead of going through the list of rules once, applying each rule throughout a phrase when it is time to apply that rule, one goes through the list once at each syllable of the phrase, beginning at the left end, applying the rules in order there, then moving to the next syllable to the right and starting again with the first rule in the list. Specifically, a mark (*) is placed before some syllabic vowel in the statement of context for application of each rule. Before the first pass through the cycles of rules is begun, the same mark (*) is placed just before the first vowel in the underlying phonological phrase to be operated on. These marks must match in position if a rule is to be applicable. Before the beginning of the next pass through the cycle of rules, the mark in the underlying phrase is shifted to lie just before the next following vowel.

With this *left-to-right syllabic cycle*, the rules are as follows:

$$\text{(GRAD)} \quad T * V \text{ (i) } C \begin{Bmatrix} C \\ \# \end{Bmatrix} \text{ produces gradation of } T.$$

$$\text{(DELE)} \quad *V \text{ t } V \text{ produces deletion of } t.$$

The derivations are as follows:

1st cycle:	*ohtakkeh	t*alota	*ammattin	h*arakkatin
GRAD:	————	————	————	————
DELE:	————	————	————	————
2nd cycle:	oht*akkeh	tal*ota	amm*attin	har*akkatin
GRAD:	d	— — — —	————	————
DELE:	————	∅	————	————
3rd cycle:	ohdakk*eh	talo*a	ammatt*in	harakk*atin
GRAD:	k	————	t	————
DELE:	————	————	————	∅
phonetic:	ohdakeh	taloa	ammatin	harakkain

It is clear that with this type of rule-application many rules will often apply vacuously. The same is true of the Chomsky-Halle theory of cyclic application of rules. For some discussion of this question see Coats and Lightner 1975, Lightner 1969.

2.3 Let us return now to the alternate lengthening rule of Tübatulabal. Within the Chomsky-Halle framework (details of which can be found in the first eight chapters of *The Sound Pattern of English*), the rule must be written approximately as follows:

$$\text{(14)} \quad V \rightarrow \bar{V} \; / \; \begin{Bmatrix} \# \\ \bar{V}CV \end{Bmatrix} \; (CVCV)_0 \; C \; \rule{1cm}{0.4pt} \; C \; \begin{Bmatrix} \# \\ V \end{Bmatrix}$$

McCawley (1969) has observed that this rule can be written in a straightforward manner if one adopts the left-to-right iterative procedure suggested by Anderson and the neighborhood convention suggested by Bach:

$$(15) \quad V \rightarrow \bar{V} \text{ except } / \text{ C } \bar{V} \text{ C } \text{[left-to-right iterative]}$$

Consider a string like C V C V C V C V C V $\bar{V}$. Rule (15) lengthens the first vowel because there is not an adjacent syllable either to the left or to the right containing a long vowel. But (15) does not apply to the second vowel because the syllable to the left now contains a long vowel. The third vowel will be lengthened. The fourth vowel will not be lengthened because the syllable to the left contains a long vowel. And, finally, the fifth vowel will not be lengthened because the syllable to the right contains a long vowel.

One must, of course, answer the question as to whether iterative application of rules and the neighborhood convention are to be incorporated within linguistic theory.

I have discussed iterative application of rules at length in PTP and argued there that *all* phonological rules should be applied iteratively. Further discussion, see Kenstowicz and Kisseberth 1973, Lightner 1971, 1976b. Let us turn now to the question of the neighborhood convention.

My initial reaction is one of wariness because there are not a large number of straightforward examples that require the use of this convention. It is important to note that the first example given by Bach—that of the point of articulation of velars in English—is not so clear-cut as Bach makes it out to be. There are not merely two points of articulation, but a very large number; as many, at least, as there are vowels. Thus before $\bar{i}$ there is one point, before *i* another, before $\bar{e}$ a third, before *e* a fourth, before *ae* a fifth, and so on. The point of articulation of the velar follows the front-back quality of the following vowels very closely. When vowels both precede and follow, the situation is, of course, even more complex. McCawley once remarked to me that he doubted that a person could consistently interchange the *k* before *e* with the *k* before *i*, pronouncing *ken* [k^{i}en] and *kin* [k^{e}in], where the vowel-superscripts indicate the point of articulation of the velar. Apparently we are dealing here with the type of rule that Postal (1968) calls *detail-rules*. That is to say, there is something basically universal about this rule; the exact details, perhaps, are language-specific.[6]

With respect to the obstruent devoicing rule (13) one can again find fault. If rule (13) is more highly valued—more to be expected—than either (16) or (17) given below, one would expect languages with either (16) or (17) to develop historically to have rule (13). But I can find no examples of such historical development (the case of Tübatulabal cannot be counted as evidence because this is the language whose analysis is in question).

$$(16) \quad [+\text{obstr}] \rightarrow [-\text{voice}] / \underline{\hspace{2cm}} \#$$
$$(17) \quad [+\text{obstr}] \rightarrow [-\text{voice}] / \# \underline{\hspace{2cm}}$$

All other things being equal, one would expect to find languages with either rule (18) or with rule (19) to develop historically to have rule (20):

(18)   [+obstr] → [+voice] / _____#

(19)   [+obstr] → [+voice] / # _____

(20)   [+obstr] → [+voice] / #

Needless to say, there are few languages with either (18) or (19), although Winnebago seems to have rule (18). I know of no language that has both (18) and (19)—i.e., the presumably highly valued rule (20).

Further discussion of the neighborhood convention, see PTP, 352-355, 366-367, and the references mentioned there.

2.4   Another problem that has been raised recently has to do with the abstractness of underlying representations. Kiparsky (1968) has proposed (roughly) that if a segment of a morpheme always has a single phonetic representation, then that phonetic representaiton must also be the underlying representation.

Consider the sequence of rules (3) and (4) mentioned in Section 1 shifting velars to palatals, and long $\bar{e}$ to $\bar{a}$ after a palatal in Russian. There are a large number of alternations which lead one to postulate such rules (details, see PTP). To give but a single example, superlative forms end in $-\bar{e}j\check{s}ij$ except for velar stems; with velar stems the superlatives end in $-\bar{a}j\check{s}ij$ and the velars appear as palatals. Thus one finds typical forms like *nov/novējšij, bogat/bogatējšij, slab/slabējšij,* and so on, but *dīk ~ dīčajšij, strog ~ strožājšij, tīx ~ tīšajšij* etc.

The problem has to do with forms like *čās* 'hour'. Regardless of what precedes or follows, the morpheme in this word is ALWAYS realized with a phonetic palatal *č* followed by the vowel *ā*.

If Kiparsky's proposal is correct, no problem arises: the underlying representation of this morpheme can only be /čās/.

But it is evident that two other underlying representations are also possible: /kēs/ or /čēs/. The advantage of choosing an abstract underlying representation like /kēs/ is that one can then predict ALL palatals from underlying velars (in some cases from dentals; details, PTP) by application of a few simple, natural, independently-motivated rules. The lexicon in this analysis will be roughly one in which any underlying segment can be contiguous to any other underlying segment (details, Lightner MS, henceforth *IEPM*).

There is, of course, another possibility that must be investigated: that underlying representations vary from speaker to speaker and that some speakers analyze [čās] as /čās/, other as /kēs/, and still others, perhaps as /čēs/.

If this is correct, then within the Chomsky-Halle-Kiparsky framework the problem is indeterminate. I should not find such a result surprising. After all, indeterminateness has been found in the physical world (as shown in some of the results of quantum theory) and in mathematics (as shown by some of the results of Gödel, Post, Turing, Church, and others in the 1930's); why should it be surprising to find indeterminateness in certain aspects of linguistics?

Acceptance of this particular notion of indeterminacy in linguistics, however, will call for revision of the notion 'grammar'. For example, linguists have distinguished what a person actually does—performance— from what a person is capable of doing—competence. A grammar up to now has been viewed as a reflection of the competence of a native speaker. Introduction of this particular notion of indeterminacy will require that a grammar be viewed as a reflection of the competence that a native speaker MIGHT have (cf. Lehmann 1975, Lightner 1975). If one goal of linguistics is to specify to at least some extent the innate intellectual capacity of man, then we will surely be interested in writing abstract grammars because these grammars will be the most interesting from a theoretical point of view. In the absence of a major breakthrough in some field like psychology or neurophysiology, it is not clear what limits to impose on the abstractness of grammar. But it is clear that the major goals of linguistics will have to be set from a different viewpoint.

2.5 James McCawley (1967) has made some interesting comments on the evaluation criterion. He suggests that the criterion mentioned above forces one to view child language-learning as a field-method analysis: the child takes in data for several years and then, when he considers that he has obtained enough raw data, begins his analysis, rejecting a solution with more feature-specifications than some other solution with fewer feature-specifications. Presumably, however, the child does not operate in this way; presumably he begins analysis the moment he begins learning. After a very short period of learning he will have constructed a grammar. By adult standards, this first grammar will be quite inadequate. Given new data, the child must revise his grammar in such a way as to keep it consistent with all the old data and yet to permit it to incorporate the new data. The basic process here, McCawley argues, is not one of minimization of feature- specifications, but rather one of changing grammars in such a way as to permit them to incorporate new data. The thing to look for, McCawley argues, is some type of constraint on how grammars can be changed; it is not at all clear if minimization of symbols plays any role whatever.

3.   A Few Problems in Analysis.

3.1 It has long been known that restricting the phonological component to apply only to surface syntactic forms prevents the derivation of certain well-formed sentences in a number of languages. It seems that at least intonation and stress are intimately connected with deeper syntactic structures. I give a few examples.

Sentences with restrictive and non-restrictive (appositive) relative clauses presumably have the same surface structure. But the intonation envelopes are different. Compare the following two sentences:

(21)   The Chinese, who are industrious, are polyglots.

(22)   The Chinese who are industrious are polyglots.

Not only intonation is involved, but stress placement as well, as can be seen from:

(23)   The industrious Chinese are polyglots.

In (23), *industrious* can have heavier stress than *Chinese* only when *industrious Chinese* is from a restrictive relative clause. More discussion, Lightner 1976a and the references mentioned there.

John R. Ross has pointed out a number of examples of this type. Consider the following ambiguous sentence:

(24)   Haj is too big to climb over.

In (24), heavy stress can go on *climb* only if *Haj* is object of *climb over*; on the other hand, heavy stress can go on *over* only if *Haj* is subject of *climb over*.

In German there is apparently a rule something like the *Nuclear Stress Rule* (NSR) in English. It places primary stress on the end of the sentence, as in:

$$1$$
(25)   Hans schrieb ein Buch.

There is also a syntactic rule which moves verbs in subordinate clauses (cf. *Weil Hans ein Buch schrieb,...* and not **Weil Hans schrieb ein Buch,...*); the main stress in such clauses, however, is still on the object:

$$1$$
(26)   Weil Hans ein Buch schrieb,...

One wants, presumably, to apply the phonological NSR before the syntactic verb-movement rule. But the Chomsky-Halle theory does not permit such an ordering.

Another example is:

(27)   John hit Harry, and then Bill hit him.

The ambiguity here centers on the word *him*. If *him* is stressed, however, *him* may refer only to *John*, whereas if *Bill* is stressed, *him* may refer only to *Harry*. This example is a bit different from the others in that the *him* is presumably indexed in the surface representation (cf., e.g., Mc-Cawley 1968).

Many further examples, all from German, are given in Bierwisch (1968).

Bresnan (1971) has considered examples somewhat like those cited above and has proposed a solution for some of these problems. Consider:

1
(28)   John left directions for Harry to follow.

1
(29)   John left directions for Harry to follow.

The meaning of (28) is that John left directions which Harry is supposed to follow, opposed to (29) which means that John left directions saying that Harry should follow. Bresnan suggests that the NSR is ordered after all syntactic transformations on each transformational cycle. With this intermixture of syntactic and phonlogical rules, one has derivations of roughly the following form:

(28)		$_s$[John	left	$_{NP}$[directions	$_s$[for Harry	to follow	directions	]$_s$]$_{NP}$]$_s$
word stress:		1	1	1	1	1	1	
cycle 1 = NSR:					2	2	1	
cycle 2 = syntax:							∅	
cycle 3 = NSY:		2	2	1	3	3		

(29)′		$_s$[John	left	$_{NP}$[directions	$_s$[for Harry	to follow	]$_s$]$_{NP}$]$_s$
word stress:		1	1	1	1	1	
cycle 1 = NSR:					2	1	
cycle 2 = NSR:				2	3	1	
cycle 3 = NSR:		2	2	3	4	1	

Bresnan writes that "the stress difference in (28) and (29) is predictable from the fact that in the deep structure of (28) *follow* has a direct object, while in (29) *follow* has no direct object and hence receives primary stress as the rightmost constituent."

This analysis is the obvious one mentioned above in connection with sentences like (25) and (26), and this analysis presumably works for those sentences. In (28) and (29), however, it is not clear that the analysis works because the underlying structure proposed for (29), i.e. (29)′, is not correct:

follow is a pure transitive and the structure of (29) should be:

(29)″ $_s$[John left $_{NP}$[directions$_s$[for Harry to follow $\begin{Bmatrix} smb \\ smth \end{Bmatrix}$]$_s$]$_{NP}$]$_s$

Evidence for the correctness of this claim comes from the fact that (29) *means* (29)″ and not (29)′. Perhaps one can sidestep this difficulty by requiring that the unspecified dummy object of *follow* is not to be stressed by the NSR.

3.2 A different type of analysis suggested by some of the work of Kisserberth seems to be relevant to some of the problems mentioned in section 3.1 above. He has shown that in some languages a rule must apply to certain segments but only if those segments are the result of application of a rule, not if those segments are underlying segments. He permits phonological rules to look back in the derivational history of forms. McCawley (1973) has proposed similar rules for tones in Bangubangu: some of his rules must refer to earlier derivational history of segments. If this approach is correct, then some of the problems mentioned above can be easily solved:

(30) Assign comma-intonation to clauses of non-restrictive origin.

(31) Put Stress on *over* if *Haj* is the subject of *climb*.

(32) Put stress on *climb* if *Haj* is the object of *climb*.

It is not clear how these so-called *global* rules differ from rules that can be applied among syntactic rules. And it is not clear how either of these two types of rules differ from using syntactic rules that place certain phonological markers on strings (the phonological rules would then refer to these dummy markers).

3.3 Consider not the exceptions mentioned in Section 1 above: 3 sg. *tkët, skët* for expected **tčët, *sčët* (the forms here are in transliteration). There are a number of 3 sg. forms from velar stems: *možet, pečët, sečët, berežët, strižët* &c. With the underlying velar intact there is only *tket* and the extremely rare form *sket* (inf. *skät*′). It is interesting to note that the two exceptions are the only forms with a consonant immediately preceding the velar. One might think, therefore, that the rule to shift velars to palatals is incorrectly formulated: it should not apply to velars in position after a consonant (one is reminded of Grimm's Law, which does not apply to obstruents following an obstruent).[7] Again, there seems to be a tendency in the development of Russian to eliminate paradigmatic alterations. Thus the imperative of a velar stem like *pek-* was at one time *peci* with a dental affricate in place of the underlying velar; today, the imperative is *peki* with the velar intact. Again, in declension one had alongside nom. sg. *ruka* forms like *ruci* and *ruče*: within a paradigm there was a *velar ∿ dental affricate ∿ palatal affricate* alternation. But today one finds only velars (*ruka, ruke, ruki*).[8] Furthermore, if (*K→Č*) were to apply to underlying *tk + e + t*, resulting in *tč + e + t*, the initial dental would assimilate to the following palatal, resulting in a phonetic representation something like *[č'č'ot]*; Dean Worth has suggested that since there are no forms with initial long palatal affricates in Russian, there would be a feedback mechanism to block the shift of velar to palatal in this form.

One can suggest, in other words, a number of possible *reasons* why the velar in *tkët* fails to shift to a palatal. If one simply lists the root as an exception to rule (*K→Č*), one fails to make explicit the reasons why the form is an exception.

The problem is even more complex. At the point in the derivation when (*K→Č*) applies, the underlying representation of *tkët* is not **tk + e + t*, but *tuk + e + t*, with a vowel between the dental and the velar (this vowel appears in derived imperfectives in *– tykat'*). Thus it cannot simply be the case that rule (*K→C*) is restricted to apply to velars which are not preceded by a consonant.

On the other hand, if one is permitted to look behind in derivations (the global rules mentioned in Section 3.2 above), one might guess that rules are also permitted to "look ahead" in derivations, and, in fact, such rules have been proposed (cf. Hill 1970).

Now, if it is correct to permit rules to look ahead in derivations, then one can simply state that rule (*K→Č*) cannot apply if the final phonetic representation is going to end up with a consonant before the velar. Such a restriction would not explain the tendency to avoid phonological alternations in paradigms, but it would give at least a tentative explantion for the other two reasons why the velars in *tkët* and *skët* fail to undergo palatalization. The tendency to avoid phonological alternations within a paradigm might be explained by appeal to some other principle (see, e.g., Kiparsky's contribution to the present volume, although one notes that this observation goes back at least as far as the famous paper by Verner—see the references at the end of this paper for a precise citation).

If the theory permits looking ahead in derivations and also permits marking certain morphemes as exceptions to rules (for interesting generalizations of the latter technique, see Coats 1970, Kisseberth 1970), then we face a problem in analysis. The problem reduces, I think, to the following: how explanatory should a grammar be? Suppose, for example, that the reasons given above for the retention of the velar in *tkët* are the correct reasons and are the only correct reasons. Is there any evidence which would lead us to believe that a native speaker would incorporate such explanations in his grammar? Might not it be the case that such explanations are solely the property of linguists, explanations to be incorporated in the metatheory of language?

3.4 I return now to the Sanskrit retroflection problem. The difficulty here reflects an incipient difficulty with all phonological theories that attempt to explain things rather than merely give lists: they are on the one hand not powerful enough—witness the attempt to make the theory more powerful by introducing global rules—and on the other hand too powerful. They are too powerful, e.g., in that there are really no constraints on what kinds of rules can be written.[9] The following "rule," for example, is easily written and is very highly valued according to the Chomsky-Halle evaluation criterion:

(34)   [−syllabic] → [+nasal] *everywhere*

Aside from the above—the "unnatural" but easily written rule—there is a difficulty in writing rules containing the Greek-variables. Zwicky (1970) has observed that in most phonological descriptions such variables are used to relate features "of the same type—either two cavity features (back and round, grave and compact, round and low, diffuse and grave, coronal and anterior, or diffuse and compact) or two manner features (vocalic and consonantal, vocalic and continuant, or continuant and strident). The Sanskrit *ruki* class, however, is specified by variables relating a cavity feature (compact) and a manner feature (consonantal). In general, such uses of variables yield classes that are highly unnatural, for example, the $\begin{bmatrix} \alpha\text{cons} \\ \alpha\text{round} \end{bmatrix}$ segments, i.e., the class consisting of labialized consonants and unrounded vowels" (p. 552).

Linguists are lucky in dealing with this specific example of retroflection in Sanskrit because it turns out that while there are exceptions to *s*-retroflection when the conditioning segment is *r, u,* or *i,* there are NO exceptions to the rule when the conditioning segment is *k.* If one agrees with Zwicky's discussion of exceptions (p. 553), then one can at least separate *k* from the so-called *ruki* class. But it is important to note that the argument is very indirect, and, moreover, that it really doesn't do much beyond help us with the formulation of the rule in Sanskrit. It does not give us any theoretical device(s) for handling the general language-independent problem. Zwicky, incidentally, remarks that in the feature-system proposed by Chomsky and Halle (1968), the *ruki* class can be simply stated without the use of variables as $\begin{bmatrix} \text{-anterior} \\ \text{-low} \end{bmatrix}$

All that the introduction of exceptions to the discussion has resulted in is further evidence to support the fact that most of us already knew anyway: that *ruki* is not a natural class. Moreover, the argument is, in a certain sense at least, specious. Suppose we agree that *rui* forms a natural class and follow Zwicky's suggestion that there are two separate processes governed by "different rules, not subrules of the same rule" (p. 554). This analysis fails to explain why there are no exceptions to the rule retroflecting *s* after *k*. Most rules, after all, *do* have exceptions; why should this particular rule, which looks so similar to the rule retroflecting *s* after *rui*, have no exceptions?

In several other languages, original **s* is affected by a preceding *ruki*. Meillet (1964: 96) writes that "si le slave a *x* devant voyelle dans tous les cas ou le sanskrit a *ṣ*, et l'iranien *š*, le baltique a souvent *s* après *i, u* (sans qu'on puisse poser une règle), par exemple la≪puce≫est en lituanien *blusà* en regard de v.sl. *blŭxa,* et en arménien, où l'on a trace de la prononciation *š* apres *k*, le traitement de l'intervocalique est **h*, d'où zéro, et non *š*, après *i* et *u*; ainsi à lat. *nurus*≪bru≫(de **nusus, *nuzus*), v. ang. *snoru* (de **snusā*) et skr. *snuṣā́*, v. sl. *snŭxa*, l'arménien répond par *nu* (de **nuhos*), génit. *nuoy* (de **nuhohyo*), tout comme gr. *nuós*. En somme, la chuintante apparaît en indo-iranien, en slave, en baltique et un peu en arménien, c'est-à-dire dans les langues du groupe oriental quie offrent un même type de traitement des gutturales." But it is clear even from this brief statement that the exceptions are quite different in the different languages that witness the process. For Slavic, Meillet (1965: 30ff.) gives a reasonably large number of examples of *x* (*š* before front vowels) from original **s* after *ruki*. He cites analogical extension of this treatment of **s* in certain grammatical forms (aorist and locative plural) and notes (p. 33) that "cette généralisation de *x, š* dans les formes grammaticales montre que le sens de l'alternance de *x, š* avec *s* s'est perdu en slave avant la période historique. Au moment où se sont réglées les actions analogiques, la prononciation *s* n'était pas admise après *i, u, ĭ, ŭ, y, r*; les consonnes *x, š* toujours possibles ont été généralisées; à l'époque historique, *s* est admis après *i, u, r*, etc." But see Lightner 1963.

It seems doubtful to me that a real solution to the problem of retroflection of *s* in Sanskrit will be found without consulting the neighboring languages. A first step in this direction would be the compilation of a list of all the attested forms in the various languages for each word in which **s* is found after **ruki*. Obvious care will have to be taken to separate *bona fide* forms from forms resulting from analogy from forms in which *s* is reintroduced in the historical periods. The data from Armenian, while obviously relevant, are particularly difficult to interpret (cf. Meillet 1936: 39-40)

3.5 A major problem in phonology today is that no one knows exactly what is the subject matter of phonology. No one knows exactly what phenomena the rules of phonolgy are supposed to cover. Few, I suspect, doubt that *sane* and *sanity* are related in the sense that the root morpheme in both is the same. But it is not at all easy to state what principle shows us that the root morpheme in any two given words is or is not the same.[10] For example, there is some evidence to show that in certain prefixed verb-noun pairs in certain dialects the stress falls after the prefix in the verb, on the prefix in the noun :[11] *convict, transfer, refund, permit,* and so on, can all be read in two ways: with initial stress (= noun) or with non-initial stress (= verb). An entirely similar pair, it would seem, is the pair *rébel* (= noun) vs. *rebél* (= verb). Since this stress pattern is restricted to prefixed verbs and nouns, it seems that the *re-* in rebel must be a prefix, although perhaps not the same prefix *re-* as in *refund*. Although this is not too surprising, we must now include in the lexicon of English a root *bel*. If one asks what other words are derived from this root, the obvious answer is *bellicose, belligerent.*[12] If this be accepted, we are well on the way to the child of footnote 9 above.

If we return, however, to the view of Section 2.4—that a grammar should reflect the competence a native speaker MIGHT have—synchronic derivation of *rebel, bellicose, belligerent* from the same root is in no way surprising. If the grammar is not to miss phonological and semantic generalizations—if it is to make explicit general relationships between sound and meaning—then quite a number of historical phenomena will have to be reflected in the synchronic analysis. Consider, for example, the pair *cardiac, heart: card-* and *heart* mean the same thing, but if the words are derived from the same root, one has to deal with a $k \sim h$ and a $d \sim t$ alternation. The fact that one finds other semantically similar pairs of words with the same alternations (*unicorn, horn* etc. and *sedentary, sit* etc.) suggests that there is a real synchronic relation here and that the synchronic grammar will have to include a reflection of Grimm's Law. In fact, one can find alternants for all the obstruent stops: *peril $\sim$ fear, tri- $\sim$ three,*[13] *bursar $\sim$ perser, erg $\sim$ work, gynecology $\sim$ queen, afferent $\sim$ bear* etc. (see IEPM for full lists and analysis).

The numerals, as always, are interesting: one must invoke a reflection of Verner's law (!), for example, to relate *hundred* with *century* (cf. fn. 13). Even more complex is the triplet *five $\sim$ quinque- $\sim$ pente-* (all from underlying *penk$^{\prime\prime}$-;* in the Greek reflex, *k$^{\prime\prime}$* shifts to *t* before *e;* in the Latin reflex *p* assimilates to the following *k$^{\prime\prime}$;* in the Germanic reflex *k$^{\prime\prime}$* assimilates to the initial *p* giving *pempe* (cf. Bennett 1969) which, by vowel raising, nasalization, and Grimm's Law results in (fīfe = fīve), ultimately [fajv] by final *e*-dropping and Great Vowel Shift).

Perhaps even more interesting is the synonymous pair *behead $\sim$ decapitate,* in which an entire syllable is missing in the Germanic reflex (cf. OE *hēafod;* note the similar loss in *poor $\sim$ poverty, impoverish, ten $\sim$ decimal* &c.).

One must include the Greek rule shifting *s* to *h* to account for the *s* ∼ *h* alternations in clearly related pairs like *semi-* ∼ *hemi-*, *sweet* ∼ *hedonism* (Grimm's Law), *six* ∼ *hexa-*, *serpent* ∼ *herpetology*, *solar* ∼ *helio-*, *super-* ∼ *hyper-*, *saline* ∼ *halogen, septet* ∼ *hepta-*, and so on. Discussion, Lightner 1974, 1975, Gross 1975: 229-230.

The negative prefixes *a-* (= the Greek reflex before consonants, as in *amoral, apolitical* &c.), *an-* (= the Greek reflex before vowels and *h*, as in *anarchy, anhydrous* &c.), *in-* (= the Latin reflex, as in *incapable, inconvenient* &c.) and *un-* (= the Germanic reflex, as in *unlikely, ungraceful* &c.) are all derived from an underlying /n/. Discussion, see Lightner 1976a and the references cited there.

Once one admits a synchronic relationship between any of these pairs (= between *rebel* and *belligerent*, or *cardiac* and *heart*, or *semi-* and *hemi-*, or *a(n)-* and *in-/un-* etc.), all the other pairs would seem to have to be related. For example, it would make little sense to have a rule relating *k* and *d* with *h* and *t* (as in *cardiac* with *heart*) and not also *t* with θ (as in *tri-* with *three*), and so on.

3.6   The effect that phonetic representations have on underlying representations is difficult to capture in any explicit theory of phonology. A particularly interesting example of this comes from long consonants in Russian.

In Russian there is a division of the vocabulary into native and foreign words (details, see Saciuk 1969, PTP, and the references cited there). In the native vocabulary, geminates arise only when consonants of the same type come together across morpheme boundaries.[14] Thus, for example, *ssylat'* [ss...] 'to banish' from *s + sylat'*, where the first *s* is prefixal, the second radical. The situation is a bit more complex than this (cf. PTP), but not in ways that affect the present discussion.

If one turns now to foreign loan words, one notices that there are many orthographic geminates: *gamma, abbat, effekt, dollar* & c. These orthographic geminates occur morpheme-internally, and it is necessary to determine whether the orthographic geminates are realized as phonetic long or phonetic short consonants. Glovinskaja (1968) gives an informative introductory study of this question. As she points out (p. 81), one of the difficulties with formulating rules for loan words is that a great deal of free variation occurs in these forms. Nevertheless, she found certain clear-cut tendencies:

The following phonetic long consonants were found to occur (in order of decreasing frequency): [tt, ss, nn, d'd', cc, t't', s's', kk, mm, m'm', bb, ll, pp, f'f', rr, l'l', ff]. Long [tt] was pronounced 55% of the times *tt* appeared orthographically, but [ff] only 15.4%. The first half of the above list—those consonants which occur phonetically long in the native system—had the greatest frequency of occurrence; the second half of the list—those consonants which never occur long in the native system—had a significantly decreased frequency of occurrence.

The problem of the precise frequency of occurrence of a particular long consonant (figures for all the consonants are unfortunately not given by Glovinskaja) is the kind of problem that has been discussed by Labov in several publications (but see his answer to may question on pages 373-374 of this volume and see also Kiparsky's contribution), and I have nothing new to add to this difficult question.

But Glovinskaja's article raises a new problem:

Long consonants in the native system arise only across morpheme-boundaries; so far as I know, there are no underlying geminate consonants in the native system. But within the foreign system, geminates occur in underlying representations within morphemes: *massa* from /mass + a/, *getto* from gett + o/, and so on. But according to Glovinskaja's article, there is a significant decrease in the occurrence of phonetic long consonants in the foreign system if these long consonants do not occur phonetically in the native system. Apparently the phonetic representations of the native system have a strong effect on possible underlying representations of the foreign system. As I said earlier, this does not seem strange to me. But I do not know how phonological theory should be formulated so that a fact like this can be explicitly captured within the grammar of a language.

3.7 A problem related to the one discussed in Section 3.6 above has recently been raised by Dinnsen and Garcia-Zamor (1971). They have shown through careful measurement of vowel-length in four native speakers of German that there are not two, but three distinct vowel-lengths in that language. The standard analysis of forms like *baten* 'asked (pl.)', *bat* 'asked (sg.)', *baden* 'to bathe', and *Bad* 'bath' requires the underlying representations *bāt + en*, *bāt*, *bad + en*, and *bad*, respectively, and the following two ordered rules:

$$(35) \quad V \rightarrow \bar{V} / \underline{\hspace{2cm}} \quad [+\text{voice}]$$

$$(36) \quad [+\text{obstr}] \rightarrow [-\text{voice}] / \underline{\hspace{2cm}} \#$$

These two rules, when applied to the representations given above, result in the following phonetic representations: [bāten] 'asked (pl.)', [bāt] 'asked (sg.)', [bāden] 'to bathe', and [bāt] 'bath', with all forms having the same length of the root vowel [ā]. Dinnsen and Garcia-Zamor found that the vowel-lengths of *baten, bat,* and *Bad* were the same (to within 15 msec.), but that the vowel-length of *baden* —the only form with a PHONETICALLY voiced consonant following the vowel—was longer than the vowels of *baten, bat, Bad* by an average of 46 msec.

Assuming the reliability of these data, one can only conclude that there are two lengthening rules—both of the form given in (35) above. One rule is a phonological rule which accounts for the homophony of *bat* and *Bad*; the other rule is a purely phonetic rule which accounts for the difference in vowel-length found in pairs like *baten* and *baden*.

3.8   In this paper two well-known rules dealing with voicing in obstruents have been frequently mentioned. Ironically, it is not clear exactly how even these rules should operate. Consider a language in which all word-final obstruents are voiceless and in which voicing in obstruent clusters assimilates to the voiced/voiceless quality of the final obstruent in the cluster. There are several possible interpretations of data like these.

One could say that in a word-final obstruent cluster, all the obstruents are devoiced in one step; a form like *uzb* would be directly interpreted as *usp*. On the other hand, one could say that it is only the final obstruent which is devoiced (*uzb* > *uzp*) and that the voicing-assimilation rule devoices any obstruents preceding the final voiceless obstruent (*uzp* > *usp*). But if one considers the voicing-assimilation rule, there is again a difficulty in interpreting how the rule should apply. Should the assimilation be done in one step (*vzt* > *fst*) or should it be done in more than one step? And if it is correct to have the assimilation take place in more than one step, which consonant should assimilate first: should the derivation be *vzt* > *vst* > *fst* or should it be *vzt* > *fzt* > *fst*?

If phonological rules are thought of as conditions imposed on lines in a derivation, it seems most reasonable to have one-step changes. But if phonological rules are meant to mirror processes, then the many-stepped derivations seem most natural. I have tried to answer this question in PTP, 338-340.

The types of questions that are being asked now—questions in part exemplified in Sections 1-8 above and in the work of investigators like Bailey, Drachmann, Stampe, and others—are of quite a different nature than those asked in the early 1960's. The concern today seems not to be with the formulation of precise rules but rather with discovery of the nature of phonological changes and with the delimitation of the field of phonology itself. We seem to be reaching the point at which Grammont's oft-cited remark is at last being given its due: "Une loi sans exemple peut-être aussi solide que celle qui est vérifiée par le plus grand nombre."

The phonology of the early 1960's was both an answer to the sterile approach of the neo-Bloomfieldians and at the same time an explicit statement of a theory of phonology whose application led to a number of insights about the nature of individual languages and about language in general. The effort was not to list facts about different languages, but to attempt an explanation of the facts.

But there are many approaches to explanation. If a language exhibits only word-final voiceless obstruents, one type of explanation is given by the statement that the grammar of the language contains a rule which devoices word-final obstruents. More recently, linguists have asked directly for explanation of a different nature: in case after case, one assumes the existence of a rule—without knowing exactly how to formulate the rule—and asks for an explanation as to *why* a language should have such a rule. With rules like the one mentioned above, one searches for an explanation as to why the rule should appear over and over again in the grammars of numerous languages throughout the world, but not in the grammars of *all* languages.

The search for an acceptable answer to questions raised in the early 1960's has led to a search for a deeper type of explanation. The difficulties inherent in finding deeper reasons for observable phenomena have led to a broadening of the base of linguistics. To answer questions about synchronic grammar, for example, linguists are now examining not merely the synchronic data of the language in question, but problems dealing with language-acquisition, language-deformation (as occurs in poetry, for example, and in secret languages, many of which are far more complex than Pig Latin), language-loss (as in aphasia), and diachronic language-change. It is important to see that the search for explanation in these deeper terms is not an original move. These, for example, are the questions that Roman Jakobson has for many years been investigating, an investigation which led to his seminal work, far ahead of its time, *Kindersprache, Aphasie, und allgemeine Lautgesetze.*

As regards the difficulty inherent in these investigations, I can do no better than cite Martin Gardner, who, in discussing the fall of parity in his remarkable book *The Ambidextrous Universe*, remarks that "every 'true' theory contains an element of falsehood. 'Nothing is perfect,' says the Philosopher in James Stephen's *The Crock of Gold*. 'There are lumps in it.' The history of science can be described as a continual, perhaps never-ending, discovery of new lumps. It was once thought that planets moved in perfect circles. Even Galileo, although he placed the sun and not the earth at the centre of the solar system, could not accept Kepler's view that the planetary orbits were ellipses. Eventually it became clear that Kepler had been right: the orbits are *almost* circles but not quite. Newton's theory of gravity explained why the orbits were perfect ellipses. Then slight deviations in the Newtonian orbits turned up and were in turn explained by the correction factors of relativity theory that Einstein introduced into the Newtonian equations. 'The real trouble with this world of ours,' comments Gilbert Chesterton in *Orthodoxy*, 'is not that it is an unreasonable world, nor even that it is a reasonable one. The commonest kind of trouble is that it is nearly reasonable, but not quite... It looks just a little more mathematical and regular than it is; its exactitude is obvious, but its inexactitude is hidden; its wildness lies in wait'."

4. The Wildness That Lies in Wait.

Five years have passed since the above was written. In that time the wildness around us has never ceased to impress me. Recently, for example, the physicists have discovered a particle that is magnetized on only one end. It is difficult for me even to understand what this means. But I am sure it is just the beginning. To give an example from morphophonology, I pose below a problem which will at first seem inordinately simple, but which on closer examination is found to be of extreme complexity. In fact, we will not be able to solve the problem here, although a suggestion will be made and at the same time we will be able to make some observations about the appropriateness of using "intuition" in analysis. The problem is:

What is the underlying phonological representation (UPR) of the root in the word tooth?

One's intuition—my intuition, at least-answers /tūθ/. One realizes that *teeth* causes a minor problem; but clearly there will have to be some kind of rule to shift the vowels in singular vs. plural. Perhaps the UPR of the root in *tooth* is /tīθ/.

The point I want to make is that neither /tūθ/ nor /tīθ/ are reasonable choices. If one starts with either /tūθ/ or /tīθ/, there is no reasonable way to make explicit the sound and meaning relationships between *tooth/teeth* and *dental, dentifrice, dentist, denture, edentate* 'toothless' (with *ex-* 'out'), *trident, orthodontist* (*ortho-* 'straight'), *macrodontia* (*macro-* 'long'), and so on.

Still clinging to the notion 'intuition', one might—in the face of these examples—propose /dent-/ as the UPR of the root in *tooth*. One would then need to include a reflex of Grimm's Law in the synchronic analysis of English. This seems to be not such a bad idea. When one stops to think about it, it turns out there are quite a number of examples (*pedal* ∼ *foot, fraternity* ∼ *brother, patronymic* ∼ *father, pipe* ∼ *fife*, and so on, cf. Section 3.5 above), and once one grasps the general ideal of the consonant shifts, the entire analysis becomes 'intuitively' correct.

Moreover, when one considers these examples one notes a vowel- alternation (*dent-* ∼ *dont-*) reminiscent of the vowel-alternation in *tooth* ∼ *teeth*. The entire situation seems clear and very intuitive. One starts with /dent-/ (or perhaps /dont-), and Grimm's Law gives the *t-*θ consonant-frame in *tooth/teeth*. One can use the same vowel-shift rule in both *tooth/teeth* and *dont-/dent*.

Despite the intuitive appeal of such an analysis, it is entirely unrealistic. Under such an analysis there is no way whatever to account for the *o-* in *odontoid* 'resembling a tooth', *odontology* 'study of teeth', and so on.

The *e-* in *endentate* 'toothless' must be derived from prefixal *ex-* 'out', but there is no known prefix which will result in the *o-* of *odontoid, odon-*

tology. Moreover, one notes that the *o-* plays no semantic role. The affix
-oid (which is complex) means 'resembling' and the affix *ology* (also complex) means 'study of'. The *o-* of *odontoid/odontology* contributes nothing
to the meaning.

How does 'intuition' handle a situation like this? I suppose the intuitive
way to solve this problem would be to "invent" a new "zero-meaning"
prefix *o-*. but this is a dangerous move: prefixes in general *do* have meaning.
Moreover, how could such a "zero-meaning" prefix have arisen: Often loss
of meaning is due to an element's being overworked (Russian *PO-*, English
-ment etc.), but there are few cases when a meaningless element is
gratuitously added. At this point I think intuition—at least the type I have
been discussing here—leads one to incorrect analysis.

One is obliged to leave one's intuition behind. Rationally, there is no
other explanation for the *o-* in *odontoid* than to say it is part of the root.

Reference to Latin *dēns, dentis* 'tooth' reveals that the *-ēns, entis* has
the same shape as the participle. Thus we could analyze everything to the
right of *d-* as verbal. How could *tooth* be verbal? Possibly through eating.
This suggestion leads to quite a different analysis; one which is far from
one's intuition.

Once the notion 'eat' is introduced, there are three sets of forms to consider: those in *ed-*, those in *od-*, and those in *d-*;

ed-: *edible, comestible, eat* (Grimm's Law), *obese* (prefixal *ob-*),...[for the long vowel in *eat, obese*, see Lightner 1973c and IEPM].

od-: *odontoid, odontology, periodontist, mastodon, orthodontists,...*

d-: *dental, denture, tooth,...*

The data arranged in this fashion reveal a distributional regularity we
had not noticed before: ALWAYS when *dont-* appears, an *o* precedes.
Before, we had analyzed *ortho-dont-ist*, presumably because this was intuitively correct (cf. *ortho-dox, ortho-pedics* etc.). Now we must analyze
ortho-od-dont-ist and must drop the final *o* of *ortho-* before the *o* of radical
-od-. But we would have needed a rule to do this anyway because of forms
like *orthoptic* 'pertaining to straight/correct vision' from *orthø-op-t-ic*.
Similarly, our earlier division *macro-dont-ia* was incorrect; we need *macrø-od-ont-ia*, with the final *o* of *macro-* dropped (cf. *macro-molecule, macro-cephalic* etc.).

Thus by leaving intuition behind and solely by examining the distribution of sound and meaning we have been led to find a new distributional
regularity and to correct an earlier mistake (the *ortho-dontist* division).

Still, we have not yet solved the original problem: what is the UPR of
the root in the word *tooth*? We know that—whatever it is—it is realized as
[t] on the surface. But the *underlying* representation could be any of /ed-/,

/od-/, /d-/—or perhaps something altogether different.

The choice /od-/ would seem to be a poor one because of the correlation between *od-* and *-ont-*. We will somehow or other have to explain why *-ont-* occurs in *odontoid* but *-ent-* in *dental*. Once we have done this we might derive *odont-* from *ed-ent-*. Whatever we had decided about *-ent-/-ont-* would give us *ed-ont-* from *ed-ent-*, and it might now merely be a simple matter of phonology to make the first vowel like the second, to change *ed-ont-* into *od-ont* by assimilation. This is one possibility, and if this is correct then there will never be a root spelled /od-/ and therefore /od-/ could not possibly be the UPR of the root of *tooth*. This would leave us with /ed-/ or /d-/ (or perhaps something else) as the possible choices.

Although the analysis of the preceding paragraph is a possible one, we do not know that it is right. And we do not yet have enough data at our disposal to decide whether it is right or not. We will have to find at least one other root which acts roughly like this one and see what happens there. This will have to be done in exhaustive detail, and to keep the length of this paper within reasonable bounds I will just make a suggestion without giving the detailed work necessary to solve the problem : in *synonym, synonymous* etc. (cf. *name, nom-enclature, nominal, mis-nom-er* etc. from the same root), there is no source for the *-o-*; the prefix is *syn-* (cf. *synthesis, sym-biosis, syllogism* etc., sometimes with consonantal-assimilation, but never with an *-o-*). Thus the *-o-* in *synonym* (like the *o-* in *odontoid*) must be part of the root. This observation about the *-o-* in *synonym* does not solve the problem; it merely gives an indication that a trivial phonological rule might not suffice to shift *ed-ont-* to *od-ont-* because the *-o-* in *synonym* is not followed by *o* but by *y*. No doubt Greek *y* comes from underlying *u* so that *synonym* is from *sun-en-um*, and one might argue that radical *e* is shifted back to *o* before *any* back vowel (i.e., before either *o* or *u*). To test this hypothesis we would have to look at more data. It is clear what type of work would have to be done and it is equally clear that this work would have nothing whatever to do with 'intuition'. Here I will just assume (perhaps incorrectly) that the hypothesis is wrong.

The choice of /ed-/ as the UPR of the root of *tooth* would seem to be a poor one because the underlying vowel would have somehow to be deleted. But this is a problem in any event— some of the Latin forms show *e-* and some don't (*edible* vs.*dental*); some of the Germanic forms show *e-* and some don't (*eat* vs. *tooth*). This is the problem of ablaut: when does one find the *zero-grade* and when the *full-grade*? This problem is at present beyond my ability to solve.

There is another way of getting at the UPR of the root in *tooth*: by inquiring into the nature of the structure of the root. This has been masterfully done for IE by Émile Benveniste (1935) who concluded (roughly) that the root in IE had the general shape $*CeC$-. This is a bad sign for us because we are proposing a shape $*eC$- or perhaps simply $*C$-. Lehman (1955), however, has suggested that there were no underlying vowels in IE (his suggestion is a bit more complex) and that the shape of the root was (roughly) *CC-.

We might suggest, then, that the UPR of the root in the word *tooth* is $X°d$-, where $X°$ is a consonant, an *o*-coloring laryngeal, which colors Greek vowels and which never appears in the surface phonetic representations. For *odontoid*, vowel-insertion would give $X°ed$-, whence $X°od$- by coloring and *od*- by loss of laryngeal. *Edible* would come from $X°ed$- simply by loss of laryngeal. And *tooth*, finally, would come from $X°d$-, the *zero-grade* of the ‹ root.

Although this is merely a suggestion, it is quite unintuitive and therefore stands a chance, at least, of being correct. *Synonym, patronymic, name, nominal, noun* etc. of course, come from a root spelled $X°n$-.

One sees that to explain the $p \sim b$ alternation in *potable* $\sim$ *beverage, bib(ulous), imbibe* etc., one must proceed from the root $pX°$-, where $X°$, the *o*-coloring laryngeal, is a voiced obstruent. Voicing-assimilation gives $bX°$-, whence *b*-, whence *bib*- by reduplication. *Potable* involves vowel- insertion (= $peX°$-), whence $poX°$- by coloring, and *poo*- (= the *pō*- in *potable*) by complete assimilation of the laryngeal to the preceding vowel. Details on these derivations, together with long lists of supporting examples are given in IEPM.

5. Conclusion.

In reviewing the contribution of generative phonology to our knowledge of language, we can see that the contribution is primarily to be found in a few suggestions for explicit formal devices, most of them wrong.

One notes a similar failure in generative syntax, where an entire battery of useless formal suggestions were made (*trees*, units like *VP*, various unmotivated types of *Adv*'s and so on); for discussion see Gross 1975, Lightner 1976a.

The entire notion behind Figure 1 collapses, and it may be profitable to examine why the generative/transformational school of linguistics has resulted in failure. I think there are two major reasons. The first is that little attempt was made to examine the factual data. In syntax no one even bothered to make a list of the sentences so that all claims were on a hit-or-miss basis. Even in phonology very few studies were exhaustive. Another extremely serious gap in the thinking of this school was the total neglect of derivational morphology (DM); this neglect alone shows the impossibility of the simple-minded device of Figure 1.

In phonology the goal was to find UPR's and a set of rules to derive the phonetic representations of what seemed to be individual words, for example, *egg*. But it was not taken into consideration that the noun might have a different source from the verb (which occurs only before *on*); the two *egg*'s might therefore have different UPR's. There are many similar examples. Without examining DM it is not possible to know whether the *math*'s in *mathematics* and in *aftermath* have the same source. Thus it was not realized that one cannot hope to arrive at a satisfactory UPR given merely the pronunciation of a world. That *lay* is pronounced [lej] gives little information about the lexical representation. One *lay*, for example, must go with *lie* 'be prostrate', and another (the one that comes before *-man*) with *laity*. These two *lay*'s might have the same UPR, but there is no *a priori* reason why they should; one cannot tell without examining all the sound-meaning relationships. English is far more complex than any of the generative phonologists had conceived. Does the third *lay* 'song, ballad', for example go with the *lude* in *interlude, prelude* &c. or not? It is just not possible to answer this question before the requisite research has been done. Thus it is not sufficient to note, for example, that *shine* may have preterite *shined* or *shone* when intransitive but only *shined* when transitive (*He shined/ *shone his shoes*). One has to look at all the verbs to see if there is a generalization to be grasped.

Given the absence of DM, it is hardly surprising that no contributions whatever were made in semantics. The role of DM, it turns out, is crucial to all the major divisions of linguistics. To such a degree that DM is the key component of a grammar: phonology, syntax, and semantics are the ancillary techniques.

All the philosophies and mysticisms of India teach that knowledge has no value if its object is not the "salvation" of man (see, e.g., Eliade 1975: 21ff.). The *Svetasvatara Upanishad* (I, 12) says: "Beyond that nothing is worth knowing". I am not sure if knowledge which results from the type of study suggested here can attain to such a high ideal; but it might offer a beginning, a starting point in the search.

Notes

*This work has been partly sponsored by the Laboratoire d'Automatique Documentaire et Linguistique (E.R.A. n° 247 de C.N.R.S.) and in part by The Linguisitics Research Center, University of Texas at Austin.

[1]Actually, of course, this often cited claim is false: the first morpheme in *pterodactyl*, for example, begins with *p-* (not *s-*), as can be seen from related forms like *apterous, archaeopteryx, hemipteroid, trichopteran, dipteron, ornithopter, helicopter*, and so on, all of which have phonetic [-pt-]. This example is not isolated; thus *chthonian* ∼ *autochthonous* [-kθ-], *phthalic* ∼ *naphtha* [fθ- ∼ -pθ-], and so on. In any event, MS-rules have been shown to be ill-conceived (Lightner 1973b), and I shall therefore not discuss such rules in this paper. A possible analysis of forms like those mentioned above is given in Lightner MS (henceforth *IEPM*).

[2]The question of larger units (= discourse analysis) was always avoided by the Chomsky-Halle school, an avoidance presumably justified by a consideration such as the following: since there is no upper-bound on sentence-length, anything that occurs in discourse will occur also within the domain of a single sentence; therefore linguistics need not deal with discourse but can restrict its investigation to units whose maximal length is that of a sentence. The problem is difficult, but it is not clear to me that the correct decision was made here. For example, in Beneveniste's fascinating paper (1952), one of the arguments he gives to distinguish the "language" of bees from human language is: "Une différence capitale apparaît aussi dans la situation où la communication a lieu. Le message des abeilles n'appelle aucune reponse de l'entourage, sinon une certaine conduite, qui n'es pas une réponse. Cela signifie que les abeilles ne connaissent pas le dialogue, qui est la condition du language humain. Nous parlons à d'autres qui parlent, telle est la réalité humaine. Cela révèle un nouveau contraste. Parce qu'il n'y a pas dialogue pour les abeilles, la communication se réfère seulement à une certaine donnée objective. Il ne peut y avoir de communication relative à une donnée ≪linguistique≫; déjà parce qu'il n'y a pas de réponse, la réponse étant une réaction linguistique à une manifestation linguistique; mais aussi en ce sens que le message d'une abeille ne peut être reproduit par une autre qui n'aurait pas vu elle même les choses que la première annonce. On n'a pas constaté qu'une abeille aille par exemple porter dans une autre ruche le message qu'elle a reçu dans la sienne, ce qui serait une manière de transmission ou de relais. On voit la différence avec le langage humain, où, dans le dialogue, la référence à l'expérience objective et la réaction à la manifestation linguistique s'entremêlent librement et à l'infini."

[3]Actually, I have given three different types. The influence of neighboring vowels on velars is in at least some sense universal (cf. 2.3 below). Languages with phonetically nasalized vowels often (always?) have different degrees of nasalization; this is found not only in English dialects, but in many French dialects and among less well-know languages such as Ewe (cf. Westermann 1907, Westermann and Ward 1933, esp. p. 43). The matter of the voiced/voiceless distinction in consonants is intricately connected with the tense/lax distinction and the aspirated/unaspirated distinction. Meillet (1964: 83), for example, writes that "les sonores sont toujours douces et les fortes toujours sourdes, mais l'inverse n'est pas vrai; les Alsaciens par exemple ont des douces qui ne sont pas sonores. Si l'émission d'air continue après l'explosion, sans vibrations glottales, avant que la voyelle commence, l'occlausive est dite ≪aspirée≫; une occlusive aspirée est ordinairement douce." Whether the onset of voiced consonants is voiced or voiceless is no doubt language-specific; it seems, for example, that in Slavic languages the onset is voiced, in Germanic languages voiceless.

[4]This is, of course, a technical mistake; what they meant was *the empty string*.

[5]Discussion of some of the work in pre-generative phonology, see Lightner 1968.

[6]It is interesting to note that Baudouin de Courtenay (1894) attributes the palatalization of velars in Slavic after *i* to the initial fronting of such velars due to the preceding front vowel.

[7]The reference to Grimm's law is meant merely to be suggestive of some general tendency; there can be no absolute universal constraint here, for the Ukrainian form corresponding to Russian *tkët* is *tče*, with a palatal from the underlying velar.

[8]There are still a few forms with alternants: *oko* ~ *oči* 'eye(s)', *drug* ~ *druz'ja* 'friend(s)'. Details, see PTP.

[9]Chomsky and Halle's evaluation criterion does, of course, constrain some types of rules; thus (7) and not (6) must be written. But this is a trivial constraint. There is no constraint against writing the following rule (the apostrophe indicates palatalization, the accent mark pharyngealization):

$$(33) \ \text{b'} \rightarrow \acute{\text{a}} \ / \ \text{ti} \underline{\hspace{2cm}} \text{us'elo\#}$$

Such a rule would be "expensive", but not excluded. Until such time as one understands better the nature of language acquisition, McCawley's suggestion fares no better than the Chomsky-Halle suggestion. Consider the case of a "normal" child who learns English and whose father is an Indo-Europeanist. At the age of, say, 8 the child is subjected to lessons in linguisitics and Indo-European. A large number of relationships are made exlicit to the child: *warm, furnace, thermal* are all from the same root, whereas *lupine, wolf, vulpine, lycanthropy* may not be; *arctic* has nothing to do with *arc* but rather with *ursine* (cf. Gk. *arktikos*, the adj. from *arktos* 'bear'), and so on. Does the child change his grammar of English to incorporate all this new knowledge? And if so, exactly how? Does the answer to this question vary with the age of the child? with the native intelligence of the child? with whether the child likes/dislikes his father? with how good an Indo-Europeanist the father is? Are such questions even relevant to linguisitics?

[10]One is reduced, I suppose, to the claim that related forms must be both phonologically and semantically relatable. I return to this question in 4 below.

[11]I dodge the embarrassing question of what the word 'stress' means—embarrassing because no one really knows what stress is. For our purposes, however, it is sufficient to note that native speakers of English, for example, will always agree that there is *something* that distinguishes the first syllable from the second in a word like *comma*, and that this same thing distinguishes the first syllable from the second in a world like *giraffe*, although in these two particular words that something appears on the first syllable of *comma*, on the second syllable of *giraffe*.
In the examples given below, I refer to the stress of my own idiolect of English. The facts vary from dialect to dialect, and within each dialect there are numerous exceptions. Neither of these facts have any bearing on the point at issue, however.

[12]Historically, *revel* is also related (from Old French *reveler* 'to revolt, make noise, make merry'). In the verb *rebel* the stress is final; in the verb *revel*, initial. Perhaps the words are not synchronically related (?); discussion of questions like this, see IEMP. There are a few *b* ~ *v* alternations in English (*probate* ~ *prove*, *gubernatorial* ~ *governor*, *web* ~ *weave*, *imbibe* ~ *beverage* etc.); but it is not immediately clear how any of these alternations should be treated synchronically. One notes the Greek form *cybernetics* from the same root as in *govern*.

[13]No doubt related to *three* is the ordinal *third* with metatheses (cf. German *dritte*). The *-d* in *third* is due to Verner's Law (cf. *-θ* in *fourth, fifth* etc.). Discussion in IEPM.

[14]There are a few forms where phonetic geminates arise because two different consonants are subjected to phonological rules which make them identical. In the 1 sg of *ezdit'*, from the root /ezd/, for example, the root final *d* is shifted to *ž* and the preceding *z* assimilates to the following palatal, resulting in *ežžu* [ježžu] or [jež'ž'u]. Such forms are not relevant to the present discussion; the important point here is that there are no underlying representations which contain geminates within a native morpheme: there are no native morphemes with underlying sequences like *-ss-, -tt-, -nn-*. When such sequences occur phonetically, the first consonant always belongs to one morpheme, the second to a different morpheme.

Bibliography

Anderson, Lloyd. 1967. "A Left-to-Right Syllabic Cycle," *Chicago Journal of Linguistics*.

Bach, Emmon. 1968. "Two Proposals Concerning The Simplicity Metric in Phonology," *Glossa* 2, 128-149.

Baudouin de Courtenay, J.A. 1894. "Einiges über Palatalisierung und Ent-palatalisierung," *Indogermanische Forschungen* 4, 45-57.

Bennett, William H. 1969. "Pre-Germanic /p/ for Indo-European /kʷ/," *Lg.* 49:2, 243-247.

Benveniste, Émile. 1935. *Origines de la Formation Des Noms En Indo-européen.* Paris: Adrien- Maisonneuve.

_____. 1952. "Communication Animale et Langage Humain," *Diogène*, I. Reprinted in Venveniste, *Problèmes de Linguistique Générale*, 56-62. Editions Gallimard (1966).

Bierwisch, Manfred. 1968. "Two Critical Problems in Accent Rules," JL 4, 173-178.

Bloomfield, Leonard. 1939. "Menomini Morphophonemics," *ICLP* 8, 105-115.

Bresnan, Joan W. 1971. "Sentence Stress and Syntactic Transformations, " *Lg.* 47:2, 257-281.

Chomsky, Noam, and Morris Halle. *The Sound Pattern of English*. Harper & Row.

Coats, Herbert S. 1970. "Rule-environment Features in Phonology," *PIL* 2:1, 110-140.

_____, and Theodore M. Lightner. 1975. "Transitive Softening in Russian Conjugation," *Lg.* 51:2, 338-341.

Dinnsen, Daniel, and M. Garcia-Zamor. 1971. "The Three Degrees of Vowel Length in German," *PIL* 4:1, 111-126.

Eliade, Mircea. 1962. *Patañjali et le Yoga*. Paris: Editions du Seuil. The reference in the text is to the English translation *Patanjali and Yoga*. N.Y.: Schocken Books (1975).

Glovinskaja, M. Ja. 1968. "O Nekotoryx Osobennostjax Proiznošenija Zaimstvovannyx Slov," *Russkij Jazyk V Škole* 1, 81-84.

Gross, Maurice. 1975. *Méthodes En Syntaxe: Régime Des Constructions Completives.* Paris: Hermann.

Hill, Jane H. 1970. "A Peeking Rule in Cupeño," *LI* 1:4, 534-539.

Jakobson, Roman. 1939. "Observations Sur Le Classement Phonologique Des Consonnes," in *Proceedings of the Third Internatinoal Congress of Phonetic Sciences*. Reprinted in Jakobson 1962, pp. 272-279.

_____. 1940. *Kindersprache, Aphasie und Allgemeine Lautgesetze*. Reprinted in Jakobson 1962, pp. 328-401. English translation: *Child Language, Aphasia, and Phonological Universals*. Mouton (1968).

_____. 1962. Selected Writings, vol. I. Mouton.

_____. Gunnar Fant, and Morris Halle. 1963. *Preliminaries to Speech Analysis*. MIT Press.

Katz, J.J., and Paul M. Postal. 1964. *An Integrated Theory of Linguistic Descriptions.* MIT Press.

Kenstowicz, Michael J., and Charles W. Kisseberth. 1973. "The Multiple Application Problem in Phonology," in *Studies in Generative Phonology,* ed. C.W. Kisseberth, pp. 13-41. Edmonton: Linguistic Research, Inc.

Kiparsky, Paul. 1968. "How Abstract is Phonolgy?" Unpublished MS.

Kisserberth, Charles W. 1970. "The Treatment of Exceptions," *PIL* 2:1, 44-58.

———. 1973. "On The Alternation of Vowel Length in Klamath: A Global Rule," in *Issues in Phonological Theory,* ed. M.J. Kenstowicz and C.W. Kisseberth, pp. 9-26. Mouton.

Lehmann, Winfred P. 1955. *Proto-Indo-European Phonology.* Univ. of Texas Press.

———. 1975. "Observations on Trubetzkoy's Contributions to Phonological Studies," *Romance Philology* 29:1, 40-57.

Lightner, Theodore M. 1963. "The Shift of *s* to *x* in Old Church Slavonic Verb Forms," *QPR* 70, 298-300.

———. 1968. "Review of *Readings in Linguistics,* ed. Martin Joos," *General Linguisitics* 8:1, 44-61.

———. 1969. "Review of *Phonologie der Gegenwart,* ed. Josef Hamm et al.," *Slavic and East European Journal* 13:4, 489-494.

———. 1971. "On Swadesh and Voegelin's *A Problem in Phonological Alternation,*" IJAL 37:4, 227-237.

———. 1972. *Problems in the Theory of Phonology: Russian Phonology and Turkish Phonology.* Edmonton: Linguistic Research, Inc.

———. 1973a. "Five Forms of the Russian Word For *Rouble,*" in *Issues in Linguistics: Papers in Honor of Henry and Renée Kahane,* ed. Braj B. Kachru et al., pp. 548-553. Univ. of Illinois Press.

———. 1973b. "Against Morpheme-structure Rules," in *Issues in Phonological Theory,* ed. M.J. Kenstowicz and C.W. Kisseberth, pp. 53-60. Mouton.

———. 1973c. "On Vowel Lengthening in English," *PIL* 6:2, 257-258.

———. 1974. "Preliminary Remarks on Derivational Morphology of French," in *Actes du Colloque Franco-allemand de Grammaire Transformationnelle,* ed. Christian Rohrer and Nicolas Ruwet, pp. 142-164. Tübingen: Max Niemeyer.

———. 1975. "The Role of Derivational Morphology in Generative Grammar," *Lg.* 51:3, 617-638.

———. 1976a. "Review of *The Goals of Linguistic Theory,* ed. Stanley Peters," *Lg.* 52:2.

———. 1976b. "On Deglottalization in Klamath," *IJAL* 42:1, 14-16.

———. MS. *Introduction to English Phonology and Morphology.*

McCawley, James D. 1967. "Can You Count Pluses and Minuses Before You Can Count?" *Chicago Journal of Linguistics.*

_____. 1968. "The Role of Semantics in Grammar," in *Universals in Linguistic Theory,* ed. Emmon Bach and Robert T. Harms, pp. 124-169. Holt, Rinehart and Winston.

_____. 1969. "Length and Voicing in Tübatulabal," *CLS* 5, 407-415.

_____. 1973. "Global Rules and Bangubangu Tone," in *Issues in Phonological Theory,* ed. M.J. Kenstowicz and C.W. Kisseberth, pp. 160-168. Mouton.

Meillet, Antoine. 1936. *Esquisse d'une Grammaire Comparée de l'Arménien Classique.* Wien.

_____. 1964. *Introduction a l'Étude Comparative des Langues Indo-européennes.* Univ. of Alabama Press.

_____. 1965. *Le Slave Commun.* Paris. Russian translation: *Obšče-slavjanskij Jazyk.* Moscow.

Postal, Paul M. 1968. *Aspects of Phonological Theory.* Harper and Row.

Saciuk, Bohdan. 1969. "The Strata Division of the Lexicon," *PIL* 1:3, 464-532.

Sapir, Edward. 1949. "The Psychological Reality of Phonemes," in *Selected Writings of Edward Sapir,* ed. David G. Mandelbaum, pp. 46-60. Univ. of Calif. Press.

Swadesh, Morris, and Charles F. Voegelin. 1939. "A Problem in Phonological Alternation," *Lg.* 15:1, 1-10.

Verner, Karl. 1875. "Eine Ausnahme der Ersten Lautverschiebung." The references in the text are to pp. 144, 147, 158 of the English translation in W.P. Lehmann (ed.), *A Reader in Nineteeth Century Historical Indo-European Linguistics.* Indiana Univ. Press (1967).

Westermann, D. 1907. *Grammatik der Ewe-Sprache.* Berlin.

_____, and Ida C. Ward. 1933. *Practical Phonetics for Students of African Languages.* Oxford Univ. Press.

Zwicky, Arnold M. 1964. "Three Traditional Rules of Sanskrit," *QPR* 74, 203-204.

_____. 1970. "Greek Variables and the Sanskrit *ruki* class," *LI* 1:4, 549-555.

Chapter Two

Historical Linguistics

Paul Kiparsky

Historical investigations in the framework of generative grammar have generally aimed at developing a theory of change which could hook up to the existing synchronic theory, so as to correctly characterize the possible forms of linguistic change, and the constraints to which they are subject. Much of the earlier work on this problem is summarized in King's book (1969). Since then, there has been much debate, for example, on the question of constraints on sound change: can rules be added to the middle of grammars (King 1970; Demers 1970)? Can the added rule be one that interchanges the values of a feature (Chomsky and Halle 1968; Matthews 1970)?

I will not try to cover this work here. I will limit myself to a parallel, and perhaps equally important line of research, which attempts to deepen our understanding of linguistic change by removing the obstacles that presently lie on the synchronic side. We cannot simply take the theory of grammar for granted and hold it constant while we "apply" it to change. This is because many of the most central problems in historical linguistics, e.g., *when does restructuring take place?* or *what determines the direction of analogical change?* are really questions about language itself. However, the present state of linguistics is such that the synchronic theory is often rather indeterminate in exactly the respects that would be most relevant for historical linguistics. For this reason much progress in historical linguistics depends on sharpening the synchronic theory so that it will provide the right basis for diachronic explanation.

It is interesting that most work that has so far been carried out along these lines points to one general conclusion. This is that the function of the "evaluation measure" in linguistic theory is carried out by a series of *substantive* conditions in addition to (not instead of) the *formal* condition of simplicity. Chomsky originally suggested that the language learner has two sorts of things available to him:

(1) formal devices for expressing rules
(2) a way of picking the right analysis from the many analyses that these formal devices allow (an evaluation measure).

The usual claim (e.g., in Chomsky and Halle 1968) has been that the formal devices are very rich, and that the evaluation measure is very simple, viz.

pick the shortest description, where length in phonology is defined in terms of the number of feature specifications in the grammatical description. It is especially the historical facts which show conclusively that this cannot be right, and that the "evaluation" of grammars involves their substantive properties. I will discuss these substantive properties under three headings:

1. Abstractness conditions
2. Paradigm conditions
3. Rule opacity.

1. Abstractness Conditions

The first modification of the theory that is suggested by historical facts is some constraint on abstractness. I discussed such a constraint in *How abstract is phonology?* (1968b), and it has been debated repeatedly in the recent literature. The type of theory that was proposed in the *Sound pattern of English* (henceforth: SPE), and on the basis of which analysis of other languages than English were proposed in the sixties, led to a number of analyses that many people find implausible. For example: the analysis of *boy* in English as being underlying [œ̄] with an open, front, rounded vowel; the epsilon glide. i.e., the segment that is [-cns, -voc, -hi] that is claimed for the underlying forms of words like *tolerance,* or *menu;* or the distinction between the final vowels of *veto* and *motto* which in SPE is that between open ɔ and mid o. All of these posited forms do not correspond in any direct way to anything that is present on the surface in any allomorphs of the words or morphemes that are analysed as having these underlying segments. Similarly, in Lightner's analysis of Russian, a word like [šum] has the analysis / xeumos / with several abstract segments. Considerable methodological importance is, in fact, given to these analyses in SPE.

In many of these cases, arguments have subsequently been given within the theory of SPE that refute or at least weaken the evidence for the analysis that posits such abstract segments (McCawley 1974; Harada and Imai 1970; Hoard, 1972). Still, one might go on to ask whether there might not be some deeper, principled reason why these analyses are not right. Is there a *substantive* constraint limiting the relation between underlying and surface representations in some fashion? Such a constraint might say either that underlying representations which don't correspond directly to anything on the surface are HARD to learn for a child or, more strongly, that such representations are IMPOSSIBLE to learn. If such purely abstract segments in underlying representations are hard to learn, the theory will have to reflect this formally by making them expensive. There will be a clause in the evaluation measure that places a high cost on them. The other possibility, that they are impossible to learn, would require setting up some absolute constraint in the theory that excludes such analyses completely. In *How abstract is phonology?* I considered both of those versions without really saying which one I preferred, the reason being that I was not sure myself. Subsequently, there has been a lot of discussion of this proposal. Some modifications to it were suggested in Vetter (1968), Smith (1969), Davison (1971), and Piggott (1971). It was argued against in Hyman (1970a, b), Brame (1968), Kisseberth (1969), Kim (1972). Campbell (1969) and Crothers (1971) have reviewed and countered some of this criticism, favoring some sort of constraint on abstraction. A view similar (in this respect) to mine was also proposed independently by Andersen (1969).

The evidence given in *How abstract is phonology?* consisted of *historical* facts. These facts seemed to indicate that the rules and underlying representations which are postulated in certain kinds of abstract analyses differ from other rules and underlying representations postulated in generative phonologies in not functioning in any linguistic changes, and that there is hence some reason to doubt their existence. The analysis I was specifically concerned with were those involving *absolute neutralization,* i.e., the context-free merger of an underlying phonological contrast on the phonetic surface. I concluded that absolute neutralization either contributes a great amount of linguistic complexity to a grammar (the *weak alternation condition*) or is excluded outright (the *strong alternation condition*). This amounts to saying that the present evaluation measure, which is based on formal simplicity, is giving the wrong answers in some cases and needs to be revised by incorporating some version of an abstractness condition.

What some of the replies to *How abstract is phonology?* showed was that there are languages in which the (strong) alternation condition leads to more complex analyses than would otherwise be possible. But showing that introducing the alternation condition can lead to more complex analyses cannot by itself refute the alternation condition, since the point at issue is precisely whether simplicity is the correct evaluation measure. The claim is that analyses involving absolute neutralization, however simple they may be, are still in some sense difficult or impossible for a child to learn; that simplicity is not the only criterion for evaluating a grammar and should be augmented by some substantive constraint on abstractness.

To avoid begging the question in investigations of this problem we must look for *external evidence* as to the correctness or incorrectness of specific analyses which are required or forbidden by the constraints at issue. The papers by Hyman (1970a, b) and Piggott (1971) went right to the heart of the matter. Hyman's papers are important in introducing another aspect of historical linguistics, viz. facts about borrowing, into discussion of phonological theory. However, as argued in Crothers (1971) and, in more detail, in Kiparsky (1973), both the internal and the external arguments for Hyman's analysis are inconclusive. I should like to discuss Pigott's paper briefly here.

A major flaw in my paper was that it dealt mostly just with cases in which wholly abstract segments had been set up in order for ONE rule to have a phonological context. All the actual evidence given there pertains to such cases. True, the majority of cases in which wholly abstract segments had been used at that time were of this type, and it is these where the legitimacy of the device is most questionable. But obviously there exist cases in which wholly abstract segments are motivated by SEVERAL distinct phonological processes, e.g., in the Spanish vowel system (Harris, 1969); a clear example is Newman (1968). As pointed out especially by Brame (1968) and Kisseberth (1969), who gave other such examples, the internal justification for abstract analyses is much stronger here. We might, accordingly, assume that wholly abstract segments are to be allowed when more than one rule refers to them crucially. From the viewpoint of language acquisition this would be very natural. We would expect, in general, the ease with which absolute neutralization is learned to go up with the amount of evidence which the phonological processes of the language provides for the neutralized distinction. In effect, this amounts to the weak alternation condition, viz. that absolute neutralization adds complexity to the grammar, but is not categorically excluded.

Since there is evidence for SOME constraint on absolute neutralization, it can be fairly said that the burden of proof falls at least in part on one who wishes to argue for a limitation on this constraint. At any rate, as noted above, internal justification is not enough, because the theory itself is at issue.

We have to find *external* evidence which shows that the abstract analyses posited in certain cases do have psychological reality. Of course, this cannot and need not be done in every single example. Once we have provided external justification in a few clear ones, we can provisionally adjust phonological theory so that it will require the abstract analyses in these cases. The resulting theory will then lead to specific predictions about what the correct analysis is in many other cases, where external empirical evidence may or may not be available to test the theory.

The beginnings of this external empirical justification have been provided by Piggott (1971). Piggott analyzes a series of phonetic mergers in the history of the Algonquian languages. The cases which Piggott investigates involve segments which before the merger behave differently with respect to at least one phonological rule. For example, Proto-Algonquian */θ/, which palatalized to */š/ before */i/, became */l/, thereby falling together with Proto-Algonquian */l/, which was not affected before */i/. Similarly, Proto-Algonquian */i/, which caused palatalization of certain preceding segments (including */θ/), merged with */e/, which did not cause palatalization before it. Some of these phonetic mergers subsequently resulted in morphophonemic mergers. Changes took place which eliminated the need for making a morphophonemic distinction between the *l* from */θ/

(which turned to š in the palatalizing environments) and the original *l* (which was not subject to change). The way this happened in some Algonquian languages was that all *l*'s, including those from */l/, started to become š in the palatalizing environments. In Delaware, the opposite happened: the *l*'s from θ became like the original *l*'s and stopped being palatalized to š.

	basic	in palatalizing environment	basic	in palatalizing environment
Proto-Algonquian	θ	š	l	l
After merger	l	š	l	l
Usual reanalysis	l	š	l	š
Delaware reanalysis	l	l	l	l

We can interpret the reanalyses as the result of language learners failing to retain the underlying phonological distinction in their synchronic grammars, and instead setting up a rule l → š, which some *l*'s have to be marked as not undergoing. Subsequently, this mark is either removed from all *l*'s (i.e., all *l*'s become regular—the usual change) or the rule itself is eliminated (the Delaware change). I.e., *the reanalyses proceed from a non-abstract synchronic analysis of the merged segments.*

In other cases, such reanalysis does NOT take place. For example, modern Algonquian languages still show the distinction between original *i*, which causes palatalization, and *i* from */e/, which does not cause palatalization. Piggott now observes the following correlation: phonetic merger leads to reanalysis where the distinction is relevant to the operation of just one rule; phonetic merger does not lead to reanalysis where the distinction is relevant to the operation of several rules. For example, palatalization is the ONLY process that distinguishes original *l* and *l* from */θ/. But the two *i*'s are distinguished by processes of vowel coalescence IN ADDITION TO the palatalization rule. If the abstract analysis is permissible in this latter kind of case, then the preconditions for reanalysis are not met there. We then have an explanation for why these cases do not in fact undergo reanalysis.

If this idea proves to be generally valid (and it is certainly consistent with the examples known to me), then my claim in *How abstract is phonology?*, that absolute neutralization is unstable, must be qualified. The instability seems to show up mainly just where the neutralized distinction is weakly embedded in the grammar, making a difference for only one rule. This suggests a version of the alternation condition which has the effect of ruling out absolute neutralization under these conditions, but which allows absolute neutralization where the internal evidence involves several phonological processes of the language. There is no need to emphasize the lack of solid evidence as to the exact nature of the alternation condition, and the tentative nature of conclusions even as vague as those suggested here.

Another constraint on the relation between underlying and surface phonological representations has recently been proposed by Hale (1971), on the basis of ample synchronic and historical evidence from various Polynesian and Australian languages. Hale considers the type of morphological situation illustrated by the following data from Maori:

verb	passive	
awhi	awhitia	'to embrace'
hopu	hopukia	'to catch'
aru	arumia	'to follow'
tohu	tohuŋia	'to point out'
mau	mauria	'to carry'
wero	werohia	'to stab'
patu	patua	'to strike, kill'
kite	kitea	'to see, find'

If we wanted an "A" on our exam, we would, of course, say that the underlying forms are /awhit/, /hopuk/, /maur/, etc., and that the suffix is /ia/. We would then have a rule that consonants are deleted word-finally, but stay otherwise. Another rule would say that /ia/ turns to a after stems ending in a vowel, e.g., /patu + ia/ → *patua*. More support for this analysis would be the fact that the gerundive ending /aŋa/ also is preceded by the consonant postulated for the stem, e.g., *awhitaŋa, hopukaŋa* etc.

If someone were to say that the underlying forms are / awhi /hopu/, /mau/ etc., and that there are large numbers of different passive suffixes, /tia/, /kia/, /ria/ etc., he'd flunk. What Hale shows is that Maori children learning their language flunk this "exam" and in fact set up underlying forms in which stems all end in different vowels and there are large numbers of different passive endings. There is strong evidence that the "clever" analysis is not psychologically correct. The psychologically correct grammar of Maori has /tia/ as the basic ending and /kia/, /ria/ etc., as a set of allomorphs used in verbs that have to be lexically marked as taking them. We have, in other words, a regular /tia/-conjugation and a number of subsidiary conjugations. In support of this analysis, Hale cites the following facts:

"(1) Stems which are basically nominal are often used verbally in spontaneous discourse; when they are so used, in the passive, they regularly take the ending /-tia/. (2) Derived causatives (formed with the prefix /whaka-/) take /-tia/ in the passive even if the basic verb stem takes another alternant when not in the causative. (3) There is a rule whereby certain adverbials are made to agree in voice with the verbs they modify; these adverbials take /-tia/ in the passive regardless of the shape of the passive ending which the verb itself takes. (4) Borrowings from English, including unassimilated consonant-final ones, take the ending /-tia/ in the passive.

(5) Compound verbs derived by incorporating a noun from an adverbial phrase regularly form their passives in /-tia/. (6) In general, /tia/ can be used when the conventional passive termination for a given verb is not remembered. These facts are entirely consistent with the suggested reanalysis. Only with difficulty can they be made consistent with the phonological alternative in the synchronic description of Maori. The situation is similar in other Polynesian languages—the extreme case of regularization is exemplified by Hawaiian, which now has a single passive ending /-ʔia/ (from *-kia, presumably)."

These facts are inexplicable under the "clever" analysis. For example, why should we have *mau* ∿ *mauria* but causative *whakamau* ∿ *whakamautia*? The analysis which sets up underlying /maur/ must say in addition that the causative prefix triggers a change of the stem-final consonant to *t* (and, presumably, in vowel-final stems, epenthesis of *t*). Under the "stupid" analysis the causatives behave exactly as expected. The fact that we get *whakamautia* is just a special case of the general fact that derived words tend to be morphologically regular as compared to simple words. For example, causative verbs are weak in English and other Germanic languages, belong to the first *a*-conjugation in Sanskrit, etc.

Historically, there is no doubt at all that the consonants were indeed originally part of the stem, and were lost by the historical analog to the rule which the "clever" analysis postulates as a synchronic process. This sound change has taken place in the other Polynesian languages, too. Interestingly enough, they seem to have undergone the same kind of change as Maori, with the consonant being reanalyzed as part of the ending. But the fact that the various languages each pick a different consonant for the basic ending shows that the reanalysis has taken place independently in each of the languages. This is very strong evidence in support of Hale's claim.

What we must do now is to change linguistic theory so that this "wrong" solution will be the right solution. Hale notes that Polynesian languages have no final consonants on the surface, and ascribes the reanalysis to a tendency for the canonical shape of the underlying representations to mimic the canonical shape of surface representations. Hale considers stating this as an absolute constraint:

(A′)   "An underlying phonological representation of stems is disallowed if it violates a universal (i.e., exception less within the language) surface canonical pattern."

but suggests that it may be more correct to regard it as a RELATIVE constraint:

(A)   *"There is a tendency in the acquisition of a language for
linguistic forms to be analyzed in a way which minimizes
the necessity to postulate underlying phonological representations of morphemes which violate the universal surface canonical patterns of the language."*

This formulation brings out the relationship to the weak alternation condition very clearly. Just as the alternation condition says that underlying
distinctions which do not directly correspond to surface distinctions are
hard to learn, so Hale's principle says that underlying canonical forms
which do not correspond to surface canonical forms are hard to learn. The
motivation of both principles in the process of language acquisition is readily apparent.

2. Paradigm Conditions

Another type of substantive constraint that is needed to account for the
historical facts has to do with the relation between the allomorphs in a
paradigm (for more detailed discussion, see Kiparsky (1972); cf. also Miller
(1971)). The first of these is essentially the traditional notion of "leveling".
(See Harris (1970, 1973).) A standard example of analogical change is the
elimination of s in the inflection of certain Latin s-stems like *honōs* ~ *honor*.
The stems that underwent this change were basically masculine and feminine
polysyllables. In the oblique cases they were originally subject to the rule:

$$s \rightarrow r \; / \; V \text{_____} V$$

The s/r alternation due to this rule was eliminated by generalizing *r* in the
nominative:

N.	honōs	honor
G.	honōris	honōris
A.	honōrem	honōrem

(The shortening of $\bar{o}$ to o is due to a general rule of Latin which says that
vowels are shortened before consonants word-finally.) In my thesis (Kiparsky 1965) I said that the change was formally a reanalysis of the base form
from /honōs/ to /honōr/. Thus the $s \rightarrow r$ rule would no longer be needed
in this derivation, although it continues to operate where the change did not
take place, i.e., in monosyllables (*flōs* ~ *flōris*) and in neuters
(*genus* ~ *generis*).

What I forgot was that some of the changing stems retain *s* in
derivatives, e.g., *honor* ~ *honestus*. To account for this, some *ad hoc*
measures must be taken. Two come to mind as possibilities: (1) The
underlying form is indeed restructured with /r/, but there is a special minor

rule that sends *r* to *s* in derivatives like *honestus*. This cannot be a general process in the language and must be restricted to a fairly small number of words. (2) We do not have a restructuring of the underlying form after all, and /s/ is retained. Instead, there is a special additional clause on the *s* → *r* rule, which states that the rule must be also applied in the nominative (even though no vowel follows the *s*) in masculine and feminine polysyllables. Either way we have a complication of the grammar. And yet we would like to say that this is basically the same type of change that generally involves optimalizing the grammar. How can we change the theory to make this a good thing to happen to a language, in spite of the formal complexity that results? The obvious way is to say that in the child's acquisition of language there is a cost attached to having alternations in a paradigm:

(B) *Allomorphy tends to be minimized in a paradigm.*

The existence of some such principle as (B) is shown by the fact that it can, in cases such as this, override *formal* considerations of simplicity. There are others in which it does not. Given that there is some such substantive principle as (B), it becomes our task to delimit the relative force of this substantive principle and the formal principle of simplicity in cases such as this where there is conflict between them, so as to be able to predict which one will win out. Obviously we are not even close to being able to do this yet.

Principle (B) also solves some problems which arise in rule reordering. There are cases which do not fit the characterization of unmarked order in terms of the *feeding* and *bleeding relations* defined in Kiparsky (1968a). For example, in German the final devoicing rule

$$Devoicing: [+obstr] \rightarrow [-voiced] / - \begin{cases} +C \\ \# \end{cases}$$

is ordered both ways, depending on the dialect, with respect to the rule that drops *g* after *ŋ*.

$$g\text{-}deletion: g \rightarrow \emptyset / [+nasal] \underline{\hspace{2cm}}$$

Depending on the order, we get [laŋ] or [laŋk] for /laŋg as follows:

Dialect group I

	/laŋg/	/laŋg + e/
1. Devoicing	laŋk	—
2. g-deletion	—	laŋe

Dialect group II

	/laŋg/	/laŋg + e/
1. g-deletion	laŋ	laŋe
2. Devoicing	—	—

Historically, *Group I* seems to represent the original order, from which *Group II* has changed by reordering. (Cf. Vennemann (1969), for a detailed dicussion of these rules.) However, the relation between the rules is one of *mutual bleeding*. Only one of the two rules can apply to any one input representation, and this is always whichever rule applies first. Yet this formally symmetrical ordering relation is not functionally symmetrical. The innovating order is in conformity with principle (B). This case of reordering therefore furnishes supporting evidence for minimization of allomorphy as an independent functional principle which is not reducible to formal properties of the generative system of a language.

A second paradigm constraint has to do with preservation of semantic information on the surface (Kiparsky 1972). For example, in Labov's data on Black English (Labov *et al.* 1968:158), final *s* is deleted much more frequently in genitives and third person singulars than in plurals. This fact has echoes in historical linguistics. In German, *-e* drops optionally in the singular dative but not in the plural. In Middle High German, the rule was optional in both cases but was applied more frequently in the dative. In Middle English, *-n* dropped more frequently when it was a case marker than when it was a plural marker. It seems to be a general phenomenon, then, that plural endings are more resistant to deletion than case and agreement endings. One would like to relate this to the fact that plural is selected in the deep structure and has a direct semantic interpretation, whereas (surface) case and agreement are inserted by transformational rules and have no direct semantic interpretation. Loss of the plural distinction hence impedes meaning more than loss of other categories. A consideration of analogical change supports this point. When lost, plurals are more likely to be re-introduced by analogical change than are cases or agreement morphemes. We can then formulate the following principle:

(C)   *Morphological material which is predictable on the surface tends to be more susceptible to loss than morphological material which is not predictable on the surface.*

In the light of this last point it is worth reconsidering the significance of the kinds of facts that Labov and his collaborators have been unearthing. They found that if you measure the frequencies with which optional rules are applied, you get very systematic results. The relationship between the frequencies in different cases is fairly constant. If one speaker deletes case more often than plural, that will be the case for any other speaker, or for the same speaker one day later. There is a real question as to how such facts are to be accounted for in linguistic theory. There are basically two ways one could see this done. Labov's proposal is to devise a new sort of linguistic rule, the *variable rule*, in which the frequencies of rule application, or at least something from which these frequencies can be deduced, are attached to the rule. This amounts to saying that the frequencies have to be learned by the child, and are simply part of the linguistic information you have to acquire when you learn your phonology. An alternative, which is suggested by the cross-linguistic validity of the factors that control the frequency of application, is the following: the frequencies are *not* learned by the child, but predictable from exactly the kinds of substantive constraints we have been considering here. This may well be too strong. There are intermediate possibilities, for example, that the child must learn the "basic strength" of an optional rule, i.e., its overall frequency of application, whereas the variations in frequency of application in specific environments follow from general functional considerations such as those discussed here.

The paradigmatic factors interact with phonotactic factors that have to do with maximizing the naturalness of the output sequences. For example, when consonants are deleted optionally at the end of a word, they are dropped more frequently when the next word begins with a consonant, less frequently when it begins with a vowel, i.e., the frequencies of deletion are such as to favor CVCV sequences in the output.

In addition, such factors as style, social class and tempo play a role. It will be useful to distinguish these as *non-grammatical* conditioning factors from the *grammatical* factors, i.e., phonotactics and paradigm structure. The justification for making this distinction is that the grammatical factors play a role elsewhere in grammar, for example in characterizing the possible targets of phonological "conspiracies".

The alternative hypothesis, then, is:

(D) *Grammatically conditioned variability in the application of optional rules favors optimal outputs.*

where optimality should be characterizable independently of any particular language in terms of paradigmatic and phonotactic properties of the output. For example, we would not expect to find a dialect of English in which plural -*s* drops MORE often than genitive or third singular -*s*. More generally, NO language should show a bias in favor of deleting a deep structure category rather than a transformationally introduced category. No language should drop final consonants more often when the next word begins with a vowel, or drop final vowels more often when the next word begins with a consonant, etc. So far the available facts seem to be compatible with this hypothesis.

More unclear is the question whether we can also predict the relative force of the different factors that jointly condition variability. For example, could two dialects differ in that paradigmatic factors were more important in one dialect but phonotactic factors were more important in the other? The answer may be no. There is some reason to believe that the strength of the factors is itself predictably variable. Conditioning by grammatical category becomes relatively more important in more formal speech (Labov *et al.* 1968). This suggests that the strength of the conditioning factors is dependent on the functional requirements of the speech situation.

The closest I have seen to a counter-example is the tensing and raising of /æ/ in New York, on which Labov (1972) has reported (cf. Bailey (1970) for further discussion of this example). This happens before voiced non-nasal stops (*bad, bag, cab*), voiceless fricatives (*laugh, bath, pass, cast*), and front nasals (*man, ham, land*). The raising is to some extent variable in all environments. For speakers over about seventy, there is more raising before fricatives and voiced stops than before nasals (i.e., the vowel is higher on the average in *pass, bad* than in *man*); but for younger speakers the situation is reversed: there is more raising before nasals than before fricatives and voiced stops. In addition, there is some less clear fluctuation in the relative strength of the fricative and voiced stop conditions. Before concluding that there is a genuine reversal of the nasal constraint, one should bear in mind two additional facts which are probably involved: (1) The tensing before fricatives in *pass, last*, etc., is a historically older process which is clearly related to the British English development of [a:] in these words (Luick 1964:704-9). It is evidently a separate rule from the other tensing. In the speech of seventy years ago this was the primary process of tensing which operated. (2) Presumably the increasingly strong raising before nasals parallels the increasing nasalization and concomitant lengthening and tensing of vowels before nasals in American English. Evidently, then, there is more going on here than a simple reversal in the strength of the conditioning factors. The raising of /æ/ actually involves several separate processes.

Hypothesis (D) leads to a reexamination of the theory of sound change. Labov's work on sound change indicates that it typically proceeds in two stages. The first is a stage in which the new rule is optional and the frequency of application in particular cases is governed by a complicated interaction of different grammatical paradigmatic and phonological and non-grammatical social and stylistic factors. In the second stage, the rule becomes obligatory in some cases, in which it was frequently applied at the previous, optional stage, and it becomes inapplicable in other cases, in which it was less frequently applied before. The conditioning now becomes relatively simple, generally with either paradigmatic, or phonological, or social, or stylistic factors being selected as the single conditioning factor of the rule. I suggest the following interpretation of this phenomenon: in the first stage, the rule is optional and is subject to the systematic and predictable variability of optional rules in general. The complex interaction of conditioning factors at this stage is not learned as part of the grammar of the language, but follows from the nature of optional rules. In the second stage, the conditioning factors become part of the acquired grammar of the language. But the variability is too complex to learn as such. The

changeover necessitates a *polarization* and *simplification* of the conditioning: some conditioning factors are eliminated and for the others the high
and low frequencies get sorted out as respectively obligatory and inapplicable cases of the new rule.

Generally the conditioning factor that wins out is the phonological one.
This gives the regular case of phonologically conditioned sound change.
When the paradigmatic, social, and stylistic conditioning factors win out we
get cases which neogrammarian theory handles variously as "analogy" or
"dialect mixture". It has long been noted that sound changes can depend on
grammatical categories. We can add that particular KINDS of grammatical
categories are going to block sound changes from taking place. This
strengthens the theory of sound change considerably by subjecting it to the
same constraints that hold on rule variability. In the same way, lexical splits
should reflect factors of style or emphasis. Examples of stylistic split are the
split between lengthening in everyday words like *grass, glass, ass,* versus
short vowel in special words like *crass, lass, gas;* the earlier dropping of *r* in
everyday words like *ass, cuss, bust* versus the retention of *r* in special words
like *parsley, hoarse* (note the doublets *cuss/curse, ass/arse, bust/burst*). The
erudite/vulgar splits known from many languages belong here. Split of
emphatic versus non-emphatic is e.g., the lengthening (reported by Ferguson
(1971) for Philadelphia) of the affective words *mad, bad, glad,* versus *lad,
add, ad, Brad, Tad, fad, cad,* with *sad* varying for the two Philadelphia
speakers I have checked with. Closely related are also splits along major
versus minor category such as the English voicing of θ to ð in pronouns.

Bhat's (1969) observations on Indian caste dialects are also naturally
explicable in these terms. Bhat compared geographic and social (caste)
dialect differentiation in Tulu, a Dravidian language. He noted that, whereas
regional isoglosses are formed by both regular and sporadic sound changes,
all caste isoglosses are formed by regular sound changes. Bhat proposes to
explain this by the assumption that regular sound changes are carried out by
children (who rarely associate with children of other castes) whereas
sporadic sound changes take place in adult speakers (who do interact with
members of other castes). However, probably a simpler way of explaining
Bhat's observation is that polarization of speech differences between social
classes is naturally a powerful factor in a society where the boundaries
between the classes are drawn very sharply.

Further work will have to show whether this is the right approach. It
remains to be seen, for example, whether this framework can account for the
facts that have led Wang and his collaborators to postulate the "diffusion" of
sound changes through the vocabulary, for such cases of grammatical
conditioning of sound change as that cited by Postal (1968) from Mohawk,
and many others. And even if it does turn out to be the right approach, there
is no doubt at all that it will have to be greatly enriched and elaborated before
it is nearly adequate to account for the complexities of synchronic variability
and diachronic change.

3. Rule Opacity and Reordering

The reordering conditions proposed in Kiparsky (1968a), that feeding order tends to be maximized, and bleeding order tends to be minimized, in most cases correctly predict the direction of reordering. The unmarked status of feeding order is not subject to any serious doubt. Still, a number of examples have turned up where these conditions are inadequate. There are three sorts of cases like this: (1) reordering contrary to the conditions; (2) reordering where the concepts of feeding and bleeding are inapplicable; (3) reordering in cases of "mutual bleeding". Some examples have been collected in Kenstowicz and Kisseberth (1971).

In this section I will review the examples known to me where the previously proposed conditions do not work. We shall see that they reveal an inadequacy in the concept of bleeding order. I will tentatively suggest a reformulation of the conditions which accounts for the problematic cases as well as for those which the old conditions handle. This reformulation will make use of the concept of *rule opacity,* which I will argue has an important role to play elsewhere in linguistic theory as well.

I will begin with the syntactic example analyzed in Klima (1964). Klima wrote this paper before it had been shown that reordering of rules is a primary form of linguistic change. His analysis is therefore formulated solely in terms of rule addition and subsequent restructuring. However, it is now easy to recognize that the historical process Klima describes is essentially a series of downward shifts in the order of case marking, which makes case in English dependent on increasingly superficial configurations. For example, the shift from *whom did you see?* to *who did you see?* is a shift from a grammar in which case marking applies before Wh-movement (i.e., to a representation of the form *you past see Wh + PRO)* to a grammar in which case marking applies after Wh- movement (i.e., to something like *Wh + PRO you past see).* From the drift-like progression of this reordering of case marking we can conclude that it constitutes a natural development in the grammar of English. This raises the question, what general principle lies behind the directionality of the drift. The ordering asymmetries of feeding and bleeding order (Kiparsky 1968a) do not help us here. If anything, Klima's analysis shows a drift towards LESS application of the case marking rule.

We can make an initial approximation to the required principle in the following way. Let us make a distinction between *reordering transformations,* which move constituents around, and *feature changing transformations,* which add some morphologically realized mark onto a constituent. Consider tentatively a principle which says:

> (E') Feature changing transformations preferably follow reordering transformations.

This implies that the evaluation measure assigns a higher value to a grammar in which a feature changing rule follows a reordering rule than to the otherwise identical grammar in which the two rules apply in the reverse order. This should, if correct, have the usual consequences in terms of directionality of change, language acquisition (children should make mistakes in the direction of the preferred order but not in the other direction), and frequency in the world's languages.

The study by Hale (1970) of the ergative and passive in Australian languages gives some support of principle (E '). On the basis of a comparative diachronic analysis of several languages Hale tentatively concludes that the ordering:

Pronominalization
Passive

is unstable. He shows that languages having this order tend either to reorder the rules or to make the passive structure obligatory and basic. It is possible, as Hale suggests, to attribute the reordering to the antifeeding nature of the unstable order. However, perhaps a more natural way of looking at the change is that the drift is toward making pronominalization, a feature-changing rule, follow the passive transformation.

There is a phonological analog to this type of asymmetry in the order of transformations. In recent papers, Kisseberth and Kenstowicz (1971) and Kaye (1971) have discussed cases in which the unmarked order of phonological rules is not characterized by the bleeding or feeding relations. The examples of Kenstowicz and Kisseberth are of the following sort. In Yokuts, vowels are shortened in closed syllables:

$$ V \rightarrow [\text{-long}] \ / \ \underline{\hspace{2cm}} \ C \begin{Bmatrix} \# \\ C \end{Bmatrix} $$

e.g., *do:s-ol* 'might report' but *dos-hin* 'reports'. This rule is critically ordered with respect to an epenthesis rule:

$$ \emptyset \rightarrow i \ / \ C \ \underline{\hspace{2cm}} \ C \begin{Bmatrix} \# \\ C \end{Bmatrix} $$

which breaks up clusters and thereby turns closed syllables into open ones. Epenthesis bleeds shortening, but as Kenstowicz and Kisseberth note, the bleeding order:

1. Epenthesis
2. Shortening

in which the rules actually apply is quite natural, and the one which one would expect them to apply. In at least some cases, then, bleeding order seems to be unmarked.

Kenstowicz and Kisseberth do not actually give evidence that bleeding order really is unmarked in such cases. However, there are cases of historical change which support their conjecture. Wayne O'Neil (personal communication) has noted that Faroese has two rules:

1. Intervocalic spirantization
2. Vowel syncope

which originally apply in the given order, e.g., *heidiner→heiðinir→heiðnir* 'heathen (pl.)', and have been reordered into a bleeding order:

1. Vowel syncope
2. Intervocalic spirantization

giving *heidnir,* where spirantization no longer applies.

Another possible example where diachronic evidence may point to the unmarked status of a bleeding order is discussed briefly in Hurford (To appear). Cockney English drops initial *h*. According to Hurford, there is an older dialect which says *a 'ouse,* whereas younger speakers say *an 'ouse*. We might say, then, that the non-bleeding order:

1. an → a / _____ C
2. h → ∅ / # _____

has changed into the bleeding order:

1. h → ∅ / # _____
2. an → a / _____ C

There are a couple of ways out. In the first place, we might say that the second dialect actually has no underlying *h*, but that words formerly ending in *h* have been restructured with an initial vowel. Secondly, we might argue that the rule for the indefinite article reads:

a → an / _____ V

in which case we no longer have a bleeding relationship. But it seems to me that these objections are really beside the point. Suppose that it is possible to motivate the underlying representations which Hurford assumes for the second dialect. Clearly this is a POSSIBLE analysis. The change from *a 'ouse* to *an 'ouse* should be predicted under this analysis as well as under the other possible analysis. That this is the case is a flaw in the theory.

Kenstowicz and Kisseberth discuss two distinct ways in which the theory of phonology might be amended to characterize the markedness of ordering relations in the correct way. The first is that:

(E″)   Where one rule A stands in a bleeding relation with another rule B by virtue of A's altering a structure so that it no longer satisfies the environmental conditions of B, bleeding order is unmarked.

That is, a rule of the form:

K → L / M _____ N

is preferably bled (i.e., preceded) by a rule which destroys M or N (the environment), although it is preferably NOT bled (i.e., followed) by a rule which destroys K (the input proper).

However, they note that (E″) does not take care of the following sort of case. In some Slavic languages there is a vowel copy rule of the form:

(C) V R C → 1 2 3 2 4
    1 2 3 4

This rule, known to be a dialectal innovation of East Slavic, has to apply before an old rule which accents the initial vowel of certain words, as shown by the following derivations:

	/vórn + u/	/golv + u/
vowel copy	vórón + u	golov + u
accent insertion	"	gólov + u
later rules	vorónu	gólovu

It seems evident that this is indeed the expected ordering of vowel copy and accent insertion. But here bleeding order is completely irrelevant. Both rules will apply to underlying /golv-u/ in either order, but with different results.

In view of this example, Kenstowicz and Kisseberth suggest an alternative principle (E‴), in terms of the *substantive* effect of the rules. I formulate it here as follows:

(E‴) Rules which affect syllabic structure (e.g., metathesis, epenthesis, deletion) preferably apply before rules that refer to syllabic structure (e.g., assimilation).

It is clear that Kenstowicz and Kisseberth are generally on the right track. However, neither (E″) nor (E‴) can be correct. This is shown by Kaye's Ojibwa example.

Kay discusses the following two rules in Ojibwa:

vowel coalescense

$$aw + i \rightarrow \begin{cases} \bar{a} \ / \underline{\hspace{1cm}}k \\ \bar{o} \ / \underline{\hspace{1cm}}n \end{cases}$$

n-assimilation $n \rightarrow k \ / \underline{\hspace{1cm}}k$

He presents evidence that certain Ojibwa dialects have gone from the above order to the reverse order. Underlying /nontaw + in + k/ has thereby changed from *nōntōkk* to *nōntākk*. Again, the bleeding (and feeding) relations are inapplicable, so that principle (E″) cannot be invoked However, principle (E‴) also gives the wrong result, since this reordering puts an assimilation rule *before* a rule that changes syllable structure, whereas (E‴) says that assimilation rules preferably go AFTER rules that change syllable structure.

In place of these principles, which are still somewhat unsatisfactory, I would like to put forward tentatively a principle which accounts for all the examples, including the syntactic ones. Define the concept *opacity of a rule* as follows:

> *DEFINITION.* A rule A → B / C _____ D is opaque to the extent that there are surface representations of the form
> (i)   A in environment C _____ D
> or (ii)   B in environment other than C _____ D

(The first of these two conditions has been referred to by structuralists as an alternation being "non-automatic" and by Stampe (1969) as a rule being "contradicted on the surface".) Note that both cases can arise in several ways. For example, CAD might arise through a rule E → C / _____AD, or a rule E → A / C _____ D. B might appear in environments other than C _____ D either through some process that changes CBD to EBD, or through a process that introduces B in other environments, etc. Of course, exceptions add opacity to a rule according to the above definition. The definition can be extended to syntax in the obvious way. Opacity as here defined is a matter of degree, although I have no suggestions as to how to quantify it formally. I suspect that the concept will ultimately turn out to be more complicated than the above definition indicates.

Let us refer to the converse of opacity as *transparency*.

The hypothesis which I want to propose is that opacity of rules adds to the cost of a grammar; more concretely, that opacity is a property of rules that makes them, and the underlying forms to which they apply, harder to learn. In particular, I conjecture that transparent rules are learned first, and that the acquisition of phonological rules proceeds roughly in the order of increasing opacity.

As regards unmarked ordering, we can now derive, as a special case, the following principle:

(E)   *Rules tend to be ordered so as to become maximally transparent.*

This principle seems to cover the hitherto recalcitrant examples of ordering asymmetry, capturing what is correct about the three principles (E'), (E"), and (E''').

For example, in Yokuts the preferred, unmarked order is that in which shortening applies to the superficial, more phonetic representations reached after epenthesis, rather than the deeper, more abstract representations that the derivation shows before epenthesis. If shortening came before epenthesis, it would be a more opaque rule by *DEF., Case* (ii). In Slavic, the rule "accent the first vowel in words of the *golv class*" would be opaque if it preceded copying, since copying would introduce a stressed vowel on the second syllable of these words as well (*DEF., Case* (ii). In Ojibwa, the awi → ō /____n rule is more opaque in the ordering that gives *nōntōkk* than in the innovating ordering that gives *nōntākk (DEF., Case* (ii)). Similarly, in Klima's syntactic example the drift is towards making case marking an increasingly transparent process.

The reader will have noticed that these examples all involve *Case* (ii) of the definition of opacity. The same is true of the syntactic examples of Klima and Hale, and of the other examples discussed in the paper by Kenstowicz and Kisseberth. What about *Case* (i), then? *This is simply a characterization of non-feeding order;* the consequence that feeding order tends to be maximized is given by including *Case* (i) in the definition of opacity.

For example, suppose we have the two rules:

1. $\gamma \rightarrow \emptyset$ / V _____ V
2. $\begin{bmatrix} V \\ -lo \end{bmatrix} \rightarrow$ [+ hi] / _____ V

Now the order given is the unmarked feeding order, in which we get derivations like *eye* → *ee* → *ie*. This is also the order in which both rules are maximally transparent. Reversing the order would result in an output *ee* for the input *eye*, making the vowel raising rule opague by *Case* (i).

Our revised characterization of the ordering asymmetries now takes care of feeding order, one type of bleeding order, and certain cases where the concepts of feeding and bleeding are not applicable. Then what about cases of marked bleeding order of the type discussed in Kiparsky (1968a), namely those in which two rules potentially apply in the *same* segment? For example, in Swiss German there is a reordering from

	/bode + Sg./	/bode + PL./
1. Umlaut (e.g., in env.____Pl.)	—	böde + Pl./
2. o → ɔ / ____[+ coronal]	bɔde + Sg.	—

to

	/bode + Sg./	/bode + Pl./
1. o → ɔ / ____[+ coronal]	bɔde + Sg.	bȫde + Pl.
2. Umlaut (e.g., in env.____Pl.)	—	bɔde + Pl.

But these are exactly the cases in which the *paradigm* condition that allomorphy tends to be minimized, which we have seen to be needed on independent grounds, will give the correct result! In the Swiss German example, the innovating order preserves the stem shape between singular and plural. A review of the examples given in Kiparsky (1968a), King (1969), and elsewhere, shows that the cases which have been cited as reordering from bleeding into non-bleeding order are all of this type.

The proposed reformulation seems necessary in order to account for the examples brought up by Kaye and by Kenstowicz and Kisseberth, and the syntactic cases discussed by Klima and Hale. It has at least as clear a ιunctional basis in language acquisition as the notion of maximal applicability which it replaces. In addition, it has some important further advantages which I will now mention briefly.

The notion of rule transparency enables us to establish a profound relationship between the two historical phenomena of rule reordering and rule loss.

It has been pointed out by Stampe (1969) and Andersen (1969) (cf. also Darden (1970)) that rules tend to be lost from grammars through historical change only under certain specific conditions. Basically, we can say that rules are susceptible to loss *if they are hard to learn*. And one of the major factors that makes rules hard to learn (though not the only one) is precisely *opacity* as defined above.

Consider the first condition that leads to opacity (*Case* (i) in the *DEFINITION*). A rule is opaque if representations of the sort which it eliminates exist on the surface. Loss under this condition is common (cf. the Algonquian example cited from Piggott (1971) in Section 1 of this paper). To give just one more case, a similar situation arose in early Iranian. The Iranian languages once had Bartholomae's law, by which voiceless stops were subject to progressive assimilation of aspiration and voicing after voiced aspirates, e.g., /drugh + ta/ → *drugdha*. Voiced *unaspirated* stops did not cause progressive assimilation, and were themselves subject to regressive assimilation of voicing (with velars in addition being spirantized), e.g., /bhag + ta/ → *bhaxta*. Subsequently the voiced aspirates were deaspirated. The resulting situation is one in which some voiced stops (the old aspirates) cause progressive voicing assimilation, but others (the original unaspirated stops) do not, e.g., (assuming rephonemicization) /drug+ta/ → *drugda,* but /bag+ta/ → *baxta*. This stage essentially survives in older Avestan. In later Avestan, however, the now opaque progressive assimilation rule is simply lost, giving /drug+ta/ → *druxta* like /bag+ta/ → *baxta*. Bartholomae's Law is lost as a rule and survives only in isolated words in lexicalized form, e.g., in *azda* 'thus'. Other examples are given in Andersen (1969).

We would also expect the second type of opacity (*Case* (ii)) to lead to rule loss. There is not a great deal of evidence for this being so. But a tentative analysis by Erteschik (1971) is, if correct, exactly such a case. The Hebrew spirantization rule, apparently applicable originally to all stops, has been limited to *p, b,* and *k*. Erteschik suggests that *p, b,* and *k* were, at the time when the rule became restricted in this way, exactly the stops whose spirantized cognates were not phonemic, the system being:

$$
\begin{array}{cccc}
p & t & k & ? \\
b & d & g & \\
s & & & X \\
z & r & &
\end{array}
$$

In support of this conjecture she notes what happens when children learn spirantization in modern Hebrew. Here *X* has lost its pharyngealization, thereby merging with *x*, the spirantized form of *k*. This means that spirantization of *k* has become opaque with respect to *Case* (ii), since the output of spirantization of *k* now has another source in the grammar. Spirantization of *p*, *b*, on the other hand, remains transparent. According to Erteschik, children make mistakes with spirantizing velars (but not, apparently, with labials). For *lexabes* ∿ *kvisa* she has observed children saying both *lexabes* ∿ *xvisa* and *lekabes* ∿ *kvisa*. That is, children find it harder to learn the opaque part of the modern Hebrew spirantization rule (and the underlying forms insofar as they are subject to this rule) than the transparent part of the same rule.

Stampe has suggested other factors which make a rule susceptible to loss, in particular the *unnatural* status of a rule. For example, certain natural processes of vowel lengthing or shortening may be unnatural as the corresponding tensing or laxing processes when the length opposition changes into a tenseness opposition in the course of historical change. Such rules might also be susceptible to loss. Therefore not all cases of loss will necessarily involve rules which are opaque in the sense defined here. Opacity will, however, be ONE of the factors that bring about the loss of rules from a grammar by historical change.

Rule opacity also plays a role in paradigm changes like those discussed above. Strictly speaking, Principle (B) is inadequate by itself to deal with an example like the change of *honōs* to *honor*. The *r* which is reintroduced in the nominative causes shortening of the preceding vowel by a general rule of Latin. As a result we have actually just traded in the s/r alternation of *honōs/honoris* for the o/ō alternation of *honor/honōris*. Still, everyone would grant that there is a real levelling here. It is obvious that the new paradigm in some sense shows "less allomorphy" than the old one. But what exactly does this mean formally? I would like to suggest as the crucial difference that the shortening rule, which produces the ō/o alternation, is transparent with respect to *Case* (i), whereas the rhotacism rule, which produces the s/r alternation, is opaque with respect to *Case* (i). That is, there are no words ending in -*ōr* in Latin, but there are many words with intervocalic *s* (partly because of exceptions to the rule, e.g., *miser* 'miserable', *positus* 'put (pp.)', including loans like *basis, asinus* 'donkey', and partly because of *s* from other underlying sources, e.g., /cād + tus/ → *cāsus* 'fallen').

Finally, I should like to suggest that the concept of rule opacity may prove to be useful in *the theory of exceptions*. It is hard to find a clearcut division of phonological rules into those that may and those that cannot allow exceptions. However, it is possible to say that certain kinds of rules are much less likely to have exceptions than others. As a first approximation to the needed criterion I propose opacity. The more opague a rule, the more likely it is to develop exceptions. More specifically, opacity by *Case* (i) leads to *input* exceptions, whereas opacity by *Case* (ii) leads to *environment* exceptions (see Kisseberth (1970) and Coats (1970) for these concepts). As an example of the first case, consider Finnish consonant gradation. This is a weakening affecting consonants in the environment.

$$ \underline{\hspace{2cm}} VC \left\{ \begin{matrix} \# \\ C \end{matrix} \right. $$

The rule applies to single stops and geminate stops in the following way:

1. *Weakening of simple stops*   t→d   (e.g. /maton/→*madon* 'worm's')
                                     p→v
                                     k→∅, v

2. *Degemination*   tt→t   (e.g. /matton/→*maton* 'carpet's')
                                     pp→p
                                     kk→k

Degemination has virtually no exceptions (only certain very foreign names might not be subjected to the rule, e.g., gen. *Giuseppen,* provided they are not assimilated in any way, including stress). On the other hand, the weakening of simple stops normally fails to apply in loans (*auton* 'car's'), as well as in many native personal names (*Lempin,* 'Lempi's'), brand names (*Upon* 'of Upo'), slang and affective words (*räkän* 'of snot'), etc. It seems reasonable to correlate this with the fact that degemination is nearly completely transparent with respect to *Case* (i), whereas the weakening of simple stops is rather opaque with respect to that case. That is, the sorts of input representations that are destroyed by degemination exist on the surface only in the rare exceptions, and in a few cases where strong boundaries block the application of gradation, e.g., *Kekkosta* 'Kekkonen (partitive)' (Karttunen 1970). But the sorts of input representations destroyed by the weakening of single stops are quite frequent on the surface; indeed, they arise with every application of degemination. Thus, we might suppose that the weakening of simple stops, and the underlying forms subject to it, are harder to learn than the degemination rule, and the underlying forms subject to it. (This should be readily testable in child language.) The greater proneness of the weakening of simple stops to develop exceptions would, then, be a consequence of its greater opacity.

Examples of the second type (opacity by *Case* (ii) leading to environment exceptions) are commonplace. This case is simply the initial stage of the process of morphologization, by which rules lose their phonological conditioning and begin to be dependent on abstract features in the lexicon. The paradigm case is Germanic umlaut. The elimination of the conditioning *i* and *j* turned the umlaut rule opaque by *Case* (ii). At some point after this took place, umlaut started to be reanalyzed as a morphologically conditioned process.

Notes

This work was supported in part by the National Institutes of Mental Health (Grant MH-13390).

References

Andersen, H. 1969. A study in diachronic morphophonemics: the Ukrainian prefixes. *Lg.* 45.807-30.

Bailey, C.J. 1970. Building Rate Into a Dynamic Theory of Linguistic Description. *Working Papers of Linguistics* (Hawaii) 2.9.161-233.

Bhat, D.N.S. 1969. A New Hypothesis on Language Change. *Linguistic Survey Bulletin* No. 13.

Brame, Michael. 1968. On the Abstractness of Phonology. Unpublished MS. Cambridge: M.I.T.

Campbell, Lyle. 1969. Phonological Features: On the Horns of a Dilemma. Unpublished MS. Los Angeles: U.C.L.A.

Chen, Matthew and Hsin-I Hsieh. 1971. The Time Variable in Phonological Change. *Journal of Linguistics* 7.1-13.

Chomsky, N. and M. Halle. 1968. The Sound Pattern of English. New York: Harper and Row.

Coats, H.S. 1970. Rule Environment Features in Phonology. *Papers in Linguistics* 2.110-40.

Crothers, John. 1971. On the Abstractness Controversy. University of California (Berkeley) Department of Linguistics Project on Linguistics Analysis Reports, Second Series 12.CR 1-CR 29.

Darden, Bill. 1970. The Fronting of Vowels After Palatals in Slavic. Papers from the Sixth Regional Meeting, Chicago Linguistic Society, 459-70. Chicago: Chicago Linguistic Society.

Davison, A. 1971. A Problem Concerning the Relative Naturalness of Phonological Rules and Phonological Representations. Unpublished MS. Stony Brook: S.U.N.Y.

Demers, R. 1970. Paper presented at the First Meeting of the New England Linguistic Society. Cambridge, Mass.

Erteschik, Nomi. 1971. The BeGeD-KeFeT or BeKeF Mystery. Unpublished MS. Cambridge: M.I.T.

Ferguson, C.A. 1971. 'Short A' in Philadelphia English. Stanford Occasional Papers in Linguistics 1.2-27.

Hale, Kenneth. 1970. The Passive and Ergative in Language Change: The Australian Case. Pacific Linguistic Studies in Honor of Arthur Capell, ed. by S.A. Wurm and D.C. Laycock. Canberra: Australian National University.

Hale, Kenneth. 1971. Deep-surface Canonical Disparities in Relation to Analysis and Change: An Australian Example. Unpublished MS. [To appear in *Current trends in Linguistics, Volume II*, ed. by T. Sebeok, H. Hoenigswald and R. Longacre. The Hague: Mouton.]

Harada, S.I. and K. Imai. 1970. Where Do English Vowels Come From? Unpublished MS. [T0 appear in Energeia.]

Harris, J. 1969. *Spanish Phonology*. Cambridge: The MIT Press.

Harris, J. 1970. Paradigmatic Regularity and Naturalness of Grammars. Presented at the 45th Annual Meeting of the Linguistic Society of America.

Harris, J. 1973. On the Order of Certain Phonological Rules in Spanish. Festschrift for Morris Halle, ed. by S. Anderson and P. Kiparsky. N.Y.: Holt, Rinehart & Winston.

Hoard, J.F. 1972. Naturalness Conditions in Phonology. With Particular Reference to English Vowels. *Contributions to Generative Phonology*, ed. by Micahel Brame. Austin: U. of Texas Press.

Hurford, J. To appear. Review: *Universals in linguistic theory* (Bach and Harms (eds.)).

Hyman, L.M. 1970a. How Concrete is Phonology? *Lg.* 46.58-76.

Hyman, L.M. 1970b. The Role of Borrowing in the Justification of Phonological Grammars. *Studies in African Linguistics* 1.1-48.

Karttunen, F. 1970. Problems in Finnish Phonology. Unpublished Ph.D. dissertation. Bloomington: U. of Indiana.

Kaye, J.D. 1971. A Case for Local Ordering in Ojibwa. Odawa Language Project, First Report. University of Toronto Dept. of Anthropology: Anthropological Series No. 9.

Kenstowicz, Michael and C. Kisserberth. 1971. Unmarked Bleeding Orders. Unpublished MS. Urbana: U. of Illinois.

Kim, C.W. 1972. Two Phonological Notes: A# and Bb. *Contributions to Generative Phonology*, ed. by M. Brame. Austin: U. of Texas Press.

King, R. 1969. *Historical Linguistics and Generative Grammar*. Englewood Cliffs: Prentice-Hall, Inc.

King, R. 1970. Can Rules be Added in the Middle of Grammars? Unpublished MS. Austin: U. of Texas.

Kiparsky, P. 1965. Phonological Change. Unpublished Ph.D. dissertation. Cambridge. M.I.T.

Kiparsky, P. 1968a. *Linguistic Universals and Linguistic Change. Universals in Linguistic Theory*, ed. by E. Bach and R. Harms, 171-202. New York, Rinehart and Winston.

Kiparsky, P. 1968b. How abstract is phonology? Mimeo. Bloomington: Indiana University Linguistics Club.

Kiparsky, P. 1972. *Explanation in Phonology. Goals in Linguistic Theory*, ed. by S. Peters. Englewood Cliffs: Prentice-Hall, Inc.

Kiparsky, P. 1973. *Phonological Representations*. Tokyo: TEC Company, Ltd.

Kisseberth, C. 1969. On the Abstractness of Phonology: The Evidence from Yawelmani. Papers in Linguistics 1.248-82.

Kisseberth, C. 1970. The Treatment of Exceptions. Papers in Linguistics 2.44-58.

Klima, E. 1964. Relatedness Between Grammatical Systems. *Lg.* 40.1-20. [Reprinted in *Modern studies in English,* ed. by D.A. Reibel and S.A. Schane, 227-46. Englewood Cliffs: Prentice-Hall, Inc.]

Labov, W./ 1972. The Internal Evolution of Linguistic Rules. Historical Linguistics in the Perspective of Generative Theory, ed. by R. Stockwell and R. Macanlay. Bloomington: Indiana U. Press.

Labov, W., P. Cohen, C. Robins and J. Lewis. 1968. A Study of the Non-standard English of the Negro and Puerto Rican Speakers of New York City. Cooperative Research Report 3288, Volume I. New York: Columbia U.

Luick, K. 1964. *Historische Grammatik der englischen Sprache, Volume I.* Oxford and Stuttgart: Blackwell and Tauchnitz.

Matthews, G.H. 1970. Some Notes on the Proto-Siouan Continuants. I.J.A.L. 36.98-109.

McCawley, J. 1968. *The Phonological Component of a Grammar of Japanese.* The Hague: Mouton.

McCawley, J. 1974. Review: *The sound pattern of English* (Chomsky and Halle). *I.J.A.L.* 40.50-88.

Miller, G. 1971. On the Motivation of Linguistic Change. Papers in Linguistics in Honor of Henry and Renée Kahane, ed. by B. Kachru *et al.* Urbana: U. of Illinois Press.

Newman, Paul. 1968. The Reality of Morphophonemics. *Lg.* 44.507-15.

Nishihara, Suzuko. 1970. Phonological Change and Verb Morphology in Japanese. Unpublished Ph.D. dissertation. Ann Arbor: U. of Michigan.

Piggott, Glyn. 1971. Some Implications of Algonquinan Palatalization. Odawa Language Project, First Report. University of Toronto Dept. of Anthropology: Anthropological Series No. 9.

Postal, P. 1968. *Aspects of Phonological Theory.* New York: Harper and Row.

Smith, N.V. 1967. The Phonology of Nupe. *Journal of African Languages* 6.153-69.

Smith, N.V. 1969. Review: French Phonology and Morphology (Schane). *Lg.* 45.398-407.

Stampe, D. 1969. The Acquisition of Phonetic Representation. Papers from the Fifth Regional Meeting, Chicago Linguistic Society, ed. by R. Binnick *et al.*, 443-54. Chicago: Dept. of Linguistics, University of Chicago.

Vennemann, T. 1970. The German Velar Nasal: A Case for Abstract Phonology. Phonetica 22.65-81.

Vetter, D. 1968. Abstractness in Phonological Representations. Unpublished Ph.D. dissertation. Cambridge: M.I.T.

Wang, W. S-Y. 1969. Competing Changes as a Cause of Residue. *Lg.* 45.9-25.

DISCUSSION

JANICE REDISH: In regard to your Latin example, do you want to end up keeping the base form in *s* or in *r*?

PAUL KIPARSKY (M.I.T.): I don't really know. I don't think it is important for my point to have made up my mind on that question. I suspect that you probably keep the *s* and have a rule that *s* turns to *r* in the nominative of masculine or feminine polysyllables. The reason I think so is that in comparatives, whose stem ends in *s*, you have e.g., masc. *audacior*, neuter *audacius*. Again, the rule does not apply in the neuter. But in these comparatives, you obviously couldn't just fiddle around with the underlying form. You have to have some rule that changes *s* to *r* in a weird grammatical context. This is the solution which Martti Nyman has proposed in an unpublished paper on Latin rhotacism.

JANICE REDISH: In general, this is a much larger problem: the question of how to weight the choice of a base form that will keep a paradigm regular but will mess up the derivational forms. In talking about the complexity to the child of having allomorphs in a paradigm, is it possible to weigh the derivational section differently from the paradigm? What I am talking about is weighing the relationship betweem forms like *sane* and *sanity* on a different level than that between forms like *honor* and *honōris*.

PAUL KIPARSKY (M.I.T.): Yes, I think you're right. By paradigm, I mean the inflectional stuff NOT the derivational stuff. It is very clear that one must distinguish between derivation and inflection in dealing with the phonology of a language.

In connection with this, I might mention the work of Dick Stanley on Navaho. [Cf. Richard Stanley. 1969. The phonology of the Navaho verb. Unpublished Ph.D. dissertation. Cambridge: M.I.T.] In this language there is a hierarchy of boundaries that increase in strength as you go out from the root. The generalization which comes out from Navaho and which fits very nicely with Finnish, Sanskrit and some other languages is that: if you have AB (where A is a root and B is a suffix) undergoing some process which crosses the boundary between A and B, and you have AC and the boundary between A and C blocks that process, then you can predict the order of the suffixes B and C if they're both present. You always have ABC; never, ABC. The way you might think of representing that formally is by abandoning the boundaries that Chomsky and Halle have with features like [+ stem boundary], [morpheme boundary], etc. and replacing them by a system of bracketing that predicts the strength of boundaries. Given [[[A]B]C], we would have [[A]B], but [[[A]]C], with a stronger boundary in the latter case. This sytem would predict that the richness of the morphology will essentially give you the number of potential boundaries that are operative in a language.

WILLIAM REILLY (Georgetown U.): I want to ask for a little bit of clarification about the weighing which you talked about with regard to Labov's inherent variability and so forth. Are you saying that the main problem for a linguist with that kind of data and with using percentages is that it fails to take into account all of the factors which are responsible for the occurrence of things in different percentages? Would you say that what we should do instead of writing a variable rule is to include more data, e.g., style, tempo, social class and so forth?

PAUL KIPARSKY (M.I.T.): If something is learned, it has to be in the grammar; if something is universally predictable, it is not learned and can be taken out of the grammar, i.e., it can be made to follow from some general principle about language with a capital *L*. What I am conjecturing is that Labov's data can be taken out of the grammar of English, the grammar of German, Spanish, etc., and derived from a theory about optional rules in general. This theory says that optional rules are applied in such a way as to optimalize the output with respect to things like syllabic structure, distinctness of categories, etc. Labov's percentages actually reflect what anybody's going to do given that a rule is optional. The percentages are not something you have to actually tabulate in your mind and look up every time you're going to speak.

PATRICIA M. WOLFE (U. of British Columbia): In regard to what you were saying about distinctness, the interesting thing in English is that you have as many completely uninflected plurals left like *fish, sheep, deer,* etc. as you do forms like *oxen, children, brethren,* etc. More interestingly, the place you really get the *n* ending left is where it carries no information at all and is redundant, viz. on past participles where you already have an auxiliary verb marker; furthermore, the weak verbs manage without any kind of marker there whatsoever. The point here is that when you get *n* preserved as an inflectional ending in English, you get it preserved many, many times more where it doesn't carry any information than where it does. Without quarreling with the general idea that languages obviously preserve distinctness, I think that in some of the data you cited you're going to find not only no support for your claim but actually an awful lot of counter-evidence.

PAUL KIPARSKY (M.I.T.): Yes. There're a lot of things I don't understand about this question. Another problem is the feminine *-e* in German, which, for some strange reason, is very strong. I don't understand why that should be the case either. Sometimes you can make sense of apparent counterexamples: in languages that drop personal pronouns, agreement endings on the verb are strong and don't drop; in languages which have enclitic pronouns, they are weak. If you don't succeed in explaining all of the things we've been discussing, you're going to have to wind up having arbitrarily variable rules and arbitrary morphological conditioning in historical changes. That's essentially throwing in the towel. I prefer, at this point, not to throw in the towel and keep looking for reasons for the variability.

WALBURGA VON RAFFLER ENGEL (Vanderbilt University): I think we are basically in agreement that there are two types of simplicity: psychological simplicity and linguistic simplicity. If the two are in conflict, then the psychological simplicity prevails. Don't you agree with me?

PAUL KIPARSKY (M.I.T.): I think that perhaps we just have a different way of saying things. What you call linguistic simplicity is what I call (formal) simplicity and what you call psychological simplicity is what I call substantive conditions. The reason I don't like your terminology, although I agree with what you mean, is that I don't think there is anything linguistic which is not psychological.

WALBURGA VON RAFFLER ENGEL (Vanderbilt University): In regard to Professor Wolfe's point in substandard English, you have *I have shook, I have took.* The entire past participle drops out which would give you a point.

LLOYD B. ANDERSON (U. of North Carolina): I have a possible explanation for the data from Maori. If there is anything like an analysis-by-synthesis routine, where, when you listen, you try to match the morphemes you're hearing, then your matching routine might state that if you think, for semantic reasons, this root ought to be there, produce that root in your matching system. You don't want to produce more than is going to be there. You therefore produce *aru* rather than *arum* as your basic form. Only if you're given further conditions, can you produce the *m*. The *m* is like *a* stem-vowel in Latin *a*-stems, say, where it is part of the root, but it's not part of the root. It's controlled by the root, because the root arbitrarily causes you to produce it, but it's not there in the minimal form. Because you have to match that might be a reason why you would pick the shortest form that occurs in all forms of the paradigm as your minimal form to match or as your most basic form. I wonder if you have any ideas on whether that would work?

PAUL KIPARSKY (M.I.T.): I'm not sure whether that would cover all the cases that one would like to see handled by Ken Hale's constraint. For example, Hale's constraint would say, as a special case, that the segment types that exist in underlying representations tend to match those that occur on the surface.

HARRY A. WHITAKER (U. of Rochester): I don't have a question—just a comment. Harold Goodglass did some work which is reported in the volume by Rosenberg and Koplin [S. Rosenberg and James H. Koplin (eds.). 1968. Developments in appled psycholinguistic research. N.Y.: The MacMillan Co.] about the differences between the plural markers and some of the other kinds of affixes. He noted that there was quite a differential behavior between these two in aphasic breakdown. Unfortunately Goodglass' data is a little bit tricky because of his failure to control the population samples and as a result he also got differences in the other direction between production and reception disorders. Perhaps with a little more analysis, this work might lend some very interesting support for what I take to be the correct view, i.e., what we're really looking at is real phenomena in the brain. It would be consistent, I think, with the things that you have suggested that brain damage would cause a differential kind of breakdown if in fact there are real differences at the grammatical level.

Chapter Three

Linguistic Metatheory

Barbara Hall Partee

It is impossible to do justice to so big a topic as syntactic and semantic theory in a brief survey article, so I should begin by indicating how I intend to restrict the scope of these remarks. My chief topic will be the relation between syntax and semantics, and I will concentrate on the metatheoretical question of whether syntax and semantics are distinct components in a grammar and if so, how they fit together, thereby neglecting some of the most interesting work that has been done in syntax, since there are, fortunately, many substantive results in syntactic theory that are independent of the form of the connection between syntax and semantics.[1] I will also neglect many of the most exciting issues in semantics proper, since even to present the issues clearly in many cases requires the elaboration of an interpreted formalized higher-order logic; attention will be restricted here to examples that can be discussed with only a little elementary logic. Another omission is pragmatics, the study of the relation between sentences and their use in particular contexts, including such topics as deixis (demonstratives), pragmatic presupposition, conversational implicature, and performatives.[2] In the earliest years of transformation syntax, the undeveloped field of semantics often served as a dump for unexplained phenomena that were suspected not to be syntactic; as semantics developed, it became a less hospitable dumping ground and pragmatics was often given that role.[3] But pragmatics, too, has undergone considerable development in the last several years, and it is becoming increasingly difficult, as it should be, to avoid responsibility for unexplained data by appeal to some not-yet-worked-out component of the grammar.

At the time when the earlier version of this article was written, in 1971, I described linguistic theory as a field very much in flux. From the publication of Chomsky's *Syntactic Structures* in 1957 to the appearance of his *Aspects of the Theory of Syntax* in 1965, the evolution of transformational grammar has been relatively smooth and unified, and there was by 1965 fairly general agreement about the form of the syntactic component of a grammar, with a well-understood phonological component operating on the output of the syntax (surface structure), and seemingly plausible suggestions about a semantic component that would map deep structures onto semantic representations (see Katz and Postal (1964)). There were numerous unsolved problems to work on, particularly in the search for language universals, but the *paradigm* (in the sense of Kuhn (1962)) seemed clear. But with the challenges to this paradigm posed by Lakoff and the development of generative semantics on the one hand, and Jackendoff's interpretive semantics on the other, the field reached by the end of the 1960's a situation in which there was no theory which was both worked out in a substantial and explicit form and compatible with all the data considered important. Syntax classes were difficult to teach; one could show how elegant solutions to many exciting syntactic problems were worked out in the *Aspects* framework, but then one felt compelled to present the additional data that seemed to call the whole framework into question, without being able to offer any single equally worked-out theory that could do better.

By now, in 1976, I think it is fair to say that most linguists working in syntax and semantics would agree that there is a sense of potential convergence. Even though there are still roughly the same major competing theories that I described in 1971, they have evolved and been worked out to the point where many solutions to problems can be translated from one theory into another, and certain substantive points of disagreement are being isolated so that empirical research can be expected to resolve most of the major issues. At the same time, however, new theories are emerging which are difficult to compare with one another or with the earlier theories because of the introduction of new devices or components in one theory that have no clear analogs in other theories; I have in mind here such diverse approaches as Bever and Langendoen's 'perceptual strategies,' Fillmore's 'frame analysis,' Lakoff's 'cognitive grammar,' Chomsky's 'trace theory,' Postal and Perlmutter's 'relational grammar,' the processing models coming out of Woods' 'augmented transition networks', and research in artificial intelligence, Hintikka's 'game theoretic semantics,' and Lieb's 'axiomatic grammar.'[4] But the issues which led to the split between generative and interpretive semantics are still central with respect to the question of the relation between semantics and syntax, and for that reason, plus limitations of time and space, I will not try to discuss any of the new issues raised by the approaches just mentioned.

What I want to do here is fourfold: first, I will give a brief historical sketch of the theory of syntax and its relation to semantics from 1957 to the early 1970's; the focus of this will be the rise and fall of the Katz-Postal hypothesis. Second, I'll outline some of the main features of the generative semantics-interpretive semantics controversy as it stood in the early 1970's, with pro's and con's. Thirdly I will sketch very briefly Richard Montague's quite different approach, which comes out of the logico-philosophical tradition rather than the linguistic tradition but which addresses many of the same key issues that figure in the linguistic controversy. These three parts will be essentially as I presented them in 1971; in the final section I will describe briefly some of the progress that has been made since 1971, and indicate why I believe there is considerable convergence now among these alternative approaches, even though linguists are far from complete unanimity on central theoretical questions.

I. HISTORY

The Katz-Postal hypothesis, presented and defended in Katz and Postal (1964), can be stated essentially as in (1).

(1)   The Katz-Postal hypothesis: The level of deep structure, independently motivated as the output of phase-structure and lexical insertion rules, the input to transformational rules, and the locus of selectional and subcategorization restrictions, is the only level of syntactic structure which is needed as input to semantic interpretation rules.

The evolution of this hypothesis is outlined in Partee (1971); as representatives of the salient points in its development let me mention just the following: (i) in *Syntactic Structures*, a Negative Transformation changed an affirmative sentence to a negative one, with a consequent change in meaning; Klima (1964) gave strong syntactic arguments for the inclusion of a NEG morpheme in the deep structure of negative sentences to which the various rules affecting negative sentences were sensitive; (ii) likewise, syntactic arguments were given for including various other 'deep-structure triggers' for previously meaning-changing transformations, such as IMP for imperatives and Q for interrogatives; (iii) the abandonment of the "generalized transformations" of *Syntactic Structures* in favor of the "generalized P-markers" of *Aspects* eliminated the need to know the transformational history of a sentence in order to determine which clauses were embedded in which so as to describe the difference in meaning between sentences like (2) and (3) below, which on the earlier theory might both have come from the "kernel sentences" in (4).

(2)   That it was obvious surprised John.
(3)   That it surprised John was obvious.
(4) $\begin{cases} \text{It was obvious.} \\ \text{It surprised John.} \end{cases}$

There are two points about the rise of the Katz-Postal hypothesis that I want to mention here because they seem surprising in retrospect, one a rather significant point in Chomsky's *Syntactic Structures* and one apparently just a historical accident in the evolution of the Katz-Postal hypothesis.

The first point concerns Chomsky's view of syntax in 1957. In *Syntactic Structures,* Chomsky expressed doubts about the possibility of ANY systematic connection between syntax and semantics. Furthermore, he believed it not only necessary, but even possible, to describe syntax in completely autonomous terms. This may seem surprising in retrospect,[5] particularly from one who was so articulate in rejecting the idea of trying to do autonomous phonetics. I think his outlook was probably very much affected by his concurrent work on formal languages, where classes of languages could be very rigorously described in syntactic terms, and very interesting formal properties of the languages could be deduced from the form of their grammars. And these approaches DID bear fruit in the investigation of natural languages. In particular, it was possible, using only the most universally agreed-on judgments of *grammatical* and *ungrammatical*, to demonstrate very elegantly that natural languages were neither finite-state languages nor context-free languages. Since those were not straw men in the fifties, that was a great theoretical advance. And since that advance was made within an *autonomous syntax* approach, that approach gained at least *prima facie* plausibility, and made the Katz-Postal hypothesis seem very surprising and strong when it was introduced.

The rise of the Katz-Postal hypothesis was also marked by interesting results which similarly provided a *prima facie* justification for its adoption. In case after case it was shown that a more careful syntactic analysis led to derivations in which transformations were meaning-preserving. The surprising historical accident that I alluded to earlier is that the behavior of quantifiers was not really noticed until the Katz-Postal hypothesis had for most linguists reached the status of a necessary condition on writing rules. I think this historical accident is one of the major causes of the state of turmoil in the theory in the late 1960's. Let me give a few examples of derivations that were not noticed but were implied by the "standard theory" of *Aspects* and leave the reader to reflect on whether the Katz-Postal hypothesis would have even been suggested if these had been noticed beforehand.

(5) a. Every man voted for himself. *FROM:*
    b. Every man voted for every man.
(6) a. Every candidate wanted to win. *FROM:*
    b. Every candidate wanted every candidate to win.
(7) a. All pacifists who fight are inconsistent. *FROM:*
    b. $\begin{cases} \text{All pacifists fight.} \\ \text{All pacifists are inconsistent.} \end{cases}$
(8) a. No number is both even and odd. *FROM:*
    b. No number is even and no number is odd.

This is the kind of data that has led to the downfall of the Katz-Postal hypothesis in conjunction with the classical *Aspects* kind of *independently motivated* syntax. There are clearly two ways to react to such data: either keep the Katz-Postal hypothesis and revise the deep structure; or abandon the Katz-Postal hypothesis and keep the deep structure. The first of these is the *generative semantics approach,* the second the *interpretive semantics approach.* Of course there is another alternative, which is to try a still different model; I'll give an example of that in section III.

II. GENERATIVE AND INTERPRETIVE SEMANTICS

Although what I just said about generative and interpretive semantics is a gross oversimplification, I think it fairly represents their historical beginnings. What there seemed to be in 1965 was a maximally elegant theory, elegant in two directions: first, there was a level of deep structure which could be established on purely syntactic grounds and which had a remarkable convergence of properties: it was the level at which all the key grammatical relations could be defined, all the lexical items could be inserted, and all of their contextual restrictions defined, and it also served as input to the transformations. The other elegant feature of the theory, the contribution of Katz and Postal, was that at this same level of structure there appeared to be a one-for-one correlation between syntactic and semantic rules (not that these were ever worked out, but it certainly appeared possible in principle).

Given this two-sided elegance, it's not hard to see why it was difficult to give the theory up, and why, when it had to be given up, linguists should be divided about which part was more worth fighting for. Let me try to make this vivid by arguing for each side.

A. Interpretive semantics: PRO

Consider again the examples where certain transformations changed meaning when quantifiers were involved, such as Equi-NP Deletion in the case of (6b) → (6a).

(6) a.   Every candidate wanted to win.
b.   Every candidate wanted every candidate to win.

There's nothing ungrammatical about either sentence, so there's no purely syntactic reason to rule out such a derivation. Most of the time the rule seems to preserve meaning as in (10):

(10)   John expected John to win. →
John expected to win.

Furthermore, there's no very plausible "better" source for *every candidate wanted to win*. Moreover, the semantic change wrought by the transformation can be described perfectly well in terms of the surface structure—two independent quantifiers in one sentence, only one in the other, which is just what the difference in logical form is. Similar remarks can be made about the other examples. I'll get back to counterarguments in a minute. But the main thrust of the arguments FOR this approach seems to be as I've just sketched: the derivations which change meaning do not change grammaticality, so we have no syntactic basis for rejecting them; and further-more the semantics can be done at the surface.

This is the approach argued for in Jackendoff (1969), (1972).

B. Generative semantics: PRO

Now let me bring in a different sort of quantifier example, (11).

(11)   A hundred soldiers shot two students

Here we have a sentence which apparently has had no transformations, so there's no problem of meaning-changing transformations. But the sentence is ambiguous; it has either two or three readings depending on one's dialect: either (1) there were a hundred soldiers each of whom shot two students or (2) there were two students each of whom was shot by a hundred soldiers or (3) there was a group of a hundred soldiers who altogether shot a pair of students.[6] It doesn't have any ambiguous WORDS in it (*a hundred* isn't ambiguous and *two* isn't ambiguous), so the ambiguity must be structural. And structural means syntactic. But the standard theory only assigns one deep structure, and therefore it predicts that the sentence is unambiguous: that was a principle enunciated by Chomsky as far back as *Syntactic Structures.* The ambiguity is one of relative scope of the two quan-tifiers, so the obvious emendation to the syntax is to indicate quantifier scope in a structural way. So just as adverbs have typically been attached higher or lower in a tree to show whether they modify the *VP* or the whole *S*, so could quantifiers be given an appropriate hierarchical structure. Classical quantifier logic in fact works just this way—not with a tree representation but with a kind of bracketing which is equivalent to it. Once we have done this, it becomes clear how the derivations which appeared to change meaning can be revised in a simple way so they no longer do: a sentence like (6a): *every candidate wanted to win* can be handled by also bringing in from logic the notion of a variable, and we have as a deep structure for (6a) something like (6a'):

(6a ')   (for every x:candidate) (x wanted x to win)

Here there is just one occurrence of the quantifier *every* and a variable which is somehow attached to the noun *candidate*; the same variable occurs twice in the representation of sentence (6a), while in the representation of the sentence (6b): *every candidate wanted every candidate to win* there would be two different variables, as in (6b '):

(6b ') (for every x:candidate) (x wanted [(for every y:candidate) (y win)])

This somewhat artificial sketch might be called a *hypothetical Stage One*—each side laying out how neatly it can preserve one of the two elegant sides of the doomed Katz-Postal—*Aspects* model, and not talking too much about the other side. The interpretivists don't say much about HOW their semantics works, and the generativists don't say much about the syntactic rules that will turn their elegant deep structures into English. Now without trying to maintain this fiction of clear historical "stages", let me describe some of the subsequent arguments. (The picture is, of course, much over-simplified by the fact that I am focussing on just a small part of the data that have been fought over. There are also negation, conjunction, pro-nominalization, causatives, derived nominals, and many other phenomena talked about by one side or the other or both.).

[1] Against the interpretivist view that grammaticality is never affected by the meaning-changing transformations, there has been offered a con-siderable amount of counter-evidence. For instance, the *EACH*-HOPPING RULE which converts (12a) to (12 b):

(12) a.   Each of the men won a prize.
     b.   The men each won a prize.
sometimes changes meaning, as in (13):

(13) a.   Each of the men hates his brothers.
     b.   The men each hate his brothers.

(where the *his* in (13b) cannot be interpreted as *his own*). Dougherty (1969), (1970) and Chomsky (1971) argued for surface interpretation, on the basis of the rule itself being too clear and simple to give up. But the same rule converts the grammatical (14a) into the ungrammatical (14b):

(14) a.   Each of the men shaved himself.
     b.   *The men each shaved himself.

and in order to derive (15b) one has to posit the ungrammatical source sentence (15a):

(15) a.   *Each of the men shaved themselves.
             [acceptable in some dialects]
     b.   the men each shaved themselves.

Similarly, the interpretivist theory of pronominalization, which generates all pronouns freely in the base, and interprets pronoun-antecedent relations semantically, generates such ungrammatical sentences as (16) and (17):

(16)   *Mary asked John to help herself.
(17)   *The boy shot her own father.

The counter-argument to this line of criticism has been interesting, and is one I find both unsettling and hard to attack. It has been to retract one of the premises of *Syntactic Structures* which many people had been dubious about anyway, namely that native speakers have clear intuitions about *grammaticality*. It is claimed instead that while certain sentences will be judged in some way deviant or unacceptable by native speakers, the classification of deviance into *syntactic* and *semantic* is not part of the raw data of speaker intuitions, but will simply be a product of whatever theory attains the greatest overall simplicity. Therefore if the simplest overall theory deems the sentence *I saw himself* to be syntactically well-formed but semantically ill-formed, so be it; we have no pre-theoretic notions of syntax vs. semantics to falsify such a claim. What a linguist might take as intuitions to the contrary are just prejudices born of habit.[7] Notice how easily *colorless green ideas sleep furiously* slid over the fence and back again— grammatical in *Syntactic Structures*, ungrammatical in *Aspects*, grammatical again once McCawley showed what should have been obvious—that selection restrictions must be semantic and not syntactic.

I once asked Chomsky if the distribution of the word *please* didn't show the influence of semantic factors on grammatical well-formedness, since it is request interpretation and not interrogative or imperative form that governs its possibility of occurrence. I take his reply as typical of the new view of grammaticality: he answered in effect that the only thing that needed to be included in the syntax about *please* was that it occurred sentence-initially, in the auxiliary, or sentence-finally (at least as a rough approximation); there was no *a priori* reason to call the deviance of *will I please help you tomorrow?* syntactic.

[2] A second argument against the interpretive semantics position is that the semantics part of it is just a claim and not a theory. I believe that Jackendoff is doing some interesting and promising work to try to rectify that inadequacy, but that it has to a large extent been a fair criticism. (Certainly it was a fair criticism of the interpretivist claims that I made in Partee (1970).) I still find the interpretivist approach to semantics a plausible one, but at this point that's a matter of temperament and "gut feelings"; not a subject for polemics but simply for further work.[8]

[3] In an earlier paper (Partee 1970) I pointed out one serious defect in Lakoff's treatment of quantifiers. Lakoff had posited two different deep structures to account for the different meanings of (18) and (19).

(18)   Few men read many books.
(19)   Many books are read by few men.

But because of the way he was accounting for the ambiguity of (11): *a hundred soldiers shot two students*, his transformations would permit either deep structure to turn into either surface form, thereby NOT accounting for the fact that (in the dialect he was describing) each sentence has only one interpretation. In response there arose the *theory of derivational constraints* (Lakoff (1969, 1971)). In general, the generative semantics approach started out with a rather unspecified syntax (deep structures but very few transformations) just as the interpretive approach started with an unspecified semantics. I think generative semanticists have done more work to fill in their syntax than interpretivists have for their semantics, though it is a matter of opinion whether the syntactic innovations Lakoff and others have made have strengthened or weakened their claims for their theory. I think they have weakened them, but I accept their reply that they foresee corresponding weaknesses in interpretive semantics if and when its semantics is specified in detail.

[4] Another point at which the generative semantics view is quite specific is in its claim that semantic representations are basically of the same form as syntactic representations, namely labelled trees. I find this aspect of the theory rather mystifying. At one time, McCawley at least was saying that that abstract free structure WAS the semantic interpretation (McCawley (1968)). But I think it has been generally conceded since then that there must be more to semantics than drawing trees.[9] For instance, in addition to the notion of synonymy, which MIGHT be capturable as *same tree*, a semantic theory must indicate when one sentence entails another—e.g., it is part of our linguistic competence to know that (20a) entails (20b), whereas (21a) entails (21b).[10]

(20) a.   John barely caught the train.
      b.   John caught the train.
(21) a.   John nearly caught the train.
      b.   John didn't catch the train.

Furthermore, there are sentences like (22a) and (22b), whose equivalence is probably best captured as mutual entailment without sameness of deep structure, since I do not believe they should be regarded as synonymous.

(22) a.   The glass is half full.
      b.   The glass is half empty.

Since I see the task of semantics as consisting in large part of explicating relations AMONG sentences such as synonymy and entailment, I can only see a role for a notion like a *semantic representation* as something like *a structural representation on which semantics can be based.* Hence I feel that so far there is in fact a serious incompleteness in even the *semantic* part of generative semantics.

One potential rebuttal to this criticism is that the semantic representations give the logical form of the sentences, so the rules of logic, presumably universal, will do the rest. The counterargument to that is that logicians are only just beginning to formulate logics that will go beyond the treatment of *all, some, and, not, or, if-then, necessarily,* and *possibly,* and that even what has been done in logic so far is extremely syntax-sensitive. That is, a logic and a syntax can never be specified independently of one another, and to give abstract syntax-like structures without simultaneously specifying a logic to operate on them is almost empty. Not quite, because to give different syntactic forms to sentences with different entailment- potentials is one step in the process. I think the near-vacuousness of the theory in this respect is being recognized and worked on; but it is as far from being worked OUT, I believe, as any other linguistic approach to semantics.

In many respects, I believe that generative and interpretive semantics are in essential agreement, and jointly in opposition to the Katz-Postal-*Aspects* theory, which was more elegant than either but unfortunately wrong. The major point of agreement now is that there are many points of connection between syntax and semantics, not just one (the classical *deep structure*).[11] Derivational constraints and interpretive rules can both be designed to capture the fact that the relative scope of logical elements depends on at least the following factors:

SURFACE STRUCTURE WORD ORDER
(23) a.   Many men read few books.
      b.   Few books are read by many men.

STRESS
(24) a.   John and Mary can't come to the party.
      b.   John *AND* Mary can't come to the party.

SUBORDINATION IN SURFACE STRUCTURE
(25) a.   To please everyone is hard.
      b.   Everyone is hard to please.

IDIOSYNCRATIC LEXICAL DIFFERENCES AMONG QUANTIFIERS
(26) a.   Every soldier shot several students. [unambiguous scope]
      b.   Several soldiers shot three students. [ambiguous scope]

Part of the problem involved here is that of describing the weighting of these different factors relative to each other, and this certainly does not seem to be extremely simple.

There is also, I think, still essential agreement among generative and interpretive semanticists about the form of the syntax, though this is not entirely clear. The interpretivists have essentially retained the standard theory's PS-rules and T-rules although the PS-rules may generate more *dummy nodes* or *empty nodes* than the standard theory did (cf. especially Emonds 1970; Dougherty 1969, 1970). The generative semanticists seem less clear on this point; Lakoff (1971) talks about the grammar specifying whole derivations as well- or ill-formed, but he only mentions transformations and *global constraints* and does not specify how either the set of inputs or outputs is specified. Presumably *deep structure constraints* plus *surface structure constraints* would have to add up to something at least as restrictive as phrase-structure rules.

III. MONTAGUE'S THEORY OF GRAMMAR

Montague's theory of grammar is different from any version of transformational grammar in at least this last respect. The theory is in some ways reminiscent of the early *Katz-Fodor theory* where both PS- rules and transformations had corresponding projection rules, but Montague's view of syntax is one in which rules much like PS-rules and rules much like transformations may apply in mixed and variable orders, with the order of operations often of crucial semantic significance. There is also a notion of noun phrases substituting for variables that is unique, though it has points of similarity with several transformational theories. Thus for an ambiguous sentence like (27):

(27)   John is looking for a little girl with red hair.

in a Montague-grammar, there will be one derivation in which the noun phrase *a little girl with red hair* is generated directly as object of *look for* before the phrase-structure rules (operating "bottom-up") attach the verb phrase to the subject to make a sentence. On that interpretation, *John* is simply described as having the property of *looking for a little girl with red hair*, i.e., what linguists have called the non-specific reading. The other interpretation will be associated with a derivation which builds up a sentence *John is looking for x* and THEN substitutes the noun phrase for *x*. To take another example, consider the ambiguous sentence (28):

(28)   Some woman loves every man.

The relevant derivations in Montague's system involve three steps: building up an open sentence *x loves y*, substituting the noun phrase *some woman* for the variable x, and substituting the noun phrase *every man* for the variable y. It is the relative order of the two substitutions that determines the relative scope of the two quantifiers in the semantic interpretation: the quantifier phrase inserted last gets widest scope. There are no differences in syntactic constituents or in grammatical relations in the two cases, but only in the order of the operations. With this added dimension of "order of operations" in the syntax, Montague is able to maintain a constraint similar to the Katz-Postal constraint, namely that for each syntatic rule there is a unique corresponding semantic interpretation rule; and Montague does this with a relatively non-abstract syntax, insofar as the syntactic constituents and grammatical relations are concerned.

Although Montague, before his tragic death in 1971, had formalized only some relatively small fragments of English[12], his formalizations were complete in both syntax and semantics, including the associated logic and its model-theoretic interpretation. His overall theory (Montague (1970b)) was designed to accommodate both natural and artificial languages; he was not particularly interested in narrowing down the class of possible grammars to a subset just large enough for natural languages, but there is no reason to suppose that it will be any harder (or easier) to do so in his framework than in any of the presently far-too-rich transformational approaches even though they avow such a purpose.

In the years since Montague's death, linguists and logicians have modified and extended Montague's framework in various ways and have offered analyses of a wide range of syntactic and semantic phenomena within such frameworks. For a fuller explication of Montague's theory and some suggestions for a possible synthesis of Montague's theory with transformational grammar, see Partee (1975) or the shorter treatment in Partee (1973). A representative sample of recent work by linguists and philosophers working in more-or-less Montague-style frameworks can be found in Partee (ed., 1976). As the above citations suggest, I consider this approach a fruitful one, not least because working in it forces one to be as rigorous and explicit about semantics as about syntax.

IV. RETROSPECT AND PROSPECT

In concluding the 1971 version of this article, I listed three key problem areas that I considered crucial in the search for an adequate theory. Since they still seem to be of central importance and the issues within them are far from resolved, I will repeat them before saying anything about the progress of the last five years.

[1] The first is one I have been illustrating in my examples—the *logical form* problem, particularly the treatment of quantifiers, negation, and conjunction. This area has been receiving plenty of attention, and there have been many new insights gained about how natural language expresses logical form, but we are still waiting for an adequate and fully specified theory.

[2] The second (and none of these are really independent) is the problem of PRONOMINALIZATION, EQUI-NP DELETION, and ELLIPSIS. I lump these together because they are all parts of the problem of how best to represent the native speaker's competence in understanding as part of the interpretation of a sentence things that are missing in the surface structure. The standard theory and generative semantics both postulate fully-specified deep structures with processes of pronominalization and deletion. *SLOPPY-IDENTITY* DELETION (as in *if you can stand on your head, I'm sure I can*) is a recent addition to this repertoire. At this point discourse may become relevant in a way that it hasn't usually been taken to be for syntax. If you say to me *you're staring at me* and I reply *no, I'm not*, are we to say that the deep structure of my sentence INCLUDES a transformed version of your sentence? It certainly wouldn't include *you're staring at me*; if it included anything, it would be *I'm staring at you*, but even that hardly seems plausible. And if the deep structure of my sentence does not include as a sub-part some transformed version of your sentence, then what is my deletion based on? It might be worth working on that question as a source for new ideas about deletions in general.

[3] The third big problem area is *lexical unity vs. lexical decomposition.* It is by now abundantly clear that *dissuade* has systematic relations to *persuade...not, kill* to *cause-to-die*, etc; but the unity of lexical items also needs to be captured. *Either* as a quantifier and *either* as part of *either- or* are not unrelated. The different subsenses of *remind* are clearly closely related, and only one of them is equivalent to *strike as similar*. It remains to find a way to reconcile the two kinds of generalizations, one among distinct lexical items that share distributional and semantic properties, and the other among semantically and/or syntactically differing uses of what seems nevertheless to be a single lexical item or a family of morphologically closely related items.

In the five years since the first version of this article was written, there has been substantial progress in these areas, an opening up of many new kinds of investigations, and noticeably greater integration of the concerns of theoretical syntax and semantics with other areas of linguistics such as psycholinguistics, sociolinguistics, and language processing models. In semantics, there has been increasingly fruitful interaction between linguists and philosophers, as can be seen in collections such as Davidson and Harman (1972), Hintikka, Moravcsik, and Suppes (1973), and Keenan (1975a), as well as in the recent work on Montague grammar. Investigation of LOGICAL FORM has become increasingly sophisticated, in part because of interaction with logicians and philosophers, and also in part because of work such as that of Keenan (1975b) on questions of logical form in a wide variety of languages other than English. The area of MORPHOLOGY is beginning to regain the position of importance it had in pre-transformational linguistics, with more sophisticated methods (see e.g. Aronoff (1976), Dowty (1976)), so that questions about lexical relatedness such as those raised in [3] above are now often viewed as questions about the internal structure of the lexicon rather than simply as questions about the relation between lexical insertion and the transformation component. The relation between SLOPPY IDENTITY LOGICAL FORM, and DIS-COURSE phenomena question in [2] above has recently been explored in what appears to be a very promising way by Edwin Williams (1977) and independently by Ivan Sag (1976); Williams has proposed the interesting hypothesis that syntactic rules whose domain is restricted to the sentence form a separate component from syntactic rules which may apply either within or across sentences, with rules of the two components differeing both in their formal properties and in their relation to semantics and logical form.

I mentioned at the outset that I sense a convergence in syntactic and semantic theory, even though there are still strong disagreements about the form of linguistic theory. This is partly just from the experience of exchanging views with linguists (and philosophers) working in a number of different frameworks and finding easily expressible agreement on substantive issues (e.g. that some but not all pronouns function like bound variables in logic, and which uses of pronouns are the hardest to treat in anybody's theory[13]; or that the representation of semantic scope phenomena requires essentially different mechanisms from the representation of basic grammatical relations.) The potential for convergence is nicely illustrated by the work of Cooper and Parsons (1976), who constructed two alternative grammars provably equivalent to the grammar given in Montague (1973) both in sentences generated and in semantic interpretations assigned to them, one of their grammars in an essentially generative-semantics form and the other in an interpretive-semantics-like framework. Since the fragment of English treated in Montague (1973) is relatively small, no immediate conclusions about equivalence of whole theories can be drawn, but Cooper and Parsons' work does help to show that some of the issues on which linguists were most sharply divided in the late sixties *can* be regarded as largely notational differences. Things are still not unified to the extent that an introductory syntax or semantics course can trace the development of "*the* theory" from 1957 to the present, but I am presently very optimistic about concerted progress on the hard substantive questions in the course of the ongoing search for a new and better unified theory. At the height of the generative semantics-interpretive semantics polemics, it seemed almost impossible to discuss any issue or consider any application of linguistic theory to related disciplines without taking a stand on that controversy; not the least of the benefits of the present progress toward convergence is that interaction between linguistic theory and related disciplines is apparently becoming easier, to the benefit of everyone. There are still innumerable unexplained phenomena, so the field is as exciting and challenging as ever; but it is certainly pleasant to see attention focussed mainly on how to explain the phenomena and how to fit the explanations into a strong and coherent theory, rather than focussed on whose theory we should be looking for explanations in. Whether the next approximation to "the best theory" looks ι re like generative semantics, interpretive semantics, relational grammar, Ν.ontague grammar, trace theory, a processing model, or something else, I am confident that it will include important insights gained from research in many of the current alternative theoretical approaches.

Notes

*The present article is a revised version of "Linguistic Metatheory," in Dingwall (1971). The principle changes are in the introductory and concluding sections; other changes consist mostly of minor modifications and added footnotes.

¹For example, the investigation of constraints on the form and functioning of syntactic rules which received a major impetus from the work of Ross (1967) has borne a great deal of fruit in cross-linguistic studies and in the development of important hypothesis such as Emonds' Structure-Preserving Constraint (Emonds 1970), Bresnan's Relativized A-Over-A Constraint (Bresnan 1976), and the family of constraints proposed recently by Chomsky (1973, 1975a). The existence of such constraints on syntactic rules seems to be largely independent of the relation of syntax to semantics, although the question of whether analogous constraints hold for semantic rules is bringing the two issues together. For a good introduction to central theoretical issues in syntax proper, see Bach (1974).

²For an indication of some of the interesting recent work in semantics and in pragmatics, the following references provide good starting points: Fillmore and Langendoen (1971), Steinberg and Jakobovits (1971), Hockney et al (1975), Davidson and Harman (1972), Fillmore, Lakoff, and Lakoff (1974), Cole and Morgan (1975).

³See Bar-Hillel (1971).

⁴For more about the approaches just mentioned, see the following works and references cited therein: for perceptual strategies, Bever (1970), Langendoen and Bever (1973); for frame analysis, Fillmore (1975); for cognitive grammar, Lakoff and Thompson (1975); for trace theory, Chomsky (1975a, 1975b, 1975c, forthcoming); for augmented transition networks and processing models, Woods (1973), Kaplan (1972), Kaplan (1973), Wanner, Kaplan,

and Shiner (1975); for relational grammar, Postal (1976), Perlmutter and Postal (to appear); for game theoretic semantics, Hintikka and Saarinen, (1975); for axiomatic grammar, Lieb (1974).

[5]Since Chomsky returned to a very similar view in Chomsky (1975b), (1975c), it may not seem so surprising any more, but I am leaving these remarks intact because I think they give a fair view of the perspective in 1971.

[6]Bennett (1974) suggests that with verbs such as *visit* where we can distinguish 'group-level' from 'individual-level' readings for both subject and object, sentences parallel to (11) are seven-ways ambiguous rather than three. But the main point above does not change.

[7]These comments reflect my understanding of some remarks in class lectures by Chomsky in the fall of 1970, and similar remarks appear in Jackendoff (1972); but Chomsky (1975c) appears to take a different view in arguing for the thesis of the autonomy of syntax, and the issue is discussed in Partee (1975b).

[8]This paragraph is intact from 1971; in the subsequent five years I believe the polemics *have* gradually decreased, and Jackendoff in particular did a great deal to make the semantics of the interpretive system more explicit; see Jackendoff (1972), (1976). However, it has remained unclear how to fit the various parts of Jackendoff's semantic representations (such as thematic relations, modal structures, tables of coreference) into a coherent whole in order to compare them with, say, a semantic interpretation which includes a representation in some formalized language such as a higher-order modal logic, which is in turn interpreted by means of a well-understood system of model theory. Up until very recently, however, virtually *all* linguists' theories of semantics were open to this sort of complaint, which generally came from logicians and philosophers, and which has only recently begun to be generally appreciated by linguists.

[9] Cf. footnote 8. Many generative semanticists have been willing to accept a logicians' type of model-theoretic semantics as a necessary part of semantic theory, although in only a very few cases (see Dowty (1972) for one) has enough detail in both the underlying structures and the logic been given for one to be able to tell whether the proposed analyses are compatible with the intended logic.

[10] The second of these inferences has recently been challenged (by Jerry Sadock, pers. comm.; his examples were with *almost,* but I am assuming he would say the same about *nearly.*) This is one of many areas where the issue is whether a semantic or pragmatic explanation is more adequate. Rather than replace the example in the text by one which *this year* looks like a paradigm example of semantic entailment, I will just remark that it *can* happen that a whole field gets abandoned because all of its paradigm examples turn out to be examples of something else, but so far as I am aware, this is not an imminent danger for semantics.

[11] More recently, Chomsky (forthcoming) has suggested that the theory of traces may make it possible to do semantic interpretation entirely at the level of ("enriched") surface structure, but much remains to be spelled out before it can be determined whether such a claim is tenable and whether it is in fact a substantive change from the earlier interpretive theories. Jackendoff (1975) showed how traces would make it possible to do certain parts of semantic interpretation either cyclically or at the surface, but without claiming any substantive differences were involved.

[12] See Montague (1970a), (1970b), (1973), all reprinted in Montague (1974).

[13] The problematic cases I have in mind are those illustrated by Bach-Peters paradox sentences like (i) (Bach(1970)), and Geach's "donkey-sentence" (ii) (Geach (1964)).

(i) The man who shows he deserves it will get the prize he desires.
(ii) Any man who owns a donkey beats it.

Bibliography

Anderson, S.R. and P. Kiparsky, eds. (1973), *A Festschrift for Morris Halle,* Holt, Rinehart, and Winston, New York.

Aronoff, Mark (1976), *Word Formation in Generative Grammar,* MIT Press, Cambridge.

Austerlitz, Robert, ed. (1975), *The Scope of American Linguistics,* The Peter de Ridder Press, Lisse.

Bach, Emmon (1970), "Probleminalization," *Linguistic Inquiry* 1, 121-2.

Bach, Emmon (1974), *Syntactic Theory,* Holt, Rinehart, and Winston, New York.

Bach, Emmon and Robert Harms, eds. (1968), *Universals in Linguistic Theory,* Holt, Rinehart, and Winston, New York.

Bar-Hillel, Yehoshua (1971), "Out of the Pragmatic Wastebasket," *Linguistic Inquiry,* 2, 401-406.

Bennett, Michael (1974), *Some Extensions of a Montague Fragment of English,* unpublished Ph.D. dissertation, UCLA (available through Indiana Univ. Linguistics Club).

Bever, Thomas G. (1970), "The Cognitive Basis for Linguistic Structures," in Hayes, J. (ed.), *Cognition and the Development of Language,* John Wiley and Sons, New York.

Bresnan, Joan (1976), "On the Form and Functioning of Transformations," *Linguistic Inquiry* 7, 3-40.

Chomsky, Noam (1957), *Syntactic Structures,* Mouton, The Hague.

Chomsky, Noam (1965), *Aspects of the Theory of Syntax,* MIT Press, Cambridge, Mass.

Chomsky, Noam (1971), "Deep Structure, Surface Structure, and Semantic Interpretation," in Steinberg and Jakobovits (1971).

Chomsky, Noam (1973), "Conditions on Transformations," in Anderson and Kiparsky (1973).

Chomsky, Noam (1975a), "Conditions on Rules of Grammar," to appear in R. Cole, ed., *Current Issues in Linguistic Theory,* Indiana University Press.

Chomsky, Noam (1975b), *Reflections on Language,* Pantheon Books, New York.

Chomsky, Noam (1975c), "Questions of Form and Interpretation," in Austerlitz (1975), 159-196.

Chomsky, Noam (forthcoming), "On Wh- Movement," to appear in Culicover, P., A. Akmajian, and T. Wasow, eds., *Formal Syntax,* Academic Press, New York.

Cogen, C. et al., eds. (1975), *Proceedings of the First Annual Meeting of the Berkeley Linguistics Society,* Berkeley Linguistics Society, Berkeley.

Cole, Peter and Jerry Morgan, eds. (1975), *Speech Acts,* Academic Press, New York.

Cooper, Robin and Terence Parsons (1976), "Montague grammar, generative semantics, and interpretive semantics," in Partee, ed. (1976).

Davidson, D. and G. Harman, eds. (1972), *Semantics of Natural Language,* Synthese Library, D. Reidel, Dordrecht.

Dingwall, Willian, ed. (1971), *A Survey of Linguistic Science,* Linguistics Program, University of Maryland.

Dougherty, Ray (1969), "An Interpretive Theory of Pronominal Reference," *Foundations of Language* 5, 488-519.

Dougherty, Ray (1970), "A Grammar of Coordinate Conjoined Structures: I, *Language* 46, 850-98.

Dowty, David (1972), *Studies in the Logic of Verb Aspect and Time Reference in English,* unpublished Ph.D. Thesis, University of Texas, Austin.

Dowty, David (1976), "Montague grammar and the lexical decomposition of causative verbs," in Partee, ed. (1976).

Emonds, Joseph (1970), *Root and Structure—Preserving Transformations,* MIT Ph.D. Dissertation (mimeo, Indiana Univ. Linguistic Club).

Fillmore, Charles J. (1975), "An Alternative to Checklist Theories of Meaning," in C. Cogen et al., (1975).

Fillmore, Charles and D. T. Langendoen, eds. (1971), *Studies in Linguistic Semantics,* Holt, Rinehart, and Winston, New York.

Fillmore, C., G. Lakoff, and R. Lakoff, eds. (1974), *Berkeley Studies in Syntax and Semantics,* Vol. 1, Department of Linguistics, University of California, Berkeley.

Geach, Peter T. (1964), *Reference and Generality,* Cornell Univ. Press, Ithaca.

Hintikka, J., J. Moravcsik, and P. Suppes, eds. (1973), *Approaches to Natural Language,* D. Reidel, Dordrecht.

Hintikka, Jaakko and Esa Saarinen (1975), "Semantical games and the Bach-Peters Paradox," *Theoretical Linguistics* 2, 1-20.

Hockney, D., W. Harper and B. Freed, eds. (1975), *Contemporary Research in Philosophical Logic and Linguistic Semantics,* D. Reidel, Dordrecht.

Jackendoff, Ray (1969), *Some Rules of Semantic Interpretation for English,* unpublished Ph.D. dissertation, MIT, Cambridge.

Jackendoff, Ray (1972), *Semantic Interpretation in Generative Grammar,* The MIT Press, Cambridge.

Jackendoff, Ray (1975), "*Tough* and the Trace Theory of Movement Rules," *Linguistic Inquiry* 6, 437-446.

Jackendoff, Ray (1976), "Toward an Explanatory Semantic Representation," *Linguistic Inquiry* 7, 89-150.

Kaplan, Ronald (1972), "Augmented Transition Networks as Psychological Models of Sentence Comprehension," *Artificial Intelligence* 3, 77-100.

Kaplan, Ronald (1973), "A General Syntactic Processor," in Rustin (1973).

Katz, Jerrold and Jerry Fodor (1963), "The Structure of a Semantic Theory," *Language* 39, 170-210.

Katz, Jerrold and Paul Postal (1964), *An Integrated Theory of Linguistic Descriptions,* MIT Press, Cambridge.

Keenan, Edward, ed. (1975a), *Formal Semantics of Natural Language,* Cambridge University Press, Cambridge.

Keenan, Edward (1975b), "Logical Expressive Power and Syntactic Variation in Natural Language," in Keenan (1975a).

Klima, E.S. (1964), "Negation in English," in *The Structure of Language,* J. Fodor and J. Katz (eds.), Prentice-Hall, Inc., Englewood Cliffs (246-323).

Kuhn, Thomas (1962), *The Structure of Scientific Revolutions,* The University of Chicago Press, Chicago.

Lakoff, George (1969), "On Derivational Constraints," in *Papers from the Fifth Regional Meeting of the Chicago Linguistics Society* (ed. by R. Binnick et al.), Chicago.

Lakoff, George (1970), *Irregularity in Syntax,* Holt, Rinehart, and Winston, New York.

Lakoff, George (1971), "On Generative Semantics," in Steinberg and Jakobovits (1971).

Lakoff, George and Henry Thompson (1975), "Introducing Cognitive Grammar," in C. Cogen et al. (1975).

Langendoen, D. Terence and Thomas G. Bever (1973), "Can a Not Unhappy Person Be Called a Not Sad One," in Anderson and Kiparsky (1973).

Lieb, Hans-Heinrich (1974), "Grammars as Theories: The Case for Axiomatic Grammar (Part 1)," *Theoretical Linguistics* 1, 39-115.

McCawley, James D. (1968), "The Role of Semantics in a Grammar," in Bach and Harms (1968).

Montague, Richard (1970a), "English as a Formal Language," in B. Visentini et al., *Linguaggi Nella Societa e Nella Tecnica,* Edizioni di Communita, Milan.

Montague, Richard (1970b), "Universal Grammar," *Theoria* 36, 373-98.

Montague, Richard (1974), *Formal Philosophy: Selected Papers of Richard Montague,* edited and with an introduction by Richmond Thomason, Yale Univ. Press, New Haven.

Montague, Richard (1973), "The Proper Treatment of Quantification in Ordinary English," in J. Hintikka, J. Moravcsik, and P. Suppes, eds. (1973).

Partee, Barbara (1970), "Negation, Conjunction, and Quantifiers: Syntax vs. Semantics," *Foundations of Language* 6, 153-165.

Partee, Barbara (1971), "On the Requirement that Transformations Preserve Meaning," in Fillmore and Langendoen (eds.) (1971).

Partee, Barbara (1973), "Some Transformational Extensions of Montague Grammar," *Journal of Philosophical Logic* 2, 509-534. Reprinted in Partee (1976).

Partee, Barbara (1975a), "Montague Grammar and Transformational Grammar," *Linguistic Inquiry* 6, 203-300.

Partee, Barbara (1975b), "Comments on C.J. Fillmore's and N. Chomsky's Papers," in Austerlitz (1975), 197-209.

Partee, Barbara, ed. (1976), *Montague Grammar,* Academic Press, New York.

Perlmutter, David and Paul Postal (to appear), *Relational Grammar.*

Postal, Paul (1976), "Avoiding Reference to Subject," *Linguistic Inquiry* 7, 151-191.

Ross, J.R. (1967), *Constraints on Variables in Syntax,* M.I.T. Ph.D. Dissertation.

Rustin, R., ed. (1973), *Natural Language Processing,* Prentice-Hall, Englewood Cliffs.

Sag, Ivan (1976), "A Logical Theory of VP Deletion," in *Papers from the Twelfth Regional Meeting of the Chicago Linguistic Society,* Chicago Linguistic Society, Chicago.

Steinberg, D. and L. Jakobovits (eds.) (1971), *Semantics: An Interdisciplinary Reader,* Cambridge University Press, Cambridge.

Wanner, E., R. Kaplan, and S. Shiner (1975), "Garden Paths in Relative Clauses," ms., Harvard University, Cambridge.

Williams, Edwin (1977), "Discourse and Logical Form," to appear in *Linguistic Inquiry* 8.1, 101-139.

Woods, W. (1973), "An Experimental Parsing System for Transition Network Grammars," in Rustin, R. (1973).

Chapter Four

Mathematical Linguistics

Robert E. Wall

Much of the early writings of Chomsky and his colleagues is concerned with pointing up the inadequacy of phrase-structure grammar as a system of linguistic description and showing how these defects can be overcome by the proposed theory of transformational grammar. (See, for example, Chomsky (1957); Postal (1964); Lees (1960).) Transformational grammar has, of course, developed along various divergent paths in recent years, and many of its fundamental tenets have been disputed, but the arguments against phrase-structure grammar have proved so widely persuasive that scarcely any serious, card-carrying linguist today still espouses it, at least not in its simple unadorned form. It was therefore particularly dismaying to mathematical linguists—those who are concerned with investigating the formal properties of linguistic theories—that although the study of phrase-structure grammars proved fairly tractable and a substantial body of results about them could be achieved, the more interesting and relevant theory of transformational grammar seemed to present overwhelming difficulties. Chomsky remarked on this state of affairs in the introduction to his survey of the field of mathematical linguistics in *Handbook of mathematical psychology,* (Chomsky 1963: 325-6):

> This survey is largely restricted to weak generative capacity of constituent-structure grammars for the simple reason that, with a few exceptions, this is the only area in which substantial results of a mathematical character have been achieved. Ultimately, of course, we are interested in studying strong generative capacity of empirically validated theories rather than weak generative capacity of theories which are at best suggestive. It is important not to allow the technical feasibility for mathematical study to blur the issue of linguistic significance and empirical justification. We want to narrow the gap between the models that are accessible to mathematical investigation and those that are validated by confrontation with empirical data, but it is crucial to be aware of the existence and character of the gap that still exists.

So long as the field of mathematical linguistics was in this state, it could be characterized, not entirely unfairly, as the formal study of irrelevant aspects of hopelessly inadequate grammars. Mathematical linguists were very like the man in the old joke who was seen searching for a lost coin under a street lamp. He confessed that he had actually dropped the coin some distance away but had decided to look for it here because the light was better.

In 1969 an interview with Chomsky appeared under the title: *The intellectual as prophet* (Staal 1969). The topics ranged from war in Viet Nam to the future of mathematical linguistics. On the latter subject Chomsky had this to say (19):

> Now mathematical linguistics I think came to a rather critical point in its extremely brief career about two or three years ago, when some simple ideas were basically exhausted...The early work in mathematical linguistics was concerned with ideas which are simple enough to study from a mathematical point of view, but which are not complex enough to have very much to do with real language structure.

He then goes on to say that in his opinion his work in this field did, nonetheless, accomplish something:

> [It] made some contribution to our understanding of natural languages, it sharpened up some issues, provided some models against which the empirically oriented work could be compared, and that's very useful.

He also credits the work in mathematical linguistics with giving "some intellectual reference points" and suggesting "some problems to look at" and says that perhaps it "spurred some empirical work." He then notes that the subject "developed into an obscure branch of mathematics which will be as interesting as its practitioners will make it." Chomsky is pessimistic about future progress in the field insofar as linguistic relevance is concerned, and he indicates that perhaps a period of benign neglect (not his words) is in order, at least:

> ...until further empirical work on language structure manages once again to formulate concepts which are amenable to mathematical study, more intricate and complex concepts that are more well-motivated empirically.

Those who agreed with this dismal forecast a couple of years ago have been considerably encouraged by some recent developments. Peters and Ritchie (1973) and Ginsburg and Partee (1969) have achieved formalizations of transformational grammar as outlined in *Aspects of the theory of syntax* (Chomsky 1965), and several linguistically important consequences have been deduced from them. I will sketch some of these results below in the hope that this will constitute a convincing demonstration that the field of mathematical linguistics is still alive and well. In order to provide some of the background within which the recent advances were made, I will begin by summarizing very briefly a few of the principal results which had been obtained previously in mathematical linguistics. More extensive and detailed summaries can be found in Chomsky (1963) and Hopcroft and Ullman (1969).

The basic model of *phrase-structure grammar* which was the focus of these investigations is a quadruple $G = (V_T, V_N, S, P)$, where V_T and V_N are finite, disjoint sets of symbols, the *terminal* and *non-terminal* alphabets, respectively; S is a designated member of V_N; and P is a finite two-place irreflexive and asymmetric relation on strings of $V_T \cup V_N$, the *rewriting rules* or *productions*. G generates the terminal string x if and only if there is some finite sequence of strings beginning with S and ending with x such that 1) each string except the first is obtained from the immediately preceding string by a single application of one of the rules in P, and 2) x is a string of terminal symbols. The set of all terminal strings generated by G is the *language generated by G.*

If the rules are further restricted so that only a single symbol is rewritten, there is a relatively straightforward way to associate with a derivation of a terminal string a phrase-structure tree having S as the root node and the terminal symbols as leaves. Considerations of this sort led to the establishment of the following hierarchy of types of grammars:

Type	Form of rules allowed
0 (unrestricted rewriting system)	$\varphi \rightarrow \Psi$ (φ, Ψ, arbitrary strings)
1 (context-sensitive)	$\varphi A \Psi \rightarrow \varphi \omega \Psi$ (φ, Ψ, arbitrary strings; $A \in V_N$; ω not null)
2 (context-free)	$A \rightarrow \omega$ ($A \in V_N$; ω not null)
3 (right-linear)	$A \rightarrow xB$ (A, $B \in V_N$; x, y strings on V_T) $A \rightarrow y$

In this hierarchy each grammar of type n is a special case of the grammars of type $n-1$, but not conversely. Thus, if we denote by $\mathcal{G}_n$ the set of all grammars of type n, we obtain the following sequence of proper inclusions as an immediate consequence of the definitions:

(1) $\quad \mathcal{G}_0 \supset \mathcal{G}_1 \supset \mathcal{G}_2 \supset \mathcal{G}_3$

Among the earliest and most fundamental results achieved in mathematical linguistics was the fact that the classes of languages generated by these successively more restricted classes of grammars are also restricted in the corresponding way. Denoting by $\mathcal{L}_n$ the set of all languages that can be generated by some grammar of type n, we have the proper inclusions:

(2) $\quad \mathcal{L}_0 \supset \mathcal{L}_1 \supset \mathcal{L}_2 \supset \mathcal{L}_3$

To put it another way, there are languages which can be generated by a context-free grammar which cannot be generated by any right-linear grammar; context-sensitive languages which cannot be generated by any context free grammer; and so on. This collection of results is not at all obvious, and considerable ingenuity was required in some cases to achieve the proofs.

The class of right-linear languages, $\mathcal{L}_3$, was shown to be identical with the well-known mathematical class of regular sets (Kleene 1956; Chomsky 1956). $\mathcal{L}_0$ is coextensive with the recursively enumerable sets, i.e., those which can be accepted (or generated) by some Turing machine (Davis 1958, Ch. 6, Sec. 2). $\mathcal{L}_1$, the context-sensitive languages, are properly included in the recursive sets (Chomsky 1959), those for which there exists a decision procedure for the problem of membership, and these, in turn, are properly included in the recursively enumerable sets. Evidently neither $\mathcal{L}_1$ nor $\mathcal{L}_2$ corresponded to any previously known mathematical class.

Another rather important advance was the establishment of correspondences between these classes of languages and the abstract automata which accept them. Recursively enumerable sets are, by definition, accepted by Turing Machines, and in view of the aforementioned equivalence, so are the type 0 languages. Regular sets are accepted by finite-state automata; hence, right-linear languages are accepted by the same devices. The discovery of the context-free and context-sensitive languages led naturally to a search for appropriate accepting automata intermediate in power between Turing machines and finite state automata. Schützenberger and Chomsky (1963),demonstrated that the context-free languages are accepted by non-deterministic pushdown-store automata, and Kuroda (1964), extending a result of Landweber (1963),showed that the class of context-sensitive languages is accepted by non-deterministic linear-bounded automata. Incidentally, whether this also holds for deterministic linear-bounded automata remains to this day an open question, despite the efforts of a number of highly ingenious researchers.

By relaxing certain of the restrictions on the form of the rewriting rules or adding others one can produce a virtually endless series of variations within this paradigm. Some of these types of grammars, such as linear, metalinear, and sequential, have received relatively little attention, but the paradigm has also spawned a great deal of work in the "obscure branch of mathematics" mentioned earlier. This deals primarily with infinite hierarchies of languages lying, for the most part, in the area between the context-free and context-sensitive languages. There has been a similar burgeoning of studies of automata corresponding to these languages. For a survey of this field the reader is referred to Hopcroft and Ullman (1969).

The remainder of what has traditionally comprised the field of mathematical linguistics falls into three general areas:

1) *Closure properties of classes of languages under various operations* such as union, intersection, complementation, mapping by finite transducers, and so on. For example, it is known that the intersection of two arbitrarily chosen type 2 languages is a type 1 language but not necessarily type 2 (Bar-Hillel, Perles, and Shamir 1960).

2) *Decidability or undecidability of various questions.* For example, it is decidable (i.e., there is a general algorithm for determining in every case) whether the language generated by an arbitrarily chosen type 2 grammar is finite, infinite, or empty, but it is undecidable whether two arbitrary type 2 grammars generate the same language (Bar-Hillel, Perles, and Shamir 1960).

3) *Ambiguity properties.* A grammar is ambiguous if it assigns some generated string two or more distinct structural descriptions. A typical result of this sort is that there exist type 2 languages which cannot be generated by any unambiguous type 2 grammar (Parikh 1961).

As I indicated earlier in quoting Chomsky's remarks, theorems such as these are, in themselves, of only marginal linguistic interest. They are concerned solely with phrase-structure grammars, and, moreover, they are in nearly every case theorems about *weak generative capacity* (the sets of strings generated) rather than *strong generative capacity* (the sets of structural descriptions assigned to grammatical strings). However, in one or two instances it has been possible to make a mathematical result directly applicable to a question of linguistic theory; specifically, by showing that a proposed type of grammar is not powerful enough to generate the sentences of some natural language. The theory which specifies that all natural languages have grammars of the proposed type must therefore be rejected. Chomsky (1956) did this for grammars of type 3 by an argument with the following structure:

First premise: No grammar of type 3 is capable of generating all and only strings containing dependencies nested within each other to an arbitrarily large degree.

Second premise: English is a language whose strings exhibit nested dependencies of this sort.

Conclusion: No type 3 grammar generates English, and therefore a linguistic theory which prescribes type 3 grammars for all natural languages cannot be maintained.

We observe that while the second premise in this argument must be established by empirical investigation, the first depends on showing that all grammars of type 3 share a certain property, and this cannot be established empirically, but only by mathematical means. Since the class of type 3 grammars is infinite, no number of unsuccessful attempts to construct a grammar of this type for a certain language would suffice to show that it is impossible. Rather, our repeated failures might indicate merely a lack of ingenuity. With a mathematical characterization of the class of grammars, however, we can hope to discover some property of the entire class which will render it demonstrably inadequate as a linguistic theory. (Of course, one cannot in general prove the correctness of any theory, linguistic or otherwise, which is intended to encompass an infinite range of data, since every unobserved case is a potential counterexample.) While it is not particularly surprising that a theory of right-linear grammars is linguistically inadequate (this could have been shown on other grounds anyway), this case does illustrate the sort of reasoning that is involved in proving that some proposed linguistic theory is too weak, i.e., too narrowly restricted, and it indicates how mathematical methods enter crucially into the solution of the problem (but cf. Fidelholtz 1974).

On the other hand, it is sometimes possible to show mathematically that a proposed linguistic theory is too strong, i.e., insufficiently restricted. This brings us back to the formalizations of transformational grammar mentioned earlier. I will here be concerned primarily with the formalization of Peters and Ritchie (1973) since its consequences have been more thoroughly explored than that of Ginsburg and Partee (1969). the two formulations are alike in most essential respects.

In the so-called "standard theory" outlined in Chomsky (1965) the principal characteristics of the syntactic component are the following. The base consists of a finite set of context-free rewriting rules and a lexicon composed of sets of semantic, syntactic, and phonological features. Lexical entries are inserted by context-sensitive rules in the position of the leaves of the phrase-structure trees generated by the rewriting rules. The base rules are recursive through the symbol S, thus permitting structures with "base sentences" nested (and presumably also co-ordinated) to an arbitrarily large extent. The transformational rules are linearly ordered and apply in cyclic fashion from the lowest base sentence to the highest to produce surface structures. The transformations also reject or *filter out* certain structures generated by the base, and only those which are not filtered out count as deep structures underlying some surface structure. The surface structures are converted to a phonetic output by the phonological rules, and well-formed deep structures receive a semantic interpretation from the semantic component.

Transformational rules map phrase-structure trees into phrase-structure trees. Each can be decomposed into a finite number of elementary operations of deletion, adjunction (either left or right), and substitution. The standard theory also stipulates that deletions must be *recoverable*. There are several possible interpretations of this condition, but the one Peters and Ritchie have adopted is the following. Given a transformational rule which deletes some element of a phrase marker, the deletion is recoverable if and only if:

1) the deleted element is a terminal symbol (lexical item) mentioned specifically in one of the terms in the structural condition of the transformation (e.g., the deletion of *you* and *will* in one commonly proposed scheme for deriving imperatives).

or 2) there is another copy of the deleted element at a specified place in the tree (e.g., the deletion of one of a pair of identical noun phrases by the Equi-NP-Deletion transformation).

Using this formulation of the theory of transformational grammar, Peters and Ritchie were able to prove the following theorem (Peters & Ritchie 1973):

3) Every recursively enumerable language is generated by some transformational grammar with context-sensitive base rules, and conversely.

In other words, the weak generative capacity of a transformational grammar is the same as that of an unrestricted rewriting system. Although this is again a theorem about weak rather than strong generative capacity, Peters and Ritchie observe that it nonetheless presents certain difficulties for the standard theory. They point out that there are some rather compelling reasons for believing that every natural language must be at least a recursive set of strings. First, it is reasonable to suppose that given any arbitrary string x, a person who commands a natural language grammar G

can determine whether or not x is generated by (is grammatical in) G. (In fact, one would probably want to impose the even stronger requirement that the speaker is able to determine in just what ways an ungrammatical sentence deviates from full grammaticality.) This amounts to saying that the speaker-hearer has available to him a decision procedure for the language generated by G, and if such a procedure exists, the language is necessarily recursive.

A second difficulty concerns children's acquisition of language. It has been suggested that a child brings to the language learning task as part of his innate endowment a set of hypotheses concerning the linguistic data whose underlying system (i.e., the grammar) he is to discover. This set of hypotheses would be just the set of possible transformational grammars, and the child would learn a grammar, in effect, by selecting one from the available set on the basis of the data he encounters and perhaps certain other criteria. If this rough account of language acquisition can be maintained, then it seems rather implausible that the child should be innately equipped to construct a grammar for any arbitrary recursively enumerable set. It is of course possible that some mysterious element in the criteria for selection might restrict the child to actually learning only recursive languages, but until there are some concrete proposals concerning the nature of these criteria of selection, it seems that the theory would predict that a child could construct a grammar for non-recursive sets. Thus, the standard theory appears to be too powerful.

Which features of the theory allow transformational grammars to generate languages which are non-recursive? Peters and Ritchie have shown that making the base rules context-free rather than context-sensitive does not reduce the class of languages generated. The theorem given above holds even in this case (Peters and Ritchie 1971), although with a context-free base it is essential to make use of the filtering effect of tranformations to achieve this result. A context-sensitive based transformational grammar, on the other hand, need not use the filtering function at all to generate the recursively enumerable sets. (Ginsburg and Partee (1969) have also proved that in their formulation, which contains, in effect, context-free base rules, the grammar generates all recursively enumerable sets. See also Salomaa (1971)). In any event, whatever the type of base rules, the non-recursiveness arises solely from the fact that there is no upper bound on the number of base sentences which can occur in the deep structure underlying any given string. That is, the theory allows the transformational component, without violating the condition of recoverability of deletions, to pare down large deep structures containing many base sentences to produce very short strings. (One is reminded here of the many-layered deep structures proposed by G. Lakoff and J.R. Ross for such sentences as *Floyd broke the glass,* which can easily be accommodated by the apparatus available in the standard theory.) It is clear, then, what must be achieved if transformational grammars are to be made to generate at most recursive sets: one must be able to determine for any given grammar and any given sentence the maximum number of cycles which could be involved in the derivation of that sentence by the grammar. How to add constraints on grammars which will produce this effect is, of course, still an open question, but pinpointing the source of non-recursiveness does at least open the way to a potentially fruitful line of investigation.

Peters and Ritchie (1971) also showed that because of the power allowed to transformational rules by the standard theory the weak generative capacity of a grammar is remarkably insensitive to restrictions on the base component. In fact, a right-linear base composed of just the two rules:

$$1) \quad S \rightarrow S\#$$
$$2) \quad S \rightarrow a_1a_2...a_nb\#$$

together with a small number of transformational rules suffices to generate any recursively enumerable language on the alphabet $\{a_1, a_2, ..., a_n\}$ (see also Kimball 1967). (In the rules '#' is a boundary symbol which plays an important role in the filtering out of deep structures by the transformations, and b is any terminal symbol distinct from #, $a_1, a_2, ..., a_n$). This result is enough to establish a weak form of the *Universal Base Hypothesis* which Peters and Ritchie (1969) state as follows:

4) There is a version of the theory of transformational grammar in which there is a fixed base grammar B which will serve as the base component of a grammar of any natural language.

The theory which they have formalized is, of course, one such version. The only other premise needed in the argument is the rather indisputable one that natural languages are (at least) recursively enumerable sets. This shows that within the standard theory the *Universal Base Hypothesis* in its weak form is devoid of empirical content since even so linguistically absurd a base grammar as the one just given would suffice for any natural language.

Further, Peters and Ritchie claim that the same result holds even for the following strengthened form of the *Universal Base Hypothesis*.

5) In the transformational theory θ of grammar, the base grammar B will serve as the base component of a descriptively adequate grammar of any natural language.

Here the theory is fixed and the grammar is required to be descriptively adequate. Peters and Ritchie take the latter condition to mean that the grammar must agree with the native speakers' intuitions in:

1) specifying which sentences are grammatical and which are ungrammatical
2) assigning the correct number of distinct structures to ambiguous sentences
3) specifying which sentences are paraphrases of each other on at least one reading

Making only the very weak assumption that each of these specifications can be made by a recursive function, Peters and Ritchie have shown that for any version of the theory of transformational grammar that has been proposed, there are a number of base grammars which satisfy the *Universal Base Hypothesis* in this stronger form. Thus, given the sort of data which linguists customarily use in determining descriptive adequacy, the *Universal Base Hypothesis* cannot be falsified (Peters 1970).

Bach, in a recent paper, makes this explicit (Bach 1971). It is impossible, he points out, given the current state of the theory and the kinds of data considered relevant, to argue for the correctness of a set of base rules for a particular natural language. For, if we were able to do so, we could also argue that the base rules of some pair of languages were different, and this would disconfirm the *Universal Base Hypothesis*. But this is, of course, just what Peters and Ritchie have shown to be impossible. Bach then goes on to argue that the current controversy surrounding generative vs. interpretive semantics is likewise an empirically undeterminable question in view of the powerful nature of the current theory. I will not recapitulate Bach's arguments here, since the point is merely to note that results arrived at by purely mathematical means can have profound implications for linguistic theory. Peters and Ritchie did no empirical investigations of natural language at all; yet they were able to establish that the standard theory allows so much latitude in what can constitute a grammar that, at least in its weak generative capacity, it fails to distinguish natural languages from arbitrary recursively enumerable sets. More importantly, the theory is seen to be so powerful that certain questions which ought to have empirical content, such as whether or not all languages have the same base rules, in fact do not.

An immediate consequence is that any theory less restricted than the standard theory will suffer from the same defects. This is true, for example, of theories which differ from the standard theory only in having syntactic rule features, deep-structure constraints, surface-structure constraints, *anywhere* rules, etc., and also of theories which allow even more general and powerful devices such as derivational constraints and trans-derivational constraints. The work of Peters and Ritchie indicates that ways must be found to limit linguistic theory more narrowly rather than to make it worse by making it even less restricted. Ross' proposals for general constraints on variables in transformational rules are evidently steps in the right direction (Ross 1967). One should also note that Peters and Ritchie's results not only show *that* the standard theory is inadequate but to some degree also *how* it fails.

I think there can no longer by any question that mathematical studies can have great relevance to linguistics. Indeed, they can be considered essential if we are at all interested in learning the consequences of our proposals.

Notes

*Actually, several theories differing somewhat in their details are presented in *Aspects*. I choose the one adopted by Peters and Ritchie.

References

Bach, E. 1971. Syntax Since *Aspects*. Georgetown University Monograph Series on Languages and Linguistics 24.

Bar-Hillel, Y., M. Perles, and E. Shamir. 1960. On Formal Properties of Simple Phrase Structure Grammars. *ZfPSK* 14.143-72.

Brainerd, B. 1971. Introduction to the mathematics of language study. N.Y.: American Elsevier Publishing Co.

Chomsky, N. 1956. Three Models for the Description of Language. IRE Trans. on Inform. *Theory*, IT-2.113-24. A revised and corrected version appears in *Readings In Mathematical Psychology,* ed. by R.D. Luce, R.R. Bush and E. Galanter, 105-24. N.Y.: John Wiley and Sons, 1965.

Chomsky, N. 1957. Syntactic Structures. The Hague: Mouton.

Chomsky, N. 1959. On Certain Formal Properties of Grammars. *Information and Control* 2.137-67.

Chomsky, N. 1963. *Formal Properties of Grammars. Handbook of Mathematical Psychology*, ed. by R.D. Luce, R.R. Bush and E. Galanter, 323-418. N.Y.: John Wiley and Sons.

Chomsky, N. 1965. *Aspects of the Theory of Syntax*. Cambridge: The MIT Press.

Davis, M. 1958. *Computability and Unsolvability*. N.Y.: McGraw-Hill.

Fidelholtz, J. L. 1974. On the non-context-freeness of natural languages, with some comments on the competence/performance distinction. Bloomington, Ind.: Indiana U. Linguistics Club.

Ginsburg, S. and B. Hall Partee. 1969. A Mathematical Model of Transformational Grammar. *Information and Control* 15.297-334.

Gross, M. 1972. Mathematical models in linguistics. Englewood Cliffs: Prentice-Hall, Inc.

Hopcroft, J.E. and J.D. Ullman. 1969. *Formal Languages and Their Relation to Automata*. Reading: Addison-Wesley.

Kimball, J.P. 1967. Predicates Definable Over Transformational Derivations by Intersection With Regular Languages. *Information and Control* 11.177-95.

Kimball, J. 1973. The formal theory of grammar. Englewood Cliffs: Prentice-Hall, Inc.

Kleene, S.C. 1956. Representation of Events in Nerve Nets and Finite Automata. *Automata Studies*, ed. by C.E. Shannon and J. McCarthy, 3-41. Princeton: Princeton U. Press.

Kuroda, S.-Y. 1964. Classes of Languages and Linear-bounded Automata. Information and Control 7.207-23.

Landweber, P.S. 1963. Three Theorems on Phrase Structure Grammars of Type 1. Information and Control 6.131-36.

Lees, R. 1960. The Grammar of English Nominalizations. Supplement to I.J.A.L. 26, No. 3.

Parikh, R. 1961. Language Generating Devices. M.I.T. Res. Lab. Elect., Quart. Prog. Report. 60.199-212. Reprinted as: On Context-free Languages. J. Assoc. Comput. Mach. 13.570-81.

Peters, P.S. 1970. Why There Are Many 'Universal' Bases. Papers in Linguistics 1.27-43.

Peters, P.S. and R.W. Ritchie. 1969. A Note on the Universal Base Hypothesis. *Journal of Linguistics* 5.150-52.

Peters, P.S. and R.W. Ritchie. 1973. On the generative Power of Transformational Grammars. Information Sciences 6.49-83.

Peters, P.S. and R.W. Ritchie. 1971. On Restricting the Base Component of Transformational Grammars: *Information and Control* 18.483-501.

Peters, P.S. and R.W. Ritchie. 1973. On the Generative Power of Transformational Grammars. *Information Sciences* 6.49-83.

Postal, P. 1964. Constituent Structure: A Study of Contemporary Models of Syntactic Description. Supplement to *I.J.A.L.* 30, No. 1.

Ross, J.R. 1967. Constraints on Variables in Syntax. Unpublished Ph.D. dissertation. Cambridge: M.I.T.

Salomaa, A. 1971. The Generative Capacity of Transformational Grammars of Ginsburg and Partee. *Information and Control.* 18.227-32.

Salomaa, A. 1971. The Generative Capacity of Transformational Grammars of Ginsburg and Partee. *Information and Control* 18.227-32.

Salomaa, A. 1973. Formal languages. N.Y.: Academic Press, Inc. Wall, R.E. 1972. Introduction to mathematical linguistics. Englewood Cliffs: Prentice-Hall, Inc.

Schutzenberger, M.P. and N. Chomsky. 1963. The Algebraic Theory of Context-free Languages. *Computer Programming and Formal Systems,* 118-61. Amsterdam: North-Holland Publishing Co.

Staal, J.F. 1968. The Intellectual as Prophet. *Delta* 11.3.5-23.

Chapter Five

Computational Linguistics

Charles J. Rieger

1. Introduction

The study of natural language via computer has traditionally meant developing models of syntax and semantics in forms which are effectively codifiable on digital computers. The input to such models is typically a single sentence, and the output is some description of the syntactic structure of the sentence, expressed, e.g., by a phrase structure parse tree. This school of modeling has existed for quite a number of years, and there is still much active research in computer models of syntax (see for example [M1], [M2], [SS1], [W4], [W5]). Although many benefits have been derived from these explorations into syntax and semantics, as a class, this approach to language is prone to a serious loss of overall perspective, in that analysis often stops with the parse tree, rather than proceeding to deeper levels of understanding.

The thrust of any theory of syntax or semantics is to compress language into a set of unifying principles—to seek out the regularities and express them in as elegant rules as possible. In this paper we will develop the thesis that this is a fundamentally incorrect approach to language, and that, rather than compression, the thrust of a language comprehension model should be distribution. That is, rather than a concise framework for expressing rules of syntax, what is instead called for is a concise framework for allowing language to sprawl throughout a larger system of intelligence.

Although it is generally counterintuitive in scientific thinking to prefer distribution to compression as an explanation of some phenomenon, we will argue that language is too complex to compress; it is inherently a very highly distributed system of phenomena and must be modeled as such. Syntax no doubt exists, and perhaps even in some compressed and elegant form, but it is secondary, something which accrues from a more primary language phenomenon.

This phenomenon, we will propose, is the organization and selection of *word senses*. We will argue that, if a model has the ability to organize word senses, then use this organization to discriminate and identify uses of a particular sense of each word of each sentence in some context (to be defined), then that model has the primary mechanism of language. Some elements of syntax will be essential to the word sense identification process (as will elements of semantics and context), but since we will argue that such syntax evolves from the word sense organization with time, syntax plays a weak secondary role which is more an artifact than anything else. A corollary of our point of view is that most of the complexity in natural language, in fact most of its information content, lies in the individual word sense, rather than in any central or uniform system of rules.

It is indeed surprising that most computational theories of language have essentially ignored the problems involved with the organization and discrimination of word senses, especially since many of the difficulties in developing syntactic models seem to trace back to multiple meanings for words. Even some of the highly semantic and conceptual models of language comprehension (such as [S3], [R6], [RS1], [W1], [W2], [W4], [C1]) have focused primarily on issues other than those of word sense discrimination, preferring instead to concentrate on meaning or syntax structures for particular senses of particular words, then developing the techniques of semantic parsing which would map language onto such structures.

All of these models have made important contributions to our overall understanding of language. However, in this paper we want to discuss one of the centralmost issues which, we feel, has not been emphasized enough in most computational theories of language, namely, word sense discrimination and selection. Since we believe that word sense discrimination is the key to language comprehension, we will develop a model which regards the discrimination and organization of word senses as central, rather than a nuisance. Also, since we are addressing the theory from an Artificial Intelligence (AI) point of view, we will propose some specific mechanisms for carrying out the theory, knowing fully well (alas) in advance that such mechanisms will probably require quite a bit of revision and refinement.

2. Background

The ability to select or discriminate one pattern from another is one of the human abilities most closely identified with intelligence. A pattern can be any collection of symbols from the relatively simple firings of sensory neurons which occur when a person touches an object, to relatively complex patterns of social plans. Admittedly, the processes of recognizing or choosing some social pattern are probably quite a bit more complex than the processes of touch sensation recognition; but they must surely be two forms of the same general phenomenon.

For the past year or two, a group of us at Maryland has been working with a theory of human problem solving and language comprehension called the Commonsense Algorithm (CSA) Project. In this research, we have defined a representation for commonsense cause-effect world knowledge which can express many forms of "active" knowledge (knowledge about actions and their cause-effect characteristics). We presently have a theory and implementation of problem solving whose primary tenet is analogous to our tenet of word sense primacy. This is the tenet that intelligent strategy selection from among a broad spectrum of possible alternate strategies is centralmost to any theory of problem solving, and that the key issue in problem solving is the organization of alternate strategies in a way which facilitates the selection process relative to some given context. Our philosophy for problem solving was motivated by the same observations we have made for language analysis: that too much emphasis was being placed on distilling out elegant principles in limited domains at the expense of ignoring the breadth of human problem solving strategies.

To illustrate, consider how many strategies we all possess for moving objects about. There are surely hundreds (if not thousands), each best suited for a situation which is usually different in one or more respects from all the others. If the object, X, we wish to move is a carrot, we employ a strategy altogether different from the one we employ if X is a truck, a person, some gas, or some fluid. If the destination of the carrot is the counter, we do one thing; if the destination is our stomach, we do another. If the distance X is to be moved is great, we may decide to mail it instead of pick it up and carry it; or if the object is "self," we may decide to walk, drive, bicycle or fly, depending on the circumstances. It is this phrase "depending on the circumstances" which is important.

Strategy selection in the real-world (open-ended) environment is to be contrasted with strategy selection in the environment of a limited-domain problem solver (see [F1], [S1], [S2], [S4], [W4] for example) where, say, the only possible goals are to move "self" or some small, graspable, solid physical object from one point on a table to another. We suggest that the set of issues in the open-ended domain is qualitatively different from the set of issues in a domain where the act of selection has been obviated.

2.1 Strategy Selection

Because of this belief, in developing the CSA problem solver, our energies have been focused on investigating how large numbers of alternate strategies might be organized so that at any moment, "depending on the circumstances," the most appropriate strategy for some subgoal can be selected. This has given rise to a construction we call a *causal selection network* (CSN).

We have a running computer model which implements CSN's. In the model, there is one CSN to represent each state and statechange concept known to the model. For example, there is a CSN for causing a statechange in the location of an arbitrary object from some starting point to some destination along some (possibly unspecified) path, in some time limit, and by some potential actor. This is the LOCATION statechange CSN. Since goals will always be expressed as a state or statechange (or as a composition of states and statechanges), there will be one CSN for each goal predicate. When a goal such as "Construct a plan wherein actor John moves carrot 23 from refrigerator 17 to counter 13," the STATECHANGE-LOCATION CSN is called up to select a strategy.

A CSN is a tree-like structure of nodes. The terminal nodes of a CSN are all the various strategies which could possibly be relevant to the solution of a goal involving the concept the tree represents (e.g., for the LOCATION CSN, a statechange-location goal). The strategies themselves are represented in the CSA cause-effect language described in [R2], [R3], [R4] and [RG1]. Non-terminal nodes of a CSN are multiple-choice questions, and each arc out of a non-terminal node, representing one of the possible answers to the question, leads to another node in the CSN. Strategy selection is thus effected by following some path from the top of the CSN to some strategy at the bottom, heeding the answers to the questions posed at each non-terminal node along the way.

The questions at the non-terminal nodes probe the context in which the goal is to be solved. For a statechange in location, things such as the class membership of the object to be moved (person, small physical object, fluid, etc.), its size, the distance the object is to be moved, and so forth, are posed. In this manner, the strategy referenced at some terminal node of the CSN will eventually be selected. By our definition, if the questions in the CSN cannot be answered, then the statement of the goal is not well-formed enough to be solved in the first place, and there is hence no theoretical problem of the network "locking up" (e.g., we cannot really decide on an appropriate strategy for moving a carrot unless we know the distance involved).[1]

The crucial point of the CSN structure is that it is a repository and organizing influence for knowledge about appropriateness conditions (context) for other knowledge, namely, the alternate problem solver strategies for each general goal class. Having a central locus at which to organize this knowledge of appropriateness makes it possible to discriminate various strategies at selection time with respect to their applicability in the current context. Furthermore, having such a central decision-making structure makes possible the augmentation of that structure (i.e., the learning of a new strategy and its appropriateness conditions, or the refinement of the appropriateness conditions for existing strategies). We will discuss this more later.

We will not describe CSN's any further in this report. CSN's are discussed and illustrated in more detail in [R3] and [R4]. These discussions also cover other interesting aspects of CSN's as they are used in the inference and prediction components of the language comprehension phases of our CSA project.

2.2 CSNs and Language Comprehension

In developing the CSN idea, our thinking was influenced by a second purpose: that the model's knowledge of cause-effect as required by the problem solver should be one and the same as the cause-effect knowledge evoked during Language comprehension. This seems obvious enough, but, surprisingly, AI systems seem to have overlooked it; problem solvers use one form of knowledge, either procedurally encoded or expressed via, say, first-order logic assertions, whereas models of Language comprehension use altogether different structures (semantic or conceptual nets, for instance).

How should the cause-effect knowledge used by the problem solver be brought to bear on the process of language comprehension? Suppose we read: "John needed to get to work. He walked to the bus terminal." From the first sentence, we can make predictions that John might employ some strategy for getting to the office. The CSA model makes such a prediction by calling up the statechange location CSN in hypothetical reasoning mode, asking it to build as much of a prediction (plan) as possible within the limits of what the model presently knows about John (his current location, whether he has money with him, etc.). Sometimes the prediction can be fairly specific (e.g. "John will probably use the TAKE-A-BUS strategy), while sometimes the prediction must be retained in a very general form (i.e., "John will probably do something to cause himself to be located at his office"). In either case, the prediction is added to the current pool of predictions—a list of future events (or their absence) currently expected by the model.

When the second sentence of our example is input to the model, all strategies which would involve John being at a bus terminal are accessed. This set of strategies represents all the possible interpretations of the second sentence, hopefully including the "correct" one. By considering each occurrence in turn, tracing backwards (from bottom to top) through CSN's in which the candidate strategies occur as terminal nodes, it is usually possible to make an eventual connection with some prediction (i.e. "Being at the bus terminal could be part of the TAKE-A-BUS strategy because it enables one of the actions in that strategy, namely the action that places John on the bus."). So by consulting in reverse the same knowledge that is useful in problem solving, our model puts one body of knowledge to use both in constructing plans for itself (and others) and in fitting perceptions (sentences) together in contextually meaningful ways. We are currently applying this idea to the understanding of a Walt Disney children's story called the Magic Grinder [WD1]. This research will be described in a forthcoming report.

We will not delve too deeply into the CSA problem solving or language comprehension models here. However, it is this very same idea of selection, we propose, that serves as the basis of word sense selection/discrimination, and hence of language comprehension.

3. Word Sense Networks

The philosophy behind the development of the CSN's is one of centralization of intelligence, wherein there is one expert decision maker for each possible class of problems to be solved. The alternative would have been to cast possibly hundreds of competing strategies for, say, statechange location into the model independently, then to have them vie for control each time a statechange location goal appeared. [2] We feel that this alternative is not particularly attractive either in theory or in practice, because it is computationally costly and it provides no cohesive structure through which most appropriate strategy selection (and in reverse, interpretation) can be carried out.

Let us now think of words of a language as "goals", and all the senses of some word as alternate "strategies" for that word. Let us call the resulting tree which is analogous to a CSN a *sense selection network* (SSN). Then what would we have?

The analogy between a CSN and SSN is almost total. Just as a CSN represents an aggregation of expertise about a class of potential goals, a SSN represents an aggregation of expertise about one word of language. This might seem to imply a need for a staggering number of SSN's, some quite complex. And indeed it does! But SSN's will provide exactly the organizing influence which we feel the breadth-wise complexity and depthwise simplicity of language demands.

To "apply" a causal selection network is to select a most relevant strategy. What will it mean to apply a SSN? Recall that to apply a CSN means to follow some path from the root to some terminal strategy, heeding the outcomes of context-probing questions at the various nodes along the path. Such questions will ensure that the chosen strategy is, within the model's abilities to probe the semantics and context of the goal to be achieved, the most appropriate strategy.

By this analogy, to apply a SSN is to request that it diagnose its environment (syntax, semantics, context) enough to select—in some environment—the most appropriate (i.e. intended) sense for the word. Suppose then that the relevant SSN were applied to each word of an input sentence. Then the activity that would result would be analogous to a group of human experts cooperatively interacting in an attempt for each to arrive at an identification of which of his possible senses was being referenced by the sentence. [3]

We will pursue the details of SSN's in a moment. But before we do, we should reflect on what this approach amounts to. A human possesses a staggering amount of information about his language. Where is the bulk of that information? It is probably not in the syntax, because, we have learned from experience, it seems to be possible to capture most of any language's syntax in a relatively small number of rules, say, 100 or 1000 or 10,000.

Clearly, this cannot be the bulk of a human's linguistic knowledge! Instead, it seems reasonable to assume that the bulk of our knowledge of a language lies in the words and word senses *as individuals,* each having a character of its own.

Since we will be considering a SSN for the verb "take," let us consider what we know about this word and all its senses: we know the meaning of each sense, we know the classes of environment in which each sense is appropriate, we know the word's syntax, its pronounciation, its spelling, its idiosyncratic uses by our friends, and on and on. Is it sensible to attempt to represent something as incredibly complex as a word or word sense as simply an entry in a syntax or semantics dictionary? We think not, and the alternative is to provide some central structure into which *all* our knowledge about each word (at least insofar as it is relevant to the extraction of meaning from sentences) can be integrated. The SSN idea, whether or not it proves ultimately adequate, is our proposal toward this goal.

3.1 SSN Structure and Methodology

Suppose then that each word is represented by a SSN, and that a SSN will be applied at some stage of the parse to determine word sense. (We will consider later at what stage SSN application is most appropriate.) What kinds of questions about the word's environment must be posed in order to discriminate senses? Since we want to take a no-holds-barred approach to language understanding,[4] the answer is: any question at all is fair (i.e. if we are talking with George about hogs and it is Tuesday, we may know there is a special interpretation of the verb "take"!). Yet all questions will fall into one of the following classes:

(1) questions about adjacent words
(2) questions about the syntax or semantics of adjacent word senses
(3) questions about invariant general world knowledge
(4) questions about dynamic expectancies in the model

To see how we might go about constructing a SSN, let us pursue the verb "take." Our strategy, as humans who are attempting to construct "take"'s SSN, is simply to begin considering all possible constructions in which "take" can participate, then to assemble a set of diagnostics which, if answered, would be capable of discriminating take's senses. Then we will organize these as best we can into a SSN (optimality of this organization is an engineering issue and not a theoretical one) and communicate this new SSN to the model in machine readable form. Engineering-wise, this approach to language will be very time consuming. But since it will tolerate considerable variability from SSN to SSN, it lends itself to development by a large group of researchers, each contributing several SSN's. Such development is also possible, but logistically far more difficult where tightly interrelated systems of syntactic rules are being developed.

We feel the best methodology is to gather together and analyze a small corpus of sentences involving the word under consideration. In our own research, since our goal is to build a comprehension system for The Magic Grinder, we have a ready-made, closed corpus for each word. Our task then becomes simply writing SSN's which are exactly rich enough to discriminate the uses of each word as found in this single story. Typically this means very small networks, say, on the order of five or ten non-terminal nodes. But since, as we will discuss later, an important characteristic of the SSN concept is that SSN's are easily extended and modified, we will not be cheating by encoding only what we need. When we move on to another story, we will simply augment or transform the existing nets to accommodate any new senses of existing or new words. We will also hypothesize that this is how language is learned: one word sense at a time, growing new context-probing branches on existing SSN's, and that syntax and semantics gradually emerge as recurring patterns throughout a system of SSN's that are originally very distributed and unorganized.

Let us work with the following corpus in the development of the SSN for the verb "take" (we will exclude the noun senses of "take," although they too would be integrated into a more complete "take" SSN):

A1 *took* the X from A2.
> John took the ball from Mary.
> John took the hint from Mary.
> John took the cold from Mary.

A1 *took* to X.
> John took to drinking.
> John took to the puppy.

A1 *took* X out.
> John took Mary out (on a date).
> John took Mary out (to the backyard).
> John took the ad out.
> John took his anger out on Mary.

A1 *took* X.
> John took the apple (instead of the orange).
> John took the aspirin.
> John took Mary (for all she was worth).

This mixture of both conventional and idiomatic uses of "take" will serve to illustrate a very small prototype of the "take" SSN.

3.2 Syntactic Case Frameworks

Our first observation is that many of the interesting discriminations are possible using only a level of "shallow" semantics, questions about the semantics of the objects "take" binds. For this class of context-probing SSN nodes, we will have to make reference to a case framework for the verb "take."

A case framework (e.g. [F3], [F4] for a verb is a specification of the syntax and/or semantics of the concepts that can be associated with that verb. Nearly every model of language presupposes some sort of case frame for each verb (in fact for each word), although in some models it is highly syntactic, with perhaps some shallow semantics (e.g. [SS1], [F3], [M1], [W2]), while in other models (e.g. [R6], [RS1], [S3]) it is highly semantic.

Frequently, it is unclear whether the case frame is being intended as a property of the verb itself, or as a property of one of its senses. In limited domains, this is no problem, since words are generally equated with one particular sense. However, there is a real problem in an unrestricted domain. Is there to be one case frame for each verb, or one case frame for each of its senses? In discussions with Mitch Marcus a while back, it seemed reasonable to assume that there could be one case frame for each verb. Cases in such a system would be Fillmore-like: Agent, Beneficiary, Recipient, etc. However, this assumption always seems to force one into misusing these case labels. Although it seems to be possible to force the case frames for all senses of a verb into one generic case frame with specified optional and required cases such as these, because of the diversity and subtleties of all the senses of the verb, the labellings would have to mirror very superficial syntax more closely than the semantics in order to embrace all the variety. This would result in such erroneous labellings as calling "his cold" as the Beneficiary case in the sentence "John took the medicine for his cold." One could argue that this type of problem is caused by an overly naive syntax or semantics, but we feel this is not the case. Choose any level of sophistication, and there will always be large numbers of case-frame mislabellings such as this.

But what, in fact, is so disasterous about a case-frame mislabelling? After all, the main purpose of a case framework, at least from an AI point of view, is to impose some initial structure on an unstructured sequence of words. This will provide slots into which later comprehension processes may look without having to contend with the onerous complexity of the original sentence, with all its passivization, tensing, tedious noun and prepositional phrases, etc. If we intend to pass the initial case frame through more semantic comprehension phases anyway (rather than stopping with the case frame labellings and having to worry about their absolute correctness at that point), then it doesn't really make any difference that cases are mislabelled (much less what the cases are called!). Instead of using the term "Beneficiary case," for an intermediate case framework we might just as well use the term "the first noun phrase after the verb."

3.3 Semantics that Second-Guess the Syntax

Our proposal, therefore, is this: use any case labellings that are expedient; any level of syntactic or shallow semantic processing would more often than not mislabel things anyway. But equip the next level of comprehension in the system (i.e. the SSN's) with a model of the kinds of foulups the syntactic or shallow semantic case frame builders are liable to make, operating in the absence of meaning as they must. In other words, build a system in which the deeper semantic components, having a model of the syntactic or shallow semantic parse process and its potential pitfalls, will know where to look to unscramble the mislabelled cases and undifferentiated word senses.[5]

Since, in our model, the SSN's are the next step of the comprehension, each SSN must reflect a model of the syntactic component's potential foulups for the particular verb the SSN represents. Thus, for example, the "take" SSN will know that, whenever the object of "take" can be regarded as a medicine (i.e. the syntactic object can be mapped onto a model concept which is a medicine), there is the possibility of a following mislabelled Beneficiary case which resulted from a "for" prepositional phrase farther down the sentence ("John took an aspirin for his cold."). It is a simple matter to round this mislabelled component up and package it into a final correct interpretation. The crucial step is simply to identify the (possibly mislabelled) case as a syntactic unit the SSN can then examine in a larger context.

It is our feeling, therefore, that if the system is going to pass the initial case frame rendering through more semantic levels of the system anyway, it makes very little difference what the cases are called, or how they were constructed at parse time, as long as the semantic component of the system has an accurate model of how the syntax goes about its business. We submit that this is how humans parse also: syntax at the level of grouping noun and prepositional phrases and extracting· tense, etc., bundling everything together into a "false" case frame for the verb, then applying a SSN to unravel the semantics and context.

Of course, comprehension surely does not occur in such a strict, one-way sequence as this description might imply. There is probably quite a heavy interaction between the SSN level and the syntax that will provide a strong predictive component at times, amounting to "syntax on demand". So we will try to imagine the SSN for each word as being applied at the earliest possible moment in the parse (e.g., as soon as there is reason to believe that the word's part of speech has been correctly identified), and that the SSN process proceeds in parallel with the syntactic processes. We are still unclear on how this should occur, but will discuss some of the issues later. There are also some intriguing questions about when to do reference conversions (i.e., convert a phrase into the model concept to which the phrase refers). We will expose some of these issues in a later section.

Our digression into case frameworks has been necessary because each verb SSN will have to make reference to the entities its verb senses are capable of governing—entities like "the first noun phrase after the verb", or the "Object" case, or whatever we decide to call the noun phrases and prepositional phrases in the case framework.

3.4 Meaning Case Frameworks

There is another notion of case framework that will be essential to the system of meaning representation. This is, of course, the *meaning* case framework associated with each word sense. Unlike the false case frameworks (FCF's), we will demand that the meaning case frameworks (MCF's) reflect a semantically accurate labelling of all concepts they bind. Also, as has been pointed out in [S3] and [R1], cases in MCF's are always mandatory, in the sense that it is impossible to "conceptualize" a word sense fully without all its meaning cases. Much of the time, cases will be un-fillable because of incomplete information, or fillable by phrases which cannot be converted to model referents at the time, but each case is nevertheless required.

In our SSN model, such meaning case frameworks will represent each sense of a given word at some terminal node of the word's SSN. Thus, the role of our SSN parser will be to map the false case frame's cases into the meaning case frame of the sense selected as most reasonable by the SSN. A flow diagram of the SSN parser concept is shown below.

FIGURE 1

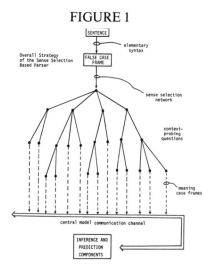

3.5 Identifying some Senses of "take"

We will illustrate the SSN idea by describing how we would go about constructing a prototype SSN for the verb "take". In constructing the "take" SSN, we will first identify all the senses of "take" required by the corpus presented earlier, then adopt some specific meaning case frames for these senses. The meaning case frames will be in the form of n-tuples, with the predicate first, followed by conceptual cases in some standard order. One or more of these MCF's, suitably selected and instantiated for any particular input sentence, will be the output of the SSN, and hence the input to the deeper inference and prediction components of the model.

In this section, we develop some concepts and representations needed to capture our corpus in meaning case frames. We will make no attempt to be exhaustive in specifying these case frames, and, in fact, the primary reason for discussing specific senses and their representations will be to provide a framework for digressions into some related issues of the CSA-SSN language comprehension model. Because it is not our main purpose to construct a final SSN, there will undoubtedly be details of our meaning case frameworks which are missing or incorrect, as well as omissions of issues we have tactily chosen to ignore.

In the following discussions, square brackets will be used to denote the model concepts referenced by the constituents of the false case frameworks. Reference conversions which transform phrases into model concepts will be carried out both during and after SSN applications. We will say more about this point later.

CLASS 1: A1 *took* the X from A2.

SENTENCE 1: John took the ball from Mary.

> *SENSE:* one actor gains control of an object from another actor
> *MCF:* (CSC-PHYS-CONTROL A1 X A2 A3 T L)
> Actor A1 causes a statechange (CSC) in physical control over object X from actor A2 to A3 at some time, T, and location, L. In this sentence A1 and A3 are both John

> *SSN OUTPUT:* (CSC-PHYS-CONTROL [JOHN] [THE BALL] [MARY]
> [JOHN] [PAST] UNKNOWN)

SENTENCE 2: John took the hint from Mary.

> *SENSE:* one actor is caused to be aware of something by another actor (in a subtle manner)

MCF: (C-INHEAD A1 A2 X T L (MANNER SUBTLE))

actor A1 causes information X to go into the head of actor A2 at time T and location L; we use the convention of including other less central markings in parentheses at the end of the standard cases; in this case, an additional marking conveys the manner in which the action was carried out

SSN
OUTPUT: (C-AWARE [MARY] [JOHN] [THE HINT] [PAST] UNKNOWN (MANNER SUBTLE))

SENTENCE 3:   John took the cold from Mary.

SENSE: one actor acquires a physical condition as the result of physical proximity to another actor

MCF: 1. (HEALTH—STATE A1 C T1)
2. (LOCATION A2 A1 T1)
3. (RESULT (1 2) (HEALTH—STATE A2 C (*D* T2 (CLASS T2 TIME) (AFTER T2 T1))))

A1 is in some health state C at time T1; A2 is at A1's location at this time; these two conditions result in A2's assuming A1's condition at some later time, T2

SSN
OUTPUT: 1. (HEALTH-STATE [MARY] [THE COLD] TIME 1)
2. (LOCATION [JOHN] [MARY] TIME1)
3. (RESULT (1 2) (HEALTH-STATE [JOHN] [THE COLD]
(*D* TIME2 (CLASS TIME2 TIME)
(AFTER TIME2 TIME 1))))

We should pause here and say some more about the terminal nodes of SSN's. In this last example, there are three meaning assertions: one which predicates that [MARY] was ill at some time TIME1, a second one which predicates that [JOHN] was located at [MARY] at this time, and a third one which predicates that the illness was transferred to [JOHN] because of these first two conditions. All three assertions are necessary here because of the presupposition that [MARY] in fact had a cold, and the inference that [JOHN] must have been near her at that time. Rather than restrict the terminal nodes of SSN's to contribute a *single* meaning assertion, we allow any terminal node to contain any number of assertions. These will reflect any presuppositions, inferences which can be made on the basis of language use exclusively, mood or tone of the speaker implied by the use of certain language constructions, and so forth. In other words, a SSN's terminal nodes are the sole point of entry of linguistic information into the model, and, being experts, are allowed to inject any secondary inferences in addition to the primary meaning of the sentence. This ability, it is felt, makes the SSN idea a very powerful one, because it allows particular presuppositions and inferences to be tailored on an individual basis for each word sense rather than appealing to some less expert, more uniform strategy of presuppositions or linguistic inference.

It should be noted that, since there are many alternate expressions of any given idea, there will be a need to share SSN terminal nodes. This will allow multiple SSN terminal nodes (in the same or different SSN's) to reference *one* MCF. For example, "Mary gave John a cold" conveys essentially the same information as "John took a cold from Mary." Hence, the "give" SSN would have as one of its numerous terminal nodes a pointer to the identical terminal node referenced by the "take" SSN, as above. Sometimes, rather than a direct sharing, it will be necessary to extend or alter the shared component in order to convey subtleties implied by the expression of one idea but not by another. This will demand some sort of hierarchical organization of the MCF's referenced from the terminal nodes of the system's SSN's.[6]

Another concept used in the "take a cold" MCF is that of a "descriptor." In assembling MCF's, it is often necessary to reference some concept obliquely by describing it instead of naming (pointing to) it directly. From a description, it ought usually to be possible to identify the object at SSN application time, or to use the descriptor to identify a specific candidate whenever an actual model concept is required.

The internal model construction employed for referencing concepts obliquely is, not surprisingly, commonly called a *descriptor*[7]. In our system, descriptors are notated by the form:

$$(*D* <var> <feature1> ... <featureN>)$$

Such a form describes a model concept (which we give some arbitrary reference name, $<var>$) that satisfies $<feature1>$, ..., $<featureN>$. In the "take a cold" example, the descriptor

$$(*D* T2 (CLASS T2 TIME) (AFTER T2 T1))$$

described a model concept which is a time and stands in an AFTER relation with another time T1. (Actually, T1 would also be represented by a descriptor with the features (CLASS T1 TIME) and (BEFORE T1 PRESENT), where PRESENT stands for whatever the reference time for the present is in the current context. However, we omit this type of model detail to avoid the snakepit of symbols that would result! The bracketed expressions such as [JOHN] are simply our (human) shorthand for descriptors which in the model would actually look like:

[JOHN] = (*D* X (CLASS X HUMAN)
(SEX X MALE)
(FIRSTNAME X JOHN))

Associated with descriptors is the notion of "converting a descriptor" to a model concept or set of model concepts at some point during comprehension. As we will see, many descriptor conversions will be forced by SSN application. Those descriptors that are not converted at SSN application time will simply be left unconverted, and will be passed along to the deeper levels of the model (inference and prediction) as is. In general, there will be an intimate interaction between the SSN's and the reference mechanism which converts descriptors, and, even beyond this, between the reference mechanism and the inference and prediction components themselves. Some interesting types of interaction were described in [R1], and later we will have a little more to say about the timing of descriptor conversion in the present model.

Let us now resume our identifications of senses of "take" in the limited corpus we have chosen:

CLASS 2:   A1 *took* to X.

SENTENCE 4:   John took to drinking.

    SENSE: an actor begins a habitual activity

    MCF: (HABITUAL⁻PATTERN A P T)
              actor A begins habitual pattern P at time T

    SSN
OUTPUT: (HABITUAL-PATTERN [JOHN] [ALCOHOLISM-
              PATTERN]   (PAST] BEGINS))

We should describe what the referent of ALCOHOLISM-PATTERN actually is in the CSA model. In our model, we are able to represent algorithmic patterns via a small number of links relating to causality and enablement concepts [R3], [R4], [RG1]. Once we have represented an algorithmic pattern in these terms, we can name it (internally), and use the entire (possibly complex) pattern as though it were a single "macro" action. Therefore, when we reference ALCOHOLISM-PATTERN from a terminal node in a SSN, we mean simply a pointer to the internal definition of this activity (See [R2].

[R3], [R4], and [R5] for more details and other example patterns expressed in the CSA cause-effect representation.) Hence, because CSA provides a hierarchical system for defining complex action patterns, we are not merely playing games with suggestive symbols when we reference concepts such as ALCOHOLISM-PATTERN![8]

SENTENCE 5:   John took to the puppy.

    SENSE: an actor begins to like something

      MCF: (EFEEL A LIKE X (T BEGINS GRADUAL))
actor A begins gradually to feel the emotion "like" toward object X at time T; the BEGINS and GRADUAL here are time aspect markings which, as symbols, represent special model concepts

         SSN
   OUTPUT: (EFEEL [JOHN] LIKE [PUPPY] ([PAST] BEGINS GRADUAL))

CLASS 3:   A1 *took* X out.

SENTENCE 6:   John took Mary out (on a date).

    SENSE: one actor initiates a mutual activity with another actor for the purpose of having fun

      MCF: (GO-DATE A1 A2 LOC T)
A1 and A2 go to LOC as a date at time T; here again, the predicate GO-DATE is a reference to a rather complex activity which would be expressed elsewhere in the model as a larger CSA pattern, but which we reference here as though it were a single action

         SSN
   OUTPUT: (GO-DATE [JOHN] [MARY] UNKNOWN [PAST])

SENTENCE 7:   John took Mary out (to the back yard).

    SENSE: an actor causes the change in location of an object; the particular strategy employed is unspecified, but is often predictable by applying the appropriate causal selection network as though the comprehension model itself were attempting to effect a change in the object's location;

MCF: (CSC-LOCATION A1 OBJ L1 L2 PATH T)
actor A1 causes a statechange (CSC) in the location of object OBJ from L1 to L2 along PATH at time T

SSN
OUTPUT: (CSC-LOCATION [JOHN] [MARY] UNKNOWN 1 [OUT] UNKNOWN 2 [PAST]

SENTENCE 8: John took the ad out.

SENSE: an actor agrees to pay another actor if the other actor will transmit information on the first actor's behalf

MCF: (CONTRACT A1 A2 (PAY A1 A2 AMT T1) (C-INHEAD A2 A3 INFO T2) T3)
a contract exists between A1 and A2 at time T3; A1's side of the contract is to pay A2 some amount of money AMT at time T1; A2's side of the contract is to cause some piece of information INFO to go into the head of A3 at time T2; this notion of a contract appears as an example in [R4]

SSN
OUTPUT: (CONTRACT [JOHN] UNKNOWN1
(PAY [JOHN] UNKNOWN1
UNKNOWN2 TIME1)
(C-INHEAD UNKNOWN1
UNKNOWN3 UNKNOWN4 TIME2)
TIME3)
(We have omitted all descriptors for the sake of visual clarity.)

SENTENCE 9: John took out his anger on Mary.

SENSE: one actor attempts to decrease his level of anger by causing a negative change to some object

MCF: 1. (EFEEL A1 (*D* E(CLASS E NEG-EMOTION)) A2 T1)
2. (MOTIVATES 1 (C-NEGCHANGE A1 OBJ ATT T2 LOC))
actor A1 feels some negative emotion at time T1 toward some actor A2, motivating A1 to cause a negative change (C-NEGCHANGE) to some object OBJ with respect to some attribute ATT, at some time T2 and location LOC;

MOTIVATES is one of the CSA primitive link types, described in [R4]; note that we have employed a descriptor to represent the entire class of possible negative emotions that A1 could be experiencing

SSN
OUTPUT: 1. (EFEEL [JOHN] ANGER UNKNOWN1 TIME1)
2. (MOTIVATES 1
(C-NEGCHANGE [JOHN] [MARY]
UNKNOWN2 TIME2 UNKNOWN3))

CLASS 4:   A1 *took* X.

SENTENCE
10:   John took the apple (instead of the orange).

SENSE: an actor selects one object from among several alternatives

MCF: (SELECT A OBJ ALTS T LOC)
actor A selects OBJ from among alternatives ALTS at location LOC and time T

SSN
OUTPUT: (SELECT [JOHN] [THE APPLE] UNKNOWN1
[PAST] UNKNOWN2)

SENTENCE
11:   John took the aspirin.

SENSE: an actor ingests some medicine

MCF: (INGEST A OBJ T LOC)
actor A ingests object OBJ at time T, location LOC

SSN
OUTPUT: (INGEST [JOHN] [THE ASPIRIN] [PAST]
UNKNOWN1)

SENTENCE
12:   John took Mary (for all she was worth).

SENSE: one actor causes another actor to lose money to him

MCF: 1. (CONTRACT A1 A2 OB1 (PAY A2 A1 AMT T1) T2)
2. (PAY A2 A1 AMT T3)
3. (NOT (ACHIEVE A1 OB1))

again, we see a MCF which contributes several facts: there was a contract between A1 and A2; A2's side of the contract was to pay A1 some amount of money, and this in fact occurred; A1's side of the contract was obligation OB1, and A1 never achieved it; ACHIEVE is a predicate in the CSA system which denotes that some actor achieves some goal (via unspecified means)

SSN
OUTPUT: 1. (CONTRACT [JOHN] [MARY] UNKNOWN1
(PAY [MARY] [JOHN] UNKNOWN2 TIME1)
TIME2)
2. (PAY [MARY] [JOHN] UNKNOWN2 TIME3)
3. (NOT (ACHIEVE [JOHN] UNKNOWN1))

3.6 Construction of the "take" SSN

Let us now assume that we have some target meaning structures onto which to map sentences involving the verb "take". Of course, the particular representations we have developed have the appearance of being ad-hoc. In fact, this is partly the case, since we have not developed the entire system and made some convincing arguments that its predicates are consistent and of use to later phases of comprehension. However, in that the general style of these representations is directly compatible with the CSA theory of representation, we have tried to be as rigorous as possible in our attempt to capture the meanings of these various senses of "take".

The last order of business before constructing the "take" SSN is to define a format for take's false case frameworks as they might be produced by an unintelligent case-frame-like parser. This will provide the framework of slots which will be probed by the tests in the SSN.

We will adopt the simplest and least biased labeling scheme possible, namely, labels which simply denote the relative positions of sentence constituents. We will use the following notation in describing the false case frames:

(NP...) a noun phrase
(PP...) a prepositional phrase
(ADV...) an adverbial phrase

and will assume that the occurrence of "take" has already been identified as a verb sense. We will ignore time aspects of these sentences. When we represent each sentence of the corpus in these terms, here is what we get:

SENTENCES: John took the ball from Mary.
                John took the hint from Mary.
                John took the cold from Mary.

FCF: ((NP JOHN) TAKE (NP THE BALL) (PP FROM (NP MARY)))
            (NP THE HINT)
            (NP THE COLD)

SENTENCES: John took to drinking.
                John took to the puppy.

FCF: ((NP JOHN) TAKE (PP TO (NP DRINKING)))
                        (NP THE PUPPY)

SENTENCES: John took Mary out on a date.
                John took Mary out to the back yard.

FCF: ((NP JOHN) TAKE (NP MARY) (ADV OUT) (PP ON (NP A DATE)))
            (PP TO
            (NP THE BACK YARD))

SENTENCE: John took the ad out.
FCF: ((NP JOHN) TAKE (NP THE AD) (ADV OUT))

SENTENCE: John took out his anger on Mary.
FCF: ((NP JOHN) TAKE(ADV OUT) (NP HIS ANGER) (PP ON (NP MARY)))

SENTENCES: John took the apple.
                John took the aspirin.
                John took Mary.

FCF: ((NP JOHN) TAKE (NP THE APPLE))
                    (NP THE ASPIRIN))
                    (NP MARY)

We will reference the various slots in the FCF's via the following predicates and objects:

SELF   the slot which holds TAKE itself

(RIGHT X)	the slot to the right of slot X
(LEFT X)	the slot to the left of slot X
(WORD X)	the actual word in slot X
(CON X)	the syntactic constituent in slot X
(NOUN NP)	the main noun of a noun phrase
(PREP PP)	the preposition of a prepositional phrase
(PREP-OBJ PP)	the object of a prepositional phrase
(SYN-CLASS X)	the syntactic class of the constituent in slot X
(SEM-CLASS X)	the semantic class of the constituent in slot X
(REF X)	the model referent of the constituent in slot X

We now decide upon a set of discriminations which will differentiate the senses of "take" in this limited corpus, and synthesize them into the prototype sense selection network. Doing this yields the net shown below. It should be noted that there are in general many acceptable orderings for SSN's; we have chosen a natural one, and another individual might choose another equally natural one. The singularly important characteristic of the SSN is simply that it be able to accomplish the discrimination *somehow*.

In the "take" SSN below, we have used some English in the question asking. In the computer model, we would of course not do this, but instead always phrase questions in a form suitable as input to the database and deductive components of our model. These components are described at various points in [R3] and [R5]. Notice that the questions in even this simple net cover a spectrum from the very syntactic, to "shallow semantics", to contextual and predictive. It is this multi-level approach to sense discrimination that we feel is the key to the human language comprehension phenomenon.

There are several noteworthy points about this SSN we have just constructed. First, it reflects only those discriminations necessary for this particular corpus of structural forms. There are clearly many variations in structural ordering (i.e. "John took the book out" vs. "John took out the book") which we have simply not incorporated. The feeling is that the SSN must anticipate all acceptable structural orderings. This means that SSN's really are more graph-like than tree-like, as this simple one might tend to indicate. A graph-like organization would allow multiple paths through the net to a single terminal node, and we feel this is an adequate solution to structural ordering variations.

Another incompleteness of this SSN is obviously its content. For every discrimination here, there are undoubtedly ten that we have not considered. The strength of the SSN is that we can see pretty much how and where to augment it to accommodate new entries.

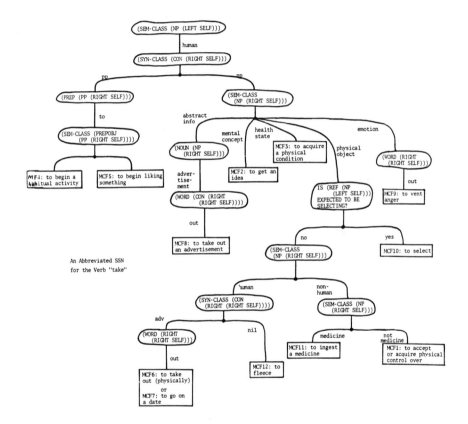

(SEM-CLASS (NP (LEFT SELF)))

human

(SYN-CLASS (CON (RIGHT SELF)))

pp   np

(PREP (PP (RIGHT SELF)))

(SEM-CLASS (NP (RIGHT SELF)))

to

abstract info

(SEM-CLASS (PREPOBJ (PP (RIGHT SELF))))

mental concept

health state

emotion

(NOUN (NP (RIGHT SELF)))

MCF3: to acquire a physical condition

physical object

(WORD (RIGHT (RIGHT SELF)))

MF4: to begin a habitual activity

MCF5: to begin liking something

adver-tise-ment

MCF2: to get an idea

out

(WORD (CON (RIGHT (RIGHT SELF))))

IS (REF (NP (LEFT SELF))) EXPECTED TO BE SELECTING?

MCF9: to vent anger

out

MCF8: to take out an advertisement

no

yes

An Abbreviated SSN for the Verb "take"

(SEM-CLASS (NP (RIGHT SELF)))

MCF10: to select

human

non-human

(SYN-CLASS (CON (RIGHT (RIGHT SELF))))

(SEM-CLASS (NP (RIGHT SELF)))

adv

nil

medicine

not medicine

(WORD (RIGHT (RIGHT SELF)))

MCF11: to ingest a medicine

MCF1: to accept or acquire physical control over

out

MCF12: to fleece

MCF6: to take out (physically) or MCF7: to go on a date

Another feature of the net is that it does only enough discrimination work to discriminate the senses it knows about at any given moment in its historical evolution. Terminal node processing (i.e. that which transforms constituents from the false case frame into the selected meaning frame) is responsible for any final testing. This is testing that must turn out true, but which was not necessary for discrimination... the leftovers, so to speak.

A final observation about the structure of this SSN is that it always poses multiple-choice questions. We feel this is a crucial aspect of question-asking that has largely been ignored. Cognitive models should simply not ask internal questions (of the database/deductive component) without some preconception of the range of possible acceptable answers. For one thing, without specifying a list of acceptable alternatives, the question asker leaves himself vulnerable to possible responses with which he might not be able to cope (i.e. computer symbols that he is not prepared to recognize). For another thing, with no guidelines, the database/deductive component might find it very difficult to determine the range of acceptable answers. Multiple choice questions, which always ask: "which, among these alternatives, is the most appropriate characterization; what is the best fit?", are easier both for humans, and, we propose, for a model's database/deductive component. So, for example, rather than asking "What is X's location" and leaving ourselves open to a range of responses we may not be able to deal with, it is better to ask: "what is X's location: CITY, WILDERNESS, HOME?, because now some effective procedures for "differencing" are suggested to determine the best characterization of X's location. We are presently working on a theory of how a "smart middleman" question answerer would difference the multiple choice responses to provide direction to the database/deductive component.

4. Perspectives and Implications of the SSN Theory

Let us assume that we carried through such an analysis for each word in our language. Besides a HUGE data base and this nucleus of an ability to discriminate word senses, what in fact would we have? Let us step back from the theory of sense discrimination a moment to consider other implications and uses of SSN's. After this, we will attempt to describe the relationship between syntax (which SSN's obviously rely upon to some extent simply to get started) and sense discrimination; finally, we will describe a small example of SSN parsing that was done by our computer model.

4.1 Context

It is always tempting to search for a central, homogeneous theory of context in an attempt to attempt to discover a uniform theory of context switching in which one large "switch" can be set, so as to condition subsequent system behavior along certain lines. For example, to take one of Riesbeck's [R6] favorite examples ("John went on a hunting trip and shot two bucks..."), if we go on a hunting trip, we would like to be able to throw the big context switch to the "hunting trip" position, and thereby bias the system in its interpretation of words which have special meanings in this domain toward those meanings. When we exit that domain, we simply throw the big switch to another setting.

Such a system is quite elegant to describe, but, we feel, not theoretically viable. (Riesbeck does not necessarily endorse this approach either! We have merely used his good example.) For one thing, how many contexts are there, and what delimits a context? These questions seem to have no answer, and even if they did, the resulting theory would probably require billions of contexts. Also, there is the problem of contexts within contexts, and related pattern matching problems in detecting which parts of which contexts are in effect at any one moment.

The SSN theory is very nearly the antithesis of the "big switch" approach to context. Our theory implies that context cannot be homogeneous or central. It must instead be distributed throughout the thousands and thousands of small units (the SSN's), each of which is an expert at the very small task of discriminating the senses of exactly one word in all conceivable contexts. The trick, of course, is that, although there are many contexts, for each SSN there are only a relatively small number of aspects which will have the potential to influence the SSN's discrimination procedure. Insofar as constructing SSN's is concerned, this means that if the sense identification of a given word can ever be influenced by some "global context," the expert SSN which performs this identification must explicitly ask whether or not it is in fact within such a global context every time it is called to perform a sense discrimination. In other words, we cannot broadcast to the system "now we are talking about hunting...please condition all subsequent activity as appropriate." Instead, each unit whose interpretation could possibly be influenced by this context must know on its own to ask whether it is in a context in which there are known to be hunting activities.

This literally means that the SSN for each word whose interpretation might be affected by some specific aspect of context must include a very specific probe which would uncover that aspect. The implication of this approach is startling at first: does a human really ask all these "irrelevant" questions about every word in every context in each sentence he hears, just so that he can decide on the right sense? The SSN theory says, and intends to say, *yes*! Of course, since we are seldom aware of all this churning beneath the surface, we must believe that it is highly associative, and, hence, subconscious in some sense of that word. We take puns to be evidence that such a process is occurring: one necessary ingredient of a pun is that it result in more than one path down a SSN. When this happens, some alarm goes off; the fact that it happens so infrequently suggests that SSN's are very expert, and very complete indeed. The fact that a child fails to recognize puns might also have an explanation in SSN terms: either his SSN's are not complete enough and do not include discriminations for alternate senses, or his SSN access mechanisms are not fully developed enough, say, to follow multiple paths in parallel.

4.2 SSN Adaptation to Context

As we have pointed out, the structure and theory of SSN's are quite similar to the structure and theory of the causal selection networks used to organize cause-effect knowledge for the purposes of language comprehension and problem solving in the CSA system. The CSN model suggests a method whereby the process of strategy selection during plan synthesis can be made to adapt to "ambient context." The effect of such an ability is to route answers to questions about context which have been uncovered during the synthesis of one plan to all other points of the system which might be interested. Relative to CSN's, what this means is that, as one question at some node in some CSN is posed and answered, the answer is routed to all other nodes of all other CSN's that would have posed the same question, and which also include the answer just received as one alternative beneath them. At such nodes, a "bypass" is implanted. The bypass will remain as long as the aspect of context for which it exists remains, and has the effect in principle of reducing the amount of context-probing the network of which it is a part must do to make a context-sensitive strategy selection if ever the net is asked. It is conceivable in such an environment that some CSN's will come to contain many bypasses. The interpretation of such a state of affairs is that, through the synthesis of other, possibly unrelated plans, the system has learned so much about the environment that, if ever asked to synthesize a plan using this heavily bypassed CSN, it will be "obvious" how to select the best strategy: the bypasses will skip over most of the questions that would ordinarily be asked.

We suggest that this mechanism is of theoretical interest within the SSN framework as well. Although we have discussed the SSN idea only with respect to verbs, we must imagine there to be an SSN for every word of the language, not just verbs. The combined, cooperative efforts of a collection of networks will produce the parse result for any given sentence. Since, in doing this job, any given network might ask, and receive an answer for, questions that other networks involved in the parse might also eventually ask, we have an obvious use to which we might profitably put this same notion of bypasses. For example, in helping to construct the noun phrase in which it is embedded, the SSN for the word JOHN might decide that, based on the context *as seen from that vantage point* in the sentence, JOHN refers to John Smith. Assuming that some of the questions the JOHN network used in this determination are also asked by, say, the "take" network

("John took..."), bypasses can be implanted to condition the "take" network along the lines relevant when its left-adjacent noun phrase refers to a male human; in this way, the "take" network will implicitly "know" enough about its left-adjacent noun phrase to proceed with its questioning about its other cases, context, etc.

We feel the concept of a bypass is an appropriate metaphor for a process that seems to occur in humans: having heard the beginning of an average sentence, we usually are able to predict what will follow. As more of the sentence comes in, the predictions can become more specific. Therefore, perhaps the reason that we do not notice ourselves applying a sense selection network for each word as it enters is that many of the later SSN's become heavily bypassed—"set" in certain directions by what has been processed up to that point.

Bypasses seem to be a possible explanation for larger contextual influences on sentences as well. If we are indeed in a hunting context, and this fact is discovered by some SSN having posed the question, then routing bypasses to all points in the system which ask this same question, will amount to something like "throwing a big switch." But now we have a computational definition of this term: the "hunting context" is the union of bypass sets which would be implanted as the result of asking and answering questions about activities in some way related to hunting ("Has there been any reference to guns?", "Are any actors out in the woods?", etc.). The reason this works, of course, is that it does not force us into identifying something so well-formed as a "hunting context," but rather it defines such a context by sets of bypasses, some or all of which may be present in varying degrees.

Interaction with context need not always be on this large a scale. For example, if sentence 1 is: "John asked Mary which piece of fruit she wanted," we will generate a very strong prediction that Mary is now in an environment where she has been asked to make a selection. If sentence 2 is: "Mary picked the apple," we seem automatically to know what sense of "pick" to expect (i.e., *not* "pluck," as in "She plucked the apple," or "She plucked the guitar," etc.). This, we propose, is simply another manifestation of bypass implantation, where, in this case, the bypass has its origins in the deeper levels of prediction and inference.

4.3 Generation

Application of SSN's top-down maps words onto word senses. However, an important characteristic of SSN's is that, being an openly-accessible data structure, they can be searched and manipulated in arbitrary ways. This is in contrast to, say, a procedurally-encoded model of grammar or problem solving, in which experts are black-box programs.

Because of this openness, it is equally convenient to traverse SSN's bottom-up, starting from some terminal node, seeking the root. This process will amount to a mapping of *senses* of words (i.e. meaning n-tuples used in the deeper parts of the model) onto *words* of the language. We propose that such a reverse application of SSN's provides a reasonable theory of language generation.

To illustrate, suppose we wish to express one of the meaning n-tuples involved in the "take" SSN analysis. We assume that, in addition to the "take" SSN, there are numerous other sources from which this meaning n-tuple might have sprung (i.e. SSN's for other words which would map those words down to the same meaning n-tuple). We assume also that each meaning n-tuple knows (is backlinked to) all SSN terminal nodes which make reference to it. Whenever the system wishes to express this meaning n-tuple, it first locates all relevant SSN terminal nodes. Then, it chooses one and begins to ascend the SSN. At each discrimination node, it observes the question that would have been posed on a downward application of the SSN, and notes what answer would have had to obtain in order to select as next node in the downward direction the node from which the upward climb is climbing. (I am aware that that was a tough sentence to parse...It was even tougher to compose!) Then, if possible, the system "makes things that way," i.e., it uses the question and its answer to add a new constraint to the sentence being generated. If the upward climb encounters a node which cannot be satisfied, this is an indication that this path is inappropriate for expressing the meaning n-tuple. In this case, another alternative is begun.

For paths which can be traversed back to the SSN's root, there will be a set of constraints on the form of the sentence, this set having accumulated during the upward traversal. These constraints form the input to a syntactic generation component which is free to express the sentence in any way it deems fit, but using this verb, and keeping within the limits of the contraints derived from the SSN.

This reverse use of SSN's is actually nothing of a surprise, since it is a property of any declarative representation that it is accessible in numerous directions. Simmon's and Slocum's use of ATN grammars in generation [G1], where the very same grammar can also be used during analysis, is directly analogous to our reverse use of SSN's.

4.3.1 Relationship to Goldman's Model of Generation

Neil Goldman [G1] wrote the theory and program for the generator in the MARGIE model, developed by Schank et. al [SGRR]. Goldman's task was to accept as input a conceptual dependency graph [S3] which represented the meaning of some thought, and, in the context of the memory and inference component's current state, produce an ATN graph representation of an English sentence which would most appropriately reflect the meaning of the graph. Having constructed such an ATN graph, an adaptation of Simmon's and Slocum's ATN generator was applied to generate surface English.

In this first phase of conceptual generation, the spirit of Goldman's approach was very much in the spirit of our proposal for language analysis. He perceived the main task as one of selection from among a set of known alternatives for expressing any given underlying concept in the input graph. By filtering the graph down a discrimination net which asked questions about the conceptual roles present in the graph and about general world knowledge, he arrived at a terminal node which contained the skeleton of some English verb's case frame, together with information concerning how to extract role-fillers from the meaning graph in fleshing out the verb's skeleton. Although most of the details of his system were different from the details of ours, his point of view was, we feel, a very sound one for deep generation tasks.

4.4 Reference

"Reference" refers to that process wherein a description of some model concept is used to identify that model concept. "Model concept" means the internal location in the model at which the concept and all its associated features are stored. Descriptions may be elaborate[9] or simple; but in either event, a descriptor can generally be thought of as simply a list of features which an object must possess in order to be considered as a candidate for the referent.

There are several very interesting and very tough problems relating to reference. Two important ones are: when are reference conversions performed, and what is the nature of the interaction between reference and inference? The reference-inference problem has been discussed to some extent in the AI literature (see [C1], [R1], [W4] for example), and one general conclusion seems to be that the system ought to have the ability to defer referent conversion in uncertain environments until inference has had a chance to make contributions which might assist in the conversion. [R1] describes one possible strategy for reference conversion. But an unsolved problem still remains: namely, how can what is needed for referent conversion for various pending unconverted referents serve to influence the inference component along lines which would be of help in the conversions? We will not attempt to treat this aspect of the reference-inference problem in this paper.

However, the other question of reference, namely, that of *when* to perform reference conversion, is partially addressed by this theory of SSN's. Generally speaking, there are two possibilities: (1) perform all reference conversions immediately after the syntactic case framework has extracted all the relevant descriptions (noun and prepositional phrases, etc.), or

(2) perform reference conversions on demand from some more goal-directed source. The first possibility suffers from chicken-egg problems, since the meaning environment in which the referent is to be identified is not known until later phases. Although syntactic intersection searches from the descriptions present at this level can often yield satisfactory results, most of the interesting issues of reference are bypassed by this strategy.

The second alternative, reference on demand, seems more in line with the strategy humans surely employ. The question is: what is the source of this demand? Abstractly, the demand source is quite simple: some reference must be converted in order to understand (i.e., make inferences or predictions from) the sentence in which it is embedded.

Such a demand source is inherent in the SSN model: the questions being posed by the net in its attempt to identify, say, the sense of a verb. For example, suppose a net asks the question "Does X own his own home?", where X refers to the referent of one of the verb's "false cases." (We assume that the network has already determined that X must refer to a human.) Then, if X has not already been converted from a description to a model concept as the result of a prior question, it certainly must in general be converted at that point in order to answer this kind of question. In other words, the act of asking a question about something not yet converted is what causes reference conversions.

In the case where the reference conversion of some syntactic constituent is not required during the application of the various SSN's in the meaning translation of a sentence, then the reference is simply not converted at all by the language-related functions. Rather, it is passed along as-is to the inference and prediction levels, and converted only when some question about it at these levels requires. We feel that this is the way a human parser works; if there is no need to convert some description in order to understand the sentence, why waste time and energy? The approach is also compatible with our philosophy of modeling: a model ought to have a "good" reason for everything it does. If it wastes time on some unessential reference conversion simply because there is a step in the comprehension at which all references must be converted, the model is not behaving "intelligently."

Of course, we would expect most descriptions to be converted either at the SSN stage, or during inference and prediction. It will usually happen that the relevance of any given description can only be determined after a partial (i.e. discovery of candidates) or full (discovery of a unique model concept) conversion.

4.5 Learning

Our view is that language is learned one word sense at a time. Rather than syntax, the things that concern a child in the earliest phases of language are the times (contexts) at which it is appropriate to utter a word. We suggest that the child's knowledge of language is at first a collection of relatively shallow SSN's in which not much organization (i.e. not many discrimination nodes) is called for, but which simply serve as a storage medium for new word senses as the child picks them up. As the child's experiences continue, he encounters new words (more correctly, some particular sense of the new word), and new senses of existing words. In the case of new senses, somehow the child adds one or more new nodes to an existing SSN. We say "somehow" because we as yet have no adequate theory of how the child determines what is relevant and what is not relevant when he builds new discrimination nodes. Differencing must certainly be a key operation, but this in itself is probably not a sufficient mechanism. (See [F2] for some insights into discrimination network evolution.)

Even though there are no completely adequate theories of discrimination network evolution, we suggest that simply having a place to store and organize new word senses as they are acquired is half the battle. If this is the primary language process, where then does syntax enter the picture? We propose that, in time, some "meta" process which observes the repeated application of SSN's during parsing notices that certain classes of questions are posed over and over. With time, these come to be distilled out of the SSN's and into a more central location where they can be shared by all SSN's. That is, syntax is a secondary phenomenon which makes the original, and primary, phenomenon run more efficiently and compactly. However, only a very small percentage of our knowledge of language can be bundled together and shared this way. This is why models of syntax are in fact deceptively small and compact. In fact, the vast majority of SSN questions are not unifiable into a compact set of rules, and remain distributed throughout individual SSN's, even in the adult.

4.6 Syntax

Our discussion has been focused primarily on the selection process that occurs "after" some sort of syntactic (or mildly semantic) case frame has been built. In particular, our discussions focussed on verb sense discrimination. There are two important points to be made in these regards. First, we envision there to be a SSN for every word of the language, with the possible exceptions of the several hundred function words which must be used as purely syntactic guideposts. Second, false case frame construction needn't necessarily occur *in-toto* before the SSN phase.

4.6.1 Sequencing

Noun and prepositional phrases have very stereotyped syntax. There are some well-known, and indeed pretty good, grammars for parsing them

([W4], [W5]). There are equally developed procedures for morphological and simple transformational processing. If we restrict the syntax to these types of tasks, it seems we run no severe risk of an overly naive syntactic component interfering with comprehension, especially if the individual sense nets incorporate models of potential parser pitfalls on an individual word basis.

We imagine the nature of the syntax/SSN interaction to be as follows. The syntax begins parsing noun and prepositional phrases left to right, collecting them as units of a potential false case frame. When the first unit which could be interpreted as a main verb appears, the syntax alerts the relevant SSN which then begins applying itself. If we arrange to have the first questions in the SSN pose queries about the phrases to its *left*, then it will be able to start interacting with the false case frame immediately. Meanwhile, the syntax continues forming noun and prepositional phrases at its own pace, noticing clause structures and initiating other SSN's where appropriate.

A running SSN has the option to bow out if it cannot make sense of what it has available to it at the moment. This would direct the syntax to attempt another suggestion concerning the role of the entity it had originally thought was a candidate for the main verb. (This probably would not happen very often.)

As the various SSN's run in parallel on the verbs of the sentence and its clauses, they will pose multiple-choice questions about the phrases collected as the false case framework. Some of these questions can be answered on the superficial evidence contained in the structure of the phrase, but many of them will require a more thorough analysis of the phrase, in particular, the concept or individual it references. This is where the SSN's for other word categories come in.

4.6.2 Preposition, Adjective and Noun SSNs

When questions cannot be answered on the basis of the syntax and shallow semantics of the phrase itself, some level of comprehension must be applied to the phrase. There are two possible levels: (1) concept identification, and (2) referent identification. Identifying the concept of the phrase means disambiguating the senses of the nouns, adjectives and prepositions that appear in the phrase. To illustrate, the *concept* underlying the phrase "the cold red man" could be one of several alternatives, according to the sense interpretation of the adjectives cold and red. Suppose that in some context the intended concept was : "an American Indian who was experiencing a state of physical coldness." Then, we would certainly want to identify this as the underlying concept, and model is by an appropriate descriptor:

```
(*D* X   (CLASS X HUMAN)
         (SEX X MALE)
         (NATIONALITY X AMERICAN-INDIAN)
         (BODY-TEMPERATURE X REL-LOW))
```

in which all the relevant concepts appear as unambiguous meaning assertations about this X, whatever it is.

It is precisely the role of adjective and noun SSN's (in this case, the nets for "cold" and "red") to probe the sentence and meaning environment and arrive at translations of these words. Except that their outputs are *descriptors* instead of instantiated MCF's, adjective and noun networks are identical in structure and concept to verb SSN's.

Thus, whenever a verb SSN poses a question about some FCF constituent, and this question cannot be answered superficially, a *concept conversion* is undertaken by applying preposition, adjective and noun SSN's, informing them of the context in which they are being called (e.g. to answer a question posed by the "take" SSN of its third phrase to the right), and expecting a meaning-based descriptor (i.e. a concept conversion) as output.

Other questions posed by the verb net might be so specific that they demand full conversion to a model referent. Examples of this type of question might be: "Does this individual know Mary Smith," or "How old is this individual?" For these, the descriptor which is derived as the converted concept is given to the model's reference processes to perform an "intelligent" intersection search for such an individual, again, passing along as much of the "upper" context as possible (e.g. it is conjectured that, whoever it is, it is someone who may have been involved in a "take" action with Mary Smith). Successful referent conversions will open the door to the wealth of detail which is typically stored with each model concept, and make possible the answering of many detailed questions posed by various SSN's.

There are many interesting problems about SSN coordination and interaction, particularly where information sharing is concerned. It is expected that we will be working on these problems for quite some time!

5. An Example

In conclusion, we will describe a very skeletal implementation of the ideas described in this paper. In AI literature, examples typically come at the beginning of the paper, so that the reader will be impressed before putting the paper down. We include this example here at the end rather than at the beginning for two reasons: first, it is neither a final result nor a general model yet, and hence is not intended to impress; second, readers of linguistics literature are generally more faithful about finishing articles than AI literature readers!

This example was the result of 3 months of system building at MIT. We took our CSA system and merged Marcus' "Wait and See" case frame parser [M1], [M2] into it. Because of vocabulary mismatches, at the end, the system did exactly one sentence in full glory; although much of the theory was there, we never equipped the system with much data.

The single example was: "The big greedy red man gave poor Minnie a headache." (Actually, it would also deal with "cold," "idea," "book" instead of "headache," and with some adjectives other than "greedy," "poor" and "red.") Marcus' parser was first run, without interaction with the CSA model, to produce a fairly semantic case frame rendering of the sentence:

```
G0:   CLAUSE
      VERB: GIVE
        AGENT: G1
        RECIP: G2
        NEUTRAL: G3
        TENSE: (PAST SIMPLE)
G1:   NOUN-PHRASE
      DET: THE
      ADJS: (BIG GREEDY RED)
      NOUN: MAN
G2:   NOUN-PHRASE
      PROPER-NOUN: MINNIE
      ADJS: (POOR)
G3:   NOUN-PHRASE
      DET: A
      NOUN: HEADACHE
```

Next, the main verb of the top clause was retrieved, and used to call up the "give" SSN. The arguments to the SSN were formed from the three cases AGENT, RECIP and NEUTRAL, and were referenced by variables named W, X and Y within the SSN's test nodes. The net was then applied, and in this example (because the NEUTRAL case was a PHYSICAL-CONDITION), selected the MCF representation:

$$(\text{C-HEALTH-STATE G1 G2 HEADACHE})$$

In the simple SSN used, no references were made to the agent or the recipient (G1 or G2) in selecting this meaning interpretation. Therefore, the G1 and G2 in the output of the SSN were still pointers to parts of Marcus' case frame structure. Since it was the purpose of that prototype model to carry a sentence from its input form to a completely internal meaning representation, but not to perform inference or predictions beyond that stage, the model always caused any remaining unconverted referents to be converted after SSN application.

In converting G1, the reference to the red man, three adjective SSN's were applied, in the order RED, GREEDY then BIG. The RED SSN decided that, because the noun was MAN, a reference to a human, the interpretation should be:

(NATIONALITY X AMERICAN-INDIAN)

and added this feature to the descriptor for the noun MAN (already begun by retrieving the meaning definition of the noun MAN from the system's dictionary of noun definitions). The original definition of MAN in the dictionary was:

```
(*D* X  (HUMAN X)
        (SEX X MALE)
        (AGE X ORDER-DECADES))
```

so, when the new feature was added, the descriptor became:

```
(*D* X  (HUMAN X)
        (SEX X MALE)
        (AGE X ORDER-DECADES)
        (NATIONALITY X AMERICAN-INDIAN))
```

After the other two adjective nets had made their contributions, the descriptor looked like:

```
(*D* X  (HUMAN X)
        (SEX X MALE)
        (AGE X ORDER-DECADES)
        (NATIONALITY X AMERICAN-INDIAN)
        (SIZE X REL-LARGE)
        (PERSONALITY X GREEDY))
```

A similar conversion occurred for Minnie, yielding:

```
(*D* X  (HUMAN X)
        (SEX X FEMALE)
        (NAME X MINNIE)
        (WEALTH-STATUS X REL-LOW))
```

These two descriptors (converted concepts) were then attached to G1 and G2 in the parse tree for future reference (i.e. as a record of the meaning conversions which resulted from the original phrases in the parse tree). Finally, both were augmented with the new assertion made by this sentence itself (since this too could be valuable in referencing), and both were passed along to the reference mechanism.

For definite noun phrases, the reference mechanism always attempted to match the input descriptor to an existing model concept via an intersection search across the features of the descriptor. Finding none, or when the phrase was indeterminate, a new model concept was created, with starting feature set the descriptor itself. In the case of our simple example, the conversion of the red man phrase resulted in the introduction of a new model concept, whereas the "poor Minnie" phrase resulted in the identification of the existing concept (which had been loaded by hand beforehand) for Minnie, the protagonist of the Magic Grinder story. The net effect of this identification was to add two features to the Minnie concept not previously known: she was poor, and someone had given her a headache! The results of both reference conversions were finally also recorded under the original G1 and G2, so that at the end, three levels of processing were evident within the parse tree: syntactic phrases, meaning descriptors, and converted referents.

The system was of interest primarily because it demonstrated a path through some potentially complex processes. The path was admittedly very narrow, but opened the door to many issues that would not otherwise have been easy to discover.

6. Conclusions

In an unrestricted-domain language comprehension system, the single most important function is word sense discrimination. Hence, we feel, any theory of language comprehension by computer must make sense discrimination central. Only very rudimentary, high-stereotyped syntax should precede the word sense discrimination process; other more complex syntax gradually emerges as macro patterns which recur as the discrimination process evolves with time. Learning and context have natural definitions in a system where there is primacy of sense discrimination, and the theory also suggests approaches to deep generation of language, we must instead explore the organizational principles which will better cope with the breadth-wise vast, but depth-wise shallow irregularities of language.

The SSN theory is an ongoing project of the CSA AI group at Maryland. Over the next months we expect to be writing SSN's which will be adequate for the corpus evident in the Magic Grinder story (approximately 200 words). Our hope is that the SSN's we build for this story will be readily extensible to the next story, and the next, and so on, until we have some reasonably sophisticated SSN's. Anyone who would like to come and help us is welcome!

References

Becker, J., The Phrasal Lexicon, Proc. Workshop on Theor. Issues in Nat. Lang. Processing, M.I.T., 1975. **[B1]**

Bobrow, D., and Winograd, T., An Overview of KRL, a Knowledge Representation Language, Xerox Palo Alto Research Center, 1976. **[BW1]**

Charniak, E., Toward a Model of Children's Story Comprehension, Doctoral Dissertation, M.I.T. A.I. Memo 266, 1972. **[C1]**

Charniak, E., Organization and Inference in a Frame-like System of Common Sense Knowledge, Proc. Workshop on Theor. Issues in Nat. Lang. Processing, M.I.T., 1975. **[C2]**

Fahlman, S., A Planning System for Robot Construction Tasks, M.I.T. A.I. Memo 283, 1973. **[F1]**

Feigenbaum, E., The Simulation of Verbal Learning Behavior, in Feigenbaum Feldman (eds.), *Computers and Thought,* McGraw Hill, 1963. **[F2]**

Fillmore, C., The Case for Case, in Bach Harms (eds.), *Universals in Linguistic Theory,* Holt, Rinehart Winston, 1968. **[F3]**

Fillmore, C., Some Problems for Case Grammar, Proc. Georgetown Linguistics Roundtable, 1971. **[F4]**

Goldman, N., Computer Generation of Natural Language from a Deep Conceptual Base, Doctoral Dissertation, Stanford A.I. Memo 247, 1974. **[G1]**

Marcus, M., Wait-and-See Strategies for Parsing Natural Language, M.I.T. Working Paper 75, 1974. **[M1]**

Marcus, M., Diagnosis as a Notion of Grammar, Proc. Workshop on Theor. Issues in Nat. Lang. Processing, M.I.T., 1975. **[M2]**

Minsky, M., A Framework for Representing Knowledge, in Winston (ed.), *The Psychology of Computer Vision,* McGraw Hill, 1975. **[M3]**

Rieger, C., Conceptual Memory: A Theory and Computer Program for Processing the Meaning Content of Natural Language Utterances, Doctoral Dissertation, Stanford A.I. Memo 233, 1974. **[R1]**

Rieger, C., The Commonsense Algorithm as a Basis for Computer Models of Human Memory, Inference, Belief, and Contextual Language Comprehension, Proc. Workshop on Theor. Issue in Nat. Lang. Processing, M.I.T., 1975. **[R2]**

Rieger, C., An Organization of Knowledge for Problem Solving and Language Comprehension, *Artificial Intelligence,* vol. 7, no. 2, 1976. **[R3]**

Rieger, C., The Representation and Selection of Commonsense Knowledge for Natural Language Comprehension, Proc. Georgetown University Linguistics Roundtable, 1976. **[R4]**

Rieger, C., Spontaneous Computation in Cognitive Models, Univ. of Maryland TR-459, 1976. **[R5]**

Rieger, C., and Grinberg, M., The Causal Representation and Simulation of Physical Mechanisms, Univ. of Maryland TR-495, 1976. **[RG1]**

Riesbeck, C., Computational Understanding: Analysis of Sentences and Context, Doctoral Dissertation, Stanford A.I. Memo 238, 1974. **[R6]**

Riesbeck, C., and Schank, R., Comprehension by Computer: Expectation-Based Analysis of Sentences in Context, Res. Rpt. 78, Yale Univ., 1976. **[RS1]**

Rumelhart, D., Lindsay, P., and Norman, D., A Process Model for Long-Term Memory, CHIP TR-17, Univ. of Ca., San Diego, 1971. **[RLN1]**

Sacerdoti, E., Planning in a Hierarchy of Abstraction Spaces, Proc. 3rd International Joint Conf. on A.I., Stanford, 1973. **[S1]**

Sacerdoti, E., The Nonlinear Nature of Plans, Proc. 3rd International Joint Conf. on A.I., Russia, 1975. **[S2]**

Schank, R., Conceptual Dependency: A Theory of Natural Language Understanding, Cog. Psychology, 3, 4, 1972. **[S3]**

Schank, R., Goldman, N., Rieger, C., and Riesbeck, C., MARGIE: Memory, Analysis, Response Generation, and Inference on English, Proc. 3rd International Conf. of A.I., Stanford, 1973. **[SGRR]**

Simmons, R., and Slocum, J., Generating English Discourse from Semantic Networks, *CACM*, vol. 15, no. 10, 1972. **[SS1]**

Sussman, G., *A Computational Model of Skill Acquisition*, American Elsevier, 1975. **[S4]**

Walt Disney, *The Magic Grinder*, Random House, 1975. **[WD1]**

Wilks, Y., An Artificial Intelligence Approach to Machine Translation, in Schank Colby (eds.), *Computer Models of Thought and Language*, W.H. Freeman, 1973. **[W1]**

Wilks, Y., Preference Semantics, Stanford A.I. Memo 206, 1973. **[W2]**

Wilks, Y., Seven Theses on Artificial Intelligence and Natural Language, *ISSCO 17*, 1975. **[W3]**

Winograd, T., *Understanding Natural Language*, Academic Press, 1972. **[W4]**

Woods, W., Transition Network Grammars for Natural Language Analysis, *CACM*, vol. 13, no. 10, 1970. **[W5]**

Notes

*The research described herein is being supported by the National Aeronautics and Space Administration, under grant NSG-7253. Their support is gratefully acknowledged.

¹There will, of course, be times when we might wish to make some assumptions about missing information and proceed with the selection anyway. Although this will involve a large knowledge base about "best default assumptions", it will be essentially the same as acts of selection in a certain environment.

[2]This approach has been quite popular in AI modeling over the past several years; see, for example, [C1], [F1], [RG1] and [S4].

[3]A group of us actually played this game at a seminar by giving each person one word from a 13 word sentence, requesting that he attempt to anticipate all possible meanings of the word (actually, all general larger contexts in which the word could be participating). In this process, each person was permitted to ask questions of his neighbors about their words. Each person, by asking only several questions, was able to arrive at a surprisingly accurate judgment of both the sense of his word and how it fit into the context of the sentence. In fact, several people accurately guessed the thrust of the entire sentence, using only very local cues.

[4]This philosophy follows Joe Becker's Razor [B1]: "Elegance and truth are inversely related!"

[5]In this type of arrangement, it will be important that the syntactic or shallow semantic component attempt to do no more than that of which it can be certain. The level of syntax we have in mind is one which can deal with noun and prepositional phrases, make suggestions about which words are likely to be the central verbs, cope with tensing, passivization and morphology, and so forth. No substantial semantic analysis should be attempted at this stage, because it has a greater potential for digging itself into deeper holes! Some degree of shallow semantics might attempt to map the syntactic constituents into more meaningful case frames at this level, but any uncertainties should be deferred to the SSN's.

[6]We should point out that this is the very same organization as is called for in the CSA plan synthesizer mentioned earlier: terminal nodes of the causal selection networks reference pieces of cause-effect patterns which are possibly shared by numerous other CSN's. This is because one strategy might be applicable to the solution of two different types of goals. For example, the goals "cause" a statechange in temperature of a piece of glass," and "cause the glass to change from a solid to a liquid" both can be effected by applying the strategy "hold the glass over a flame." The only difference in this case might be the goal state criterion, i.e. the length of time which may be required.

[7]The notion of a descriptor is central to all symbolic cognitive models. For a more comprehensive treatment of the ideas, see [BW1], and chapters 3, 4 and 8 of [R1].

[8]Hierarchical systems are more the rule than the exception in AI research (see [M3], [R3], [R5], [RLN1], [BW1] for example). Schank's Conceptual Dependency theory [S3] is an exception, and calls for maintaining all knowledge in terms of a small number of primitive actions. We believe that a mixture of the two approaches is correct: namely, that a system of primitives that provides an ultimate basis of definition for every concept in the model must exist, but that larger patterns, once defined, ought to be manipulable as though they were primitive. Deeper aspects of the comprehension process, such as inference and prediction, will sometimes key on the details of the primitive definition of a concept, and other times key on the concept itself, as though it were in fact primitive.

[9]See, for example, the KRL project [BW1], which has invested much time and energy in providing an expressive language for referent description.

Chapter Six

Towards a Reconstruction of the Methodology of Experimental Linguistics

William Orr Dingwall

Goals and Methods

There is an intimate and obvious relationship between the goals of any undertaking and the methods adopted to attain these goals. If one desires to build a house, it would appear reasonable to first ascertain what methods have proved most effective in this endeavor. At least, if one wishes the house to stand. Similarly, in an undertaking such as linguistics where goals invariably involve the search for knowledge and understanding of various types of behavioral phenomena, it seems reasonable, as a first step, to investigate those epistomological methods which have proved most effective within other areas of inquiry.

Some have been inclined to appeal to *common sense* in their search for insight. Surely it is common sense to say that language is learned solely by imitation or that the more primitive the society the less complex its language. The only trouble is that both these statements as well as countless others based on this criterion have proven to be false upon close attention to the facts. Likewise, *appeal to authority* has shown itself an untrustworthy guide to knowledge. For example, Mary Brazier, in a recent discussion of the history of neurophysiology, notes "the stultifying effect of the immoderate worship given to Aristotle" on progress within this field:

> If Aristotle is to be evaluated as a scientist, it must be admitted that he was almost always wrong in every inference he made from his vast collection of natural history and numerous dissections...(Brazier, 1959: 1)

The *a priorist method* involving inference from propositions accepted as self-evident while of indubitable value in the formal sciences is fraught with danger when applied to empirical investigations. If the premises, despite being self-evident, are false, then all conclusions validly derived from them are also false. Yet within this method, as the French physiologist, Claude Bernard, points out "the one condition is that the starting point [the premises] shall remain immutable and shall not vary with [one's] experiences and observations, but on the contrary that facts shall be so interpreted as to adopt themselves to it.'' (Bernard, 1957: 49) A 'classical' example of this stance within linguistics is afforded by the following statement of Fodor and Garrett:

> A grammar is simply an axiomatic representation of an infinite set of structural descriptions, and the internal evidence in favour of the structural descriptions modern grammars generate is so strong that it is difficult to imagine their succumbing to any purely experimental disconfirmation. (Fodor and Garrett, 1966: 152)

It will be noted that all of the above methods of 'fixing belief', to use Pierce's phrase, involve the unquestioning acceptance of opinions—an acceptance which abdicates any right of examining relevant facts. It is an unwillingness to accept the pronouncements of others on faith, a requirement that no claims be entertained without proof, an elevation of doubt over all including one's most cherished 'insights' that characterizes the most efficacious epistomological method known, viz., that of science to which we now briefly turn.

Scientific Method

The method of science involves essentially a cyclic process rooted in the world of facts as schematized in (1)[1]:

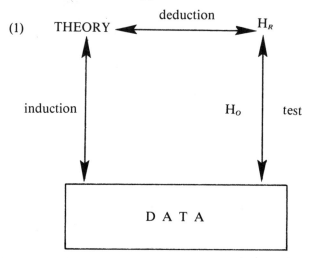

(1)   THEORY ⟷ deduction ⟶ H_R

induction H_O test

D A T A

The arrows in this schema are all double-headed as there is interplay between each facet of the method. It may at times be claimed that pure serendipity results in an important law or theory but it usually turns out that observation has been guided if not by some vaguely formulated hypothesis at least by considerable experience in the field under investigation. It should be noted that what is termed *induction* here will inevitably involve, *inter alia*, an initial stage of classification but that such a taxonomy only has empirical content to the degree that it figures in subsequent stages of the method.

Let us define *hypotheses* as statements from which at least one empirical generalization may be logically deduced. Some philosophers of science such as Caws (1965) differentiate hypotheses from *laws* by holding that only the former contain theoretical terms.[2] *Scientific theories* may be rather informally defined, at this point, as deductive systems with initial hypotheses "at the summit and empirically testable generalizations at the base" (Braithwaite, 1962: 224). They are more general in their coverage of a given data domain than a single hypothesis, which often forms the basis for experimentation in the human sciences, and they evince a formal structure which will be discussed in more detail below.

In order to test the empirical generalizations derived from theories, hypotheses or laws, they must be translated into a form amenable to statistical analysis. Typically this may involve some relation among population means or variances. Thus, in a dichotic listening test, an empirical generalization might be stated in terms of a relation between the mean number of errors reported from inputs to the left and right ears. The statistical generalization might be stated as follows:

(2) (a) $\mu L > \mu R$
      (b) $\mu L < \mu R$
      (c) $\mu L = \mu R$

where μL and μR represent the population error means for the left and right ears respectively. Since the argument form in (3) is invalid:

(3) $p \supset q$
     q
     _____
     p

i.e., hypotheses can never be confirmed but only disconfirmed, an indirect method of proof is adopted in statistical analysis. This involves setting forth all possible statistical hypotheses as in (2), postulating that one, the so-called null or alternative hypothesis (*H*o) is true, and in Fisher's words giving the facts a chance of disproving this hypothesis (cf. Fisher, 1971). If we find that generalization (c) can be rejected with some high degree of confidence and furthermore that $\overline{X}_L < \overline{X}_R$ thus disconfirming (a), then we may accept the only remaining logical alternative (b) as receiving confirmation.

This interplay between research hypotheses, null or alternative hypotheses and data is indicated by the double-headed arrow at the right of the schema in (1).

Experimentation involves a complex interplay between theory, experimental design and statistical analysis of data. Not all empirical generalizations derived from a theory are equally interesting. Not all terms in such generalizations can be provided operational definitions. Having isolated some interesting aspect of the theory that is capable of being tested, one is still confronted by the formidable task of selecting appropriate independent and dependent variables, of eliminating, as much as possible, experimental error, of constructing adequate stimuli, etc. At the same time one must constantly keep in mind how these aspects of experimental design are to mesh with available statistical methods for data analysis (cf. Kerlinger, 1973 and Hays, 1963 for insight into these problems of behavioral research).

The emphasis which scientific method places on data invariably leads to an increased reliance on instrumentation. Not only must the scientist be familiar with the intricacies of theory formation, experimental design and statistics, but he finds that he might have done well to study electrical engineering. Instrumentation is important not only in extending the acruity of our senses but increasingly in the presentation of stimuli and the analysis of data. Thus, e.g., in event-related potential experiments, presentation of stimuli, monitoring of the EEG from predetermined sites and averaging can all be done mechanically (cf. Sidowski (ed.), 1966).

The final double-headed arrow in (1) represents the interaction between experimental results and theory. If the elimination of alternative hypothesis results in confirmation of the research hypothesis, then we are justified in feeling increased confidence in the theory from which this hypothesis is derived—confidence which either grows or diminishes depending on the results of replications of the experiment in question. It should be noted that the ability to replicate forms an important part of the method. The essential ingredient of doubt which causes the scientist to reject statements about the real world not based on fact often arouses in him the desire to re-test findings in which he has a particular interest. It is for this reason that in reporting experiments careful descriptions of methods, stimuli and even data protocols must be provided. If replication fails or our research hypothesis is rejected at the outset and we are reasonably certain of the reliability and validity of our experimental technique, then we must be prepared to alter our theory either in part or *in toto*. This willingness to expose our theories to disconfirmation and to modify them in case of negative results is the hallmark of science. Thus, we see that the schema in (1) must be replaced by a less static view such as that provided in (4):

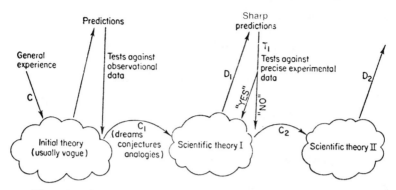

The scientific approach illustrated graphically. From à theory one makes predictions, deducing (steps D) logically what the theory predicts in certain circumstances. One then uses observational data to test (steps T) these predictions. If there is no agreement, a new theory must be conjectured (steps C).

(From J. T. Davies 1973. With permission)

Theory

Our earlier definition of scientific theory may now be made more precise. In sciences which have reached what Caws terms the *hypothetical stage,* a scientific theory is equivalent to a formal deductive system with the following defining characteristics:

(5) (a)   a set of elements
    (b)   a subset of well-formed formulae (wffs) which makes up the axioms of the system
    (c)   another subset of wffs disjoint with the subset in (b) which makes up the theorems of the system
    (d)   rules of definition

Such a system or calculus is to be distinguished from *formal language systems* and *axiomatic systems.* The former generate all and only the well-formed (grammatical) formulae of some language L via a set of formation rules.[3] The latter selects a subset of wffs as axioms and derives some (but not all) the remaining wffs as theorems. A *deductive system* is distinguished by one additional feature, viz., it guarantees that for each possible interpretation of the calculus if the axioms are true, then the theorems will likewise be true.

A somewhat informal example of such a deductive system adopted from Kemeny (1959) is presented in (6):

(6) *Deductive System*

A-1. There is an x such that no other x bears the relation R
to it.
A-2. No x has more than one x bearing the relation R to
it.
A-3. Each x bears the relation R to just one other x, and
never bears this relation to itself.

Theorem: There are infinitely many x's.

Such an uninterpreted system could easily be restated in terms of the first-order predicate calculus. When variable 'x' and relation 'R' are interpreted in terms of 'the year A.D.' and 'precedes' respectively, we see that both the axioms and the theorem are true; if they are interpreted in terms of 'dog' and 'bites' then not all the axioms are true and the theorem is thus false. It might be noted in passing that a theory is said to be *formalized* when it is presented in terms of a calculus such as that described above with all descriptive signs replaced by marks such as 'x' and 'R'.

The advantages of such a system within the framework of scientific method should be obvious. The translation of informal hypotheses into formal language provides a way of fereting out inexplicitness and of assuring us that the research hypotheses we are testing follow logically from the axioms of the theory.

Although linguistic systems or grammars share many features of the formal calculae we have discussed above, as well they might in that both have their origins in the work of Post, Carnap and other logicians, it is clear that they are not deductive systems in that there is no explicitly defined subset of axioms from which it makes sense to say that theorems may be derived preserving truth-value. This is not to say that there may not be some way of converting linguistic systems into this form, as we shall see later, nor is it to say that no branch of linguistics has developed formal theories of the type we are discussing. Clearly theories in mathematical linguistics constitute deductive systems in the proper sense, but these deal with properties of generative grammars and not with natural language phenomena. Such theories are clearly non-empirical (cf. Ringen 1974; also Wall in this volume).

If linguistics does not evince the characteristics of the *hypothetical stage* in Caws' hierarchy, perhaps it can be said at least to have reached the earlier *nomological stage*—a stage "...at which classification and correlation have been completed to the point where well-confirmed generalizations (that is, empirical laws—nomological is from the Greek 'nomos', 'law') emerge, but at which as yet the lines of a fully developed and axiomatized theory are not firmly laid down..." (Caws 1965: 280). This does, in fact, appear to be what Chomsky has in mind when he states:

> A grammar of the language L is essentially a theory of L. Any scientific theory is based on a finite number of observations, and it seeks to relate the observed phenomena and to predict new phenomena by constructing general laws in terms of hypothetical constructs such as (in physics, for example) "mass" and "electron". Similarly, a grammar of English is based on a finite corpus of utterances (observations), and it will contain certain grammatical rules (laws) stated in terms of the particular phonemes, phrases, etc., of English (hypothetical constructs). These rules express structural relations among the sentences of the corpus and the indefinite number of sentences generated by the grammar beyond the corpus (predictions). (Chomsky 1957: 49)

The problem with this definition is that scientific laws and linguistic rules are in no way similar. The former are simply empirical generalizations which are accepted as truths. As such the term 'law' is inappropriate, in that there is no sense in which such laws can be violated and still remain laws. It is obvious that linguistic rules are not laws in this sense; they are clearly violable. If they were not, linguists would be unable to generate ungrammatical sentences, and we would be deprived of information relayed to us by children, speakers of other dialects as well as non-native speakers of our language. The term 'rule' itself is used in a number of different ways—none of which are equivalent to its use in linguistics. Computers can be programmed to follow all and only the well-formed statements in various high-level languages. Thus, an appropriately programmed computer can be said to be unable to disobey the formation rules of, say, FORTRAN, as any of us who have worked with computers have learned to our chagrin. We are not programmed in such a manner vis-à-vis linguistic rules. The rules of a game can, of course, be violated as can linguistic rules—usually the repercussions are different—but they can also be stated while linguistic rules cannot. Of course, some of us can state linguistic rules if we have learned them in school or just formulated them, but generally we don't follow these explicit rules in speaking or understanding. In some sense linguistic rules are like social conventions or moral codes. It would appear that de Saussure looked at *la langue* in this fashion. If I were of different character, I might decide to appear in public without my clothes or, fully clothed, enter my neighborhood grocery and declare: "A head of lettuce want I." In both instances, it would appear that I have willfully broken some social covenant, as may be gauged by the response of my audience. In the first case, I might be arrested; in the second case, I might be looked upon askance although I would be surely understood. In the first case, if I am sane, I am well aware of the rule I have violated; in the second, I am not. Further linguistic rules and moral codes have different aims presumably. In neither case are we dealing with scientific laws. Such laws, if they can be formulated for linguistic behavior, would apply to *la parole* not to *la langue* (cf. Wartofsky, 1968: 38-9). Thus, we see that linguistic grammars do not qualify as nomological deductive systems either.

At this point, we might be tempted to relegate linguistics to the earliest stage of science set forth in Caws' hierarchy, viz., the *descriptive stage* "at which explanation proceeds mainly by classification and correlation, and at which generalizations and hypotheses, if formulated at all, have comparatively low degrees of confirmation..." (Caws, 1965: 280). This, I think, would be a mistake, as linguistic systems do make available to us empirical generalizations which can be tested but in a round-about manner. In order to understand this, we must explore the concept of model.

Model

A model is nothing more than one of the possible interpretations within some data domain of a *mathematical theory*. Often this means setting forth a deductive system such as given in (6) and providing it via rules of interpretation, as we did, with alternative instantiations in the real world—instantiations which, as we have seen, can turn out to be either true or false. Mathematical theories, however, cover a much broader range than deductive calculae. They need only involve the names of relations, the names of variables and the properties of the relations. (7) is a mathematical theory in this sense and one of its models is given in (8).

(7)   *Mathematical Theory*

$$T = \langle R_1, R_2; P_1, ..., P_7 \rangle$$
$P_{1\ 2}: (\forall x)(x\ R_i\ x)$
$P_{3\ 4}: (\forall x)(\forall y)(x\ R_i\ y \Rightarrow y\ R_i\ x)$
$P_{5\ 6}: (\forall x)(\forall y)(\forall z)((x\ R_i\ y\ \&\ y\ R_i\ z) \Rightarrow x\ R_i\ z)$
$P_7\ : (\forall x)(\forall y)((x\ R_1\ y\ \&\ x\ R_2\ y) \Rightarrow (x = y))$

(8)   *A Model of T*

$M = \langle M; R_1, R_2 \rangle$ where M is the set of word-forms of Russian nouns, R_1 the relation: 'to appear in a common paradigm', and R_2 'to have identical gender, number and case.'

It should be easy to see how grammars of particular languages constitute models of a mathematical theory, e.g., that of transformational generative grammar within a particular data domain, viz., some particular language. Alternative mathematical theories of grammar can be studied abstractly as is done in mathematical linguistics. One can speak of the *validity* of a given Theory T for a particular Class K of objects if every object in the Class is a model of Theory T. The Theory T can be said to be *complete* for a particular Class K if all (finite) models of this Theory are isomorphic to at least a potential object of Class K (cf. Šrejder, 1973 for further discussion). It appears that context-free phrase structure grammars may be invalid in the above sense and that transformational grammars are incomplete.[4]

Modeling in linguistics can be schematized as in the left part of diagram (9) where shifts due to invalidity or incompleteness are represented by horizontal arrows and the interplay between models and theories is indicated by double-headed vertical arrows. Particular grammars ('theories', in Chomsky's terminology) are thus equivalent to models of a mathematical theory in terms of some data domain. The mathematical theory is equivalent to what Chomsky terms: *general linguistic theory* or *linguistic metatheory*. In that such modeling does involve some aspect of the real world, it can be said to be empirical, but it is clearly not experimental in the sense we have discussed above.

Modeling of this sort would constitute essentially an empty endeavor were it not for the psychological claims expressed via the competence/performance distinction to which we now turn.

(9)

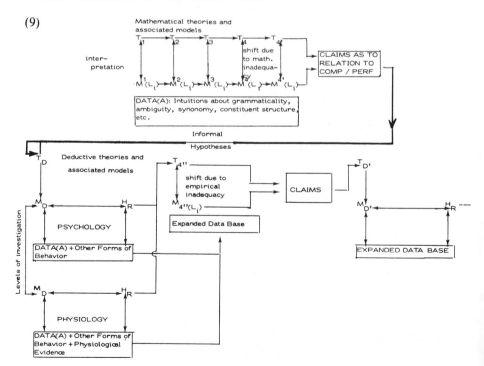

Competence/Performance

One sure way of sparking endless debate in linguistics is to propose some dichotomy. Competence/performance joins emic/etic, synchronic/diachronic, paradigmatic/syntagmatic *inter alia* in lending support to this maxim. After years of intense and often acrimonious discussion, three general views of this distinction have evolved.

1) The first holds that models of competence and performance have little or no relationship to one another. This view which embodies a reasonable, if *a priori*, rejection of Plato's assumption that *knowing what* necessarily involves *knowing how* was first hinted at by Fodor and Garrett (1966) and then elaborated by Bever (1970) and more recently by Sanders (1974) and Dretske (1974). The latter represents this view as in (10):

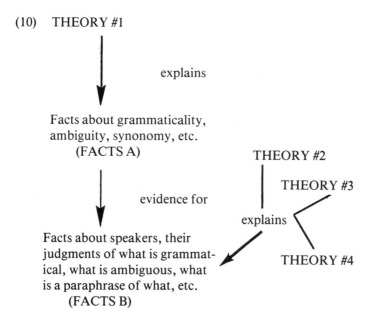

(10) THEORY #1

    explains

Facts about grammaticality,
ambiguity, synonymy, etc.
(FACTS A)

    THEORY #2

    THEORY #3

evidence for

explains

Facts about speakers, their
judgments of what is grammatical, what is ambiguous, what
is a paraphrase of what, etc.
(FACTS B)

    THEORY #4

The grammar (Theory #1) accounts for certain 'facts' produced by speakers (i.e., it accounts for the *what*); Theories #2, #3 and #4, psychological, neurological, perceptual theories, account for the *how*. Theory #1 and the others are not to be confused as they have different data domains. At the outset, it should be pointed out that Theory #1 in no way can be said to explain FACTS A. For explanation, laws are necessary and the grammar is not a nomological system as we have seen. Rather Theory #1 constitutes but one of many possible descriptions of FACTS A. The Theories explaining FACTS B might simply involve the claim that speakers had internalized Theory #1, but Dretske holds such a claim to be unfounded. As he puts it:

> A grammar...is not a theory about people; it is a theory about grammaticality. And rules are not in the head any more than the legal code is in the head. What is in the head or in the brain (if one wants to put it this way) is a knowledge of the grammar, a certain set of perceptual limitations, a certain set of habits, expectations, memories, etc. that help to account for speakers' competence and performance in speaking the language (Facts B). (1970: 40)

The initial impetus for holding this position that models of competence and performance are unrelated or related in an extremely abstract manner stems from negative experimental findings, findings that have continued to accumulate as we shall see, that the rules postulated in the grammar are not reflected in performance. These findings, it seems to me, were to be expected in that processes being tacit, as Chomsky puts it, are not included in FACTS A. Insofar as FACTS A are valid, an assumption which at present seems in doubt (see p. 151 below), then Theory #1 can be interpreted so as to provide hypotheses for a scientific theory of linguistic behavior (pace Dretske). These hypotheses will provide empirical generalizations not about the processes involved in producing or recognizing sentences or learning a language but about structures and their relations, as it is judgments about these that form the data base for this mathematical theory.

2) A second stand on the competence/performance dichotomy is that the competence model forms a subpart of the performance model. As Chomsky puts it:

> No doubt, a reasonable model of language use will incorporate, as a basic component, the generative grammar that expresses the speaker-hearer's knowledge of the language; but this generative grammar does not, in itself, prescribe the character or functioning of a perceptual model or a model of speech production. (Chomsky, 1965: 9; also Chomsky, 1976)

This view is reminiscent of the algorithm *cum* heuristics approach which has enjoyed a certain vogue in artificial intelligence circles. What is usually proposed here is some programmatic version of analysis-by-synthesis plus, oftentimes, an even more vaguely specified set of procedures relating utterances produced or received in an appropriate manner to their context, a pragmatics component in effect.

While this view of competence/performance is that most often adopted by linguists and psychologists, it makes even more unreasonable *a priori* assumptions than the first. Whenever analysis-by-synthesis procedures are spelled out in any detail, they are immediately revealed as being so cumbersome and time-consuming as to be in total dissonance with the observed rapidity and accuracy of speech processing behavior. Moreover, Occam's Razor surely dictates that we at first entertain a more direct relation between the competence model and behavior before adopting this less economical proposal. (This is in fact what the computer scientists did. Only after the pure algorithmic approach proved impractical was the heuristic approach adopted.)

3) The third stand on the competence/performance dichotomy regards the competence model as an idealized model of performance. This stand has been perhaps most forcefully asserted by Bartsch and Vennemann (1972) who state:

> A grammar is to us a system of rules which convert semantic representations into phonetic representations and conversely, where the semantic representations and phonetic representations are models of structures, and the grammar rules models of processes, which occur in the minds of speakers. (1972: 35-6)

This view is not only the most parsimonious of the three, making the least number of *a priori* assumptions, but, in part because of this fact, allows for the most straightforward conversion into a scientific theory for the purposes of testing. The first stand, in that it amounts to more than the claim that linguistics is a purely descriptive discipline, leads in Bever's formulation to the postulation of so-called 'perceptual strategies' which are imagined as intervening freely between the competence model and behavior whenever there are discrepancies between the two. Thus, as Watt (1972) puts it, the competence model '...moves ever further from the possibility of experimental confirmation; but, by way of compensation, concomitantly further from the possibility of *dis*confirmation' (1972: 9). It also results in such oddities as sentences which are fully acceptable but not grammatical and the converse. The second stand is not only uneconomical, as we have pointed out, but is so vaguely formulated as to be almost untestable.

Thus, the third interpretation is the most tenable. The idealization involved in it is no different from that intervening between any psychological theory and its subject matter. In statistical theory, this abstraction is captured by the concept of experimental error. Such error, which is included in the statistical models for individual scores, accounts for the intrinsic variability in human behavior which can never be totally controlled for.

Thus, the mathematical theory of linguistics and its associated models can be said to constitute a scientific theory to the extent that one can derive hypotheses from the former from which in turn testable empirical generalizations can be deduced. This conversion from mathematical to scientific theory is mediated via the claims made as to the competence/performance relation as illustrated in the center section of diagram (9).

Thus, e.g., we might derive the informal hypothesis that constituent structure, specifically surface structure bracketing, plays a role in language processing. This is, of course, far too vague a formulation. We would want to take over various axioms and theorems from the mathematical theory defining constituent structure and its properties and combine these with our hypothesis or hypotheses concerning how such structures might be reflected in behavior to produce a formal deductive system (T_D) of the type we have discussed above. Next, we would interpret this calculus (M_D = Theory in schema (1)) in terms of some data domain (including, perhaps, English sentences) and proceed to deduce testable empirical generalizations (H_R). If these tests confirmed T_D and indirectly T_4', then we would retain both. If the test was disconfirmatory, then we should be prepared to alter or abandon T_4' and T_D in favor of a new set of theories T_4'' and T_D'. Thus, modeling in terms of mathematical theories and the construction of a scientific theory of linguistic behavior proceed in tandem each contributing to the advancement of knowledge. The modeling stage, as Gross (1972) has pointed out, plays somewhat the same role as atomic particle accelerators in physics—revealing new insights about language and allowing for the formulation of new hypotheses which, if confirmed, become part of a general scientific theory of linguistic behavior.

Levels of Investigation

The investigation of a complex form of behavior such as communication among organisms can be and, indeed, is carried on at a number of different levels and for a number of different reasons. As indicated in diagram (9), the two levels which appear to me most crucially involved in the undertaking I would term *experimental linguistics* are psychology and physiology (or more generally biology).[5] To understand why this is so, a brief review of the origins of modern psychology as they relate to linguistics is in order.

As in the case of linguistics, the origins of modern psychology are manifold. It is perhaps not too great a distortion, however, to follow Boring (1950) in the view that its most immediate antecedent is to be found in the experimental physiology of the first half of the 19th century. Although the physiology of Wundt and his followers may have been more "fanciful" (to use Hebb's term) than that of a Bell or Müller, psychology continued to be basically physiological until a turning point was reached in 1929.[6] In that year, Karl Lashley published his monograph on brain mechanisms and intelligence in which he set forth the twin principles of equipotentiality and mass action. For a general task such as maze running, it was found that performance was diminished in direct proportion to the extent rather than the location of the ablation of cerebral cortex (in rats). This finding appeared to cast grave doubt on the neurological speculations of the preceding period which dealt in circumscribed localization of function, establishment of memory traces and the like. Although physiological psychology survived, it had suffered a heavy blow from which it was not to recover until fairly recent times. Psychology became largely anti-physiological and the stage was set for the entrance of behavioristic psychology personified by such scholars as E.C. Tolman and B.F. Skinner. These new arrivals accomplished the remarkable feat of creating a psychology largely devoid of ψυχή and were concerned with techniques for manipulating their subject matter rather than explaining it.

Exactly thirty years after the publication of Lashley's monograph—years which witnessed the rise and rout of the descriptive tradition of Bloomfield and his followers—psychology underwent another shift in direction with Chomsky's critical assessment of Skinner's attempt to elevate his techniques for behavior modification to the status of an explanatory theory of language acquisition and use. It may seem paradoxical on the basis of what has been said that Chomsky devotes a portion of his review to a favorable resume of Lashley's paper on serial order in behavior. But it turns out that Lashley neither denied the existence of cortical localization of function nor subscribed to some of the major contentions of S-R psychology such as associative chaining, as many had mistakenly assumed. Chomsky's review did not signal a return to physiological psychology but rather a return to the study of ψυχή on a more abstract, model-oriented level (cf. P. Carey's remarks on p. 311-2 below). The usefulness of neurological investigations was either denied or held to be millennia off in the future. This new branch of research which may be termed rationalistic or mentalistic psychology (or psycholinguistics for short) has attracted many former behaviorists perhaps not so much out of love for Chomsky's models as out of aversion for Skinner's arid philosophy of science. The course of events described here is graphically displayed in figure (11). Some may wonder why behavioristic psychology is shown here moving off seemingly unscathed in a divergent direction from psycholinguistics and physiological psychology. This is due not so much to the fact that old trends never die but just fade away but that behaviorism by and large in its conscious rejection of any attempt at explication of language or other behavior is not antithetical to these trends but simply irrelevant. The term "irrelevant" is not meant here in a derogatory sense; in this author's view, behavior modification techniques have been firmly established as valid and useful tools of clinical psychology.[7]

Two natural bridges—experimental phonetics and neurolinguistics—one old, one quite new (at least in name), serve to link physiological psychology with modern psycholinguistics. With the increasing attention being paid by experimental phoneticians to the neurological aspects of articulation and audition (cf. Kim's contribution to this volume), it is not unlikely that these two bridges will merge to form the avenue by which psycholinguistics will eventually become one with physiological psychology or, more likely, some greater union of the human sciences along the lines discussed by Wilson (cf. footnote 5).

Further, this conjunction of disciplines can be expected to become increasingly aware of the dynamic aspects of the behavior they study. As I have stressed elsewhere, language is in no sense unitary. It does not spring forth as a whole in children; it does not decline as a whole in pathology; it seems increasingly evident that it did not evolve as a whole. It is subject to the same laws of evolution, to the same complex equation involving the genotype, the total environment and their interaction that all other forms of behavior obey (cf. Dingwall, 1975, 1978; Lieberman, 1975, as well as his contribution to this volume).

(11)

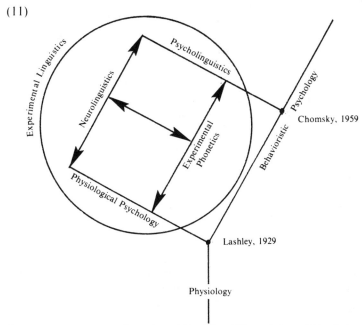

The emergence and domain of experimental linguistics within psychology: A historical perspective.

Fallacies of Modeling *Sans* Experimentation

Failure to link mathematical modeling to scientific theory in linguistics leaves us with an endeavor which is purely descriptive and largely arbitrary. That this is the case can be made clear by examining briefly a number of fallacies which have been pointed out in the literature from time to time (cf. Botha, 1968; Hutchinson, 1974).

1) *MODEL* = *MECHANISM FALLACY.* Just because a mathematical theory makes available a model for the output of some device does not imply it is this model which enables the device to produce such an output. Schwartz (1969) provides a nice example of this fallacy by noting that a device which accepts spheres as input and outputs pluses if their density is greater than 1.0 and minuses if it is less might, *inter alia*, be a digital device operating in terms of a set of equations or an analogue device containing liquid of density 1.0.

2) *HOW-ELSE FALLACY.* Similarly the fact that the theory appears to provide but one model for a given data base can in no way be taken as an argument that this is the only model that could be employed to produce this data. What is more likely at stake is a simple lack of ingenuity on the part of the investigator.

3) *SIMPLICITY METRIC FALLACY.* There is no *a priori* reason for believing that such a metric chooses models that are more likely to be psychologically or physiologically real—in fact, the history of discovery within these disciplines supports the contrary view (cf. Boring, 1950; Brazier, 1959). Where redundancy is the rule, logical simplicity is unlikely to lead to insight.

4) *CONSTRAINTS FALLACY.* Constraints on the mathematical theory that limit the types of phenomena which the theory can describe in no way can be said to explain these phenomena (cf. Dingwall, 1971: 777ff.).

5) *COMPLEXITY FALLACY.* Because the most highly valued model provided by the theory for a given data base is extremely complex and because the time required by a child to learn to produce this data is relatively short, it does not follow that the theory must be totally innate (cf. Dingwall, 1975).

All of these fallacies arise from the naive view that somehow the process of describing behavior in terms of a theory arrived at largely *a priori* can lead in and of itself to true insight into the nature of this behavior and the processes underlying it. The problem is that the ways of accounting for observed behavior are only limited by our creativity. We might happen upon a correct theory but the odds are against us and even if we did, without experimentation, we would never know.

The Role of Experimentation

As pointed out at the beginning of our discussion, the hallmark of science is the willingness to expose one's theories to disconfirmation and to modify them in the case of negative test results carefully evaluated. It is this step that linguists have been more often than not unwilling to undertake. Generally, experimental findings are ignored and speculation continues as usual. In part this may be due to the belief that experimentation can only play an essentially negative role forcing one to abandon elegant theoretical formulations without providing any workable alternative. This belief is without foundation. No experimentalist worth his salt simply presents negative findings without attempting to explain their occurrence and without exploring their implications for the theory under investigation. To illustrate this, let us examine some recent findings bearing on selected aspects of linguistic theory and method.

A. *GRAMMATICALITY JUDGMENTS*. These judgments form, of course, a crucial part of the data base for mathematical modeling in linguistics. In an important study, Spencer (1973) has been able to show that subjects either with or without training in linguistics agree with professional linguists' intuitive grammaticality judgments only 50% of the time. At the same time they agree among themselves in such judgments in over 80% of the cases. Their judgments are not only consistent and dependable but are unaffected to any large degree by sentential context or previous training. Spencer does not stop with this finding but goes on to explain why professional linguists' judgments might be unreliable by citing results of experimentation on satiation, reorganization and contextual stabilization. She concludes her article by noting that:

> ...linguists' intuitions should not be uncritically accepted as a secure data base for the derivation of a theory of natural language of the speech community. Intuitions of informants who are not linguists about the grammatical acceptability of exemplars which illustrate rules should be used to identify unclear cases and incorrect rules, if there is to be any confidence that the rules do reflect the formal structure of the common language being described (1973: 97).

B. *PHONOLOGICAL RULES AND BASE FORMS*. There is now a considerable body of almost totally unequivocal experimental evidence indicating that phonological rules and base forms proposed by linguists to account for such phenomena as word derivation in English and Maori, tone sandhi in Taiwanese, morpheme structure conditions in Turkish, etc. play no productive role in speech processing. What these results point to is a much more redundant lexical representation perhaps involving separate listing of allomorphs (cf. Hsieh, 1970, 1975, 1976; Steinberg and Krohn, 1975; Ohala, 1973; Zimmer, 1969; Braine, 1974; Dingwall, 1971; also Lightner and Kiparsky in this volume).

C. *TRANSFORMATIONAL RULES*. The case for transformational rules or, better, some form of sentence relatedness is less clear-cut than that for phonological rules. A nice example of this is the active/passive transformation. Language acquisition studies as well as sentence processing studies appear to indicate that full passives and truncated passives are not related. There remains evidence, however, for the active/passive relation although it is far from unequivocal. Once again it appears to be the case that many generalizations captured by the linguist elude the naive speaker, that many of the bonds between sentences postulated in the linguistic grammar fail to play a role in the mental grammar. Again, as in the previous section on phonology, we are led to a view of linguistic theory which allows for a much more redundant representation of linguistic entities and their relations (cf. the discussion in Fodor, Bever and Garrett, 1974 with Gough in this volume; Watt, 1970, 1974; Dingwall and Shields, 1973; Beilin, 1975).

D. *SEMANTICS*. Sachs (1967) and Wanner (1974) have shown that after approximately 27 seconds of interpolated material, subjects can recognize only about 50% of the time whether a test utterance is identical to one occurring just before this period or is a structurally altered version with the same meaning. Recognition of semantic changes, on the other hand, is above 80%. This finding suggests to these investigators that in normal language processing syntactic information is only stored long enough to extract the meaning. When the meaning has been extracted, it is this that is stored. This result does not pose any particular problem for current semantic theories in that the structurally altered versions of the sentences involved would be provided with the same semantic representation. (There might be some quibble about active/passive since these are often now provided with differing deep structure representations.)

Findings of Bransford and his colleagues, however, do pose problems for most current semantic theories. Consider sentence pairs (12) and (13).

(12)   PROBABLE INFERENCE
       SENTENCES
       (a) The raccoons raced up the tree and the dogs circled around them.
       (b) The raccoons raced up the tree and the dogs circled around it.

(13) NON-PROBABLE INFERENCE
SENTENCES
(a) The raccoons looked over towards the tree and the dogs circled around them.
(b) The raccoons looked over towards the tree and the dogs circled around it.

From a linguistic point of view, they differ from one another in a like manner, viz., in the replacement of one lexical item in their associated phrase markers. The semantic representation for each pair would also be different presumably. Bransford *et. al* (1972) were interested in ascertaining whether there would be no difference (in a recognition task) in the detection of the pronoun shifts involved in (12) as opposed to (13) as the linguistic view would indicate or whether inference based on knowledge of the world would result in better detection of shifts in (13) than in (12). Fourteen sentence frames were used to produce sentences such as those in (12) and (13). Half of the four sentences producible from these frames were presented (counterbalanced) to two groups as acquisition sentences. The remaining half (28) plus all the acquisition sentences were given for recognition. Filler sentences without the relations in the above sets were also used. Subjects were asked if they had seen the sentences before and to state their confidence on a five point scale. The mean recognition scores are presented with plus for YES and minus for NO in table (14). As predicted, there was no significant difference between OLD and NEW probable inference sentences.

(14) Mean Recognition Scores for the Six Sentence Categories

	OLDS	NEWS
Probable Inference	1.40	1.43
Non-prob. Inference	2.22	− 0.19
Fillers	2.19	− 4.15

What this indicates is that not only are sentences stored in terms of their meaning but that meaning structures are further collapsed so-to-speak employing inference based on knowledge of the world. If semantic theories are to truly reflect language processing, then they must contain devices allowing for such inferences to be made.

Bransford *et. al* (1971) have also been able to demonstrate that not only are inferences made in the course of semantic processing but that semantic networks are built up from sentences comprising idea-sets. No semantic theory that I am aware of (with the possible exception of Schank's (1972)) offers the machinery for accomplishing this, but at least we have an inkling of one direction in which we should move (cf. also Kintsch's model and experimental evidence bearing on semantic representation in memory (1974) which, in my view, offers a paradigm of how theory construction and experimentation should be combined).

The method of science requires much of its practitioners. It is not enough to describe, for there are many ways to describe and pure description offers no external criteria for deciding among them. It is not enough to create hypotheses and derive their consequences, for our hypotheses may be in error. Only by exposing our theories to the possibility of disconfirmation do we make any contact with the real world.

The particular models of communicative behavior proposed within the Chomskyan framework during the past twenty years may well turn out to be invalid. Such invalidity need not extend, however, to the form of investigation of rule-governed behavior outlined in diagram (9). If this proves to be the case, then the analysis presented in this paper will not have been in vain.

Notes

1. This schema is, of course, over-simplified in that each aspect of the method discussed below involves a specific theory or theories (cf. Suppes' (1962) concept of a 'hierarchy of theories').

2. The observational/theoretical dichotomy may well be untenable. Cf. Suppe (1974) for a discussion of this question as well as for an excellent overview of the nature of scientific theories.

3. In apparent ignorance of Chomsky's efforts along similar lines, Rudner (1966) illustrates how such a system might be applied to natural language. With some degree of prescience, he is not overly enthusiastic about the success of such an endeavor.

4. Such incompleteness constitutes a problem only to the extent that language and cognition can be isolated from one another. (cf. Dingwall (1975) for discussion.)

5. I do not deny that other levels may also be involved. Indeed, my view is that, at this stage in its development, the study of human behavior would benefit most from some form of synthesis perhaps along the lines suggested by E. Wilson (1975) in his *Sociobiology* rather than isolation of disciplines or some form of reductionism. This view is indicated by the increasing data base as one moves from psychology to physiology.

6. This admittedly over-simplified account of the history of psychology is based on that of D. O. Hebb in his introduction to the Dover edition of Karl Lashley's 1929 work. For further discussion see Boring (1950) as well as Whitaker (1969).

7. The irrelevance spoken of here is well illustrated by the difference in attitude and research aim with which two prominent scholars representing the divergent trends under disucssion approach two very similar cases involving congenital lack of productive speech. (Cf. Lenneberg 1962 and Sapon 1966—particularly the latter's comment in footnote #11).

References

Bartsch, R. and T. Vennemann. 1972. *Semantic Structures.* Frankfurt/Main: Athenaüm Verlag.

Beilin, Harry. 1975. *Studies in the Cognitive Basis of Language Development.* New York: Academic Press.

Bernard, Claude. 1957. *An Introduction to the Study of Experimental Medicine.* New York: Dover Publications, Inc.

Bever, T. 1970. The Cognitive Basis for Linguistic Structures. *Cognition and the Development of Language,* ed. by John R. Hayes, 279-362. New York: John Wiley and Sons.

Boring, Edwin G. 1950. *A History of Experimental Psychology.* New York: Appleton-Century-Crofts.

Botha, Rudolf P. 1968. *The Function of the Lexicon in Transformational Generative Grammar.* The Hague: Mouton.

Braine, M. S. 1974. On What Might Constitute Learnable Phonology. Lg. 50. 270-299.

Braithwaite, R. B. 1962. Models in the Empirical Sciences. *Logic, Methodology and Philosophy of Science,* ed. by E. Nagel et al., 224-231. Stanford: Stanford U. Press.

Bransford, J. and J. Franks. 1971. The Abstraction of Linguisitc Ideas. *Cognitive Psychology* 2.331-350.

Bransford, J. et al. 1972. Sentence Memory: A Constructive Versus Interpretive Approach. *Cognitive Psychology* 3.193-209.

Brazier, Mary 1959. The Historical Development of Neurophysiology. *Handbook of Physiology,* ed. by John Field (Section 1, Volume I), 1-58. Washington, D. C.: American Physiological Society.

Caws, Peter. 1965. *The Philosophy of Science.* Princeton: D. Van Nostrand Co.

Chomsky, Noam. 1957. *Syntactic Structures.* The Hague: Mouton.

Chomsky, Noam. 1959. Review: *Verbal behavior* (Skinner); Lg. 35.26-58.

Chomsky, Noam. 1965. *Aspects of the Theory of Syntax.* Cambridge: The MIT Press.

Chomsky, N. 1976. *Reflections on language.* N.Y.: Random House.

Davies, J. T. 1973. *The Scientific Approach.* New York: Academic Press.

Dingwall, W. O. 1971. Linguistics as Psychology: A Definition and Some Initial Tasks. *A Survey of Linguistic Science,* ed. by W. O. Dingwall, 758-802. College Park: Linguistics Program/University of Maryland.

Dingwall, W.O. 1975. *Species-specificity of Speech.* Georgetown U. Round Table on Languages and Linguistics, 1975. Ed. by D. Dato, 17-62. Washington, D.C.: Georgetown U. Press.

Dingwall, W.O. 1978. The evolution of human communication systems. *Studies in neurolinguistics,* ed. by H. Whitaker and H.A. Whitaker. N.Y.: Academic Press.

Dingwall, W.O. and J. Shields. 1973. From Utterance to Gist: Four Experimental Studies of What's in Between. Unpublished MS.

Dretske, Fred. I. 1974. *Explanation in Linguistics: Explaining Linguistic Phenomena*, ed. by D. Cohen, 21-41. New York: John Wiley and Sons.

Fisher, Sir Ronald A. 1971. *The Design of Experiments*. New York: Hafner Publishing Co.

Fodor, J. and M. Garrett. 1966. *Some Reflections on Competence and Performance.* Psycholinguistics papers, ed. by John Lyons and R. Wales, 133-154. Edinburgh: Edinburgh U. Press.

Gross, M. 1972. *Mathematical Models in Linguistics*. Englewood Cliffs: Prentice-hall, Inc.

Hays, William L. 1963. *Statistics*. New York: Holt, Rinehart and Winston.

Hsieh, Hsin-I. 1970. The Psychological Reality of Tone Sandhi Rules in Taiwanese. CLS 6.489-503. Chicago: Chicago Linguistic Society.

Hsieh, Hsin-I. 1975. *How Generative is Phonology] Current Issues in Linguistic Theory, Volume I*, ed. by E. Koerner, 109-144. Amsterdam: John Benjamins B.V.

Hsieh, Hsin-I. 1976. On the unreality of some phonological rules. *Lingua* 38. 1-19.

Hutchinson, L. 1974. *Grammar as Theory: Explaining Linguistic Phenomena*, ed. by D. Cohen, 43-73. New York: John Wiley and Sons.

Kemeny, J.G. 1959. *A Philosopher Looks at Science*. New York: D. Van Nostrand Co.

Kerlinger, Fred. N. 1973. *Foundations of Behavioral Research*. New York: Holt, Rinehart and Winston.

Kintsch, Walter. 1974. *The Representation of Meaning in Memory*. New York: John Wiley and Sons.

Lashley, K.S. 1963. *Brain Mechanisms and Intelligence*. New York: Dover Publications, Inc.

Lenneberg, E. 1962. Understanding Language Without the Ability to Speak: A case report. *J. Abnorm. Soc. Psychol.* 65.419-25.

Lieberman, P. 1975. *On the Origins of Language*. New York: Macmillan Publishing Co.

Ohala, J. 1973. On the Design of Phonological Experiments. Unpublished MS.

Ringen, J. 1974. Linguistic facts: A study of the empirical scientific status of transformational generative grammars. *Minnesota Working Papers in Linguistics and Philosophy of Language,* 2.106-143.

Rudner, Richard S. 1966. *Philosophy of Social Science*. Englewood Cliffs: Prentice-Hall, Inc.

Sachs, J.D. 1967. Recognition Memory for Syntactic and Semantic Aspects of Connected Discourse. *Perception and Psychophysics* 2.437-42.

Sanders, G. 1974. *Introduction: Explaining Linguistic Phenomena*, ed. by D. Cohen, 1-20. New York: John Wiley and Sons.

Sapon, S. 1966. Shaping Productive Verbal Behavior in a Non-speaking Child: A Case Report. Georgetown U. Monograph Series on Languages and Linguistics 19.157-75.

Schank, R. 1972. Conceptual Dependency: A Theory of Natural Language Understanding. *Cognitive Psychology* 3.552-631.

Schwartz, R. 1969. *On Knowing a Grammar: Language and Philosophy,* ed. by S. Hook, 183-190. New York: New York U. Press.

Sidowski, J. (ed.). 1966. *Experimental Methods and Instrumentation in Psychology.* New York: McGraw-Hill Book Co.

Spencer, N.J. 1973. Differences Between Linguists and Nonlinguists in Intuitions of Grammaticality-acceptability. *J. of Psycholinguistic Res.* 2.83-98.

Šrejder, J. 1973. *On the Contrast Between the Concepts "Language Model" and "Mathematical Model." Mathematical Models of Language,* ed. by F. Kiefer, 241-267. Frankfurt/Main: Athenaüm Verlag.

Steinberg, D. and R. Krohn. 1975. *The Psychological Validity of Chomsky and Halle's Vowel Shift Rule. Current Issues in Linguistic Theory, Volume I,* 233-259. Amsterdam: John Benjamins B.V.

Suppe, F. 1974. *The Search for Philosophic Understanding of Scientific Theories. The Structure of Scientific Theories,* ed. by F. Suppe, 1-241. Urbana: U. of Illinois Press.

Suppes, P. 1962. *Models of Data: Logic, Methodology and Philosophy of Science,* ed. by E. Nagel *et al.,* 252-261. Stanford: Stanford U. Press.

Wanner, E. 1974. *On Remembering, Forgetting, and Understanding Sentences.* The Hague: Mouton.

Wartofsky, M. 1968. *Conceptual Foundations of Scientific Thought.* New York: The Macmillan Co.

Watt, W. 1970. *On Two Hypotheses Concerning Psycholinguistics. Cognition and the Development of Language,* ed. by John Hayes, 137-220. New York: John Wiley and Sons.

Watt, W. 1972. Competing Economy Criteria. Social Sciences Working Papers, 5. Irvine: U. of California.

Wilson, Edward O. 1975. *Sociobiology: The New Synthesis.* Cambridge: Harvard U. Press.

Whitaker, H.A. 1969. *On the Representation of Language in the Human Brain. Working papers in Phonetics* #12. Phonetics Lab. Los Angeles: U. of California.

Zimmer, K.E. 1969. Psychological Correlates of Some Turkish Morpheme Structure Conditions. Lg. 45.309-21.

Chapter Seven

Experimental Phonetics

Chin-Wu Kim

Since this survey is the first of its kind in our field, I shall begin by trying to delineate briefly the progress of phonetic science in the past and to project a new course that it will likely take in the future before turning to more recent developments.

When phonetics started in Great Britain in the late 18th century, it was largely impressionistic. For example, one of those whom Abercrombie (1965) termed "forgotten phoneticians" called *p, t, c(k)* "silent stops, because their sound is instantaneous like the stroke of a hammer"; and concerning *r* he said: "Upon rendering the end of the tongue limber, so that it will shake like a rag with the bellow, it will rattle out "r"." (Abercrombie 1965: 65, 67, from *Vocal sounds* by Abraham Tucker (alias Edward Search), London 1773.) By the early 20th century, phonetics had become a science thanks to the efforts of Jespersen, Jones, Palmer, Passy, Sweet, *et al.* Their phonetics which led to the founding of the *International Phonetics Association* was mainly articulatory. They regarded, for practical reasons, phonetic segments as static, and were busy in classifying segments in the two-dimensional place-and-manner chart. With the advent of electronic instruments in the middle of the century, acoustic phonetics flourished, and roughly the two decades after World War II saw a heavy emphasis on and major achievements in acoustic phonetics. Eminent phoneticians during the period such as Gunnar Fant, Eli Fischer-Jørgensen, James L. Flanagan, Osamu Fujimura, Arthur S. House, Ilse Lehiste, Gordon E. Peterson, Kenneth N. Stevens, and the Haskins group including Franklin S. Cooper, Pierre C. Delattre, Katherine S. Harris, Alvin M. Liberman, etc. are all readily recognizable as acoustic phoneticians, and their major works appear in the journal of the *Acoustic Society of America*. (Notable exceptions are Kenneth L. Pike and Peter Ladefoged whose major writings remained audiophysiological, although the latter must have seen enough importance in acoustic phonetics to write a book entitled *Elements of acoustic phonetics* (Ladefoged 1962a).) With the acoustic trend came the realization that speech is not a stationary but rather a dynamic phenomenon. One need only look at a spectrogram to see the constantly varying nature of speech. Furthermore, when the physiological mechanisms that are responsible for the dynamics of speech were more closely examined, one came to realize that articulating speech was not something given or inborn but a function involving a rather delicate synchronization, synergism to use a more technical term, of many muscular activities that had to be learned. This realization was strengthened by studies in disorders of speech which went on simultaneously but largely independently which showed that one type of defective speech was due to the mal-synchronization of the articulatory muscles involved, although, quite surprisingly, the muscles were intact and their functions normal in non-linguistic activities.

To give an example of a dynamic aspect of speech, it is commonly known that the difference between [d] and [t] is in "voicing," the former being voiced and the latter voiceless. What this means in articulatory terms is that while the tongue tip is making a contact with the alveolar ridge and the velum is raised to block the air passage to the nasal cavity, the vocal folds are vibrating in the case of [d] but not in the case of [t]. But the matter is not as simple as it may appear to be. When looked at from a temporal plane, the difference is in relative timing of the onset of the vocal fold vibration with respect to the release of the oral closure for stops. In [t] the onset of glottal vibration lags slightly behind the oral release, while in [d] it may precede or be simultaneous with the release. In English, this difference in the delay of vocal fold closure and vibration may be as small as three or four hundredths of a second. Also, it was found that in articulating words of the type *apt, act,* etc., the two compatible closures for the final consonants are only some 20 milliseconds apart, but that they never become simultaneous, nor is their order reversed. Surely, such delicate gestures synchronizing the various muscles involved in the right temporal order must be learned and programmed beforehand prior to articulation. The problem looms larger when one looks at fluent speech which may be generated at the rate of as many as 20 segments per second. How do we do it? What sort of organization of speech in the brain must be postulated to account for this? What neuro-muscular mechanisms enable us to achieve this spectacular phenomenon? These kinds of questions naturally led to a neurophysiological inquiry into speech, for it was increasingly apparent that speech was not peripherally organized at the articulators but was centrally programmed in the higher nervous system.

To employ a metaphor, speech was viewed up to then like a cine-film, moving as a whole, yet consisting of individual, segmentalized, and stationary frames. So were segments in a stream of speech regarded. A speech stream, however, is not a film strip nor a string of beads. It is more like a stroboscopic picture. The simile is a bit exaggerated perhaps, but it is a correct one to the extent that speech is a complex of very fast moving neuro-muscular activities and that its appearance as a segmentable entity consisting of discrete elements is due to our linguistic knowledge and perceptual strategies in the nervous system, as a slowed-down or stationary appearance in stroboscopy is due to an electro-mechanical apparatus of the stroboscope.

The acoustic trend, however, seems to have reached a point approaching an asymptote ("a plateau" in Lehiste's words (1967: vi)) by 1967. I single out 1967 because that year saw the publication of two books of significance in the field of linguistics. One is an anthology edited by Ilse Lehiste titled *Readings in acoustic phonetics* and the other *Biological foundations of language* by Eric H. Lenneberg. It seems to me that these two books together form a milestone in time; one, Lehiste's, marking the end of one era, and the other, Lenneberg's, marking the beginning of a new era. (Like any historical division, this demarcation is only symbolic and a matter of convenience. No sudden break in continuous transition is implied here.)

Phoneticians are now turning their interests to physiological phonetics again. But this is not a circle but a spiral; the new trend is more than physiological; it is *neuro*physiological. One now wants to relate articulatory phenomena with neuro-muscular activities and with brain function. By examining the ways by which the human sensory and motor systems process and interpret linguistic data, one hopes to find some underlying mechanisms that would explain as yet poorly understood dynamic aspects of speech production and perception. I am not saying that phonetic laboratories will now throw their spectrographs out of the window, but merely that for the reasons which were just mentioned and that will be elaborated later, phoneticians now want to examine man's brain as much as, perhaps more than, his tongue (cf. Kim 1971a).

If we take the total chain of speech communication as beginning with a message in the nervous system of the speaker and ending with the same message arising in the nervous system of the hearer, then obviously a speech signal undergoes a series of transformations in the course of its travel from the speaker's brain to the hearer's: from neural to motor, from articulatory to acoustic, and finally from aural to neural. It becomes clear from this picture that past phonetic studies have been confined to the middle stage only, and that for a total comprehension of the speech mechanism one must add other stages of signal transmission to the domain of phonetic research. Hence, the logical necessity for examining neuro-muscular properties of speech.

Here, by saying that phoneticians now want to examine the human nervous system with respect to its linguistic functions, I am not referring to the ethological questions of what made man speak or how it is possible for men to use speech, nor am I interested in the question of brain topography and histology, i.e., localization and organization of the brain. Rather I am referring to that stage in any scientific field at which one seeks to subject the empirical consequences of theories to experimental (in)validation. Theory construction is, of course, important. Architects prepare blueprints of a building before they construct the building, and before men build airplanes, models are constructed and tested in wind tunnels. Likewise, workability of a model or a hypothesis about language can be determined only when it is tested against a real body of data, and, whenever possible, against the inner structures of the language-generator itself, i.e., the brain. In the current scene of linguistics, a number of hypotheses have been made, e.g., the hypothesis about competence vs. performance, hypotheses about language acquisition, linguistic change, the hierarchy of sentence generation, hypotheses about how sound are processed in production and perception, etc. If concepts like tacit knowledge of a native speaker, his competence, deep structures, underlying abstract representations, etc. are indeed psychologically real as some people have claimed, then they sould have neurophysiological representations in the human brain. I do not think that hypotheses like those listed above are merely heuristic and methodologically convenient assumptions which are immune to experimental verification. An organism has limited capacities that are inherently due to its self-structures. That is, an organism is only as good as its structures, and I believe that investigations of these structures and their functions will lead to discoveries of natural conditions on thoery construction and of explanatory reasons for hypotheses.

To be more specific and informative, let me illustrate, in some detail, an aspect of the dynamicity of speech production and the kinds of assumptions that must be postulated about the control system to account for the input-output relations in speech. In trying to do so, I will ask some readers' indulgence for giving in the following what may look like lecture notes for a physiological psychology class, but I do so for students of language who are not familiar with neurophysiology.

Except for some involuntary reflex actions (e.g., a knee jerk), movements in our body require specific instructions from the central nervous system. These instructions travel down the nerve fibers (axons) in the form of neural impulses. When these impulses excite peripheral muscle fibers, the muscle contracts, and we have a movement. Articulation or speaking is no different from this. Closing the lips, raising the tongue, lowering the jaw, raising the velum, closing the vocal folds, etc., all require neural commands that originate in the cortical cells. A cell is a small microscopic mass of protoplasm enclosed in a semipermeable membrane. Man's nervous system consists of about 10 billion specialized cells, called neurons, woven together into a highly complex network. Neurons appear in various forms, but certain features are common to all of them. A neuron has a cell body surrounding a nucleus. Extending from the cell body is a fine filament called an axon or nerve fiber. The axon may run for a long distance, sending off several side branches along the way, before it terminates in an even finer network of filaments called nerve endings which are capped by the terminal arbor (buttons) at a muscle spindle. Man's longest axon runs for several feet, from the spinal column to muscles that control movements of the toes. Connections between neurons are made primarily at junctions called synapses, which commonly occur where the nerve endings from one axon come into contact with dendrites, extensions that sprout from the cell body of a different neuron. One may divide the cells into two types: receptor cells and effector cells. Receptor cells, such as hair cells in the Organ of Corti, receive sensory information and help to code this information into neural signals that are transmitted to the central nervous system. Effector cells, such as those in muscle fibers, respond to the neural signals that the brain sends to them along the nerve fibers. In the case of muscles, the response is a contraction of the fiber, of course. Neural impulses are electro-chemical in nature. The interior of the cell contains positively charged potassium ions (K^+), while the surrounding intercellular fluid contains positively charged sodium ions (Na^+). Chlorine ions (Cl^-) with negative charges are present in both. These different ion concentrations on opposite sides of the membrane create an electrical potential difference between the two regions (the inside is 50 to 80 millivolts negative with respect to the outside). When a neuron is stimulated, this delicate ionic balance is upset, and a rapid exchange of ions takes place between the inside and the outside. This motion of charged particles constitutes an electric current (called action potential; the inner voltage increases by 40 to 50 mv), and this current propagates along the axon (cf. Hodgkin 1964).

Now how soon the neural signals thus generated reach their destinations depends mainly upon the following two factors:

(a) the length of the axon: the longer the axon, the longer the travel time.

(b) the conduction velocity which is proportional to the thickness of the axon. The axon's thickness in man varies from 1 micron (= 1/1000 mm) to 20 microns (in some animals it is as thick as 0.1 inch). The thicker the axon, the faster the propagation.

Speech production involves a large number of muscles, the majority of which are capable of independent control (e.g., one can do any, none, or any combination of the following: close/open the lips, raise the tongue, raise/lower the velum, close/open the vocal folds, etc.). Krmpotic (1959) painstakingly measured the lengths and the diameters of a dozen representative nerve fibers (axons) which supply neural impulses to the muscles involved in speech production, and tried to establish the order of different degrees of latency in the propagation time of nerve impulses among these axons. Krmpotic indicated these latency values in terms of what she called an *index* which is the length over the diameter of the axon. The following is a list of several nerves associated with speech production arranged according to the order of increasing index values:

(1) Facial (Cranial Nerve VII): 0.77~2.55—serves the digastric, the superior labial, etc.
(2) Trigeminal (Cranial Nerve V): 1.02~1.68—serves the pterygoid, the mylohyoid, etc.

(3)   Glossopharyngeal (Cranial Nerve IX): 1.46—serves the posterior portion of the tongue and the pharynx.

(4)   Hypoglossal (Cranial Nerve XII): 1.66∿1.69—serves the muscles of the tongue.

(5)   Recurrent laryngeal of Vagus (Cranial Nerve X): 5.80∿5.87—serves the intrinsic muscles of the larynx.

These figures do not represent any actual time units but merely indicate relative degrees of latency, implying that the greater the index value, the longer the time it takes for neural signals to reach the designated muscle, *ceteris paribus*.

In view of Krmpotic's findings, there are two assumptions one can make:

(1) The nerve impulses of a speech act leave the cortex simultaneously so that those travelling the axons of higher index values will reach their destinations progressively later than those travelling the axons with lower index values. In the absence of evidence to the contrary, this is a natural assumption. Galambos (1962: 106), for example, showed that a series of protective actions, e.g., a crouching maneuver that one makes upon hearing a loud explosive sound, has a certain temporal order which is parallel to the distance of the location of the muscle to be activated from the brain, i.e., one first closes his eyes, he then draws his chin against his chest; next, he brings his elbows together to the sides of the body, and finally, he bends his knees.

(2) In learned behavior that must require simultaneous actions of different muscles which have different latency indices, the order of neuronal firings must be different from that of the motor event. This is so because if the respective muscles are to be ready to contract simultaneously, that is, if a complex motor action is to come in time to produce an intended event, neural impulses to distant muscles must be fired earlier than those to the nearer ones to offset any time differential.

Which one of the two assumptions above applies to the act of speech? Lenneberg (1967: 100-102) is of the opinion that the orders of neuronal firings are adjusted so as to achieve a temporal coincidence at the neuromuscular juncture, and assumes that there exists in the nervous system an elaborate organization of interrelated neurons which, by some process of scanning, is capable of imposing certain types of synchronization upon a large number of widely spaced effector elements. He also attempts to explain the phenomenon of coarticulation in terms of different neuronal instructions for different segments being activated at a given time due to time differentials between motor and neuronal events. But if neuronal events are preadjusted to offset any temporal disorders in motor events, why should there be coarticulation at all? Lenneberg's schematic presentation is too abstract, and when one examines actual realization of phonic events, one even sees a glimpse of the first assumption operating. For instance, let us assume that in order to articulate the word *school* [skuwl], four muscle groups are required to function in the following way (+ = contraction, − = relaxation):

	s	k	u	w	l
lip protrusion m.	−	−	+	+	−
tongue back m.	−	+	+	+	−
tongue front m.	+	−	−	−	+
vocal folds m.	−	−	+	+	+

If we rearrange this table à la Lenneberg (1967:101 in terms of activation latency of the muscles, i.e., in accordance with the time it takes for neural signals to reach them from the brain according to the findings of Krmpotić, we get:

	1	2	3	4	5	6	7	8
lip protrusion m.	s	k	u	w	l			
tongue back m.		s	k	u	w	l		
tongue front m.			s	k	u	w	l	
vocal folds m.				s	k	u	w	l

At times *1* and *2*, there is no sound, as all muscles are as yet inactive. At time *3*, however, we have three simultaneous activations, i.e., the lips are rounding for [u], the tongue back is moving toward [k], while the tongue front is making [s]. At time *4*, the lip rounding for [u] and [w] is superimposed on [k]; at time *5*, their velic quality underlies [l], etc. This picture is close to the actual pronunciation of the word, i.e., the lips are already rounded during the initial consonantal cluster, which seems to make an almost simultaneous oral contact. (Note the near simultaneous lip and tongue positioning in the initial clusters of such words as *play, cloud,* etc. Was it this excessive simultaneity that contributed to the dropping of the initial consonant in such types of words as *psyche, knave,* etc.? Note also that when the initial cluster is all dental, e.g., *sn-, st-,* where the simultaneous tongue positioning is impossible, the dropping did not happen.) Admittedly, my presentation is as schematic and without evidence as Lenneberg's, but it does serve to show that assumption (1) is just as plausible as assumption (2) which Lenneberg adopts. Even if it were the case that assumption (2) is operative in language use, it seems to me to be reasonable to assume that readjustment in the ordering of neuronal firings represents a *marked* ordering which requires *a posteriori* learning by children, while assumption (1) represents a more natural and *unmarked* ordering.

We can further assume that since linguistic changes favor the unmarked over the marked ordering (cf. Kiparsky 1968), directionality of certain changes would be toward conforming with assumption (1) rather than with assumption (2). For example, recall that Krmpotić's finding showed that those neural impulses travelling down the recurrent laryngeal nerves would arrive at the intrinsic laryngeal muscles last. Since these muscles control the glottal closure for initiating vocal fold vibration, what the delay means is that in utterance-initial position, the voiced segment will become (partially) devoiced. It is reasonable to assume that a language learner has to learn how to prevent this devoicing, i.e., fire instructions to the glottis prior to those for the tongue or the lips. It is also reasonable to assume that the tendency toward the unmarked state will eventually prevail, giving rise to the change of voiced becoming voiceless (unaspirated), and voiceless unaspirated becoming aspirated. (Note that despite the change, functional relative differences are still kept, as [b] and [p] shift to [p] and [pʰ] respectively. A stop is unaspirated if voicing starts immediately after the oral release. If the voicing onset is delayed, there is a short period of breathy silence between the release and the onset of voicing for the following vowel. This period is aspiration (cf. Abercrombie 1967: 148; Lisker and Abramson 1964; Kim 1970a). Thus, when the delay in the onset of vocal fold vibration occurs during the closure period of a voiced stop, it would become a (partially) devoiced or voiceless stop, but when the delay occurs to a voiceless unaspirated stop, it would become a voiceless aspirated stop.)

The above predictive assumption seems to be borne out well. In historical linguistic changes involving voicing and aspiration in context-free environment, i.e., in word-initial position, the direction seems to be always [b] → [p] → [pʰ]. Rarely is the reverse direction found. It has also been observed that children often speak with [h] or with aspiration, e.g., *hi* 'I', *hice cream*, etc. (H. Winitz, in a personal communication, pointed out to me that, according to the studies of Erwin, Lind, Truby, *et al.*, non-crying utterances of infants are made with the glottis in the normal wide-open position for expiration, thereby producing /h/-like sounds with great frequency, suggesting that the skill required for glottal approximation has not been acquired.)

This serves as an example showing neurophysiological information contributing to formulating an explanatory assumption about theories of language behavior.

Granted then that speech is a complex phenomenon programmed and controlled in the central nervous system, and therefore, that the new path for phonetics to take is up the axon, rather than down the glottis, how can we go about studying the neurology of language, what experimental designs are we to construct to expose those mysterious penetralia of the brain? It is at this point that our excitement and optimism must be mitigated somewhat. In the first place, neurophysiology, though nearly a century old, has been largely an independent discipline, and we may have to wait a while yet to see significant contributions from neurophysiology to linguistic studies. Secondly, it is extremely difficult to observe the human brain; after all, exposed live brains are not easy to come by, and even when clinical opportunities arise, limitations in operation time and in accessibility to other areas are rather severe, tending to make whatever information obtained fragmentary. Furthermore, neuronal activities are not directly observable, and the search for the engram—the neurophysiological correlate of the memory trace—seems to be all but hopeless, as Lashley (1950) sadly realized.

In view of these difficulties, what one hopes to be able to do at this stage is to infer and deduce information about brain mechanisms by observing some lower level phenomena that are accessible with the instrumental techniques available today. These include use of *electromyography* to measure magnitudes of muscular activities involved in articulation and phonation (as was mentioned earlier, muscles contract upon firing of neurons, which generates minute but measurable electrical voltages); use of *high-speed cinematography*, both ordinary and radiographic using X-rays, to record and analyze the continuous movements of the articulators; *dynamic palatography* (Fujii 1970; Hardcastle 1969, 1970; Kydd and Belt 1964; Shibata 1968); use of *ultra-sonics* (ultra-sonic echo reflection is used to determine the distance, say, between the external neck wall and the lateral pharyngeal wall, as a function of time (cf. Kelsey, Minifie, and Hixon 1969; Kelsey, Woodhouse, and Minifie 1969); and *studies of speech disorders*, e.g., hesitation, slips of the tongue, aphasia, agraphia, alexia, dysphonia, etc. (malfunctions of a system can reveal as much about the system as normal functions). The last area of study is not new. There has been nearly a century of aphasiology since Paul Broca (1824-1880) and Carl Wernicke (1848-1905). But the studies in the past century were largely concerned with finding out how selective damages to the brain correlate and affect different classes of learned behavior of man. It was in Jakobson (1941) that the relevance of speech in dissolution to linguistic theories of acquisition and universals was seriously raised. For some more recent discussions on the matter, see Carterette (1966), Darley (1967), Osgood and Miron (1963), Penfield and Roberts (1959), Weigl and Bierwisch (1970), and Whitaker (1969). Electromyography (EMG) and cineradiography are both relatively recent techniques in phonetic research, and there are still problems in acquiring and interpreting EMG data (see Cooper 1965; Fromkin and Ladefoged 1966; Mansell 1970). Varying results and degrees of success in EMG studies done so far (e.g., Fritzell 1969; Harris *et al.* 1970; Knutsson and Märtensson 1969; Lubker *et al.* 1971; MacNeilage 1963; MacNeilage and Sholes 1964; Öhman *et al.* 1965, 1966, etc.) reflect this problem. The difficulty with cineradiography is of a different nature. Here the problem is not in finding the right muscle fiber in which to place an electrode but in the difficulty of obtaining sufficient data due to the hazardous nature of radiology (only a certain amount of Roentgen dosage may be safely absorbed by one subject) and the tedium of processing the data (the frame-by-frame tracing must still be done manually, and at 100 frames per second, one minute of speech will require the tracing of 6000 frames! (Cf. Kim 1970b). A computer processing technique of dynamic radiographic data is now being developed in Tokyo (cf. Fujimura *et al.* 1969; Kiritani and Fujimura 1970). For some recent studies in speech involving high-speed photography, see Fujimura (1961), Lindblom (1968a), Moore *et al.* (1962), Ohala *et al.* (1968), Soron (1967), Teter and Newell (1969), and Zemlin (1969); for a trans-illumination technique using fiber optics, see Hirose *et al.* (1969), Lindqvist (1969), Lisker *et al.* (1969), Ohala (1966), Sawashima (1968), and Sawashima and Hirose (1968); and for recent contributions in cineradiographic study of speech, see Amerman and Daniloff (1970), Daniloff (1967), Daniloff and Moll (1968), Delattre (1967), Gendron (1962), Hollien *et al.* (1968), Kim (1970a), Lubker (1968), Lubker and Moll (1965), Massengill *et al.* (1966), Moll (1960, 1962), Ondráčková and Poch (1962), Perkell (1969), Stevens (1963), Strenger (1968), Subtelny and Subtelny (1962), and Truby (1962).

Having so far pictured the general framework which guided the direction of the science of phonetics in this century, we can now turn to a review of a few specific issues that were dominant in phonetic circles in recent years.

The most dominant issue among phoneticians in recent years has been the question of the model of speech production, in particular the size of the unit of speech encoding (cf. Fromkin 1965, 1966, 1968; Henke 1966; Kozhevnikov and Chistovich 1965; Ladefoged 1967; Lindblom 1968b; MacNeilage 1970; MacNeilage and DeClerk 1969; Öhman 1967; Tatham 1971; and Tatham and Morton 1969).

Ever since Sapir advanced the notion of the "psychological reality of phonemes," the concept of a phoneme has been accepted as something real which has an invariant correlate at some level. And needless to say, the concept of the phoneme was the corner-stone of structural linguistics. The notion of phonemic reality was strengthened by the supposedly superior alphabetized writing systems of the Western world. If the language user writes two different sounds with one and the same symbol, he must regard them as mentally the same, so goes the argument. Actually, this notion is not so unchallengeable as it might seem. For one thing, I am not at all sure if awareness of this sameness is equally strong in speakers of languages which do not have writing systems. Secondly, the alphabetic system is not the only writing system that human civilization has known. As a matter of fact, the earliest writing systems were syllabic, and even now languages like Chinese and Japanese have syllabic writing systems, and even though they have been looked upon as something less economical and less optimal,

I think they should be given more merit for the reasons that will become clear shortly.

What is the unit of speech production? It would be ideally economical if our brain stored separate instructions for each phoneme and generated them in their order of occurence in a phonemic string. Note, for example, the following traditional account of the process of speech production:

> We shall assume that the speaker has stored in his memory a table of all the phonemes and their actualizations. This table lists the different vocal tract configurations or motor gestures that are associated with each phoneme and the conditions under which each is to be used. In producing an utterance the speaker looks up, as it were, in the table the individual phonemes and then instructs his vocal tract to assume in succession the configurations or gestures corresponding to the phonemes. (Halle and Stevens 1964:605)

This simple view, however, runs into many difficulties. Spectrograms do not show invariant acoustic correlates. Attempts to construct an automatic speech recognition device (e.g., a machine that will take speech as input and produce a print-out of its phonemic instantiation as output) has failed despite years of efforts. Speech synthesizers that "look up" phonemic tables produce all but natural speech.

The search for phonemic invariance at the motor level through electromyographic studies (cf. Fromkin 1965; Harris et al. 1965; Lubker et al. 1970; MacNeilage 1963; MacNeilage and Sholes 1964 etc.) has not presented cause for more optimism. One then began to speculate that the unit of speech encoding may have a different magnitude than the size of a phoneme, and there are some indications that it is perhaps something larger than the phoneme in size. There is, for example, a temporal overlap between articulations of two or more phonemes. In such words as *two, who, coo,* one can easily detect the lip-rounding beginning with or before the initial consonant, not after (compare these words with *tea, he, key*). Daniloff and Moll (1968) found that coarticulation of rounding can begin as early as four consonants before it is segmentally due (e.g., in such words as *since true* and *construe,* the lip-rounding for *u* was observed to start at *n*). One can argue that if there were a separate and independent neural command for each phoneme and if these commands were generated sequentially, how is it possible that a part of the articulation of the following phoneme is executed during the articulation of the preceding phoneme? Doesn't this suggest that our effector organs already possess information concerning the second segment at the same time as the articulation of the first segment is being accomplished? It was in this vein that Kozhevnikov and Chistovich (1965) hypothesized that the minimal unit of a motor command is syllable, not a phoneme, and accordingly, that segments within a syllable receive a simultaneous package of instructions for articulation.

At this point, I think it is appropriate to mention that their book which appeared in 1965 was the single most powerful driving force underlying the current of phonetic research in the late 60's. Hardly a phonetic paper is written these days without a reference to their monograph. I recall the air of excitement that surrounded my colleagues and myself when we first received and read the translated copies in 1966. It is difficult to say whether the numerous subsequent arguments on units of motor commands in speech production were solely derivatives from that book from Leningrad. I like to think that there was independent thinking along similar lines in the United States, and that the stage was set for bringing up the issue in any case. For example, Fromkin's dissertation which is also dated 1965 cites no Russian sources in her bibliography, yet her conclusion was that her investigation "did not support the hypothesis that a simple one-to-one correspondence exists between a phoneme and its motor commands" (160) and speculated that "the minimal linguistic unit corresponding to the motor commands which produce speech is larger than the phoneme, perhaps more of the order of a syllable." (163) It is none the less true, however, the EMG studies by the Haskins group and by the Stockholm laboratory in the middle 60's (e.g., Harris *et al.* 1965; Lindblom 1965; Liberman *et al.* 1964; MacNeilage 1963; Öhman 1967; Öhman *et al.* 1967.) were largely preoccupied with finding the motor invariants associated with phonemes, and that it was in the main Kozhevnikov and Chistovich's monograph that freed us from the spell of phonemes as far as speech production models were concerned.

One can, of course, argue that as early as 1951, Lashley theorized that certain behaviors involving rapid serial movements, e.g., piano playing, galloping, speaking, etc. must be centrally programmed rather than peripherally organized. But Lashley was never specific about the mechanisms in speech production, and phonemic realism in structural linguistics was so strong that Lashley's hypothesis went largely ignored and untested. Thus, most early EMG studies were primarily occupied with finding motor invariants of phonemes, and the so-called associative chain model dominated the thinkings of behavioral and physiological psychologists.

One can diagram the two alternative views in the following way:

THE CLOSED-LOOP MODEL [*Sawtooth model* adapted from Kozhevnikov and Chistovich 1966:94]

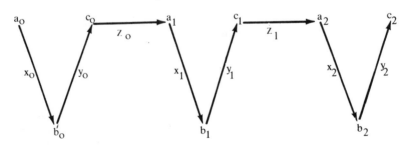

a - beginning of a neural command
b - beginning of the movement
c - moment of arrival of afferent impulsation about b
x - time interval for conduction of neural command
y - time interval for conduction of feedback signal
z - latent period until the next neural command

THE OPEN-LOOP MODEL $\left[$*Comb Model* adapted from Ohala 1970:121$\right]$

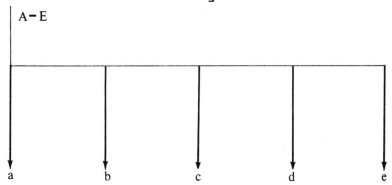

A - E, simultaneous instruction
a - e, sequential realization

Major arguments for favoring the open-loop model are that:

(1) there is an overlapping coarticulation phenomenon.

(2) there is not enough time for a round-trip transit of nerve impulses. Human motor responses to sensory stimuli take as long as 1/8 second.

(3) there are differences in nerve impulse conduction times, among articulator muscles, of up to 30 msec (Lenneberg 1967:96). A single stimulus cannot trigger a complex of commands which have to be temporally staggered.

Proponents of the phoneme theory counterargue that the lack of invariants is due to such factors as the mechanical constraints inherent in the peripheral vocal apparatus, limitations in the response capabilities of the muscular system, and overlapping in time of the effects of successive phoneme commands. As for (2) above, Ohala (1970) argued, à la Fairbanks (1954), that it is not necessary that a gesture be 100% completed before afferent information on the progress of the gesture is reported to the brain. Afferent signals are probably continuously sent to the brain which is capable of predicting on the basis of initial preliminary information. This is plausible, Ohala continues, because as speech movements become more automatic and more removed from conscious control, articulation becomes more reflexive, which requires shorter latencies. Ohala also counterargued point (3) above by saying that laryngeal synchronization is not precise in voice onset time in aspiration and in full voicing. Furthermore, Ohala's reconstruction of conduction time differences between oro-facial nerves and laryngeal nerves showed only a difference of 9 msec which Ohala doubts will present any great problem for the kind of precise coordination believed to be required by Lenneberg.

But Ohala does not consider the different response capabilities once the neural signals reach their target muscles. I would think that it would take different times for the tongue tip, for the tongue back, for the lips, for the velum, and for the glottis to travel an equal distance of, say, 1 cm. I have some data on glottis timing. If aspiration is taken to be a voice onset delay due to the time it takes for the open glottis to approximate for voicing (the view that Ohala also accepts), then my data (Kim 1970a) shows that it takes as much as 90 msec for the open glottis to travel 10mm (actually 5 mm since two vocal folds meet at the median). I doubt that it would take that much time for the lips or for the tongue tip to travel the same distance. According to Daniloff's (1967) data, it took the tongue tip 30 msec in making the closure for [t] in uttering *not* (measured from the moment of the maximum opening of the preceding vowel to the moment of the tongue-alveolar contact; distance - 1.25 cm), and it took the lips about 35 msec to close for [p] in uttering *a plume* (the lip opening at *a* was 1.6 cm).

Strong support for the closed-loop model came recently from Wickelgren (1969) who argued that Lashley's rejection of the associative-chain model was premature in that one needs to distinguish non-creative serial behavior from creative serial behavior and that Lashley's objection applies only to the latter, but not to the former to which word production belongs. Wickelgren attempts to rescue the associative-chain hypothesis by proposing a *context-sensitive associative-chain theory* which assumes that serial order is encoded by means of associations between *context-sensitive elementary motor responses* (EMR). In speech, this means that a word such as *stop* is assumed to be coded allophonically as $[_\#s_t]$ ([s] in the context of #____[t]), $[_st_o]$, $[_to_p]$, and $[_op_\#]$. In this model the basic units of production would be context-sensitive allophones, and serial ordering of these EMRs would be achieved, as Whitaker (1970:3) put it, by interlocking the preceding and following contexts in puzzle fashion. Since stress, pitch, and durational differences in otherwise identical contexts constitute independent EMRs, it turns out that one needs to store about 10^4 to 10^6 EMRs for speech production. Wickelgren claims that this is no problem because the human cortex contains about 10^{10} neurons. Regardless of the counterintuitive nature of this necessity for such an enormous cerebral storage and retrieval capacity, I think the numerology here is quite meaningless. There is no evidence whatsoever that each neuron is associated with a specific allophone or an EMR. Available evidence is rather that a complex network of neurons behaves in a multiply integrated way, and unless some specific relationships between allophones and neurons are observed, a claim that the number of allophones does not begin to exhaust the number of neurons in the brain is pointless.

Wickelgren's paper occasioned a criticism by MacKay (1970) who, citing examples from German and English spoonerisms, argued that Wickelgren's model would fail. Specifically, MacKay assumed that since association in the chain model is unidirectional, it would predict that reversed segments in spoonerisms would occur much more frequently following repeated segments, i.e., ABCBDA → ABDBCA, e.g., *Cavalerie* → *Calaverie,* and that positions of reversals would be random as long as the reversed segments share similar contexts in the chain. But MacKay found that repeated segments followed the reversed segments as often as they preceded them, e.g., *Wasserflasche→Flasserwasche,* and that, as others have also observed (Boomer and Laver 1968; Fromkin 1970), reversed segments occur only in the same positions within the syllable, i.e., the switching occurs only between two syllable-initial segments, between two syllable nuclei, or between two syllable-final segments.

In a pilot study, Tatham and Morton (1970) tested Wickelgren's model by trying to detect any EMR differences between two [k]'s in [aku], [uka] and [iku], [uki]. They reasoned that if Wickelgren was right, EMR for [k] in the former set should be different from that in the latter set; in particular, the muscle contraction for lip-rounding in the former [k] would be greater and longer than in the latter case because [a] is neutral to lip-rounding, while [i] requires lip-spreading which is antagonistic to lip-rounding. Since EMR's are context-sensitive, the two [k]'s would constitute two different EMRs and therefore would show different *EMG* patterns. But the result was negative, i.e., EMG activity in [aku] was not different from that in [iku]. Since there are nonetheless differences in spatial configurations of the lips during the two [k]'s, Tatham and Morton's conclusion was that "[aku] and [iku] exist **after** coarticulation, but only [k] exists **before** coarticulation." (121-22)

MacKay's criticism of Wickelgren was soon rebutted by Whitaker (1970) who assumed that Wickelgren could have argued that MacKay's hypotheses about reversals in spoonerisms are not relevant to the associative-chain theory because it is **after** the error has been made that the correct group of EMRs is assembled. Thus, all examples that MacKay cited against Wickelgren could no longer be damaging, since EMRs are activated after their erroneous ordering has been established. This assumption, Whitaker says, is borne out well by the fact that regardless of the cause of error, the error output is still an admissible sequence in the language obeying all the phonological constraints. (I have noted, however, the following exceptions: *comb* → *ngowp*[ŋowp] (Hockett 1967:915,fn. 11) *stick shift* → *shtick sift* (Fromkin 1970:46).) Whitaker gives a hypothetical example of a spoonerism which would crucially bear on the issue. That is, if *a loud* *spanking* spoonerized into *a poud slanking,* the model would predict that the allophone of *p* would be articulated as a word-initial aspirated [ph], not as a post-*s* unaspirated [p]. If any residues of the originally intended context remained in the realized output, the model would be disconfirmed.

It is difficult to assess Whitaker's precise position. The tone of the paper appears to be in defense of Wickelgren and against MacKay, but since he later rejects Wickelgren's model as well, his objection to MacKay was perhaps for the sake of argument, or for his own model, which follows.

MacKay, Ohala, and Whitaker propose a model of language programming in which an entire phrase is simultaneously displayed in a *buffer zone,* then is read off or scanned in a unidirectional fashion. That is, speech units are put into some kind of a *hopper* (Ohala 1970:133) where they are entered in a particular order—the order in which they will be *fed* to the appropriate muscles. In Whitaker's words, "the phonological output of the grammar is displayed in a buffer and the [tracking] mechanism tracks this display by activating the requisite vocal tract command sets."

Kozhevnikov and Chistovich's (1965) view is somewhat eclectic, eclectic in the sense that their model uses both the open-loop and the closed-loop mechanisms. They hypothesize that what makes the string of segments in a syllable be realized in a serial order is not a separate and direct instruction for each segment from the speech center, nor a proprioceptive impulsation (sensation of tension in muscles) occuring upon the movements of articulators during the articulation of the preceding segment (the so-called associative-chain model), but a sort of reflex mechanism connecting several movements such that stimulation for the following movement is subliminal, which rises above the threshold value to cause an external effect when given an additional push created by the impulsation occuring upon articulation of the preceding segment.

MacNeilage (1970) is a bit more specific about the reflex mechanism. He borrows Hebb's (1949) notion of motor equivalence which is to say that the motor system is controlled by internal specifications of certain spatial targets so as to achieve a single result, e.g., reaching for a doorknob, a tennis player reaching for the ball hit by the opponent, etc. In MacNeilage's model, the open-loop component emits a context-independent command for an articulator to reach a certain position and closed-loop control curcuits constantly sample the mechanical state of the articulator and adjust the command accordingly (speaking with a cigarette or a pipe in one's mouth provides a good example of such adjustment). MacNeilage speculates that this feedback loop is controlled by the gamma motor system, that consists of smaller diameter motoneurons which activate intrafusal muscle fibers in muscle spindles which form a monosynaptic reflex arc with the alpha motoneurons which activate the main body of the muscle. (Cf. Eldred et al. 1953).

Resolution of these different views of the model of speech will have to wait neurophysiological evidence. Personally, I find it difficult to believe that the command sequence for the word *yes* is just the reverse of that for the word *say* [sey]. Somehow, I feel that their storage and retrieval in the brain is unitary, independent, and *quantum libet.* The following will serve as a good example. Ilse Lehiste (1970) recently examined temporal organization of several English words such as *stead, stay, stayed, steady,* etc., and found that there was a temporal compensation between component segments in these words. For example, in various pronunciations of the word *steady,* there was a negative correlation between the two vowels in such a way that if one vowel was longer, the other was proportionately shorter, with all tokens maintaining the same average duration. What was more surprising was the fact that the words *stead* and *staid* had the same total duration, although the vowel in *stead* is intrinsically shorter than that in *staid.* A temporal compensation was made by longer durations of consonants. This study definitely shows that the unit of articulatory programming is larger in size than the segment, and makes it difficult to believe that articulation consists merely in the concatenation of phonemes.

There are other indications that seem to support the open-loop theory. One is the phenomenon of false starts. It has been observed that in a false start one cannot correct oneself before the completion of at least the first syllable of an utterance, even though the speaker has come to be aware of the mistake before or during the first segment of the utterance. (Cf. "Such errors are practically never corrected until a whole syllable at least has been emitted." Fry 1964:219) Again, an argument can be made to the effect that if the neural commands were phoneme by phoneme, one should be able to stop at any segment in the utterance, but if the unit of neural commands is a syllable, then one would have to complete the motor execution of that syllable once the command has been sent out, i.e., there would be no way to retrieve it in the middle of a syllable. The phenomenon may be linked to a pitcher's throw or a golfer's swing. During the final wind-up before the ball leaves his hand, the pitcher may realize that his pitch is going to be wild; likewise, the golfer may realize during his final swing before the club hits the ball that it is going to be short of the green. Despite this realization, however, he is unable to change the pattern of the swing, as neuronal commands for that final swing have already been fired, and once fired, they must be executed. And any one who has typed is probably familiar with the sensation that he has often experienced when he "had to" hit a wrong key even though the realization that it was a wrong one had come prior to the downward movement.

Another indication is that stutterers stutter (Taylor 1966) and babblers babble in terms of syllables, not in terms of phonemes. Babies for example babble in terms of the CV type, e.g., [ma, ma, ma], [da, da, da], or [ka, ka, ka]. "They do not babble in any way that indicates awareness or control of units smaller than a syllable.'' (Ladefoged 1967:148) Thus, even when they have mastered the above phrases, such independent and arbitrary sequences as [madaka], [akadam], etc. do not occur.

The rhythm in speech also appears to behave in terms of units of syllable size. Thus, iambic pentameter means that there are five sets of paired syllables in a line, e.g.:

And ALL the AIR a SOLemn STILLness HOLDS. (from Thomas Gray's Elegy. Capital letters indicate stressed syllables.) Although the role of rhythm in prose language is not comparable to that in poetry, it should not be minimized, since, although not always regular, it definitely has a tendency to maintain iambic rhythmicity. Note the stress contour in such words as ARtiFIciAliTY, DIFfeRENtiAtion, OPporTUniTY, etc. A good example of the alternating stress pattern is found in Finnish where the stress falls regularly on odd numbered syllables, e.g., TIEttäMÄttöMYYdesTÄni 'about my ignorance' (the example is from Skousen). The underlying current of rhythm is so strong that when rhythm is grossly violated, languages seem to have rules whose sole function is to readjust the stress pattern so as to maintain the rhythmicity. Thus, English has rules like STRESS AD-JUSTMENT and AUXILIARY REDUCTION (cf. The sound pattern of English, Chapter 3) that produce rhythmic contours. For example, to derive soLIDity from SOlid + ity, the original primary stress must be weakened to tertiary as the new primary stress is assigned on the next syllable in the noun form. To give another example, in Tunica (an AmerIndian language in Louisiana) TAkoMEli 'a species of tree' is derived from ta 'determiner' + KO 'tree' + MEli 'black', and the underlying form of TIyahPAni 'she was hungry, it is said' is ti + YAHpa + Ani (the example is from Kisseberth). It has also been observed that in English a lexical stress can shift to conform with the rhythmic stress, e.g., JUST fourTEEN vs. FOURteen SHILLings; QUITE unKNOWN vs. UNknown LAND (Jones 1959: 253. On the role of rhythm in a theory of language, see Allen 1968, 1970).

A neurological correlate for this organizing principle that underlies the rhythmic behavior of language is difficult to present. Although there is some discussion (e.g. Morrell et al. 1956; Wall 1959) on the mechanism and and the origin of the production of repetitive (rhythmic) neuronal firing (e.g., in cardiac ganglion cells of vertebrates) as to whether it is within the fiber itself where the arrival of an afferent volley sets up a long-lasting ex-citatory process in the region of the synapses or whether the rhythmic discharge of neurons is driven by bombardment of impulses from other in-terconnecting neurons that make up the so-called "reverberating circuit," I have nothing better than what Lenneberg (1967: 117) cites from Brazier (1960) who shows that the periodicity of the dominant brain (theta?) waves at the vertex and the temporo-parietal region which are closely associated with the speech center is about 7.3 cps, which happens to coincide, Lenne-berg notes, with the average number of syllables per second in speech of normal rate. This of course does not imply that one cannot speed up or slow down the tempo of speech without the accompanying adjustment in brain rhythm frequency, nor is there any conclusive evidence that there is a direct causal relation between brain rhythm and speech rhythm. Some correlations have been observed, however. For example, alpha waves (Berger rhythm) which characteristically appear during the wakeful and relaxed state have a frequency of 9-12 cps, which speeds up considerably to 20-30 cps (beta waves) in close attention or excitement, but slows down to 3-5 cps (delta waves) in slumber (Woodburne 1967: 292-93; Gardner 1968: 296-98).

It seems then not unreasonable to assume that brain rhythm serves as an organizing principle and a timing device for speech, and that rhythm in speech is due to biological factors rather than social or cultural factors. (One may read quite a fascinating account of rhythm subserving various types of human behavior in *The Naked Ape*, Morris 1967: 88ff.) Thus, one can strongly argue that the rhythmic unit is also a syllable, not a segment. (Recall that the frequencies of brain rhythm and speech rhythm match when the latter is measured in terms of syllables-per-second.) Since the varying pattern in brain waves represents the algebraic sum of the action potentials of cortical neurons, one is tempted to speculate that this gives supporting evidence to the claim that the brain *fires out* (encodes) speech in terms of syllables. This gives more magnitude to the status of the syllable as a linguistic unit. Indeed, in phonological rules there are some constraints that seem to be due to the nature of the syllable as a unit. For example, one can imagine rules that state: "shift the stress to the next syllable," "lengthen a vowel in every second syllable" (e.g., in Tübatulabal, cf. Swadesh and Voegelin 1939; McCawley 1969), or "destress in front of a stressed syllable," etc., but hardly such rules as "shift the stress to the next segment," "lengthen every second segment," etc.

In view of these facts it strikes me as difficult to maintain the view that speech production is a phoneme-by-phoneme Markovian process.

Having now deposed segment for syllable, one might ask what the exact nature of the syllable is, as I have been using the term in a rather loose way. Unfortunately, despite the fact that most laymen can intuitively determine the correct number of syllables within a word, we don't know yet exactly what a syllable is. Stetson's (1951) theory that each syllable is accompanied by a *ballistic chest pulse* has been refuted by Ladefoged (1962), and phoneticians are still unable to find simple physiological correlates for syllables. It seems that a syllable as a unit must have some minimum requirements. These requirements may be in terms of a certain number of segments, morae, or a certain amount of muscle work. English monosyllabic words, for example, must contain a tense vowel, e.g., *he, how, eye, may, boy,* etc., or must end in a consonant if the vowel is lax, e.g., *hid, at, met, us, bed,* etc. A similar phenomenon is found in Faroese (a west Scandinavian language) where a non-final vowel is lax and short in a closed syllable, but tense and long in an open syllable, e.g., *gert* [ʃɛrt] '(thou) dost', *gera* [ʃeːra] 'to do'; *tordi* [tɔrdi] 'dared', *tora* [toːra] 'to dare' (the example is from S. Anderson). The so-called *compensatory lengthening* of a vowel in the environment of a consonantal loss, for example, or a consonant gemination ensuing a vowel loss or shortening is also, I feel, functionally related to the effort to preserve the unity of the syllable.

Linguists like to define syllable structure in terms of language-specific surface constraints on phonemic strings. Does this mean then that each language has differently sized units of neural commands? Perhaps so, although one would like to think that neural mechanisms are basically the same for all species of man. Also, in terms of rhythm, what does it mean that a language is syllable-timed, while another is stress-timed? Exactly how does the relationship between rhythm and syllable differ in these two types of languages?

Kozhevnikov and Chistovich have advanced the notion that any number of prevocalic consonants form a syllable-unit with the following vowel (the final postvocalic consonant is said to constitute a syllable of its own). Later, they suggest that the simplest and the most basic articulatory unit is the consonant-vowel syllable complex, and that more complex combinations of the type CCV are nothing but groups of these simple complexes organized in such a way that the second complex is accomplished partially in parallel with the accomplishment of the first, supporting Fairbanks and Guttman's (1958) conclusion that multiple repetitions of a complex of movements which formally coincide with a CV syllable are very typical for artificial stuttering.

Can we say that CCV = CX + CV where X is a vowel reflex? It is certainly tempting to think that all syllables are of a simple CV type. There are certain indications that this might be a proto-type. Children say *mommy, daddy, doggy, chicky,* etc. Forms like *mom, dad, dog,* etc. are certainly later developments. I have also noticed in one of my children that when he could not produce initial consonant clusters in such words as *school, spoon, stop, snow,* etc. (he would put *s* at the end, saying *kools, poons, tops, nows,* etc.), he could say *sketi,* 'spaghetti'. Was it because there was some sort of a vowel reflex or a mental syllable between *s* and *k* in *sketi*?

This brings up the question of the syllable at two levels of representation: phonological (deep, linguistic) and phonetic (surface, physiological). Is the syllable definable at both levels or oñly at one of the two? If the latter, which one? Could it be, for example, that syllables are units only at the physiological level, while the units at the linguistic level are segments? If so, just what is the relationship between the two? (Cf. Tatham 1971.) Is it the case that the abstract underlying representations consist mainly of consonant clusters in which various vowels are inserted to derive forms at the surface level? [Semitic languages in general have consonantal verb roots from which other forms are derived by supplying different vowels, e.g., Hebrew

/ktb/ 'to write', *katab* 'he wrote', *koteb* 'he writes', *yiktob* 'he will write', *niktab* 'it was written', *hiktib* 'he dictated', *ktiba* 'writing', *miktab* 'a letter', etc. The example is from Bolotzky.] Or is it the case that, as Hofman (1967) postulates, consonant clusters are to be regarded as a complex single segment at the underlying level which is then sequentially realized as multiple segments at the phonetic level by some sort of segmentalization rules? (E.g., *pl* in *plain* would be regarded as a single segment /p^l/ 'a liquidic *p*', *kw* in *queen* as /k^w/ 'a rounded *k*', the initial cluster in *strong* as a single segment somethin like /t$_r^s$/ 'a strident liquidic *t*', etc. In the case of vowel complexes, the argument about the sequential realization of an underlying segment seems to be stronger and more plausible. For example, in English, a tense *i* is realized as [ay], (cf. *derive/derivation, collide/collision*, etc.). Or is it the case that they underlying representation consists primarily of simple CV types, deriving consonant clusters at the phonetic level by some sort of vowel deletion? The role of the distinction between a *weak syllable* and *a strong syllable* in English stress rules (Chomsky and Halle 1968:29) is interesting to examine in this respect. For example, both words *PERson* and *DIAlect* have the stress on the initial syllable but when the affix *-al* is added, the stress remains on the first syllable in *PERsonal* but shifts to the next syllable in DIAlect to give *diaLECTal*. The reason is of course given as being due to the different syllable structures of the penultimate syllable, *-son-* being a weak syllable, *-lect-* being a strong syllable. But if we assume that the consonant cluster in *lect* has an intervening vowel reflex (which is deleted after the stress rule), both forms would have the stress on the ante-penultimate syllable. Admittedly, this is a wild speculation, but I think it is worth having a fresh look at all phonological behavior, especially at prosody and exceptions, with the theory of rhythm and the syllable integrated into the current theory.

There are other linguistic implications of the syllable model. Obviously, difficulty in speaking a foreign language having the same set of sounds or in pronouncing nonsense forms violating the native morpheme structure conditions can be explained in terms of this model. That is, it would be naturally difficult to re-program serial behavior.

Furthermore, if we accept the assumption that the minimal unit of speech production is a syllable, then this assumption dictates that metathesis between segments across a syllable boundary should seldom occur, i.e., in the string *abc#xyz* where # is a syllable boundary, it should be rare for *b* and *y* or *a* and *z* to change places, while it predicts that metathesis between segments within a syllable should be more common. This follows since our peripheral organs have information about the whole syllable at the beginning of the articulation of the syllable, and one can expect cases where the sequence of segments within a syllable is realized in a different order, especially when two compatible segments become excessively simultaneous and result in a reversed order. The fact that in spoonerisms the segments which are interchanged maintain their original positions in a syllable (i.e., only *a* and *x,* *b* and *y,* or *c* and *z* may exchange places) is also predictable from the unitary nature of the syllable.

Consider now the assumption which has been favored here in connection with a familiar phonological rule of the form:

$$X \rightarrow Y / \underline{\hspace{2cm}} Z$$

If one cherishes a chain association model (a model that explains a serial behavior *ABC* as *A* eliciting *B* response which then becomes a stimulus for *C* response, and so on), then it seems to me that he cannot write such a rule, for how can he explain that what follows (*Z*) triggers a change in what precedes (*X* to *Y*), when at the time one is about to accomplish the required adjustment, one has no information at all about *Z* as *Z* has to wait for the completion of *X*? In view of the fact that there are rarely context-free rules, but that many phonological rules are context-restricted, like the above, necessitating the specification of such units as syllables or stress groups as the domain in which a change is triggered, one can only wonder what the phonological rules would look like and how many "exceptions" and "environments" one could dispense with if rules were written in terms of motor units. It is known, for example, that Verner's Law and consonant clusters are exceptions to Grimm's Law. As Ladefoged (1967: 172) speculates, if all *t*'s were the same in the sense that all *t*'s had the same storage pattern and the same neural coding in the brain, then shouldn't all *t*'s have changed in the same way without exception? But once we accept the assumption that each *t* had a different neural representation depending upon the syllabic structure of which it is a part, then exceptions may cease to be exceptions.

It impresses me as true to say that, despite much talk about the *explanatory* goal of linguistics, people have been more concerned with expression than with explanation. By and large, phonologists have been concerned with ways by which their rules may look concise, pretty, and elegant. I am hopeful that the new experimental phonetics will generate enough force to shift the current of phonology from formalism to functionalism and provide explanations that indeed look and sound like explanations.

So far, we have been discussing some aspects of speech production. Let us now look briefly at its complementary aspect, i.e., speech perception.

The area of speech perception is in obscure limbo. If speech-encoding has a message as the input and its phonetic realization as the output, perception is of course its inverse where the input is the phonetic realization and the output the message. One can imagine thousands of rules, right or wrong, that have been written relating the message input to the phonetic output. But how many rules do we have relating the phonetic input to the message output? Surely one cannot say that the subject matter of linguistics ceases at the moment of phonetic realization and that what is beyond lies in the realm of cybernetics.

From a simplistic point of view, one can assume that there is a set of acoustic signals that is uniquely associated with a phoneme. In this case, the decoding procedure would be nothing but segmenting the incoming acoustic signals into segment-sized chunks and identifying these segments with particular phonemes. Unfortunately, the matter is not as simple as this. In the first place, no acoustic signal is uniquely associated with a particular phoneme, and secondly, it is virtually impossible to segment the continuously varying acoustic signals into discrete phoneme-sized segments. As was mentioned earlier, an automatic speech recognition device is not yet a reality despite many years of efforts, although Medress (1969) reports that computer recognition of English monosyllabic words spoken in isolation has been perfected to a degree where there are but 6 errors in 240 tokens. (For some recent developments in speech and speaker recognition, see Derkach 1970; Fant 1970; Hays and Clark 1970; Ramishvili 1970; Wolf 1969, 1970; and Zagoruiko 1970.) Furthermore, experiments have shown that people could not identify the temporal ordering of segments (Ladefoged 1967; Thomas *et al.* 1970). For example, when unfamiliar nonsense segments were presented, listeners could easily differentiate between complex stimuli which differed in the order of their components. But they differentiated the stimuli as wholes and could not tell the relative times of arrival of the component parts. That is, the stimuli which differed only in the order of their components were perceived as being different simply in overall quality. An experiment with localization of a click showed the same negative results, suggesting that listeners have difficulty in determining the physical order of arrival of individual items, and therefore that immediate perception is perhaps in terms of larger units than the phoneme, which is analogous to the case of the unit in speech production.

The open-loop versus the closed-loop argument can also apply to the case of speech perception. The closed-loop model of perception would assume that the hearer in decoding the incoming speech signal will refer back to his own production mechanism. This is what is known as *the motor theory of speech perception* which hypothesizes that the listener refers the acoustic pattern to the set of motor commands required in order to utter a sound similar to the one heard (e.g., Cooper 1958; Denes 1967; Gulanov and Chistovich 1965; Liberman *et al.* 1963, 1967). Do we really, in perceiving a sound, make use of our knowledge of the articulatory gestures that are used to make that sound? And why not? If a machine makes an extraneous noise, the person who constructed or assembled the machine should certainly be able to tell more accurately which part of the machine is making the noise than someone who has never seen the device. Speech perception involves a similarly unique situation in that the listener himself knows how to make the sounds that he is hearing (in the general case that he is listening to his native tongue), and there is no reason to believe that one does not summon this useful knowledge is assisting the decoding of speech signals. The danger lies in believing that this is the only mode by which one perceives speech. I think the notion that every phonetic feature has an exclusive function assignable to it has played a rather unfortunate role in past phonetic research.

Recall, for example, such vehemently argued issues as: What is *the* distinctive feature differentiating [p] from [b]; voicing, tenseness, or aspiration? (Cf. Fischer-Jørgensen 1968; Jakobson and Halle 1964; Kim 1965; Lisker and Abramson 1964; Malécot 1970; Slis and Cohen 1969.) What is *the* crucial perceptual cue of consonants; the noise spectra or the formant transitions (loci)? (Cf. Borovičková *et al.* 1970; Delattre *et al.* 1965; Halle *et al.* 1957; Liberman *et al.* 1956; Suzuki 1970; Wang 1959.) What is *the* acoustic correlate of stress; intensity, pitch-rise, or duration? (Cf. Fry 1955; Gonzales 1970; Janota and Liljencrants 1970; Lehiste 1961; Lehiste and Peterson 1959; Lieberman 1960; Malmberg 1963: 102ff.) What is *the* physiological correlate of fundamental frequency variation? (Cf. Faaborg-Anderson *et al.* 1967; Hirano *et al.* 1969; Kim 1968; Lieberman 1967; Lieberman *et al.* 1969, 1970; Ohala 1970; Ohala and Ladefoged 1970; Vanderslice 1967, 1970.) What is wrong in assuming that there is a maximum differentiation between [p] and [b] in which voicing, tenseness, and aspiration all take opposite values? In that language constitutes a communicative code, there is a tendency to establish optimum opposition or maximum contrast between meaningful signals ("le principe de différentiation maxima," Martinet 1955: 62), as the task of comprehension on the part of the hearer is much easier if distinctive signals differ from each other as much as possible. Such distinctiveness permits signals to pass through a noisy medium without being completely drowned out. From the speaker's point of view, this optimum differentiation allows a margin of error in production, which would not be possible if all signals clustered around the same area in the acoustic spectrum (cf. Kim 1971c). In specific linguistic or nonlinguistic contexts, some cues may be weakened, in which case the remaining cue(s) will have to be amplified and assume a greater role. Note the following interesting account reported in Jakobson, Fant and Halle (1951:8):

> In Russian, the phoneme /i/ is implemented as a back vowel [ɨ] after non-palatalized consonants, and as a front vowel [i] in all other positions. These variants are redundant, and normally for Russian listeners it is the difference between the non-palatalized [s] and the palatalized [ş] which serves as the means of discriminating between the syllables [sɨ] and [şi]. But when a mason telephoned an engineer saying that the walls [sɨr'ejut] 'are getting damp' and the transmission distorted the high frequencies of the [s] so that it was difficult to comprehend

whether the walls 'were getting damp' or 'turning gray' [si̯r 'ejut], then the worker repeated the word with particular emphasis on the [ɨ], and through this redundant feature the listener made the right choice.

I tend to agree with Fant who said that "the motor theory of speech perception has perhaps gained more interest than it deserves." (Fant 1968b: 7) See also Lane's (1965) criticism of the motor theory and a recent reply to Lane by Studdert-Kennedy *et al.* (1970).

I assume that *the analysis-by-synthesis model* (Halle and Stevens 1964; Stevens 1960; Stevens and Halle 1967) is also a closed-loop theory of perception, although this model does not specifically say that one's production mechanism comes to play a role in perception. It says rather that the listener internally generates an utterance to find the best match to the incoming utterance.

In the past fifteen years or so, there was a great upsurge in the development of speech synthesizers (Cooper *et al.* 1963; Fant 1968; Fant and Mártoney 1962; Flanagan 1965; Henke 1969; Holmes *et al.* 1964; Liberman *et al.* 1959; Liljencrants 1967; Meltzer 1970; Rosen 1958), and many of the studies in speech perception employ synthetic speech stimuli (e.g. Ladefoged and Broadbent 1957, and most of the Haskins works cited in this paper; for some recent examples, see Carlson *et al.* 1970; Fujimura 1970; Hadding-Koch and Studdert-Kennedy 1964; Janota and Liljencrants 1970; Majewski and Blasdell 1969; Rabiner *et al.* 1969; Stevens *et al.* 1969; Thompson and Hollien 1970). Experimentation with speech synthesizers had two basic purposes: (1) the construction of a model and the testing of its capabilities and limitations (By mechanically simulating a natural device, one hoped to study in exact terms the process of speech wave formation and the transfer (filter) function of the articulatory organs (e.g., Stevens and House 1955, 1956).); (2) the ascertainment of what acoustic variables are perceptual determinants (cues) for identification of phonetic features and phonological units (e.g., alveolarity, nasality, rounding, stress, etc.). A speech synthesizer was particularly helpful for this purpose because the experimenter could isolate a variable and by manipulating it at his own will, he could determine, through auditory judgments of the result of this manipulation, which is most relevant to perception (Cooper 1962). But often it had an unfortunate consequence of isolating a variable not only mechanically but also functionally from its interconnecting parts. The effect was somewhat like reporting that a man possessed an auditory and olfactory sensitivity of canine acuity, except that the reporter neglected the fact that the man was blind.

Experimentation with speech synthesizers will continue (I do not think that it has reached a "plateau"), as it is an essential tool not only in perceptual studies but also in validating a phonological description (Kim 1966). But the new neurophysiological trend should eventually prevail, for I think that the ultimate task in perception research is to find out just what relationship holds between the sensory input and its interpretation in the brain. Sensation is of course the awareness of events in the sensory nerves, not necessarily in the physical environment (Johannes Müller's Law). But it is still not clearly known how those events occur at the peripheral nerves, and whether, once excited, the neuronal events are faithfully transmitted to the brain or whether the central nervous system can affect the inflow of sensory data in some way. That is, is there convergence and divergence at different stages of the sensory pathway which play a role in the coding of afferent information? Galambos is quite emphatic on this point and asserts that "the simple conception of the sensory pathway as one that delivers receptor events, unchanged, to the cortex is certainly no longer tenable. The evidence is accumulating for its extensive modification at every level from the receptor upward by events originating within the nervous system itself." (Galambos 1956: 436)

It was shown, for instance, that when a shift in *attention* from one modality to another, e.g., from auditory to visual, occurs, there was a suppression of cortical responses in non-relevant modalities. Hernández-Peón *et al.* (1956), for example, demonstrated that showing mice to a cat or blowing fish odors at him resulted in marked reduction of auditory potentials of clicks. Similarly, Davis (1964) found that auditory responses at the vertex were amplified (enhanced) in human subjects when the stimuli were involved in decision-making. This is related to what Colin Cherry (1957: 277) termed *the cocktail party problem*, the problem of explaining how one can tune in a particular speaker but tune out others in the presence of a multitude of competing noises as at a cocktail party. There is some indication that the reticular formation, a small finger-sized fiber bundle in the brain stem, is largely responsible for this kind of screening and channel-switching activity (French 1957; Woodburne 1967; 251ff.). Apparently acting like a sentinel, it monitors both ascending and descending neural pathways, regulating such responses as arousal, habituation, attention, etc., by enhancing or inhibiting the sensory inflow. Just what role, if any, the reticular formation plays in speech perception is not known, although one can ask a number of interesting questions. For example, is the reticular formation functionally related to what is called *acquired similarity* and *acquired distinction* (Liberman 1957) in phoneme perception? That is, when one tunes out allophonic differences, is it done at the cortex, at the brain stem, or at the ear? Just what does it mean, neurophysiologically, to say that:

We take for granted that phonetic representations describe a perceptual reality. Our problem is to provide an explanation for this fact. Notice, however, that there is nothing to suggest that these phonetic representations also describe a physical or acoustic reality in any detail...A speaker who utilizes the principle of the transformational cycle and the Compound and Nuclear Stress Rules should "hear" the stress contour of the utterance that he perceives and understands, whether or not it is physically present in any detail. (Chomsky and Halle 1968: 25)

How are one's internalized rules projected (again neurophysiologically) onto the incoming sensory signals to predict perceived phonetic shapes? I do not doubt for a moment that the brain is capable of hearing something which is not there, of imposing certain modes of interpretation on varying sensory data to achieve constant perception, or of adjusting its grid lines so that varying perception is made from constant stimuli (e.g., Ladefoged and Broadbent 1957). Notice, for example, a quite dramatic result in auditory perception obtained by Blesser (1969). He rotated the acoustic spectrum of natural speech at a center frequency of 1600 cps so that a component at 200 cps would emerge at 3000 cps, 300 at 2900 cps, 400 at 2800 cps, etc. Six pairs of subjects had three half-hour sessions per week of talking and listening to this inverted speech, and at the end of the seventh week, after a period of probing and readjusting, the subjects reached a stage where they could carry out normal conversation! (It reminds me of the brain's reversal interpretation of retinal images. The image made by the non-refracting X-rays and therefore *not* inverted upon the retina nonetheless would appear upside down! Cf. Gardner 1968: 207.) The linguistic implications of such findings on model building (models of sensory coding in speech) should be clear. Thus, once more, future phonetic studies point to a neurophysiological pathway.

To mention now a few more specific issues, an item of interest to note is an accumulation of indications that vowels and consonants have different modes of production and perception. Perkell (1969), for example, on the basis of his cineradiographic observations develops the notion that the vowel-producing system is different from the consonant-producing system, i.e., vowel production employs in the main the slower extrinsic tongue muscles (the genioglossus, the styloglossus, the palatoglossus, and the hyoglossus), while consonant production involves the above for gross positioning of the tongue body plus the faster, geometrically more complex, and more precise intrinsic musculature (the superior and the inferior longitudinals, the transverse, and the vertical) for local articulation.

On the perception side, the Haskins group (cf. Liberman 1957; Liberman *et al.* 1963; Stevens *et al.* 1969) found that vowels are less categorically perceived than consonants (but cf. Chistovich *et al.* 1966) and there is abundant evidence from dichotic listening tests (e.g., Halwes 1969; Kimura 1967; Shankweiler 1970; Studdert-Kennedy and Shankweiler 1970) that there is hemispheric lateralization in speech perception so that only consonants have the right-ear advantage.

These findings that there seem to be two separate neuro-muscular systems for consonants and vowels have a theoretical implication in that they mitigate one of the virtues of distinctive feature theory, i.e., having the same set of classificatory parameters for both consonants and vowels. Phonetic classification à la IPA uses two sets of criteria, one for consonants (e.g., *labial, alveolar, stop, fricative,* etc.) and another for vowels (*front, back, rounded,* etc.). Now the distinctive feature system uses only one and the same set of criteria for all speech sounds, e.g., *grave, diffuse, vocalic,* etc. (now *coronal, anterior, syllabic,* etc.). For some features like *voicing* and *nasality,* I think the uniformity of the system is desirable. There is no reason to treat vowel voicing differently from consonant voicing in stating, for example, the voiced environment in which voiceless consonants become voiced. But there is a question whether features like *grave* or *diffuse* actually constitute a natural class in any language. That is, unless one finds a case where a rule of the form [−grave] → [+grave] affects all the [−grave] segments regardless of their membership in the consonantal/vocalic class, i.e., unless a class (natural?) of sounds like *i, e, t, s, n, c,* etc. changes to *u, o, p, f, m, k,* etc. respectively, as a single process, the uniformity is not really advantageous but rather a spurious one, and the recent findings that the two classes have two different neuro-muscular systems perhaps supports the traditional way of dichotomizing speech sounds into two major classes, vowels and consonants, and of using separate criteria for further subdivisions.

It is also interesting to note that the theory of distinctive features which was in full swing by 1967 went on a parallel path. That is, symptomatic of the change in the trend from acoustics to physiology, the Jakobsonian distinctive features in *Preliminaries to speech analysis* (1951) which were largely acoustic (e.g., *flat, sharp, grave, diffuse,* etc.) took articulatory shapes in their revised system in Chomsky and Halle's *Sound pattern of English* (1968).

One last word about distinctive features. A good notational system is important in any scientific field. Note the effects and advantages of the Arabic number system over the Roman number system. In chemistry similarly, element notations such as H_2O, C_2H_4 are much more explanatory than the ordinary names of objects, 'water,' 'ethylene,' as the former notation shows individual elements in the compound and can explain why ethylene and water produce ethanol, i.e.,

$$C_2H_4 \ + \ H_2O \ \rightarrow \ C_2H_5OH \text{ (cf. Ohala 1970:13)}$$

Likewise, the distinctive feature system has a linguistically significant advantage over the atomistic IPA system (cf. Halle 1962; Kim 1971b). But

Chomsky and Halle's system is far from ideal and perfect. Just as element notations in chemistry do not show the specific bond relations among molecules within a compound, I feel that some distinctive features still do not correctly reflect many relevant facts of sound.

As an example, let us take the feature *voicing* and its related phenomena. The first series of facts to consider is that voicing and tone are related in such a way that a low tone seems to induce voicing, a high tone, voicelessness, and vice versa (e.g., "a low rising pitch (after the consonantal release) leads to perception of an initial stop consonant as voiced, while a high falling pitch leads to perception as voiceless." Haggard *et al.* 1970:617). Welmers (1970) for example observed in Kpelle that a low tone makes initial obstruents voiced and converts initial sonorants to low-tone nasals, and Maran (1971) observed that in Tibeto-Burmese languages the tone is predictable from the voicing of the syllable-final consonant. The second series of facts is that ejectives are always voiceless, while implosives are always voiced. And thirdly, voicing and aspiration are related in such a way that they form a single continuum. It is, of course, possible to account for this kind of implicational phenomena by writing a set of redundancy rules. But this would be an arbitrary way of stating the phenomena. It would be nice if our phonetic system were such that this kind of redundancy was inherently built into the system. After all, there are good reasons why these various phenomena are related. Voicing is, of course, made with the vibrating vocal folds. During the vibration, air continuously flows through the glottis from the lungs to the upper vocal tract. If the tract is wide open, as in vowels, the airflow can proceed with no difficulty. But when there is a constriction in the tract, as in obstruent consonants, there is a limit as to how much air can flow into the closed cavity. As more air flows into the oral cavity, the pressure in the cavity becomes higher. If no adjustment is made, this increasing pressure equalizes the pressure differential across the glottis and the voicing stops. In order to prevent this from happening, one can do a little adjustment in the tract; increase the cavity size to accommodate the airflow. Though one can blow out one's cheeks to achieve this purpose, this is normally not done in speaking. Instead, what is done is to lower the glottis. On the other hand, in tense voiceless consonants, high subglottal pressure will often push up the glottis. Now there is a correlation between the rate of vibration (i.e., pitch) and the pressure such that the higher the subglottal pressure, the higher the pitch. Thus, in high-pressured voiceless obstruents, the adjacent vowels tend to carry a higher tone than those adjacent to voiced segments which, due to the constantly escaping air, have a lower subglottal pressure. As for ejectives, the tightly closed glottis is raised to compress the air inside the oral tract. Loosening the tight glottal closure will result in airflow which prevents the tract air from being compressed. Thus, the tight closure is kept, and hence no voicing. In implosives, the rarefaction of the tract air is created by the lowering of the glottis. Now, this lowering of the glottis simultaneously compresses the lung air, and since air flows from areas of high pressure to areas of low pressure, the air will eventually flow from the lungs to the rarefied upper tract, resulting in the vibration of the vocal folds. As for aspiration, Kim (1970a) showed that it is a function of the glottal opening at the time of the release of an oral closure, i.e., the more open the glottis at the time of release, the more aspiration.

Taking all these facts into consideration, Maran proposed the following four *glottal features*, dispensing with voicing and pressure features: (1) raised, (2) lowered, (3) spread, and (4) constricted. Raised glottis would entail voicelessness and/or high tone, and lowered glottis, voicedness and/or low tone, and spread glottis would yield aspiration, while constricted glottis would be functional in glottalic sounds (ejectives, implosives, creaky sounds, etc.). Since combinations of $\begin{bmatrix} + \text{raised} \\ + \text{lowered} \end{bmatrix}$ and $\begin{bmatrix} + \text{spread} \\ + \text{constr} \end{bmatrix}$ are *a priori* impossible, one can have nine different combinations of these four features, corresponding to nine different types of segments. *Table 1* on the following page which is adapted from Bird (1971:155) gives bilabial stops as examples.

Although I would not assert that these proposed glottal features are absolutely correct (for a more recent suggestion on laryngeal features, see Halle and Stevens 1971), it appears to me that they at least explain a range of related phenomena in a more natural and insightful way than the *Preliminaries* or the *Sound pattern of English* system. Experimental phonetics should provide bases for revision of old features and adoption of new explanatory features. (For some recent experimental studies of features and further discussion, see Ahmed and Agrawal 1969; Fant 1969; Halle and Stevens 1969, 1971; Kim 1971b; Lieberman 1970; and Lindblom and Sundberg 1969.)

	aspirated	partially voiced	implosive	unaspirated	ejective	lax[1]	creaky[2]	voiced aspir.[3]	fully voiced
	[pʰ]	Eng. initial [b]	[b]	Fr. [p]	[p']	Kor. [p*]	Hausa [?b]	[bʱ]	Fr. [b]
raised	+	–	–	+	+	–	–	–	–
lowered	–	–	+	–	–	–	–	+	+
spread	+	–	–	–	–	+	–	+	–
constricted	–	–	+	+	+	–	–	–	–

Table 1. The specification bilabial stops of various types in terms of *glottal features.*
[1]cf. Kim 1965
[2]cf. Ladefoged 1968: 6, 10, 16
[3]cf. Catford 1964

Let me conclude. I have said that all organisms have limited capacities that are due to their self-structures. Man is not fundamentally different from other creatures in this respect. In fact, there is no device, natural or artificial, which is totally free from its own structural limitations. The capabilities of a machine or a computer are a function of its design and programming. In this respect, man's brain can be likened to a computer, and as such it serves as a biological matrix into which its output is mappable. Thus, the search for innate linguistic behavior is, as Lenneberg (1967:394) concludes, within the scope of neurophysiological inquiry. The 19th century French physiologist Fournié remarked: "Speech is the only window through which the physiologist can view the cerebral life" (quoted in Lashley (1951). Perhaps the inverse path is just as true, that is, the brain may be the only window through which the linguist can view the life of language.

Nineteenth century linguists primarily defined the subject matter of linguistics, the relationship between languages, what is regular and what is not in linguistic changes, etc. Two thirds of twentieth century linguistics was spent in determining how languages are diversified into dialects, how changes are made, how sounds are produced, how sentences are generated, how linguistic theories are constructed, how rules are formulated, etc. Perhaps it is now time to ask *why* they should be so, why languages behave as they do, and it is my belief that a reasonable answer to this question will come only from an experimental investigation of the brain which is certainly not made of green cheese (a Harvard psychologist Jerome Bruner (1957:340) confessed that once he held the view that he couldn't care less if the brain was made of green cheese. He no longer holds such a view.).

Experimentation in search of answers to these questions will involve enormous complexities and will "require the combined expertise of several disciplines which have human behavior as their subject matter" (Wang 1968:55): linguistics, phonetics, psychology, neurology, physiology, biochemistry, bioengineering, etc. Distant as the goal may be, I still retain the hope that some day we will attain it.

References

For further discussion of the general issues touched on in this paper, a reader would profit from reading Fujimura (1970a), Ladefoged (1967), and Laver (1970). For a good annotated bibliography on articulatory phonetics, see Uldall (1970).

Abbreviations

JASA	=	Journal of the Acoustic Society of America
JSHD	=	Journal of Speech and Hearing Disorders
JSHR	=	Journal of Speech and Hearing Research
MIT-RLE-QPR	=	Quarterly Progress and Status Report Laboratory of Electronics, Massachusetts Institute of Technology
RIT-STL-QPSR	=	Quarterly Progress and Status Report, Speech Transmission Laboratory, Royal Institute of Technology, Stockholm, Sweden

Abercrombie, D. 1965. *Forgotten Phoneticians*. Studies in phonetics and linguistics, 45-75. London: Oxford University Press.

Abercrombie, D. 1967. *Elements of General Phonetics*. Chicago: Aldine Publishing Co.

Ahmed, R. and S. S. Agrawal. 1969. Significant Features in the Perception of (Hindi) Consonants. *JASA* 45. 758-63.

Ainsworth, W. A. 1976. *Mechanisms of Speech Recognition*. Oxford: Pergamon Press Ltd.

Allen, G. 1968. The Place of Rhythm in a Theory of Language. UCLA Working Papers in Phonetics 10.60-84.

Allen, G. 1970. The Location of Rhythmic Stress Beats in English: An Experimental Study. UCLA Working Papers in Phonetics 14.80-132.

Amerman, J. D. and R. Daniloff. 1970. Lip and Jaw Coarticulation for the Phoneme /ae/. *JSHR* 13.147-61.

Bird, C. S. 1971. Observations on Initial Consonant Change in Southwestern Mande. Papers in African Linguistics, ed. by C-W. Kim and H.S. Stahlke, 153-74. Edmonton/Champaign: Linguistic Research, Inc.

Blesser, B. A. 1969. *Spectral Transformation as a Psycholinguistic Technique: A Summary*. [Cf. B. A. Blesser. 1969. Perception of Spectally Rotated Speech. Unpublished Ph.D. dissertation. Cambridge: MIT]. *MIT-RLE-QPR* 94.249-53.

Boomer, D. S. and J. D. M. Laver. 1968. Slips of the Tongue. *British Journal of Disorders of Communication* 3:1.1-12.

Borovičková, B., V. Malač, and S. Pauli. 1970. F2-Transition in the Perception of Czech Stops. *RIT-STL-QPSR* 1970.1:14-15.

Brazier, Mary. 1960. Long-persisting Electrical Traces in the Brain of Man and their Possible Relationship to Higher Nervous Activity. *EEG Journal Supplement* 13.347-58.

Bruner, J. S. 1957. Neural Mechanisms in Perception. Psychological Review 64.340-58.

Carlson, R., B. Grandstrom, and G. Fant. 1970. Some Studies Concerning Perception of Isolated Vowels. *RIT-STL-QPSR* 1970.2/3:19-35.

Carterette, E. C. (ed.). 1966. *Brain Function*, Vol. 3 (*Speech, Language, and Communication*). UCLA Forum in Medical Sciences No. 4. Berkeley and Los Angeles: University of California Press.

Catford, J. C. 1964. *Phonation Types: The Classification of Some Laryngeal Components of Speech Production*. In Honor of Daniel Jones, ed. by D. Abercrombie *et al.*, 26-37. London: Longmans.

Cherry, C. 1957. *On Human Communication*. New York: Science Editions, Inc.

Chistovich, L. A., G. Fant, and A. de SerpaLeitão. 1966. Mimicking and Perception of Synthetic Vowels.*RIT-STL-QPSR* 1966.3:1-3.

Chomsky, N. and M. Halle. 1968. *The Sound Pattern of English*. New York: Harper and Row.

Cooper, F. S. 1958. *Some Input-Output Relations Observed in Experiments on the Perception of Speech*. Second International Congress of Cybernetics, 930-41. Namur, Belgium.

Cooper, F. S. 1962. *Speech Synthesizers*. Proceedings of the Fourth International Congress of Phonetic Sciences, ed. by A. Sovijärvi and P. Aalto, 3-13. The Hague: Mouton.

Cooper, F. S. 1965. Research Techniques and Instrumentation: EMG. American Speech and Hearing Association Reports 1.153-68.

Cooper, F. S., A. M. Liberman, L. Lisker, and J. J. Gaitenby. 1963. *Speech Synthesis by Rules*. Proceedings of the Speech Communication Seminar, Vol. 2, Paper F2. Stockholm: Royal Institute of Technology.

Daniloff, R. G. 1967. A Cinefluorographic Study of Selected Aspects of Coarticulation of Speech Sounds. Unpublished Ph.D. dissertation. Iowa City: University of Iowa.

Daniloff, R. and K. Moll. 1968. Coarticulation in Lip Rounding. *JSHR* 11.707-21.

Darley, F. L. (ed.). 1967. *Brain Mechanisms Underlying Speech and Language*. New York: Grune and Stratton.

David, E. and P. Denes. 1972. *Human Communication: A Unified View*. N.Y.: McGraw-Hill Book Co.

Davis, H. 1964. Enchantment of Evoked Cortical Potentials in Humans Related to a Task Requiring a Decision. *Science* 145.182-83. [Reprinted in Gross and Zeigler 1969, 278-81.]

Delattre, P. 1967. A Dialect Study of American *r*'s by X-ray Motion-Picture. The General Phonetic Characteristic of Languages, 5-80. Santa Barbara: University of California.

Delattre, P. C., A. M. Liberman and F. S. Cooper. 1955. Acoustic loci and transitional cues for consonants. *JASA* 27.769-73. [Reprinted in Ilse Lehiste (ed.) 1967, 288-92.]

Denes, P., 1967. *On the Motor Theory of Speech Perception: Models for the Perception of Speech and Visual Form*, ed. by W. Wathen-Dunn, 309-13. Cambridge: The MIT Press. [Also in Proceedings of the Fifth International Congress of Phonetic Sciences, ed. by E. Zwirner and W. Bethge, 252-58 (1965). Basal, Switzerland: S. Karger.]

Derkach, M. 1970. Heuristic Models for Automatic Recognition of Spoken Words. *RIT-STL-QPSR* 1970.1:39-49.

Eldred, E., R. Granit, and P. A. Merton. 1953. Supraspinal Control of the Muscle Spindles and its Significance. *Journal of Physiology (London)* 122.498-523. [Reprinted in Gross and Zeigler 1969, 243-269.]

Faaborg-Anderson, K., N. Yanagihara, and H. von Leden. 1967. *Vocal Pitch and Intensity Regulation.* Archibes of Oto-Laryngology 85.448-54.

Fairbanks, G. 1954. *A Theory of the Speech Mechanism as a Servosystem. JSHD* 19.133-39.

Fairbanks, G. and N. Guttman. 1958. *Effects of delayed auditory feedback upon articulation. JSHR* 1.12-22.

Fant, G. 1968a. Analysis and Synthesis of Speech Processes. Manual of Phonetics, 2nd Ed., ed. by B. Malmberg, 173-277. Amsterdam: North-Holland Publishing Co.

Fant, G. 1968b. Models of Speech Perception. Zeitschrift für Phonetik, Sprachwissenschaft und Kommunikationsforschung 21.5-8.

Fant, G. 1969. Distinctive Features and Phonetic Dimensions. *RIT-STL-QPSR* 1969.2/3:1-18.

Fant, G. 1970. Automatic Recognition and Speech Research. *RIT-STL-QPSR* 1970.1:16-31.

Fant, G. (ed.). 1974. *Speech Communication.* N.Y.: John Wiley & Sons.

Fant, G. and J. Martony. 1962. Speech Synthesis. *RIT-STL-QPSR* 1962.2:18-24.

Fischer-Jørgensen, Eli. 1968. Voicing, Tenseness and Aspiration in Stop Consonants, with Special Reference to French and Danish. University of Copenhagen Institute of Phonetics Annual Report 3.63-114.

Flanagan, J. L. 1965. *Speech Analysis, Synthesis, and Perception.* Berlin: Springer-Verlag.

French, J. D. 1957., The Reticular Formation. *Scientific American* (May) 54-60. [Reprinted in *Psychobiology: Readings from Scientific American*, 232-39 (1967). San Francisco: W. H. Freeman and Co.]

Fritzell, B. 1969. The Velopharyngeal Muscles in Speech: An Electromyographic and Cinefluorographic Study. Acta Oto-Laryngologica, Supplement 250.

Fromkin, Victoria. 1965. Some Phonetic Specifications of Linguistic Units: An Electromyographic Investigation. UCLA Working Papers in Phonetics No. 3.

Fromkin, Victoria. 1968. Neuromuscular Specification of Linguistic Units. *Language and Speech* 9.170-99.

Fromkin, Victoria. 1968. Speculations on Performance Models. *Journal of Linguistics* 4.47-68.

Fromkin, Victoria. 1970. Tips of the Slung or To Err is Human. UCLA Working Papers in Phonetics 14.40-79. [= The Non-Anomalous Nature of Anomalous Utterances. Lg. 47.27-52 (1971).]

Fromkin, Victoria and P. Ladefoged. 1966. Electromyography in Speech Research. *Phonetica* 15.219-42.

Fry, D. B. 1955. Duration and Intensity as Physical Correlates of Linguistic Stress. *JASA* 35.765-69. [Reprinted in Ilse Lehiste (ed.) 1969, 155-58.]

Fry, D. B. 1964. The Functions of the Syllable. *Zeitschrift für Phonetik, Sprachwissenschaft und Kommunikationsforschung* 17.215-37.

Fujii, I. 1970. Phoneme Identification with Dynamic Palatography. University of Tokyo Research Institute of Logopedics and Phoniatrics Annual Bulletin 4.67-73.

Fujimura, O. 1961. Bilabial Stop and Nasal Consonants: A Motion Picture Study and its Acoustic Implications. *JSHR* 4.233-47.

Fujimura, O. 1970a. Current Issues in Experimental Phonetics. Studies in General and Oriental Linguistics (Presented to Shiro Hattori on the occasion of his sixtieth birthday), ed. by R. Jakobson and S. Kawamoto, 109-30. Tokyo: TEC Corporation, Ltd.

Fujimura, O. 1970b. Remarks on Stop Consonants—Synthesis Experiments and Acoustic Cues. University of Tokyo Research Institute of Logopedics and Phoniatrics Annual Bulletin 4.75-88.

Fujimura, O., S. Kiritani, and H. Ishida. 1969. Digitally Controlled Dynamic Radiography. University of Tokyo Research Institute of Logopedics and Phoniatrics Annual Bulletin 3.1-34.

Galambos, R. 1956. Suppression of Auditory Nerve Activity by Stimulation of Efferent Fibers to Cochlea *Journal Neurophysiology* 19.424-37. [Reprinted in Landauer 1967, 3-16.]

Galambos, R. 1962. *Nerves and Muscles*. New York: Doubleday. (Anchor Book Science Study Series, S25)

Gardner, E. 1968. *Fundamentals of Neurology* 5th Ed. Philadelphia: W. B. Saunders.

Gendron, J-D. 1962. La Méthode Radiographique Appliqueé à la Comparaison des Articulations Vocaliques en Français Canadien et en Français Parisien. Proceedings of the Fourth International Congress of Phonetic Sciences, ed. by A. Sovijärvi and P. Aalto, 155-66. The Hague: Mouton.

Gilbert, J. H. (ed.). 1972. *Speech and Cortical Functioning*. N.Y.: Academic Press.

Gonzales, A. 1970. Acoustic Correlates of Accent, Rhythm, and Intonation in Tagalog. *Phonetica* 22.11-44.

Gross, C. G. and H. P. Zeigler, (eds.). 1969. *Readings in physiological psychology: Neurophysiology/Sensory Processes*. New York: Harper and Row.

Gulanov, V. I. and L. A. Chistovich. 1965. Relationship of Motor Theory to the General Problems of Speech Recognition. *Akusticheskii Zhurnal*11.417-26. [English translation in *Soviet-Physics-Acoustics*11.357-65, 1966.]

Hadding-Koch, K. and M. Studdert-Kennedy. 1964. An Experimental Study of some Intonation Contours. *Phonetica* 11.175-85.

Haggard, M., S. Ambler, and M. Callow. 1970. Pitch as a Voicing Cue. *JASA* 47.613-17.

Halle, M. 1962. Phonology in Generative Grammar. *Word* 18.54-72. [Reprinted in *The Structure of Language,* ed. by J. Fodor and J. Katz, 344-52. Englewood Cliffs: Prentice Hall, 1964.]

Halle, M. G. W. Hughes, and J. P. A. Radley. 1957. Acoustic Properties of Stop Consonants. *JASA* 29.107-16. [Reprinted in Ilse Lehiste(ed.) 1969, 170-79.]

Halle, M. and K. N. Stevens. 1964. Speech Recognition: A Model and a Program for Research. *The Structure of Language,* ed. by J. Fodor and J. Katz, 604-12. Englewood Cliffs: Prentice-Hall, Inc.

Halle, M. and K. N. Stevens. 1969. On the feature "Advanced Tongue Root." *MIT-RLE-QPR* 94.209-15.

Halle, M. and K. N. Stevens. 1971. A Note on Laryngeal Features. *MIT-RLE-QPR* 101.198-213.

Halwes, T. 1969. Effects of Dichotic Fusion in the Perception of Speech. Unpublished Ph.D. dissertation. Minneapolis: University of Minnesota.

Hardcastle, W. 1969. A System of Dynamic Palatography. Edinburgh University Department of Linguistics Work in Progress 3.47-52.

Hardcastle, W. 1970. Electropalatography in Speech Research. Univ. of Essex Language Centre Occasional Papers 9.54-64.

Hardcastle, W. J. 1976. *Physiology of Speech Production. N.Y.: Academic Press.*

Harris, Katherine S., G. G. Lysaught, and M. M. Schvey. 1965. Some Aspects of the Production of Oral and Nasal Labial Stops. *Language and Speech* 8.135-47.

Hayes, J. R. and H. H. Clark. 1970. *Experiments on the Segmentation of an Artificial Speech Analogue: Cognition and the Development of Language,* ed. by J. R. Hayes, 221-34. New York: J. Wiley & Sons.

Hebb, D. O. 1949. *The Organization of Behavior.* New York: J. Wiley & Sons.

Henke, W. L. 1966. Dynamic Articulatory Model of Speech Production. Presented at the 72nd Meeting of the Acoustical Society of America. Los Angeles.

Henke, W. L. 1969. TASS—Another Terminal Analog Speech Synthesis System. *MIT-RLE-QPR* 95.73-81.

Hernández-Peón, R., H. Scherrer, and M. Jouvet. 1956. Modification of Electric Activity in Cochlear Nucleus during "Attention" in Unanesthetized Cats. *Science* 123:331-32. [Reprinted in Gross and Zeigler 1969, 270-73; and in Landauer 1967, 208-12.]

Hirano, M., J. Ohala, and W. Vennard. 1969. The Function of Laryngeal Muscles in Regulating Fundamental Frequency and Intensity of Phonation. *JSHR* 12.616-28.

Hirose, J., Z. Simada, and O. Fujimura. 1970. An Electromyographic Study of the Activity of the Laryngeal Muscles during Speech Utterances., University of Tokyo Research Institute of Logopedics and Phoniatrics Annual Bulletin 4.9-25.

Hockett, C. F. 1967. *Where the Tongue Slips, There Slip I.* To Honor Roman Jakobson, Vol. II, 910-36. The Hague: Mouton.

Hodgkin, A. L. 1964. The Ionic Basis of Nervous Conduction. *Science* 145.1148-154. [Reprinted in Gross and Zeigler 1969, 5-20.]

Hofmann, T. R. 1967. Initial Clusters in English, *MIT-RLE-QPR* 84.263-74

Hollien, H., R. Coleman, and P. Moore. 1968. Stroboscopic Laminagraphy of the Larynx during Phonation. *Acta Ota-Laryngologica* 65.209-15

Holmes, J. N., I. G. Mattingly, and J. N. Shearme. 1964. Speech Synthesis by Rule. *Language and Speech* 7.127-43.

Jakobson, R. 1941. *Kindersprache, Aphasie und Allgemeine Lautgesetze.* Selected Writings, Vol. I, 328-401. The Hague: Mouton. [English translation by A. R. Keiler. *1968. Child Language, Aphasia and Phonological Universals.* The Hague: Mouton.]

Jakobson, R., G. Fant, and M. Halle. 1951. *Preliminaries to Speech Analysis.* Cambridge: The MIT Press.

Jakobson, R. and M. Halle. 1964. *Tenseness and Laxness*. In Honor of Daniel Jones, ed. by D. Abercrombie *et al.*, 96-101. London: Longmans. [Reprinted in Jakobson, Fant and Halle 1951, 57-61.]

Janota, P. and J. Liljencrants. 1970. The Effect of Fundamental Frequency Changes on the Perception of Stress by Czech Listeners. *RIT-STL-QPSR* 1969.4:32-38.

Jones, D. 1959. *An Outline of English Phonetics*. New York: E. P. Dutton.

Kelsey, C. A., F. D. Minifie, and T. J. Hixon. 1969. Applications of Ultra-Sound in Speech Research. *JSHR* 12.564-75.

Kelsey, C. A., R. J. Woodhouse, and F. D. Minifie. 1969. Ultrasonic Observations of Coarticulation in the Pharynx. *JASA* 46.1016-1018.

Kim, C-W. 1965. On the Autonomy of the Tensity Feature in Stop Classification, with Special Reference to Korean Stops. *Word* 21.339-59.

Kim, C-W. 1966. The Role of a Speech Synthesizer. UCLA Working Papers in Phonetics 5.16-26.

Kim, C-W. 1968. Review of Lieberman 1967. *Language* 44.830-42.

Kim, C-W. 1970a. A Theory of Aspiration. *Phonetica* 21.107-16.

Kim, C-W. 1970b. Review of Perkell 1969. *General Linguistics* 10.182-93.

Kim, C-W. 1971a. A New Direction in Phonetics. *Language Sciences* 16.35-40.

Kim, C-W. 1971b. From Segments to Features. To appear.

Kim, C-W. 1971c. Opposition and Complement in Phonology. To appear in *Papers in Linguistic in Honor of Renee and Henry Kahane*, ed. by B. B. Kachru *et al.* Urbana: University of Illinois Press.

Kimura, Doreen. 1967. Functional Asymmetry of the Brain in Dichotic Listening. *Cortex* 3.163-78.

Kiparsky, P. 1968, *Linguistic Universals and Linguistic Change: Universals in Linguistic Theory*, Ed. by E. Bach and R. T. Harms, 171-202. New York: Holt, Rinehart and Winston.

Kiritani, S. and O. Fujimura. 1970. A Preliminary Experiment of the Observation of the Hyoid Bone by Means of Digitally Controlled Dynamic Radiography. University of Tokyo Research Institute of Logopedics and Phoniatrics Annual Bulletin 4.1-7.

Knutsson, E., A. and B. Mårtensson. 1969. The Normal EMG in Human Vocal Muscles. *Acta Oto-Laryngologica* 68.526-36.

Kozhevnikov, V. A. and L. A. Chistovich. 1965. *Rech: Artikulyatsia i Vospriyatiye*. Moskva-Leningrad. [English translation by Joint Publications Research Service, U.S. Department of Commerce: Speech: Articulation and Perception, 1966.]

Krmpotić, Jelena. 1959. Données Anatomiques et Histologiques Relatives aus Effecteurs Laryngo-pharyngo-buccaus. *Revue de Laryngologie* 11.829-48.

Kydd, W. L. and D. A. Belt. 1964. Continuous Palatography. *JSHD* 29.489-92.

Ladefoged, P. 1962a. *Elements of Acoustic Phonetics.* Chicago: University of Chicago Press.

Ladefoged, P. 1962b. Sub-Glottal Activity during Speech. Proceedings of the Fourth International Congress of Phonetic Sciences, ed. by A. Sovijärvi and P. Aalto, 73-91. The Hague: Mouton.

Ladefoged, P. 1967. *Units in the Perception and Production of Speech: Three Areas of Experimental Phonetics,* 143-72. London: Oxford University Press.

Ladefoged, P. 1968. *A Phonetic Study of West African Languages.* 2nd Ed., Cambridge (London): Cambridge University Press.

Ladefoged, P. and D. E. Broadbent. 1957. Information Conveyed by Vowels. *JASA* 29.98-104. [Reprinted in Lehiste (ed.) 1967, 326-32.]

Landauer, T. K. (ed.). 1967. *Readings in Physiological Psychology.* New York: McGraw-Hill.

Lane, H. 1965. The Motor Theory of Speech Perception: A Critical Review. *Psychological Review* 72.275-309.

Lashley, K. S. 1950. *In Search of the Engram.* Society of Experimental Biology Symposium No. 4: *Physiological Mechanisms in Animal Behavior.* 478-505. Cambridge (England): Cambridge University Press. [Reprinted in Landauer 1967, 287-313.]

Lashley, K. S. 1951. The problem of serial order in behaviour. *Cerebral Mechanisms in Behavoir,* ed. by L. A. Jeffress, 112-36. New York: J. Wiley & Sons. [Reprinted in *Psycholinguistics,* ed. by S. Saporta, 180-98. New York: Holt, Rinehard and Winston, 1961 and in Landauer 1967. 480-501.]

Lass, N. J. (ed.). 1976. *Contemporary Issues in Experimental Phonetics.* N.Y.: Academic Press.

Laver, J. 1970. *The Production of Speech. New Horizons in Linguistics,* ed. by J. Lyons, 53-75. Middlesex (England): Penguin Books Ltd.

Lehiste, Ilse. 1961. Some Acoustic Correlates of Accent in Serbo-Croatian. *Phonetica* 7.114-47.

Lehiste, Ilse (ed.). 1967. *Readings in Acoustic Phonetics.* Cambridge: The MIT Press.

Lehiste, Ilse. 1970. Temporal Organization of Spoken Language. Ohio State University Working Papers in Linguistics 4.95-114.

Lehiste, Ilse, and G. E. Peterson. 1959. Vowel Amplitude and Phonemic Stress in American English. *JASA* 31.428-35. [Reprinted in Ilse Lehiste, (ed.) 1967, 183-90.]

Lenneberg, E. H. 1967. *Biological Foundations of Language.* New York: J. Wiley & Sons.

Liberman, A. M. 1957. Some Results of Research on Speech Perception. *JASA* 29.117-23. [Reprinted in *Psycholinguistics* ed. by S. Saporta, 142-53. New York: Holt, Rinehart and Winston, 1961.]

Liberman, A. M., F. S. Cooper, Katherine S. Harris, and P. F. MacNeilage. 1963. A Motor Theory of Speech Perception. Proceedings of Speech Communication Seminar, Vol.2., Paper D3. Stockholm: Royal Institute of Technology, 1962.

Liberman, A. M., F. S. Cooper, Katherine S. Harris, P. F. MacNeilage and M. Studdert-Kennedy. 1967. *Some Observations on a Model for Speech Perception: Models for the Perception of Speech and Visual Form,* ed. by W. Wathen-Dunn, 68-87. Cambridge: The MIT Press.

Liberman, A. M. P. C. Delattre, L. J. Gerstman, and F. S. Cooper. 1956. Tempo of Frequency Change as a Cue for Distinguishing Classes of Speech Sounds. *Journal of Experimental Psychology* 52.127-37. [Reprinted in Ilse Lehiste (ed.) 1967, 159-169.]

Liberman, A. M., Francis Ingemann, L. Lisker, P. C. Delattre, and F. S. Cooper. 1959. Minimal Rules for Synthesizing Speech. *JASA* 31.1490-1499.

Lieberman, P. 1960. Some Acoustic Correlates of Word Stress in American English. *JASA* 32.451-54.

Lieberman, P. 1967. *Intonation, Perception, and Language.* Cambridge: The MIT Press.

Lieberman, P. 1970. Towards a Unified Phonetic Theory. *Linguistic Inquiry* 1.307-22.

Lieberman, P. 1977. *Speech Physiology and Acoustic Phonetics: An Introduction.* N.Y.: Macmillan Publishing Co., Inc.

Lieberman, P., R. Knudson, and J. Mead. 1969. Determination of the Rate of Change of Fundamental Frequency with Respect to Sub-Glottal Air Pressure during Sustained Phonation. *JASA* 46.1537-1543.

Lieberman, P., M. Sawashima, Katherine S. Harris, and T. Gay. 1970. The Articulatory Implementation of the Breath-Group and Prominence. *Language* 46.312.27.

Liljencrants, J. 1967. The OVE III Speech Synthesizer. *RIT-STL-QPSR* 1967.2/3:76-81.

Lindblom, B. 1965. Studies of Labial Articulation. *RIT-STL-QPSR* 1965.4:7-9.

Lindblom, B. 1968a. Vowel Duration and a Model of Lip-Mandible Coordination. *RIT-STL-QPSR* 1967.4:1-29.

Lindblom, B. 1968b. Temporal Organization of Syllable Production. *RIT-STL-QPSR* 1968.2/3:1-5.

Lindblom, B. and J. Sundberg. 1969. A Quantitative Model of Vowel Production and the Distinctive Features of Swedish Vowels. *RIT-STL-QPSR* 1969.1:14-32.

Lindqvist, J. 1969. Laryngeal Mechanisms in Speech. *RIT-STL-QPSR* 1969.2/3:26-32.

Lisker, L. and A. S. Abramson. 1964. A Cross-Language Study of Voicing in Initial Stops: Acoustical Measurements. *Word* 20.384-422.

Lisker, L., A. Abramson, F. S. Cooper, and M. H. Schvey. 1969. Transillumination of the Larynx in Running Speech. *JASA* 46.1544-1546.

Lubker, J. F. 1968. An Electromyographic-Cineradiographic Investigation of Velar Function during Normal Speech Production. *Cleft Palate Journal* 5.1-18.

Lubker, J. F., B. Fritzell, and J. Lindqvist. 1971. Velopharyngeal Function: An Electromyographic Study. *RIT-STL-QPSR* 1970.4:9-20.

Lubker, J. F. and K. L. Moll. 1965. Simultaneous Oral-Nasal Air Flow Measurements and Cinefluorographic Observation during Speech Production. *Cleft Palate Journal* 2.257-72.

Lubker, J. F. and Pamela J. Parris. 1970. Simultaneous Measurement of Intraoral Pressure, Force of Labial Contact, and Labial Electromyographic Activity during Production of the Stop Consonant Cognates /p/ and /b/. *JASA* 47.625-33.

MacKay. D. G. 1970. Spoonerisms: The Structure of Errors in the Serial Order of Speech. *Neuropsychologia* 8.323-50.

MacNeilage, P. F. 1963. Electromyographic and Acoustic Study of the Production of Certain Final Clusters. *JASA* 35.461-63.

MacNeilage, P. F. 1970. Motor Control of Serial Ordering of Speech. *Psychological Review* 77.182-196.

MacNeilage, P. F. and J. L. DeClerk. 1969. On the Motor Control of Coarticulation in CVC Monosyllables. *JASA* 45.1217-1233.

MacNeilage, P. F. and G. N. Sholes. 1964. An Electromyographic Study of the Tongue during Vowel Production. *JSHR* 7.209-32.

Malécot, A. 1970. The Lenis-Fortis Opposition: Its Physiological Parameters. *JASA* 47.1588-92.

Majewski, W. and R. Blasdell. 1969. Influence of Fundamental Frequency Cues on the Perception of some Synthetic Intonation Contours. *JASA* 45.450-57.

Malmberg, B. 1963. *Structural Linguistics and Human Communication*. New York: Academic Press.

Mansell, P. 1970. The Nature of EMB Variations. University of Essex Language Centre Occasional Papers 9.65-87.

Maran, L. R. 1971. Tones in Burmese and Jinpho. Unpublished Ph.D. dissertation. Urbana: University of Illinois.

Martinet, A. 1955. *Économie des Changements Phonétiques*. Berne, Switzerland: A. Francke.

Massengill, R., Jr., G. Quinn, W. F. Barry, Jr., and K. Pickrell. 1966. The development of Rotational Cinefluorography and its Application to Speech Research. *JSHR* 9.259-65.

McCawley, J. D. 1969. Length and Voicing in Tübatulabal. Papers from the Fifth Regional Meeting of Chicago Linguistic Society, 407-15.

Medress, M. F. 1969. Computer Recognition of Single-Syllable Words Spoken in Isolation. *MIT-RLE-QPR* 92.338-51.

Meltzer, D. 1970. Speech Synthesis Project. Ohio State University Working Papers in Linguistics 6.59-65.

Minifie, F. *et al.* (eds.). 1973. *Normal Aspects of Speech, Hearing, and Language*. Englewood Cliffs: Prentice-Hall, Inc.

Moll, K. L. 1960. Cinefluorographic Techniques in Speech Research. *JSHR* 3.227-41.

Moll, K. L. 1962. Velopharyngeal Closure on Vowels. *JSHR* 5.30-37.

Moore, P., F. D. White, and H. von Leden. 1962. The Importance of Ultra-High Speed Photography in Laryngeal Physiology. *JSHD* 27.155-71.

Morrell, R. M., K. Frank, M. G. F. Fuortes, and M. C. Becker. 1956. Site of Origin of Motoneurone Rhythms Physiology Congress Abstracts 20.660.61.

Morris, D. 1967. *The Naked Ape*. New York: McGraw-Hill.

Ohala, J. 1966. A New Photo-Electric Glottograph. UCLA Working Papers in Phonetics 4.40-53.

Ohala, J. 1970. Aspects of the Control and Production of Speech. UCLA Working Papers in Phonetics No. 15.

Ohala, J., S. Hiki, S. Hubler, and R. Harshman. 1968. Photo-Electric Methods of Transducing Lip and Jaw Movements in Speech. UCLA Working Papers in Phonetics 10.135-44.

Ohala, J. and H. Hirose. 1970. The Function of the Sternohyoid Muscle in Speech. University of Tokyo Research Institute of Logopedics and Phoniatrics Annual Bulletin 4.41-44.

Ohala, J. and P. Ladefoged. 1970. Further Investigation of Pitch Regulation in Speech. UCLA Working Papers in Phonetics 14.12-24.

Öhman, S. 1967. Peripheral Motor Commands in Labial Articulation. *RIT-STL-QPSR* 1967.4:30-63.

Öhman, S., R. Leanderson, and A. Persson. 1965. 1966. Electromyographic Studies of Facial Muscles during Speech. *RIT-STL-QPSR* 1965.3:1-11; 1966.1:1-4.

Öhman, S., A. Persson, and R. Leanderson. 1967. Speech Production at the Neuro-Muscular Level. *RIT-STL-APSR* 1967.2/3:15-19.

Ondráčková, Jana, and R. Poch. 1962. New Roentgenographic Methods in the Research of the Activity of Articulatory Organs. *Indian Journal of Radiology* 16.137-50.

Osgood, C. E. and M. S. Miron. 1963. *Approaches to the Study of Aphasia.* Urbana: University of Illinois Press.

Penfield, W. and L. Roberts. 1959. *Speech and Brain Mechanisms.* Princeton: Princeton University Press.

Perkell, J. S. 1969. *Physiology of Speech Production: Results and Implications of a Quantitative Cineradiographic Study.* Cambridge: The MIT Press.

Rabiner, L. R., H. Levitt, and A. E. Rosenberg. 1969. Investigation of Stress Pattern for Speech Synthesis by Rule. *JASA* 45.92-101.

Ramishvili, G. 1970. Some Problems in Automatic Identification of Spoken Utterances and Speakers. *RIT-STL-QPSR* 1970.2/3:36-40.

Rosen, G. 1958. Dynamic Analog Speech Synthesizer. *JASA* 30.201-9.

Sawashima, M. 1968. Movements of the Larynx in Articulation of Japanese Consonants. University of Tokyo Research Institute of Logopedics and Phoniatrics Annual Bulletin 2.11-20.

Sawashima, M. and H. Hirose. 1968. New Laryngoscopic Technique by Use of Fiber Optics. *JASA* 43.168-69.

Shankweiler, D. 1970. *An Analysis of Laterality Effects in Speech Perception. Perception of Language,* ed. by P. Kjeldergaard. Columbus, Ohio: Charles E. Merrill Publishing Co.

Shibata, S. 1968. A Study of Dynamic Palatography. University of Tokyo Research Institute of Logopedics and Phoniatrics Annual Bulletin 2.28-36.

Slis, I. H. and A. Cohen. 1969. On the Complex Regulating the Voiced-Voiceless Distinction. *Language and Speech* 12.80-102; 12.137-55.

Soron, H. I. 1967. High Speed Photography in Speech Research. *JSHR* 10.768-76.

Stetson, R. H. 1951. *Motor Phonetics.* Amsterdam: North Holland Publishing Co.

Stevens, K. N. 1960. Toward a Model for Speech Recognition. *JASA* 32.47-55.

Stevens, K. N. 1963. Studies of the Dynamics of Speech Production. *MIT-RLE-QPR* 71.203-5.

Stevens, K. N., and M. Halle. 1967. *Remarks on Analysis by Synthesis and Distinctive Features. Models for the Perception of Speech and Visual Form,* ed. by W. Wathen-Dunn, 88-102. Cambridge: The MIT Press.

Stevens, K. N. and A. S. House. 1955. Development of a Quantitative Description of Vowel Articulation. *JASA* 27.484-93. [Reprinted in Lehiste (ed.) 1967, 34-43.]

Stevens, K. N. and A. S. House. 1956. Studies of Formant Transition Using a Vocal Tract Analog. *JASA* 28.578-85.

Stevens, K. N., A. M. Libermann, M. Studdert-Kennedy and S. E. G. Öhman. 1969. Cross-Language Study of Vowel Perception. *Language and Speech* 12.1-23.

Strenger, F. 1968. *Radiographic, Palatographic and Labiographic Methods in Phonetics. Manual of Phonetics,* [2nd Ed.], ed. by B. Malmberg, Chapter 11, 334-64. Amsterdam: North Holland Publishing Co.

Studdert-Kennedy, M., A. M. Liberman, Katherine S. Harris and F. S. Cooper. 1970. The Motor Theory of Speech Perception: A Reply to Lane's Critical Review. *Psychological Review* 77.234-49.

Studdert-Kennedy and D. Shankweiler. 1970. Hemispheric Specialization for Speech Perception. *JASA* 48.579-94.

Subtelny, Joanne D. and J. D. Subtelny. 1962. Roentgenographic Technique and Phonetic Research. Proceedings of the Fourth International Congress of Phonetic Sciences, ed. by A. Sovijarvi and P. Aalto, 129-46. The Hague: Mouton.

Suzuki, H. 1970. Mutually Complementary Effects of Rate and Amount of Formant Transition in Distinguising Vowel, Semi-Vowel, and Stop Consonant. *MIT-RLE-QPR* 96.164-72.

Swadesh, M. and C. F. Voegelin. 1939. A Problem in Phonological Alternation. *Language* 15.1-10. [Reprinted in *Readings in Linguistics,* ed. by M. Joos, Vol. I, 88-92 (1957;. Chicago: University of Chicago Press.]

Tatham, M. A. A. 1971. Model Building in Phonetic Theory. *Language Sciences* 14.16-19.

Tatham, M. A. A. and Katherine Morton. 1969. Some Electromyography Data Towards a Model of Speech Production. *Language and Speech* 12.39-53.

Tatham, M. A. A. and Katherine Morton. 1970. Explaining some Apparently Context- Sensitive Effects in Speech. University of Essex Language Centre Occasional Papers 9.116-22.

Taylor, I. K. 1966. What Words are Stuttered? Psychological Bulletin 65.236-42.

Teter, D. L. and R. C. Newell. 1969. High-Speed Photography of the Larynx in a Clinical Setting. *Annals of Otology, Rhinology, and Laryngology* 78.1227-1233.

Thomas, I. B., P. B. Hill, Francis S. Carroll, and B. Garcia. 1970. Temporal Order in the Perception of Vowels. *JASA* 48.1010-1013.

Thompson, C. L. and H. Hollien. 1970. Some Contextual Effects on the Perception of Synthetic Vowels. *Language and Speech* 13.1-13.

Truby, H. M. 1962. Synchronized Cineradiography and Visual-Acoustic Analysis. Proceedings of the Fourth International Congress of Phonetic Sciences, ed. by A. Sovijärvi and P. Aalto, 265-79. The Hague: Mouton.

Uldall, Elizabeth. 1970. Instrumental Investigation of Articulatory Phonetics: An Annotated Bibliography. Edinburgh University Department of Linguistics Work in Progress 4.1-43.

Vanderslice, R. 1967. Larynx vs. Lungs: Cricothyrometer Data Refuting some Recent Claims Concerning Intonation and 'Archetypality'. UCLA Working Papers in Phonetics 7.69-79.

Vanderslice, R. 1970. Review of Lieberman 1967. *Journal of Linguistics* 6.138-44.

Wall, P. D. 1959. Repetitive Discharge of Neurons. *Journal of Neurophysiology* 22. 305-20.

Wang, W. S-Y. 1959. Transition and Release as Perceptual Cues for Final Plosives. *JSHR* 2.66-73. [Reprinted in Ilse Lehiste, (ed.) 1969, 343-50.]

Wang, W. S-Y. 1968. The Basis of Speech. University of California (Berkeley) Department of Linguistics Project on Linguistic Analysis Report, Second Series, No. 4.

Weigl, E. and M. Bierwisch. 1970. Neuropsychology and Linguistics: Topics of Common Research. *Foundations of Language* 6.1-18.

Welmers, W. E. 1962. The Phonology of Kpelle. *Journal of African Languages* 1.1:69-93.

Whitaker, H. A. 1969. On the Representation of Language in the Human Brain. UCLA Working Papers in Phonetics, No. 12. [Revised edition published by Linguistic Research, Inc. 1971. Edmonton/Champaign.]

Whitaker, H. A. 1970. Some Constraints on Speech Production Models. University of Essex Language Centre Occasional Papers 9.1-13.

Wickelgren, W. A. 1969. Context-Sensitive Coding, Associative Memory, and Serial Order in (Speech) Behavior. Psychological Review 76.1-15.

Wolf, J. J. 1969. Acoustic Measurements for Speaker Recognition. *MIT-RLE-QPR* 94.216-22. (Cf. unpublished Ph.D. dissertation with same title. Cambridge: M.I.T., 1969.)

Wolf, J. J. 1970. Choice of Speaker Recognition Parameters. *MIT-RLE-QPR* 97.125-33.

Woodburne, L. S. 1967. *The Neural Basis of Behavior*. Columbus, Ohio: Charles E. Merrill Publishing Co.

Zagoruiko, N. G. 1970. Automatic Recognition of Speech. *RIT-STL-QPSR* 1970.1.32-38.

Zemlin, W. R. 1969. The Effect of Topical Anesthesia on Internal Laryngeal Behavior. *Acta Oto-Laryngologica* 68.169-76.

DISCUSSION

WILLIAM LABOV (U. of Pennsylvania): I think that many of your arguments in favor of the syllable as a basic unit are, of course, persuasive. There were, however, several points which I would like to bring up which may have been overstated. (1) There is certainly no substance to the statement that false starts are limited to syllables. Anyone who has worked with natural speech has observed that it is quite common to have false starts with single consonants and, furthermore, that there are many cases where people stammer or stutter on single consonants where it is even difficult to tell whether they are producing a long consonant or releasing one. The observation that people stammer on syllables may be partly due to the fact that it's difficult to tell a released consonant from a syllable. (2) I think that your argument that *X* goes to *Y* in environment *Z* is certainly sound in that the great majority of conditioning factors in linguistic changes are following elements. But I don't know of any evidence that would support the view that the syllable is a natural conditioning factor other than stress rules. We would have to search far and wide to find examples where *Z* is a syllable. On the contrary, *Z* is usually a single consonant that seams to me a powerful argument in the reverse direction. (3) I don't notice any data from Fromkin that supports the idea that the syllable is the basic unit for spoonerisms; on the contrary, her arguments seems to show that the basic unit, if not a feature, would be limited to a segment. (4) Finally, when we begin to study variable rules which give us a powerful body of quantitative evidence on the nature of conditioning factors, we do sometimes see changes being generalized through the language with one syllable after the other being added. That would be the case with palatalization. It is more normal, however, to find that the generalization moves in larger units—e.g., the aspiration of *s* to *h* with the latter's subsequent disappearance in Spanish or the shift of final θ to *f* in English and other languages seem to proceed with relative independence sometimes conditioned by a feature of vowel position but very often irrespective of the vowel that precedes or follows. Thus, I think that we would have to add to your discussion of the importance of the syllable as a linguistic unit a fairly large number of facts which point in the other direction.

CHIN-WU KIM (U. of Illinois): (1) I have no data to cite off-hand, but I think it is generally true that most cases of hesitations and false starts occur in terms of open syllables. In artificial stuttering, e.g., due to a delayed auditory feedback, this is particularly true (cf. Fairbanks and Guttman 1958; Kozhevnikov and Chistovich 1966:142ff.).
(2) I did not mean to imply that in the rule *X* → *Y* / _____ *Z*, *Z* is a syllable. Rather, it is a segment, a part of a syllable. What I was saying was

that if only *XZ* went to *YZ*, but not *XW* to *YW*, then perhaps *X* has different neurophysiological representations depending upon its place in the syllable.

(3) You're right. Fromkin's recent article on spoonerisms does not support the syllable theory. The supporting work by Fromkin that I cited was her 1965 dissertation, an EMG investigation of linguistic units. [Cf. Victoria A. Fromkin. 1965. Some phonetic specifications of linguistic units: An electromyographic investigation. Working papers in Phonetics 3. 184pp. Los Angeles: University of California.]

HARRY A. WHITAKER (U. of Rochester): Let me clarify, as briefly as possible, that paper which I wrote on Wickelgren's context-sensitive model. The problem that Wickelgren runs into is the fact that you cannot disprove his model. What he's got is a system whereby he can completely describe everything that is outputted by the speaker. As a complete descriptive system, I have no quarrel with it. The problem is that it makes no generalizations that can be tested.

On the matter of the six cycle per second rhythm which Lenneberg quotes Brazier on, there is an incredibly serious problem here. The paper that Mary Brazier wrote dealt with EEG correlates of memory. She noted in the process of investigating these that approximately one-third and no more of her subjects exhibited this phenomenal behaviour of having a six cycle per second rhythm over the temporal lobe. She was so struck by this anomaly that she published a diagram of it. Lenneberg picked this up and then generalized it holding that this anomaly in one-third of the subjects might be responsible for the organizing rhythm. I guess this leaves the rest of us without a rhythmic base for language. [Cf. M. A. B. Brazier. 1960. Long-persisting electrical traces in the brain of man and their possible relationship to higher nervous activity. The Moscow colloquium on electroencephalography of higher nervous activity, ed. by H. H. Jasper and G. D. Smirnov, EEG Journal Suppl. 13.347-58.]

DON G. STUART (Georgetown U.): I quite agree that the role of the syllable has been neglected. Still I wonder if we are not involved in some semantic confusions in putting the syllable in competition with the phoneme as a basic unit. Certainly it is quite clear that there is some kind of productive unit in speech which is not the phoneme. If one sees phonemes, however, as simultaneous ensembles of differential choices, then it's perfectly clear that we must recognize that there are partial resemblances and differences between syllables which we should want to take account of in the phoneme. One might want to say that the syllable is a unit of speech production and the phoneme, a unit of possible sequential difference or something of this sort.

In any case, I should like to suggest with regard to the importance of the syllable that it might be worthwile to investigate the average rates of acquisition of writing systems in languages in which the writing system is syllabic and in languages which have essentially a phonemic writing system. My own experiences with a bilingual child learning to read and write in Japanese and Dutch indicate that the Japanese writing system is acquired much more rapidly than the Dutch, but this is only a single instance, of course.

WALBURGA VON RAFFLER ENGEL (Vanderbilt University): I fully agree that the syllable is the first unit the child acquires in his motor babbling, but when the child goes on to imitate actual words of the spoken language, he definitely displays phonemic substitution. I thus see two stages involved. The syllable is not the end-product, but rather constitutes the first stage in acquisition which is followed by a second stage characterized by phonemic awareness.

CHIN-WU KIM (U. of Illinois): Logically there is nothing against hypothesizing that the basic unit is a word, phrase or even a sentence. I think that investigators are simply being properly cautious. Up to now we have been pre-occupied with the notion of the phoneme. As the phoneme does not fit the model, then the next cautious step is to take the next larger unit which happens to be the syllable. [As a matter of fact, one can reasonably speculate that the word, rather than the syllable is the unit of articulatory programming. Notice, for instance, that the domain of vowel harmony, in all the languages that I know of, is always the word. Why should this be so? And also, much of the phonological component seems to be word-level phonology (cf. *The sound pattern of English*). There is in fact a small piece of evidence pointing to this. Ilse Lehiste (1970) in a recent study that I cited earlier found that the average duration of disyllabic words was the same as or even shorter than that of the monosyllabic words. E.g., *stead, steady; skid, skiddy; skit, skitty*, etc. all had the same average duration (actually in each pair, the disyllabic word was shorter). A temporal compensation was made by the shorter consonant durations in longer words. It seems to me that this finding indicates that a word, as well as a syllable, is an articulatorily cohesive unit.]

RALPH VANDERSLICE (C.U.N.Y., Hunter College): I was very glad to hear Professor Kim bring up the matter of words with variable accentuation like *unknown*. It was Daniel Jones, as far as I know who first brought up the fact that it can be *the únknown soldier* but *the soldier is unknówn*. This phenomenon in general has been discussed by Bridges and before him other metrists. It has been of great interest in determining what are the underlying constraints on iambic pentameter and so on. Bridges called it *accent reces-*

sion. The clearest discussion in recent literature has been by Bolinger. [Cf. D. Bolinger. 1965. Forms of English: Accent, morpheme, order, ed. by Isamu Abe and T. Kanekiyo. Cambridge: Harvard U. Press.] In the phrase: *we established telegraphic communication* discussed in the SPE, *telegraphic* must have the appropriate underlying form to yield the correct stress pattern. However, in another context: *they established it by telegraphic contact* you get an entirely different stress pattern on *telegraphic*, because *telegraphic* happens to be like *unknown* and a very large number of other words that can take variable accentuation according to the context they come in.

Chapter Eight

Neurolinguistics

William Orr Dingwall and Harry A. Whitaker

Introduction

The subject matter of the discipline of neurolinguistics is the relationship that pertains between man's language and his nervous system (169). Although research in this area has a history that is at least as old as neuropsychology, the term "neurolinguistics" has only recently been used to describe it (38, 80, 108, 113, 116, 180, 181). An earlier term, "biolinguistics," failed to gain acceptance even though it referred to the same endeavor (125). Theories of brain function and theories of language have had an independent as well as conjunct history which, over the centuries, reflect all the vagaries of intellectual history. Since the early 19th century, however, there has been an increasing number of investigations that directly confront the brain-language issue. One of the early concerns of neurolinguistics, and still a much-discussed topic today, is the question of which regions of the brain are responsible for or underlie the language function (61, 77, 116). Recent studies suggesting that the nondominant (usually the right) hemisphere may have some residual linguistic capacity are of interest in this regard (55, 60). Furthermore, localization of language functions is intimately related to the problem of a model of the language user—how we comprehend and produce language. Recent work on such models has emphasized one or more aspects of neurolinguistics: that of clinical neurology (20), of neuropsychology (113, 116), and of linguistics (180). Towards the latter half of the 19th century it became generally accepted that lesions to certain regions of the brain led to certain syndromes of language disorder (aphasia), which in turn has led to a still-current concern in neurolinguistics: a typology of language disorders (20, 58, 66, 70, 82, 83, 114).

A current focus in neurolinguistics, though not without historical precedent, is the application of hypotheses in psycholinguistic theory to specific aspects of aphasic language (11, 64, 69, 158, 180, 181). It is implicit in the preceding list of issues in neurolinguistics that one of the primary sources of data is and has been the aphasic patient. Neurosurgical techniques have added new dimensions to the data base by controlled mapping of the electrical activity or by electrically stimulating the brain tissue (46, 164) by sectioning the corpus callosum (55), as well as more direct knowledge of damaged brain regions in aphasic patients. Other areas of concern in neurolinguistics are: the relationship between disorders of language and disorders of movement (2, 35, 147, 175); disorders of language and impaired intelligence (27, 102); the nature of aphasia in bilingual speakers (28); and the interactions between aphasia and other factors and functions such as emotions, visual-spatial perception, and hearing (112, 129). It is apparent that the field of neurolinguistics has at this time achieved an independent status comparable to, e.g. neuropsychology, and therefore it is impossible for us to review it in its entirety. Instead, in the following sections we will consider three topics in neurolinguistics which seem to us to be of current interest: the question of localization of language function in the brain; linguistic and neurological analyses of aphasia; and manipulative studies of brain and language functions.

Localization of Language Functions in the Brain

To paraphrase Head (76), we would first observe that the history of our understanding of the functions of regions of the cerebral cortex is one of the most astonishing stories in medicine. Needless to say, it is a story filled with controversy, widely divergent viewpoints, and a great deal of misunderstanding; and the story is by no means finished (84). Observations on the relationship between language and brain, specifically on the relationship between language and brain damage, are found in the medical literature dating as far back as 3500 B.C. in an Egyptian papyrus (7). Many further observations were made in the Renaissance, the 17th and 18th centuries, such that by the beginning of the 19th century most of the sundry clinical forms of aphasia, with the possible exception of sensory aphasia, had been described and recognized as manifestations of brain disease. For various reasons, some of them religious, little attention had been given to the underlying pathology of the brain, and thus the postulations of function to specific parts of the brain had not yet been made (7, 8). In fact, as late as the mid-19th century, handbooks of physiology ascribed higher mental functions to the cerebral ventricles.

Although in one sense it could be argued that the Cartesian postulate that the soul resided in the pineal gland represented the first theory of localized function in the brain, it is more customary to recognize Gall as the first person to propose separate functions for distinct anatomical parts of the brain. Gall (52) associated the faculty of speech with the frontal portions of the brain (located behind the orbits). Earlier, in collaboration with Spurzheim (53), he outlined some of the facets of the lateralization of cerebral (motor) functions and demonstrated anatomically the decussation of the pyramid tract. Bouillaud's paper (13) was based on Gall's work and acknowledged the same. Bouillaud also noted the lateralization of cerebral functions with respect to movements of the arm, based on a case of paralysis of the arm following contralateral cerebral damage. Regarding speech, he said that the "principal lawgiver" is to be found in the anterior lobes of the brain. He had also distinguished phonological defects of speech from the neuromuscular (what we now term an expressive aphasia versus dysarthria). Auburtin, Bouillaud's son-in-law and pupil, championed the localization theories of his father-in-law and, together with Broca, took part in the famous series of papers and discussions in 1861 on the role of the frontal lobes, and in particular the left third frontal convolution, in speech. Auburtin (5) had observed a patient who had a large frontal skull defect which exposed the frontal lobes of the brain; he noted that the placement of a spatula on the frontal lobe and a slight exertion of pressure caused all speech to suddenly stop, then reappear as soon as the compression ceased. Of special interest in the case is Auburtin's specific mention that there was no accompanying paralysis or loss of consciousness when this slight pressure was exerted; speech alone was affected. Shortly thereafter, Broca (17) presented the first of his celebrated cases, exhibiting the brain of a patient who had a severe expressive impairment to the Anthropological Society of Paris. In subsequent papers (18, 19) Broca concluded, on the basis of two autopsied patients, that the faculty of articulated language (speech) could be separated from other aspects of language by lesions in the left third frontal convolution, now known as Broca's area. Broca presented these cases as support for the localizationist theories of Gall, Bouillaud, and Auburtin. In retrospect it is reasonable to assume that Broca's contribution was to identify left-sided dominance for speech in man; the observations regarding the type of expressive disorder, as well as the postulation of the role of the frontal lobes in general, were proposed prior to Broca's observations (85). A claim was made by Gustav Dax (1865), submitted in 1863, that his father, Marc Dax, had in 1836 written a paper proposing that the left hemisphere was dominant for speech. In the 1865 paper, 40 cases were cited; however, there was no pathological verification and the clinical history was very sketchy. Attempts to locate the 1836 paper were fruitless, and thus the claim of Broca's should be considered to have priority (85).

The last quarter of the 19th century witnessed an incredible number of studies on cerebral localization of language, and it is reasonable to conclude that it was during this time that the positions of the holists versus the atomists (the nonlocalizationists versus the localizationists, respectively) were consolidated and crystallized. What would be a formidable job of summarizing the research in this period (Marie, Charcot, Dejerine, Jackson, Trousseau, Kussmal, Wernicke, Lichtheim, Bastian, Meynert, Broadbent, von Monakow, Pick, et al) fortunately is obviated by the perceptive and comprehensive review of Freud (49). Using published case histories and logical arguments, Freud addressed most of the questions about localization of language functions in a detailed critique of all of the leading theories of his day. His conclusion, strikingly contemporary, is a combination of general localization of the language area and functional distinctions between the various factors of language use:

> Our concept of the structure of the speech apparatus was based
> on the observation that the so-called speech centers border exter-

nally (peripherally) on parts of the cortex which are important for the speech function, while interiorly (centrally) they enclose a region not covered by localization which probably also belongs to the speech area. The apparatus of speech therefore presented itself to us as a continuous cortical area in the left hemisphere extending between the terminations of the acoustic and optic nerves and the origins of the motor tracts for the muscles serving articulation and arm movements. The necessarily ill-defined parts of the speech region which border on these receptive and motor cortical fields, have acquired the sigificance of speech centres from the point of view of morbid anatomy but not in respect of normal function; their lesions cut off one of the elements of speech association from its connections with the others (101, 102).

Although a great deal of new information has been discovered during the course of the 20th century, the debate over localization continues to this day in much the same terms as originally. It is reasonable to conclude that there are no more strict or narrow localizationists (in the sense of cerebral topography), although there are authors who seem to profess a rather complete holist or nonlocalizationist position (104). The predominant position is best exemplified by Hécaen (77), Gloning & Hoff (61), and Luria (116).

Hécaen (77) identifies six modalities of functional localization in the nervous system:

1. A somatotopic, contralateral localization in the motor projection and sensory reception cortical zones on a point-to-area basis.

2. A system localization for ordinary type functions of instinct and affect in the limbic system and a system localization for certain aspects of memory (fixation and acquisition) in the rhinencephalic regions, inferomesial-temporal region, and the mammilary bodies.

3. Broad functional areas for speech, action, and perception in association cortex; the principles of cerebral dominance, functional asymmetry, and organizational differences obtain in this type of functional localization; Hécaen suggests an area subserving serial order performance located in the region of the parietal-occipital-temporal junction, predominantly in the left hemisphere.

4. A functional localization in the frontal lobes, not determined by dominance but possibily determined by mass effects, relating to sensorimotor adaptation. This is implied by the effects of frontal lobe lesions producing akinesia, subconfusional excitations, loss of initiative, loss of self criticism and other subtle clinical changes.

5. A complex integration system involving corticofugal fibers, the ascending reticular formation, and peripheral receptor organs relating to orienting, habituation, attention, sleep, and consciousness.

6. The possibility of nonlocalizable functional disturbances which result from damage to any part of the brain. Hécaen rejects the theories of mass action, of general figure-ground differentiation, of abstract attitude, or of general intellectual deficit as explaining the underlying basis of all brain damage, but he does recognize that there are certain performance deficits which seem to be present in all subjects with brain damage, e.g. delayed reaction time. In this regard it should be noted that delayed reaction times are also found in populations of chronic schizophrenics who have no obvious nervous system lesion.

Gloning & Hoff (61) review aspects of localization in the context of systems in the brain rather than centers, concluding that complex higher functions involve the entire brain but that syndromes of deficits can be localized to some extent (which is in fact the basis of current clinical neurology). They consider conjugate eye movements, cerebral dominance, and the analysis of space and time, providing details of various deficits associated with cerebral disease in various areas. Their schema of aphasic syndromes comprises three basic types following from lesions in frontal, temporal, and temporoparietal areas, qualified by observations on some syndromes that may not be attributed to these general regions.

Luria (116) briefly reviews the problems of the mosaicist theories of strict localization and the holist theories of undifferentiated whole-brain involvement in higher cognitive functions. His proposal is to reconsider the notion of function in terms of elementary functions of particular tissues and complex functional systems. He next restructures the concept of localization to include the systemic nature of mental functions which are organized by different cortical zones (analyzers), each having its own role in the system complex. While arguing that one cannot make simple direct correlations between a deficit, a region of the brain, and a specific normal function, Luria does conclude that careful neuropsychological analysis of the deficits that result from local brain lesions can make a major contribution to the structural analysis of normal mental functions and their cerebral organization by isolating relevant factors in these processes and the contribution of different brain areas to the system as a whole.

One of the severe limitations on cerebral localization studies has been the difficulty in locating the lesion when autopsy data is not available. The more familiar neurological techniques—brain scans, arteriograms, EEG, pneumoencephalograms, etc—have various limitations; some entail risk to the patient and are only performed when the clinical situation warrants, some are very imprecise, and some are only effective for certain kinds of lesions at a certain stage of their etiology. Therefore, although this is somewhat removed from the main focus of our review, it is with interest that we note the development of a new X-ray machine which may revolutionize clinical neurology and neurosurgery as well as localization studies *(New Scientist,* 187). Producing a total X-ray dose less than the ordinary chest

X-ray examination, requiring only about 16 minutes, and being nearly fully automated, this machine is capable of detecting such minute differences in tissue as that between the grey and white matter of the brain. Prototype machines have already been shown to be capable of locating small tumors and other lesions which escaped detection by the usual diagnostic procedures.

Neurological and Linguistic Analyses of Aphasia

Clinical neurology, psychiatry, and neurosurgery historically have contributed more to the study of aphasia than any other disciplines, although recently there has been more of a balance of contributions between them and the fields of speech pathology, psychology, and linguistics. Because of the extensive literature on the clinical aspects of aphasia and the spatial limitations of this review, we feel that a chart showing characteristics of the aphasias will generate the least amount of distortion. Any summary, whether in tabular form or not, will fail to convey an accurate picture of the complexity of aphasic disturbances. In looking at this chart, the reader should bear in mind that these listed characteristics (a) indicate the usual or typical situation for one of these syndromes; (b) in part represent an interpretation of the language behavior (e.g. grammatical formatives); and (c) in part represent judgments (e.g. degree of fluency). It should also be remembered that this chart represents what is thought to be the typical syndrome resulting from lesions that are primarily in the brain areas cited. Since in actual fact a great number of aphasic patients have lesions that involve more than one of these discrete areas or that involve one of these regions to a greater or lesser extent, these patients will of course not have the precise list of characteristics mentioned. There are a number of good books currently available from which the interested reader may obtain properly detailed information (20, 27, 58, 62, 64, 76, 78, 111-114, 129, 150, 172).

Linguistic observations of aphasic language have a much more recent history than clinical studies and are just now becoming frequent (64, 180). This fact is nowhere more obvious than in the batteries of tests used to examine for aphasia; only one aphasia test overtly employs linguistic theory in the test design and scoring (68). Aphasia researchers will, of course, occasionally use other tests like the developmentally oriented Illinois Test of Psycholinguistic Abilities (ITPA) which has sections that are based on linguistic theory. And it is possible to show how some aphasia tests reveal aspects of linguistic organization, as Whitaker & Noll (184) did for the Token Test. From the standpoint of linguistic theory, the most remarkable fact about partial brain damage is the specificity and variety of the resulting language deficits which delineate linguistic categories and operations. Data from aphasic language behavior provides us with detailed insights into the

Chart Showing Typical Characteristics of the Aphasias

SYNDROME	LOCUS OF LESION	VERBAL OUTPUT Phonological, Syntactic, Semantic	WRITING	AUDITORY COMPREHENSION Phonological, Syntactic, Semantic	READING
Broca's Aphasia	Posterior inferior frontal	Phonemic paraphasias; OK surface word order; appropriate meaning; telegraphic style	Same as verbal	Normal to limited, grammatical formatives are processed poorly	Same as auditory comprehension
Conduction Aphasia	Parietal operculum, arcuate fasc. & adjacent cortex	Some phonemic paraphasias, surface word order OK; meaning is appropriate	Same as verbal	Normal to mildly affected	Normal to mildly affected
Wernicke's Aphasia	Posterior superior temporal	Normal to complete jargon phonology; surface word order OK to severely impaired; meaning may be vacuous or irrelevant or even nonsensical	Same as verbal	Can distinguish speech from nonspeech; comprehension impaired to very severe; high-frequency words occasionally understood	Impaired to the degree of auditory comprehension
Isolation Syndrome	Association cortex in all lobes	Normal	Severely impaired	Severely impaired comprehension but does process speech	Limited to severely impaired, no comprehension
Transcortical Motor	Anterior & superior frontal lobe	Normal in repetition	Impaired	Normal	Normal to limited
Anomic or Amnestic	Posterior middle temporal, or, diffuse	Normal except on noun phrases	Unpredictable	Normal	Unpredictable
Alexia & Agraphia	Inferior parietal & angular gyrus	Normal	Impaired	Normal	Impaired
Word Deafness	Border zone of Heschl's gyrus & Wernicke's area	Normal	Normal	Hearing OK but severe impairment of speech comprehension	Normal
Word Blindness	Splenium of the corpus callosum, visual cortex of left hemisphere	Normal	Normal	Normal	Severely impaired, including inability to read own writing

Chart Showing Typical Characteristics of the Aphasias (*Continued*)

SYNDROME	SPONTANEITY OF SPEAKING & WRITING	GRAMMATICAL FORMATIVES	FLUENCY	LEXICAL FORMATIVES	REPETITION
Broca's Aphasia	Severely impaired; hesitant, frequent pause	Often missing; some incorrect use	Severely impaired	Present	Limited like the verbal
Conduction Aphasia	Limited	Usually present but may occasionally be missing	Limited	Present	Severely impaired; frequent paraphasia
Wernicke's Aphasia	Normal but often repetitious, stereotyped	Present but often incorrect or inappropriate	Normal	Frequent indefinite or nonspecific nouns; phonemic paraphasias with perseveration on syllables, lexical paraphasias, neologistic jargon	Impaired to the degree of auditory comprehension
Isolation Syndrome	Severely impaired	Present	Normal when echoic	Present	Echolalic, occasional completion phenomenon
Transcortical Motor	Severely impaired	Usually present	Normal in repetition	Present	Normal
Anomic or Amnestic	Normal	Present	Normal except block on word finding	Severely impaired in output, especially nouns, with circumlocutions	Normal
Alexia & Agraphia	Normal	Present in the verbal–auditory	Normal	Present in the verbal–auditory	Normal
Word Deafness	Normal	Present	Normal	Present	Severely impaired
Word Blindness	Normal	Present	Normal	Present	Normal

language system of man, and in addition can provide evidence that bears on the validity and generality of theories in linguistics (11, 158, 177, 180, 181).

Phonological Studies

Lecours & Lhermitte (103), using an articulatorily based set of features, analyzed phonological errors made by two jargon aphasic patients while reading. In the paradigmatic dimension, errors appeared to be determined by the distance between target and actual production: more errors are made between phonemes that are similarly articulated. In the syntagmatic dimension, they showed that a context of similar phonemes increases the likelihood that a phonological error will occur. They also observed that writing errors on the syntactic level are analogous to these phonological errors, suggesting similar neuropsychological mechanisms underlying both. A later study by Poncet et al (148) reassessed the Lecours & Lhermitte (103) study, using different experimental techniques.

Blumstein (11), using a distinctive feature analysis and the concept of markedness, studied phonological errors (consonants) in three classes of patients: the Broca, the Wernicke, and the Conduction type of aphasic. In her analysis, all three patient types exhibited the same general pattern of errors, differing essentially in the number of errors rather than the types. There was a tendency to make errors of only one distinctive feature rather than two or more features, and the unmarked member of a pair of phonemes was more frequently substituted for the marked member rather than the opposite. Blumstein also found some limited support for Jakobson's (82, 83) suggestion that features acquired later by children were more likely to be disrupted in aphasic speech.

In the first study of its kind, Schnitzer (158) analyzed the phonological errors of a patient who had a small lesion in the supramarginal gyrus, using the model of generative phonology developed by Chomsky and Halle. Schnitzer showed how a variety of errors at the phonetic level could be accounted for in terms of a small set of errors in underlying phonemic representations, coupled with occasional errors in the application of phonological rules. A discussion of other aspects of this patient's language behavior and cognitive abilities is found in Kehoe & Whitaker (86).

Syntactic and Semantic Studies

Good descriptions of agrammatism can be found in Goodglass & Geschwind (66), showing the syntactic nature of this disorder. They note that English agrammatic patients often use verbs in the infinitive (uninflected) form without modals; German agrammatic patients also use verbs in the infinitive-nominalized form, but in the German case the form requires, and receives, a derivational affix. This and other data support the conclusion that agrammatism is not simply the result of an increased difficulty of speaking which leads to reduced (telegraphic) utterances, but in fact is a linguistic/syntatic disorder. The use of the infinitive form as a nominal also supports the observation by Whitaker (182) that some patients tended to nominalize all verbs. Marshall & Newcombe (120) obtained data which showed that alexic errors can be specific to certain semantic and syntactic features; their patient's errors tended to be within the same semantic field and tended to be nouns or noun forms regardless of what part of speech the stimulus was. In a later study of this same patient, Marshall, Newcombe & Marshall (121) specifically tested certain semantic and syntactic features such as *stative, human, abstract,* etc, and found a general tendency that verbs were much more difficult than nouns, with adjectives in between.

A study by Goodglass, Fodor & Schulhoff (65) proposed that agrammatic patients demonstrate a relationship between the so-called function words (grammatical formatives) and sentence stress (in their terms, "phonological salience"). They argued that the agrammatic patient depends upon a stressed word to initiate his utterance and will delete a grammatical formative in the initial position if unstressed but retain it later in the sentence when it is stressed or between two stressed words. A review of these and similar studies on agrammatism is in Goodglass (63).

Goodglass, Hyde & Blumstein (67) found that fluent and nonfluent aphasics (approximately those with posterior or anterior lesions, respectively) differed in the proportion of picturable (= concrete reference) and non-picturable (= abstract reference) nouns used in speaking. Fluent aphasics used more nonpicturable words in conversational speech, although these were frequently in idiomatic expressions with little semantic content.

Evidence that word-finding problems in aphasia in part relate to semantic factors was presented by Goodglass et al (68a). In naming (production) tasks, object names were hardest and letter names were easiest, but in choice tests requiring auditory comprehension, the order was reversed. In some classes of patients there were significant discrepancies between naming letters or numbers on the one hand and naming objects on the other. Naming of colors can be selectively impaired (59) with little other anomic/amnestic deficiencies. Yamadori & Albert (188) presented a case report which they described as word-category aphasia—a nonmodality-specific anomia in conjunction with a comprehension deficit for words in specific semantic categories. They suggest that categories such as body parts, objects in a room, and colors (cf Geschwind 58a) may be separately disrupted as a sequel to brain damage and therefore may have independent neuropsychological status in the internal lexicon.

Some semantic and syntactic deficits are manifested in all modalities. Whitaker (179) observed a patient whose distinguishing semantic features for the personal pronouns—person, number, gender, and case—were disrupted even though the formative feature identifying (pronoun) was not;

i.e., the patient always used a personal pronoun where it was required, but he usually erred by using the wrong one or misunderstanding it.

Rinnert & Whitaker (151) compared semantic confusions by patients with a variety of aphasic syndromes to corresponding word association norms for subjects without brain damage. They showed that the two classes of data are remarkably alike, suggesting that both can provide insights into the semantic organization of the internal lexicon or dictionary. It is of course well established that word associations are not random; this study by implication also shows that aphasic patients do not randomly err in the semantic domain.

Alajouanine (4) suggested that there are three different types of jargon aphasic patients: the first is characterized by no linguistic meaning (it is generally a "babbling" type of production which nevertheless preserves normal-sounding intonational contours, phrasing with pauses, etc); the second is characterized by frequent neologisms similar to some types of schizophrenic language (there is generally a retained semblance of syntactic structure); and the third is characterized by constantly misused words. If Alajouanine is correct, there is a very rich source of linguistic data concerning the interplay between syntax and semantics in such patients (see also Buckingham & Kertesz 24 in this regard).

Weigl & Bierwisch (177) investigated the correspondence between auditory phonemic perception and the perception of graphemic structure and lip-reading in a group of aphasic patients. Their data indicated that there is only one underlying abstract representation of words in the brain's internal lexicon and that various other subsystems for particular modalities are interrelated at a lower level. Evidence was presented that supported a model in which the phonological component is distinct (neuropsychologically) from the semantic and syntactic components (cf 180 also in this regard). Weigl and Bierwisch further provided evidence that both visual and auditory speech perception need not depend on lower-level articulatory patterns, somewhat contrary to what would be predicted by the so-called motor theory of speech perception. In their analysis of some cases of alexia, which at first seemed to demonstrate a loss of the semantic distinction between abstract and concrete, further study showed that the impairment was actually dependent upon the difference between lexical and grammatical formatives (in German), again supporting the distinction between these syntactic categories. Related to this, they showed that a patient could grasp syntactic information without correctly comprehending either the semantic or the phonological information in the stimuli (cf 4, 179). Analysis of other data by Weigl and Bierwisch supported the notion that the lexicon is divided into semantic fields and that something analogous to syntactic transformations has neuropsychological validity.

Manipulative Studies of Brain Function

In this section we turn to methods of investigating the relationship between brain mechanisms and language which allow greater control over experimentally relevant variables than does the study of aphasia. Some of these methods involve what Lenneberg (106) has termed the "clinical-experimental approach" which employs as subjects patients generally destined to undergo some form of neurosurgical therapy. For well-founded ethical reasons, such techniques as surgical excision, pharmacological deactivation, and electrical stimulation cannot be employed on normal subjects and are not subject to all the experimental controls which characterize neurophysiological studies on animals. For these and other reasons having to do with the difficulty of assessing the far-reaching effects of both the initial insult to the brain as well as of the therapeutic techniques themselves—effects which may involve metabolic processes at some distance from the site of lesion—the results of such studies must be interpreted with caution (cf 128). Other techniques such as electroencephalography, electromyography, and dichotic listening do not involve any danger to the subject and can be employed under appropriately controlled conditions.

Neurosurgical Techniques

TEMPORAL LOBECTOMY—The effects of surgery involving the removal of the anterior portion of the left or right temporal lobe for the relief of epilepsy have been carefully investigated by members of the Montreal Neurological Institute and of the National Institute of Neurological Diseases and Stroke (NINDS) in Bethesda, Maryland. Immediately following left temporal lobectomy, one usually finds some degree of dysphasia which, however, rapidly disappears. As Milner (130, 132) and Meyer (127) have shown, there is a persisting deficit involving memory for both visually and auditorily presented verbal materials such as words, nonsense syllables, and three-digit numbers. Similar operations on the nondominant hemisphere produce deficits in memory for nonverbal materials including tone patterns and timbre discriminations. That the verbal learning deficits are confined to the dominant temporal lobe is clearly demonstrated by the following table comparing the results of excisions in other parts of the brain. Similar findings have been obtained using the dichotic listening procedure. Kimura (88) was able to demonstrate a significant loss in accuracy in reporting digits presented to the ear contralateral to the lobectomy, with the number of errors consistently greatest for the left-sided cases. Frontal lobectomy failed to show such an effect.

The role played by internal structuring of materials on recall has also been investigated. Weingartner (178) found that right temporal lobectomy patients perform significantly better on tasks requiring the free recall and

Table 1 Mean delayed recall scores and mean Wechsler-Bellevue IQ ratings for 56 patients tested in long-term follow-up and subdivided according to locus of cortical excision[a]

| Excision | N | Verbal Recall[b] | | Mean IQ |
		Auditory	Visual	(Wechsler)
Left temporal	22	9.6	10.0	110.3
Right temporal	13	16.5	17.4	110.1
Minor hemisphere (large)	10	17.4	16.2	101.3
Left frontal	6	18.1	18.4	109.8
Left parietal	4	15.0	15.4	111.5
Left occipital	1	20.0	16.0	96.0

[a] From Milner (132).

[b] Scores based on mean number of items recalled from two prose passages and ten paired associates presented orally and in written form.

serial learning of words. Semantic structuring of the words produced significantly better scores for *both* left and right groups in free recall but for *neither* group in serial learning. In a recognition task involving transformations of a "base" design, Spear (165) was unable to show any difference in performance between normals and right and left-temporal lobectomy patients. These experiments thus fail to provide evidence bearing on localization or dominance for either semantic or abstract visual patterning. Initial findings in a study recently conducted by Dingwall & Shields does provide some evidence that grammatical structuring aids recall in this patient population. In a task employing as stimuli anomalous and nonanomalous sentences as well as strings of unrelated lexical items, the dominant temporal lobectomy group evinced a clear deficit in the recall of the word strings, while near perfect performance was demonstrated by both left and right groups for both classes of sentences.

FRONTAL LOBECTOMY—Although frontal lobectomy does not appear to effect retention of verbal material, Milner (131) has found that subjects with left frontal lesions are impaired in their ability to produce words on the Thurstone Word Fluency Test, which involves essentially writing down words beginning with various letters. Miller (128) conjectures that this may be due to involvement of Broca's area. However, Pribram (149) observed that over 10,000 frontal lobotomies were performed in Europe during the 1940s and the 1950s using a surgical procedure that apparently injures Broca's area, yet there were no reported aphasia sequelae. In a series of 48 psychotic patients who were given various frontal lobe neurosurgical procedures, two had excisions in the region of Broca's area (126). Case #33, who had both Area 44 and Area 45 removed bilaterally, subsequently became severely dysarthric (Mettler's terminology) and remained so; Case #47, who had Area 44 removed bilaterally (subtotal resection of Broca's area), was neither dysarthric nor dysphasic following the operation. Penfield & Roberts (146) report on a case in which, in two operations 10 years apart (the first when the patient was 18 years old), Broca's area was ultimately completely removed with no residual aphasia. Their opinion was that the congenital abnormality of the left-hemisphere inferior posterior frontal lobe (the basis of the seizure disorder and the reason for the surgical removal of this area) had caused a displacement (Penfield and Roberts' terminology) of the function of speech to some other part of the cortex; therefore removal of the abnormal tissue had no further effect on speaking. It is of interest to note in this case that one of the effects of the seizures was to render the patient unable to speak. Mohr's (136) carefully researched cases of rapid amelioration of expressive aphasia after infarction of Broca's area and the underlying white matter would appear to lend support to Pribram's belief that "an intact Broca's area . . . is not necessary for normal speech" (149, p. 357), and is reminiscent of Marie's (119) paper, titled The Third Left Frontal Convolution Plays No Special Role in the Function of Language. On the other hand, Hécaen & Consoli (79) recently studied 19 patients with anatomically verified lesions of Broca's area and compared their expressive language performance with a group of 15 patients with comparable lesions in the right hemisphere. The patients with damage to Broca's area had language disturbances that could be classified into a group with articulatory and prosodic impairments (lesion limited to the cortex) and a group that had, in addition, auditory-verbal comprehension disorders and dysgraphia (lesions included white matter beneath Broca's area). The patients with comparable lesions in the right hemisphere were virtually free of language deficits.

THE SPLIT BRAIN—The neurosurgical technique which provides perhaps the richest source of information on specific aspects of language function is commissurotomy. This technique which involves sectioning of the major neural pathways between the two cerebral hemispheres, viz. the corpus callosum, the anterior and hippocampal commissures as well as the massa intermedia in some cases was introduced in 1940 as a treatment for relief of epilepsy. At first no major effects involving language could be found (3), but with more careful experimental techniques employing rapid tachistoscopic presentation of stimuli to the right and left visual fields, dramatic results were obtained. If the subject focuses on a midpoint as shown in Figure 1A, then all information flashed in the right visual field is projected to the left (generally language-dominant) hemisphere and all information flashed in the left visual field is projected to the right (nondominant) hemisphere. Exposure time must be rapid (approximately 180 msec) to prevent eye movement. The major paths of information flow under these conditions from hand and eye to brain are presented schematically in part B of Figure 1.

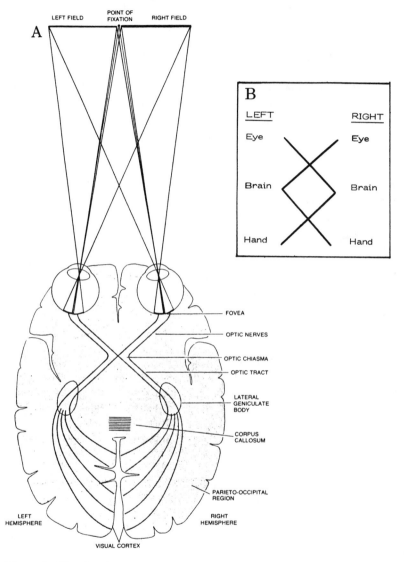

Figure 1. Visual pathways are completely crossed, so that when the eyes are fixated on a point, all of the field to the left of the fixation point excites the visual cortex in the right hemisphere and stimuli from the right visual field excite the left visual cortex. The visual cortexes can communicate via the corpus callosum, which connects the two hemispheres.

A. From The Asymmetry of the Human Brain by Doreen Kimura (91). Copyright © 1973 *Scientific American,* Inc. All rights reserved.

B. Graphic representation of A.

The major findings of this research vis-à-vis language are summarized below. Gazzaniga (55) recently has provided us with a thorough overview of split brain work; other recent articles which deal specifically with language function are those by Gazzaniga (54), Gazzaniga & Sperry (57), and Sperry & Gazzaniga (166).

With one possible exception (25), speech appears to be confined solely to the dominant hemisphere. Subjects can only name items or pronounce words flashed in the right visual field. Perception of items in the left visual field is denied. However, items flashed in either field can be found tactually behind a screen with the homolateral hand. When the left hand is involved, the items located cannot be named. If a name is volunteered by the left hemisphere, it is more often than not incorrect, whereupon the right hemisphere winces.

Simple words flashed into the left visual field can be spelled using letter cutouts behind a screen. The word spelled cannot be pronounced, however. In one instance, the investigator flashed the word: H E | A R T on the screen with the midpoint dividing the word as indicated. Subjects in this case said they had seen the word A R T and nothing more. Asked to point out with the left hand which word had been seen, subjects invariably pointed to H E rather than A R T. Drawing of three-dimensional objects is carried out best by the left hand (right hemisphere), while calculation beyond the simplest addition appears confined to the left hemisphere.

Subjects cannot write words or the names of objects flashed to the non-dominant hemisphere. The dominant hemisphere has no difficulty with any of these tasks. For two of Gazzaniga's patients, writing to dictation was possible with the left hand. This appears to be explained by the return of some ipsilateral control over this hand. That this is the case is supported by the fact that these same subjects could write the names of objects flashed to the dominant hemisphere with their left hands (cf 159).

Thus, as far as expressive aspects of language are concerned, these studies clearly point to their localization in the dominant hemisphere.

It cannot be concluded from the above that the minor hemisphere is without language. Sperry & Gazzaniga (166) have shown that acallosals are able to find items requested verbally with the left hand even when such items are described in a circumlocutory manner. Thus, requested to find the "thing that monkeys eat," subjects are able to locate a banana with their left hand behind a screen. Later, when the same piece of fruit is placed in this hand, they are unable to name it. The right hemisphere is capable of finding an item presented to it visually or tactually among a list of words. This item cannot be named, however, until it is located in the list. After all, it is not until then that the dominant hemisphere knows what it is, and only this hemisphere can initiate speech. Gazzaniga (55) has done some finer-grained testing of verbal comprehension and found that while nouns are correctly responded to, adjectives and verbs represent increasing degrees of difficulty. If subjects are requested to follow simple commands such as "smile," "nod," etc presented to the minor hemisphere, they appear unable to do so. This inability to deal with action words would seem to extend to agent nouns derived from verbs. Thus, while subjects respond correctly to words like "butter," "letter," etc, they are unable to process derived nouns such as "locker," "teller," etc. On the levels of morphology and syntax, the minor hemisphere appears able to deal with affirmative and negative constructions but not with passives, future constructions, or pluralization. (cf, however, Zaidel 1973).

The minor hemisphere also is capable of carrying out tasks which are purposely interrupted; it thus evinces memory. Emotion can also be demonstrated. When a nude photograph was mixed among neutral stimuli flashed in the left visual field, the subject's face took on a sly look of amusement. When asked why, she was unable to explain (cf 56).

Dichotic listening tests have also been carried out on acallosals by Milner et al (135) and Sparks & Geschwind (164). Although subjects were near perfect in their reporting of digits presented monaurally to either ear, scores for the left ear showed a marked drop in accuracy under dichotic presentation. This effect is shown in the following figure from Milner et al where acallosal patients are compared with other patient groups.

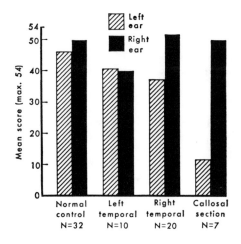

Figure 2. Mean number of digits correctly reported for each ear when different digits are simultaneously presented to the two ears. The results are for normal control subjects and for three different patient groups. From Milner et al (135).

In sum, language comprehension appears to be bilaterally represented, but this representation is by no means equipollent. If, as many hold, dominance for language is a product of maturation, then perhaps the vestiges of language evinced by the minor hemisphere are the product of earlier stages in this gradual development. A young patient studied by Gazzaniga appears to bear on this issue. This 11-year-old boy, for whom a pneumoencephalogram showed clearly established agenesis of the corpus callosum, was shown to have bilateral representation of expressive speech. Gazzaniga speculates that when the corpus callosum fails to develop, language lateralization is prevented from taking place, with the result that speech and language are bilaterally represented (cf 21). (cf Whitaker and Ojemann 1977).

HEMISPHERECTOMY—Patients suffering from the Sturge-Weber syndrome and other forms of epilepsy as well as from malignancies of the brain may indeed be better off with half a brain. Dandy introduced the operation involving total removal of one hemisphere in 1928 for the treatment of tumors. Since then hundreds of such operations have been performed in children and adults. Surveys of the effects of such operations are to be found in (185) and (6); discussions by Hillier (81), A. Smith (161), A. Smith & Burklund (162), and Ueki (170) will also be of interest. The following table from Lenneberg (104) summarizes the results of some of these operations. In all cases of dominant hemispherectomy in adults, speech, while not totally abolished, was severely affected. The same was true of

Table 2 Hemispherectomy[a]

Lesions Acquired	Hemisphere operated on	Speech not affected or improved postoperatively	Permanent aphasia
Before teens	Left	49	3 (had aphasia before operation)
	Right	38	5 (had aphasia before operation)
During puberty (single case)	Left	Slow improvement	Some residue to end of life (27 months postop.)
Adult	Left	None	6 (1 had aphasia before operation)
	Right	25	None

[a] From Lenneberg (104).

writing. Comprehension would appear to have been much less involved. As would be expected, right hemispherectomy leads to permanent impairment of various nonverbal tasks. Thus, while these cases appear to indicate some speech ability on the part of the nondominant hemisphere in contradistinction to the acallosal cases, in general they are in conformity with what we would expect from our discussion thus far. In addition, they provide some evidence (largely of an anecdotal nature) for recovery of language when the operation takes place early enough in the child's development—certainly before 5 years and perhaps as late as before puberty [cf Krashen (96, 97) and Lenneberg (104) for contrasting views of the evidence bearing on early plasticity also cf Dennis and Whitaker 1976].

Dichotic listening experiments conducted by Curry (29) and by Berlin et al (9) on hemispherectomized subjects show results comparable to those cited above for similar experiments on acallosals. The right ear achieves a score from three to four times better than the left ear.

Pharmacological Deactivation

Accurate knowledge of lateralization of speech is crucial in cases of surgery involving the classical speech areas. In 1949 Wada devised a test for language dominance which has since become widely employed (173, 174). The test involves the injection of sodium amytal into the common carotid artery, resulting in deactivation of the hemisphere ipsilateral to the side of injection. The patient who lies on a table with his legs drawn up, his forearms raised, and his fingers moving is asked to count during the injection. The injection generally produces immediate contralateral hemiplegia. In all instances, counting is momentarily interrupted, but with nondominant deactivation it resumes within 5-20 seconds, while if the dominant hemisphere is involved, dysphasic responses may continue for as long as 1-3 minutes.

Table 3 Handedness and Carotid-Amytal Speech Lateralization[a]

	Number	Speech Representation		
Handedness	of cases	Left	Bilateral	Right
Right	48	43 (90%)	0 (0%)	5 (10%)
Left or Ambidextrous				
Without early left brain damage	44	28 (64%)	7 (16%)	9 (20%)
With early left brain damage	27	6 (22%)	3 (11%)	18 (67%)

[a] From Milner et al (133).

There is now a considerable literature relating the results of this test to handedness and dominance (15,133,146,152). Typical of these findings are those reported by Milner et al (133) for 123 patients summarized in the table below.

Note the shift in dominance among patients with early left brain damage. This again provides clear support for the concept of early plasticity hypothesized by Lenneberg. Cases of bilateral speech representation are, as Milner points out, clearly also related to handedness. In 1967, she reported finding 18 such cases with only one occurring in a right-handed patient. At least one case has been cited (152) where dysphasic responses failed to develop from injection on either side!

Some extremely interesting experiments have been conducted recently at NINDS (42, 47, 110) using the Wada procedure in conjunction with a test of naming and short-term memory. This test involves a film strip with pictures of common objects joined by the word AND. Subjects are presented these stimuli at the rate of one frame every 5 seconds and are required to name the object depicted and also to recall the object in the previous frame. The AND frames serve simply as an aid to the patient in connecting utterances. Fedio and his colleagues have found that injection of sodium amytal into the dominant hemisphere produces a significant slowing in resumption of naming and an even more marked effect on short-term memory. Minor hemisphere anesthetization shows only momentary disruption of either function. In addition, if the right hemisphere is dominant, naming and recall are even further delayed. This effect they attribute to a lesser competence on the part of the right hemisphere for verbal behavior.

Electrical Stimulation of the Brain (ESB)

In 1959 Wilder Penfield and Lamar Roberts published a book on speech and brain mechanisms which did a great deal to stir interest among linguists in brain research. In this work, Penfield discusses in some detail his technique for mapping the speech cortex. A craniotomy (removing part of the skull) is performed under local anesthesia to expose the damaged portion of the brain destined for resection. While monitoring EEG activity in different parts of the brain, the neurosurgeon electrically stimulates the exposed cortex in order to determine the boundaries of the lesion, paying particular attention to the speech areas of the cortex which must not be invaded during the operation. Such stimulation at moderate frequencies (usually about 60 Hz) and intensities results in either positive signs—prolonged vocalizations (grunts or vowel sounds)—or negative signs—slurring, stuttering, difficulties in counting, misnaming, inability to name common objects, as well as complete arrest of speech. This effect is presumably brought about by inducing a disruption of the normal firing pattern in the areas involved. Vocalizations resulted from stimulation of the pre- and post-central gyri as well as of the supplementary motor area in either hemisphere. The negative signs were less specific in their localization. Based on such mapping, Penfield delineated three major speech areas which are in descending order of importance: Wernicke's area, Broca's area, and the supplementary motor area, a small zone of cortex within the longitudinal fissure in the superior part of the frontal lobe (145, 146). While the researchers cited above were never able to elicit connected speech from stimulation of the cortex, Lenneberg (105, 110) notes recent work by Schaltenbrand (156, 157) in Germany, who has been able to elicit words and phrases by means of thalamic stimulation.

Recently the research group at NINDS has been able to greatly extend and clarify much of the work of Penfield and his associates (110). Using the naming and recall task described above, Fedio & Van Buren (45) have been able to delineate in some detail the function of the temporal lobes in language and memory. Stimulation of the temporal lobe on the nondominant side failed to produce any effects on naming and immediate recall. Stimulation on the dominant side, however, produced an interesting pattern of effects. The vast majority of naming errors result from stimulation of the posterior temporoparietal area as opposed to the anterior portion of the temporal lobe which, as we have seen, can be removed without disruption of speech. Finer-grained analysis shows, however, that stimulation of this anterior region results in failure to store the items being named during stimulation, while stimulation of the posterior region produces a deficit in retrieval of an item previously named but does not interfere with storage. A similar effect holds for nonverbal, pattern-oriented tasks on the nondominant side. Based on these findings, Fedio and Van Buren speculate that what is known as Wernicke's expressive aphasia results from a breakdown in the verbal retrieval mechanism. Note that in this experiment ability to name is not lost; only recall is affected. In his recent LSA presentation, Fedio (110) notes that unlike Penfield, he has failed to observe any dysphasia from stimulation of the nondominant hemisphere. Stimulation of Broca's area produces less than half as many errors as does stimulation of Wernicke's area. The errors in Broca's area turn out to be exclusively ones of omission as opposed to substitution.

Unlike Geschwind (58), who stresses the importance of cortico-cortical connections among speech areas of the brain, Penfield and Roberts stressed cortico-subcortical ties between their three major speech areas and parts of the thalamus. These subcortical areas form what they term the *centrencephalic system,* which is responsible for integration of the functions of the cortical superstrate. Penfield and Roberts adduce as evidence for this theory the fact that excision of the convolutions around the cortical speech areas does not result in permanent aphasia, while deep trauma and strokes do. With a series of dissections by Dr. Klinger, they also clearly demonstrate that fiber tracts do indeed connect the speech areas with the thalamus. In a number of studies, the NINDS group has been able to amass considerable evidence in support of thalamic involvement in speech and language. In Fedio et al (48) and Ojemann et al (142), it is demonstrated that the thalamus displays the same sort of lateralization as the cortex. Stimulation of the left lateral as well as left superior posterior thalamus produced anomia and short-term memory disruption, while stimulation of the homologous areas on the right produced disruption in nonverbal tasks. Ojemann and associates (141, 143) show results for the left and right pulvinar, an area which Penfield and Roberts stressed in discussing their centrencephalic system. More specifically, Ojemann et al hold that the pulvinar, like the posterior portion of the temporal lobe, is involved in the retrieval mechanism for speech (cf also 142, 144, 170a). Fedio & Ommaya (44) have also done stimulation studies on the left and right cingulum. Lateralization for recall but not anomia was evinced. The experimenters postulate that unlike the pulvinar, the cingulum plays no major role in speech production or recognition. The deficit in recall may be due to involvement of the hippocampus. (cf Ojemann 1976).

Event-Related Potentials (ERPs)

Although the electrical nature of the nervous system was suspected even before Galvani, it was not until 1924 that the first brain waves from humans were recorded by Hans Berger. Even earlier, Richard Caton was aware of the effects of sensory stimuli on the brain waves of animals. Recording the effects of external stimuli from scalp electrodes in unanesthetized humans requires some method of averaging out the effects of a time-locked stimulus from the background noise generated by the brain's overall electrical activity. Such an averaging technique was introduced by Dawson in 1951 and a few years later was computerized. A thorough discussion of these important localization techniques is to be found in Donchin & Lindsley (37). Since such averaged potentials may arise not only from sensory stimulation but also as a prelude to motor activity, we adopt the cover term: *event-related potentials* to refer to both sensory and motor potentials. A considerable number of ERP studies relating speech and language activity to particular sites in the brain have recently appeared, and it is to these that we now turn.

SPEECH PRODUCTION—It has been observed that just preceding the performance of voluntary motor activity a series of negative deflections take place. In discussing such motor potentials (MPs) at a conference in 1968, Vaughan (171) called attention to their promise as a tool for the investigation of speech mechanisms in the brain. Indeed, the year before, Ertl & Schafer (40) had tested the effect of having subjects pronounce the word TEA, as well as contract their left fists, on MPs monitored from the right motor area (C_4). In both instances, a negative potential was observed before the voluntary act. However, later they (41) withdrew their finding in regard to speech production, holding it to be contaminated by a lip movement artifact. A study which yielded less equivocal results has been carried out by Whitaker & McAdam (123, 183). These investigators monitored the effect of speech (p- and k-words) vs nonspeech (spitting and coughing) production on MPs from the left and right inferior frontal areas (Broca's area and its right homologue) as well as the left precentral area 3 cm distant. No significant left-right differences were found for the nonlinguistic gestures, while significant differences with consistently greater negativity over the left hemisphere were found for the linguistic gestures. Further research indicated that this left-right asymmetry applied also to nonsense words. This study has been criticized by Morrell & Huntington (137) essentially on the basis that various myogenic artifacts were not properly controlled for (cf 124 for a response to this criticism).

A more recent study by Morrell & Huntington (138), which carefully controlled for such artifacts, does provide evidence for MPs preceding the production of various nonsense syllables. These potentials reach a maximum 10-200 msec before phonation. These investigators monitored from left and right leads over the following areas: temporo-parietal, Rolandic, anterior temporal, and frontal. The maximal negativity was recorded from the temporo-parietal sites. As in the case of speech recognition (see below), a progressive diminution of amplitude was noted the more anterior the site monitored. (For some speculation on how such a gradient might be interpreted, see the section on electromyography below.) Morrell and Huntington did not note consistent left-right asymmetries in MPs.

Another study by Low et al (109) used a cued reaction-time paradigm in which speech served as the response to a light-flash followed 1.4 seconds later by a tone. The ERP in this instance is a so-called *contingent negative variation* (CNV) which is generated by the stimuli. This slow negative potential has been shown to last until a response has been made or the intention to make a response has been abandoned. Low et al show a significant asymmetry in CNV over the temporal area (T_1, T_2). The site of maximal negativity correctly predicted lateralization as established by the sodium amytal test in 10 out of 11 patients (cf 153).

SPEECH RECOGNITION—Recording from sites on the temporal lobe (T_3, T_4), Greenberg & Graham (71) studied the effects on ERPs of the learning of linguistic (CV syllables) and nonlinguistic (piano notes) stimuli. Both sets of stimuli showed their greatest effect at first in the left hemisphere, with gradual decline in amplitude as learning progressed. At high levels of learning, a greater amplitude was present for notes in the right hemisphere. Unfortunately, no statistical analysis of this data was carried out.

An interesting experiment designed to test the contention of Studdert-Kennedy & Shankweiler (167) that the dominant hemisphere is equipped with a specific device which is only engaged in the monitoring of linguistically relevant parameters has been conducted by Wood et al (186). Stimuli differing only in formant transition [ba(low) vs da(low)] and only in fundamental frequency [ba(low) vs ba(high)] were generated on a speech synthesizer. Wood et al postulate that only the former is a linguistically relevant contrast in English. Neural activity was monitored from temporal (T_3, T_4) and central (C_3, C_4) sites during two auditory identification tasks—one involving blocks of consonant contrasts and the other blocks of frequency contrasts. Responses consisted of pressing buttons identifying which of the two possible stimuli in each block had been heard. Results indicated no difference in ERPs between the two tasks from the right hemisphere. In the left hemisphere, however, the tasks produced significant differences at both monitoring sites. The hypothesis of differential treatment of linguistic parameters on the basis of their relevance within a language system is thus supported (cf also 26, 33). More recently, Michael Dorman (37a) has provided evidence of categorical perception of speech stimuli varying in voice onset time (VOT) at the cortical level. A significant difference in average evoked responses was demonstrated between groups experiencing a category shift (20 to 40 VOT) and those in a noshift condition. Dorman suggests that language processing involves essentially the digitizing of auditory data which is in analog form. After such a transform, the auditory data is not stored. Thus, for the first time, we appear to have neurological evidence of the feature-detectors postulated by Eimas et al (39; cf also 1). The type of restructuring we see here mediating between auditory input and phonetic representation, with a resultant loss of nonessential information, also characterizes the higher level processing involved in the extraction of the "gist" (36).

Additional evidence for the differential involvement of various sites in the dominant hemisphere in speech processing comes from work by Morrell & Salamy (139). These two investigators monitored the evoked potentials to nonsense words from the left and right frontal, Rolandic, and temporo-parietal leads. Results once again supported lateralization for language processing in the dominant hemisphere. The largest contrast was, as one would expect, between the left and right temporo-parietal sites (Wernicke's area). On the left side, early negative waves over this area differed significantly from the same waves over Broca's area. There is a progressive attenuation of amplitude as one moves anteriorly in the dominant hemisphere (cf Figure 3).

VISUAL PROCESSING—Lateralization in the processing of linguistic as opposed to nonlinguistic visual patterns has also been demonstrated in a

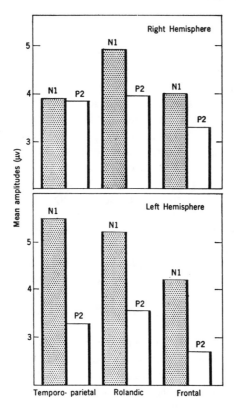

Figure 3. Mean amplitudes (in microvolts) of N1 (stippled bars) and P2 (open bars) components at temporoparietal, Rolandic, and frontal recordings for left (bottom) and right (top) hemispheres. Each mean based upon 35 observations (five stimuli for each of seven subjects). From Morrell & Salamy (139).

series of studies by the NINDS group (22, 23, 43). The stimuli in these experiments were computer-generated dot configurations which either represented three-letter words or random dot patterns produced by distorting the arrangement of dots in the letters making up such words. Geometric dot designs were also used as nonverbal stimuli. The stimuli were presented tachistoscopically in the right and left visual fields as in the split brain experiments. The finding that the verbal and nonverbal stimuli produced greater differences in the left hemisphere regardless of visual field of presentation lead Fedio and Buchsbaum to the intriguing conclusion that there is an exchange of information via the commissures and/or subcortical routes which favors reception by the left hemisphere. The left hemisphere is postulated to have an inherent comparator role in certain stages of perception.

Electromyography

In this section we turn briefly to an examination of what is known of the anatomy and physiology of speech production. Despite the fact that the importance of this area was stressed in Lashley's famous tract on serial order (101), and despite the fact that much has been learned about the mechanism of speech production, current texts in physiological psychology and neurology usually neglect this area in favor of the other topics discussed in this review. While space considerations will not allow us to totally rectify this undue neglect, at least we can call attention to some of the principal findings and alert readers to sources of additional information.

Discussions of the cranial nerves innervating the speech musculature can be found in (189) and in (94). Krmpotić (98), in an article made famous by Lenneberg (104), has performed careful measurements of these nerves indicating the great differences in length and diameter among them. Because length and diameter determine conduction speeds, Lenneberg (104) suggests that staggered firing of these nerves may be required to obtain temporal coincidence of the various speech gestures. Kim (in this volume) observes, however, that co-articulation effects in speech are perhaps best explained by *unstaggered* firing.

Recent evidence from slips of the tongue (10, 51) indicate that speech is readied for production in chunks at least as long as breath-groups or syntagma (cf 95). The size of the minimal unit making up such assemblies remains in doubt, as does the degree of monitoring or feedback that takes place once production commences (cf in this volume, 118, 140, and 163 for detailed discussions of the so-called open- and closed-loop models as well as the possible minimal unit (s) of production).

The use of electromyography (the monitoring of electrical activity during muscle contraction) has done much to pinpoint specific adaptations of physiological processes (e.g. respiration) for speech purposes (99). It has also served to clarify which particular muscles or groups of muscles are involved in producing specific linguistic parameters such as pitch, voicing, nasalization, etc. (75, 117, 154). It has not produced, however, evidence for the sort of invariance postulated by linguists for their phonetic constructs. Different neuromuscular patterns accompany perceptually identical consonant segments in pre- and post-vocalic positions (50) or before different vowels (163). What is perceptually the same vowel sound can be produced with radically different gestures (34, 100). Unrounding may involve both lips or only the upper lip. This list could easily be extended. It seems as useless to look for invariance at the muscular level in speech production as it would be in human door-opening behavior. What is clearly involved here is another problem isolated by Lashley, viz. that of motor equivalence. At the level of the cortex, we have what Pribram (149) terms an Image-of-Achievement. Such a mechanism explains how we can draw the same object, large or small, in the sand or on a blackboard; it also explains how we can speak with a pipe between our teeth or with part of our tongue removed. A promising auditory-motor theory of speech production which takes these factors into account has recently been proposed by Ladefoged et al (100). Commenting on the marked differences in articulatory gestures employed by their subjects in producing the same set of vowel sounds, these investigators propose that

. . it is useful to recall what the Haskins Laboratory group have said about the perception of consonants. According to Liberman et al (107), "articulatory movements and sensory feedback (or, more likely, the corresponding neurological processes) become part of the perceiving process, mediating between the acoustic stimulus and the ultimate perception." We would feel that it is equally true that acoustic properties and their sensory counterparts (or, more likely, the corresponding neurological processes) become part of the producing process, mediating between the possible articulatory gestures and their ultimate production. Articulatory gestures are organized within the sensory-motor cortex. The information available at this level includes not only sensory feedback information revealing dynamic and static information about the state of the muscles, but also neural projections from the auditory cortex. A speaker may be able to use an auditory image to arrive at a suitable tongue position without reference to any stored pattern of articulatory gestures.

Such a view of speech production ties in well with the findings of Morrell & Huntington (138) and Low et al (109), cited above in connection with electrical activity in the brain preceding vocalization. In both of these studies, it will be recalled that the maximal negativity was found in the temporo-parietal region with progressive attenuation of amplitude in more anterior sites. Exactly the same pattern of activity was noted in speech perception (139). [For additional suggestive discussion of voluntary motor acts as they relate to speech, see also (14) and (115).]

Dichotic Listening

We have already had occasion to refer several times to the results of dichotic listening studies. We now turn to a more detailed discussion of this experimental approach which is without doubt the most widely used in investigating the relationship of brain mechanisms to language. The basic paradigm for dichotic listening was created by Donald Broadbent (16) in connection with his ongoing studies of attention. Broadbent's technique consisted of presenting one sequence of three digits to one ear while simultaneously presenting another sequence to the opposite ear. Thus, one ear might be presented with a sequence such as 176 while the other ear re-received another sequence such as 852. It was found that subjects reported the digits they had heard in terms of sequences presented to each ear rather than in terms of order of presentation. In administering this test to patients at the Montreal Neurological Institute, Kimura (89) discovered that digits presented to the ear contralateral to the dominant hemisphere were reported more accurately irrespective of area of brain damage. The same effect was shown to obtain in normals. Kimura attributed this to cerebral dominance coupled with the greater strength of the contralateral pathways over the ipsilateral ones. This is shown in Figure 4. Evidence for such a distinction in

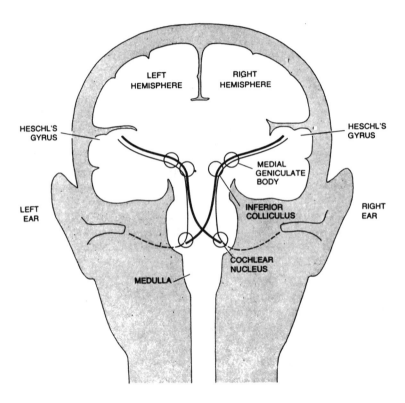

Figure 4. Auditory pathways from the ears to the cerebral auditory receiving areas in the right and left hemispheres are partially crossed. Although each hemisphere can receive input from both ears, the neural connections from one ear to the hemisphere on the opposite side are stronger than the connections to the hemisphere on the same side. When ipsilateral (same side) and contralateral (opposite side) inputs compete in the auditory neural system, it is thought that the stronger contralateral input inhibits or occludes the ipsilateral signals. From The Asymmetry of the Human Brain by Doreen Kimura (91). Copyright©1973 *Scientific American,* Inc. All rights reserved.

man has been provided by Bocca et al (12). When stimuli are presented monaurally, however, this right ear advantage is not observed. It was postulated that this was the case because only under dichotic presentation are the ipsilateral pathways inhibited. Strong support for this explanation is provided by studies of dichotic listening in acallosal (135, 164) and hemispherectomized patients (29). Such studies, as we have already pointed out, show a drastic decline in accuracy for the ipsilateral ear. This can only be attributed to inhibition at a peripheral level as all other pathways from the ear ipsilateral to the dominant hemisphere do not exist in these patients (cf 96 for a complete discussion of this topic). In normals it is assumed that speech presented to the ipsilateral ear crosses to the nondominant hemisphere via the contralateral pathway and then must be routed to the dominant hemisphere via the corpus callosum. It is generally held that this indirect route in some manner accounts for the lower degree of accuracy evinced by the ipsilateral ear (cf 167). For a discussion of some problems involved in this interpretation see (176).

The results of applying the dichotic listening paradigm to a number of modalities are presented in the table below adapted from Kimura (91; cf 90). It can be seen that these results obtained from normals are consistent with the findings of other approaches we have discussed above. In regard to auditory input, it should be noted that the dominant hemisphere is specialized not only for meaningful input but for nonsense syllables and backward speech as well (31, 72, 92, 93, 160). This has led investigators at Haskins and the University of Connecticut to speak of a specialized linguistic processor in the dominant hemisphere utilized for the extraction of linguistically encoded sounds (108, 122, 167). This view has encouraged these investigators to undertake a more fine-grained analysis of speech sounds within the dichotic listening paradigm. Studdert-Kennedy & Shankweiler (167) found significant right ear advantage for initial and final consonants but not for medial (presumably linguistically encoded) vowels. They also found significant right ear advantages for such features as voicing and place of articulation in initial stops (cf 73). Fricatives have a small right ear effect only when they evince formant transitions (32). Liquids and semivowels also show a right ear advantage but smaller than for stops (74). Such findings have led some investigators to speak of degrees of encodedness, with stops being generally the most encoded speech sounds and vowels the least (30).

If there is indeed a specialized linguistic processor in the dominant hemisphere, it does not appear to be modality-specific, as Table 4 clearly shows. In fact, it may not even be language-specific. Note the advantage indicated for skilled movements (in this regard see also 159). Dominant hemisphere advantages for nonlinguistic temporal ordering have also been noted (96). From our study of acallosals and hemispherectomized patients, it is also clear that linguistic processing is not entirely confined to the dominant hemisphere. Not only does it appear to make sense to speak of a continuum for encoding, but also of a continuum for dominance itself (168).

Table 4 Left/right hemisphere test score ratios in normal, right-handed subjects on the dichotic listening task[a]

Modality	Left/Right Hemisphere Test Score Ratio
Auditory	
words	1.88 : 1
nonsense syllables	1.73 : 1
backward speech	1.66 : 1
melodic pattern	1 : 1.19
human nonspeech sounds	1 : 1.08
Visual	
letters	1.23 : 1
words	1.47 : 1
two-dimensional point location	1 : 1.18
dot and form enumeration	1 : 1.20
matching of slanted lines	1 : 1.05
stereoscopic depth perception	1 : 1.28
Manual	
skilled movements	1.13 : 1
free movements during speech	3.10 : 1
tactile dot patterns (Braille)	Right advantage (initial findings)
nonvisual location	1 : 1.12

[a] Adapted from (91).

Acknowledgement

The authors wish to express their gratitude to Dr. Paul Fedio of the National Institutes of Health for his many valuable suggestions on the final section of this paper.

References

1 Abbs, J., Sussman, H. 1971. Neurophysiological feature detectors and speech perception: A discussion of theoretical implications. *J. Speech Hear. Res.* 14:23-36

2 de Ajuriaguerra, J., Tissot, R. 1969. The Apraxias. See Ref. 172, 4:48-66

3 Akelaitas, A.J. 1944. A study of gnosis, praxis and language following section of the corpus callosum and anterior commissure. *J. Neurosurg.* 1:94

4 Alajouanine, T. 1956. Verbal realization in aphasia. *Brain* 79:1-28

5 Auburtin, S. A. E. 1861. Discussion in *Bull. Soc. Anthropol. Paris* 4:217-20

6 Basser, L.S. 1962. hemiplegia of early onset and the faculty of speech with special reference to the effects of hemispherectomy. *Brain* 85:427-60

7 Benton, A. L. 1964. Contributions to aphasia before Broca. *Cortex* 1:314-27

8 Benton, A. L., Joynt, R. J. 1960. Early descriptions of aphasia. *Archiv. Neurol.* 3:205-22

9 Berlin, C., Lowe-Bell, S., Porter, R., Berlin, H., Thompson, C. 1972. Dichotic signs of the recognition of speech elements in normals, temporal lobectomies, and hemispherectomies. *Proc. Int. Congr. Speech Commun. Process Boston*

10 Bierwisch, M. 1970. Fehler-Linguistik. *Ling. Inq.* 1:397-414

11 Blumstein, S. 1973. *A Phonological Investigation of Aphasic Speech.* The Hague: Mouton

12 Bocca, E., Calearo, C., Cassinari, V., Migliavacca, F. 1955. Testing "cortical" hearing in temporal lobe tumors. *Acta Oto-Laryngol.* 45:289-304

13 Bouillaud, J. 1825. Recherches cliniques propres a demontrer que la perte de la parole correspond a la lesion des lobules anterrieurs du cerveau et a confirmer l'opinion de M. Gall, sur la siege de l'organe du langage articule. *Arch. Gen. Med.* 8:25-45

14 Brain, R. 1961. The neurology of language. *Brain* 84:145-66

15 Branch, C., Milner, B., Rasmussen, T. 1967. Intra-carotid sodium amytal for the lateralization of cerebral speech dominance. *J. Neurosurg.* 21:399-405

16 Broadbent, D. E. 1954. The role of auditory localization in attention and memory span. *J. Exp. Psychol.* 47:191-96

17 Broca, P. 1861. Perte de la parole. Ramollissement chronique et destruction partielle du lobe anterrieur gauche de cerveau. *Bull. Soc. Anthropol. Paris* 2:235-38

18 Broca, P. 1861. Remarques sur le siege de la faculte du langage articule, suives d'une observation d'aphemie. *Bull. Soc. Ant.* 6:330-57

19 Ibid. Nouvelle observation d'aphemie produite par une lesion de la moite posterieure des duexieme et troisieme curconvolutions frontales, 398-407

20 Brown, J. W. 1972. *Aphasia, Apraxia and Agnosia.* Springfield: Thomas

21 Bryden. M. P., Zwrif, F. B. 1970. Dichotic listening performance in a case of agenesis of the corpus callosum. *Neuropsychologia* 8:371-77.

22 Buchsbaum, M., Fedio, P. 1969. Visual information and evoked responses from left and right hemispheres. *Electroencephalogr. Clin. Neurophysiol.* 26:266-72

23 Buchsbaum, M., Fedio, P. 1970. Hemispheric differences in evoked potentials to verbal and nonverbal stimuli in the left and right visual fields. *Physiol. Behav.* 5:207-10

24 Buckingham, H., Kertesz, A. 1974. A linguistic analysis of fluent aphasia. *Brain Lang.* 1:43-62

25 Butler, S., Norrsell, U. 1968. Vocalization possibly initiated by the minor hemisphere. *Nature* 220:793-94

26 Cohn, R. 1971. Differential cerebral processing of noise and verbal stimuli. *Science* 172:599-601

27 Critchley, M. 1970. *Aphasiology.* London: Arnold

28 Citchley, M. 1974. Aphasia in polyglots and bilinguals. *Brain Lang.* 1:15-27

29 Curry, F. 1968. A comparison of the performance of a right hemispherectomized subject and twenty-five normals on four dichotic listening tasks. *Cortex* 4:144-53

30 Cutting, J. E. 1972. A parallel between encodedness and the magnitude of the right ear effect. *Status Rep. Speech Res.* (Haskins Labs.) 29/30:61-68

31 Darwin. C. J. 1969. *Auditory perception and cerebral dominance.* PhD thesis. Univ. Cambridge, England

32 Darwin, C. J. 1971. Ear differences in the recall of fricatives and vowels. *Quart. J. Exp. Psychol.* 23:46-62

33 Day, R. S. 1973. Engaging and disengaging the speech processor. *J. Psycholing. Res.* 2:283-84

34 Delattre, P. 1967. Acoustic or articulatory invariance. *Glossa* 1:3-25

35 De Renzi, E., Pieczuro, A., Vignolo, L. A. 1966. Oral apraxia and aphasia. *Cortex* 2:50-73

36 Dingwall, W. O., Shields, J. L. 1973. From utterance to gist: Four experimental studies of what's in between. Unpublished Manuscript.

37 Donchin, E., Lindsley, D. B., Eds. 1969. *Average Evoked Potentials.* Washington, D.C.: NASA SP-191

37a Dorman, M. 1972. Auditory evoked potential correlates of speech sound discrimination. *Status Rep. Speech Res.* 29/30:111-20

38 Dubois, J., Hécaen, H., Angelergues, R., de Chatelier, A. M., Marcie, P. 1964. Etude neurolinguistique de l'aphasie de conduction. *Neuropsychologia* 2:9-44

39 Eimas, P., Cooper, W., Corbit, J. 1973. Some properties of linguistic feature detectors. *Percept. Psychophys.* 13:247-52

40 Ertl, J., Schafer, E. W. P. 1967. Cortical activity preceding speech. *Life Sci.* 6:473-79

41 Ibid 1969. Erratum. 8:559

42 Fedio, P., Baldwin, M. 1969. Dysonmia and short-term memory impairment from intracarotid sodium amytal. *Experpta Med. Found. Int. Congr. Ser. 193*

43 Fedio, P., Buchsbaum, M. 1971. Unilateral temporal lobectomy and changes in evoked responses during recognition of verbal and nonverbal material in the left and right visual fields. *Neuropsychologia* 9:261-71

44 Fedio, P., Ommaya, A. K. 1970. Bilateral cingulum lesions and stimulation in man with lateralized impairment in short-term verbal memory. *Exp. Neurol.* 29:84-91

45 Fedio, P., Van Buren, J. M. 1971. Cerebral mechanisms for perception and immediate memory under electrical stimulation in conscious man. Bethesda: Surg. Neurol. Branch, Nat. Inst. Neurol. Dis. Stroke. Unpublished manuscript

46 Fedio, P., Van Buren, J. M. 1974. Memory deficits during electrical stimulation of the speech cortex in conscious man. *Brain Lang.* 1:29-42

47 Fedio, P., Weinberg, L. K. 1971. Dysnomia and impairment of verbal memory following intracarotid injection of sodium amytal. *Brain Res.* 31:159-68

48 Fedio, P., Van Buren, J. M., Ojemann, G. Asymmetry of verbal and nonverbal memory from thalamic and subcortical parietal stimulation (abstr.)

49 Freud, S. 1901. *On Aphasia.* New York: Int. Univ. Press

50 Fromkin, V. A. 1966. Neuromuscular specification of linguistic units. *Lang. Speech* 9:170-99

51 Fromkin, V. A. 1971. The non-anomalous nature of anomalous utterances. *Language* 47:27-52

52 Gall, F. J. 1818. Anatomie et physiologie du systeme nerveux en general et du cerveau en particulier. *Paris* IV

53 Gall, F. J., Spurzheim, G. 1809. Recherches sur le systeme nerveux en general et sur celui du cerveau en particulier. *Mémoire presente a l'Institut de France* 14 mars. Paris

54 Gazzaniga, M. S. 1967. The split brain in man. *Sci. Am.* 217:24-29

55 Gazzaniga, M. S. 1970. *The Bisected Brain.* New York; Appleton-Century-Crofts

56 Gazzaniga, M. S., Hillyard, S. A. 1971. Language and speech capacity of the right hemisphere. *Neuropsychologia* 9:278-80

57 Gazzaniga, M. S., Sperry, R. W. 1967. Language after section of the cerebral commissures. *Brain* 90:131-48

58 Geschwind, N. 1965. Disconnexion syndromes in animals and man. *Brain* 88: 237-94, 585-644

58a Geschwind, N. 1967. The varieties of naming errors. *Cortex* 9:97-112

59 Geschwind, N., Fusillo, M. 1966. Color naming defects in association with alexia. *Arch. Neurol.* 15:137-46

60 Glass, A. V., Gazzaniga, M. S., Premack, D. 1973. Articifical language in global aphasics. *Neuropsychologia* 11:95-103

61 Gloning, K., Hoff, H. 1969. Cerebral localisation of disorders of higher nervous activity. See Ref. 172, 3:22-47

62 Goldstein, K. 1948. *Language and Language Disturbances.* New York: Grune & Stratton

63 Goodglass, H. 1968. Studies on the grammar of aphasics. In *Developments in Applied Psycholinguistics,* ed. S. Rosenberg, J. H. Koplin, 177-208. New York: MacMillan

64 Goodglass, H., Blumstein, S., Eds. 1973. *Psycholinguistics and Aphasia.* Baltimore: John Hopkins Press

65 Goodglass, H., Fodor, I. G., Schulhoff, C. 1967. Prosodic factors in grammar—evidence from aphasia. *J. Speech Hear. Res.* 10:5-20

66 Goodglass, H., Geschwind, N. Language disorders (aphasia). In *Handbook of Perception,* ed. E. C. Carterette, M. Friedman. New York: Academic. 1976

67 Goodglass, H., Hyde, M. R., Blumstein, S. 1969. Frequency, picturability and the availability of nouns in aphasia. *Cortex* 5:104-19

68 Goodglass, H., Kaplan, E. 1972. *The Assessment of Aphasia and Related Disorders.* Philadelphia: Lea & Febiger

68a Goodglass, H., Klein, B., Carey, P., Jones, K. J. 1966. Specific semantic word categories in aphasia. *Cortex* 2:74-89

69 Green, E. 1969. Phonological and grammatical aspects of jargon in an aphasic patient: a case study. *Lang. Speech* 12:103-18

70 Green, E. 1969. Psycholinguistic approaches to aphasia. *Linguistics* 53:30-50

71 Greenberg, H. J., Graham, J. T. 1970. Electroencephalographic changes during learning of speech and nonspeech stimuli. *J. Verb. Learn. Verb. Behav.* 9:274-81

72 Haggard, M. P. 1969. Perception of semi-vowels and laterals. *J. Acoust. Soc. Am.* 46:115 (abstr.)

73 Haggard, M. P. 1970. The use of voicing information. *Speech Synthesis and Perception, Progr. Rep.* 2:1-14, Psychol. Lab., Univ. Cambridge

74 Haggard, M. 1971. Encoding and the REA for speech signals. *Quart. J. Exp. Psychol.* 23:34-45

75 Harris, K. S. 1970 Physiological aspects of articulatory behavior. SR. 23:49-67

76 Head, H. 1963 (reprint of 1926 edition). *Aphasia and Kindred Disorders of Speech.* New York: Hafner

77 Hécaen, H. 1969. Cerebral localization of mental functions and their disorders. See Ref. 172, 3:11-21

78 Hécaen, H. *Introduction to Neurolinguistics.* Springer-Verlag. In press

79 Hécaen, H., Consoli, S. 1973. Analyse des troubles du language en cours des lesions de l'aire du Broca. *Neuropsychologia* 11:377-88

80 Hécaen, H., Dubois, R. 1967. Essai d'analyse neurolinguistique des agraphies. In *To Honor Roman Jakobson,* 869-900. The Hague: Mouton

81 Hillier, W. 1954. Total left hemispherectomy for malignant glioma. *Neurology* 4:718-21

82 Jakobson, R. 1964. Towards a linguistic typology of aphasic impairments. In *Disorders of Language,* ed. A. V. S. de Reuck, M. O'Connor, 21-41. Boston: Little Brown

83 Jakobson, R. 1966. Linguistic types of aphasia. In *Brain Function,* ed. E. C. Carterette, 3:67-91. Los Angeles: Univ. California Press

84 Janzen, R. 1972. Die letzen 100 Jahre Lokalisationforschung an der Grosshirnrinde. *A. Neurol.* 202:75-93

85 Joynt, R. J. 1964. Paul Pierre Broca: His contribution to the knowledge of aphasia. *Cortex* 1: 206-13

86 Kehoe, W. J., Whitaker, H. A. 1973. Lexical structure disruption in aphasia: a case study. See Ref. 64

87 Kim, Chin-Wu 1971. Experimental phonetics. In *A Survey of Linguistic Science,* ed. W. O. Dingwall, 16-135. College Park: Univ. Maryland Ling. Program

88Kimura, D. 1961. Some effects of temporal lobe damage on auditory perception. *Can. J. Psychol.* 15:156-65

89Ibid. Cerebral dominance and the perception of verbal stimuli, 166-71

90Kimura, D. 1964. Left-right differences in the perception of melodies. *Quart. J. Exp. Psychol.* 14:355-58

91Kimura, D. 1973. The asymmetry of the human brain. *Sci. Am.* 228:70-78

92Kimura, D. 1967. Functional asymmetry of the brain in dichotic listening. *Cortex* 3:163-78

93Kimura, D., Folb, S. 1968. Neural processing of backwards-speech sounds. *Science* 161:396-406

94Konigsmark, B. W. 1970. Neuroanatomy of speech. *ASHA Rep.* 5:3-19

95Kozhevnikov, V., Chistovich, L. 1966. *Speech: Articulation and Perception.* Washington, D.C.: US Dep. Commerce

96Krashen, S. 1972. Language and the left hemisphere. *UCLA Work. Pap. Phonetics* 24

97Krashen, S. D. 1973. Lateralization, language learning, and the critical period: Some new evidence. *Lang. Learn.* 23:63-74

98Krmpotić, J. 1959. Données anatomiques et histologiques relatives aux effecteurs laryngo-pharyngo-buccaux. *Rev. Laryngol.* 11:829-48

99Ladefoged, P. 1967. *Three Areas of Experimental Phonetics.* London: Oxford Univ. Press

100Ladefoged, P., DeClark, J., Lindau, M., Papcun, g. 1972. An auditory-motor theory of speech production. *UCLA Work. Pap. Phonetics* 22:48-75

101Lashley, K. S. 1951. The problem of serial order in behavior. In *Cerebral Mechanisms in Behavior,* ed. L. A. Jeffress, 112-36. New York: Wiley

102Lebrun, Y., Hoops, R. 1974. *Aphasia and Intelligence.* Amsterdam: Swets & Zeitlinger. 1974

103Lecours, A. R., Lhermitte, F. 1969. Phonemic paraphasias: linguistic structures and tentative hypotheses. *Cortex* 5:193-228

104Lenneberg, E. 1967. *Biological Foundations of Language.* New York: Wiley

105Lenneberg, E. H. 1973. The neurology of language. *Daedalus* 102: 115-33

106Lenneberg, E. 1960. Review: *Speech and Brain Mechanism* (Penfield & Roberts). *Language* 36:97-112

107Liberman, A., Cooper, F., Shankweiler, D., Studdert-Kennedy, M. 1967. Perception of the speech code. *Psychol. Rev.* 74:431-61

108Locke, S., Caplan, D., Kellar, L. 1973. *A Study in Neurolinguistics.* Springfield: Thomas

109Low, M. D., Wada, J., Fox, M. 1973. Electroencephalographic localization of conative aspects of language production in the human brain. *3rd Int. Congr. Event-Related Slow Potentials of the Brain, Bristol, England*

110LSA Language and the Brain Tutorial. 1973. Introduction, W. O. Dingwall; Neuropsychology, E. H. Lenneberg; Neurolinguistics, H. A. Whitaker; Neurology, J. P. Mohr; Language, Memory and the Brain, P. Fedio. Available on tape from: Linguistic Society of America, 1611 North Kent Street, Arlington, Virginia 22207

111Luria, A. R. 1958. Brain disorders and language analysis. Lang. Speech 1:14-34

112Luria, A. R. 1966. Higher Cortical Functions in Man. New York: Basic Books

113Luria, A. R. 1967. Problems and facts of neurolinguistics. In To Honor Roman Jakobson 2: 1213-27. The Hague: Mouton

114Luria, A. R. 1970. Traumatic Aphasia. The Hague: Mouton

115Luria, A. R. 1970. The functional organization of the brain. Sci. Am. 222:66-78

116Luria, A. R. 1973. The Working Brain. London: Penguin Press

117MacNeilage, P. F. 1972. Speech physiology. In Speech and Cortical Functioning, ed. J. Gilbert, 1-72. New York: Academic

118MacNeilage, P. F. 1973. Preliminaries to the study of single motor unit activity in speech musculature. J. Phonetics 1:55-71

119Marie, P. 1906. The third left frontal convolution plays no special role in the function of language (in French). Sem. Med. 26:241-47

120Marshall, J. C., Newcombe, F. 1966. Syntactic and semantic errors in paralexia. Neuropsychologia 4:169-76

121Marshall, M., Newcombe, F., Marshall, J. C. 1971. The microstructure of word-finding difficulties in a dysphasic subject. In Advances in Psycholinguistics, ed. G. B. Flores d'Arcais, W. Levelt, 416-26. Amsterdam: North-Holland

122Mattingly, I. G., Liberman, A. M. 1969. The speech code and the physiology of language. In Information Processing in the Nervous System, ed. K. N. Leibovic, 97-117. New York: Springer-Verlag

123McAdam, D., Whitaker, H. A. 1971. Language production: Electroencephalograchic localization in the normal human brain. Science 172:499-502

124Ibid. Electrocortical localization ot language production (A reply to Morrell & Huntington). 174:1360-61

125Meader, C. L., Muyskens, J. H. 1950. Handbook of Biolinguistics. Toledo: Weller

126Mettler, F. A., Ed. 1949. Selective Partial Ablation of the Frontal Cortex. New York: Hoeber

127Meyer, V. 1959. Cognitive changes following temporal lobectomy for the relief of temporal lobe epilepsy. Arch. Neurol. Psychiat. 81:299-309

128Miller, E. 1972. Clinical Neuropsychology. Middlesex, England: Penguin Books

129Millikan, C. H., Darley, F. L., Eds. 1967. Brain Mechanisms Underlying Speech and Language. New York: Grune & Stratton

130Milner, B. 1958. Psychological defects produced by temporal-lobe excision. Res. Publ. Res. Nerv. Ment. Dis. 36:244-57

131Milner, B. 1964. Some effects of frontal lobectomy in man. *The Frontal Granular Cortex and Behavior,* ed. J. W. Warren, K. Akert. New York: McGraw-Hill

132Milner, B. 1967. Brain mechanisms suggested by studies of temporal lobes. See Ref. 129, 122-45

133Milner, B., Branch, C., Rasmussen, T. 1964. Observations on cerebral dominance. See Ref. 150, 200-14

134Milner, B., Branch, E., Rasmussen, T. 1966. Evidence for bilateral speech representation in some non-righthanders. *Trans. Am. Neurol. Assoc.* 91:306-8

135Milner, B., Taylor, L., Sperry, R. 1968. Lateralized suppression of dichotically presented digits after commissural section in man. *Science* 161:184-86

136Mohr, J. P. 1973. Rapid amelioration of motor aphasia. *AMA Arch. Neuro.* 28.77-82.

137Morrell, L., Huntington, D. 1971. Electrocortical localization of language production. *Science* 174:1359-60

138Morrell, L., Huntington, D. 1972. Cortical potentials time-locked to speech production: Evidence for probable cerebral origin. *Life Sci.* 11:921-29

139Morrell, L. K., Salamy. J. G. 1971. Hemispheric asymmetry of electrocortical responses to speech stimuli. *Science* 174:164-66

140Ohala, J. 1970. Aspects of the control and production of speech. *UCLA Work. Pap. Phonetics* 15

141Ojemann, G., Fedio, P. 1968. Effect of stimulation of the human thalamus and parietal and temporal white matter on short-term memory. *J. Neurosurg.* 29:51-59

142Ojemann, G., Fedio, P., Van Buren, J. M. 1969. Evidence for dominance within the human lateral thalamus. *Excepta Med. Int. Congr. Ser.* 193:260

143Ojemann, G., Fedio, P., Van Buren, J. M. 1968. Anomia from pulvinar and subcortical parietal stimulation. *Brain* 91:99-116

144Ojemann, G., Ward, A. 1971. Speech representation in the ventro-lateral thalamus. *Brain* 94:669-715

145Penfield, W. 1963. *Speech and Perception.* New York Univ. Med. Center

146Penfield, W., Roberts, L. 1969. *Speech and Brain Mechanisms.* Princeton Univ. Press

147Poeck, K., Kerschensteiner, M. 1971. Ideomotor apraxia following right-sided cerebral lesion in a left-handed subject. *Neuropsychologia* 9:359-61

148Poncet, M., Degos, C., Deloche, G., Lecours, A. R. 1972. Phonetic and phonemic transformations in aphasia. *Int. J. Ment. Health* 1:46-54

149Pribram, K. H. 1971. *Languages of the Brain: Experimental Paradoxes and Principles in Neuropsychology.* Englewood Cliffs: Prentice-Hall

150de Reuck, A. V. S., O'Connor, M., Eds. 1964. *Ciba Foundation Symposium on Disorders of Language.* London: Churchill

151Rinnert, C., Whitaker, H. A. 1973. Semantic confusions by aphasic patients. *Cortex* 9:56-81

152Rossi, G., Rosadini, G. 1967. Experimental analysis of cerebral dominance in man. See Ref. 129, 167-84

153Roth, W. T., Kopell, D. S., Bertozzi, P. E. 1970. The effect of attention on the average evoked response to speech sounds. *Electroencephalogr. Clin. Neurophysiol.* 29:38-46

154Sawashima, M. 1970. Laryngeal research in experimental phonetics. *Status Rep. Speech Res.* 23:69-115

155Schafer, E. W. P. 1967. Cortical activity preceding speech. *Life Sci.* 6:473-79

156Schaltenbrand, G. 1965. The effects of stereotactic stimulation in the depth of the brain. *Brain* 88:835-40

157Schaltenbrand, G., Spuer, H., Wahren, W., Rummler, B. 1971. Electroanatomy of the thalamic ventro-oral nucleus based on stereotatic stimulation in moan. *Z. Neurol.* 199:259-76

158Schnitzer, M. 1972. *Generative Phonology—Evidence from Aphasia.* University Park: Penn State Univ. Press

159Semmes, J. 1968. Hemispheric specialization: A possible clue to mechanism. *Neuropsychologia* 6:11-26

160Shankweiler, D., Studdert-Kennedy, M. 1967. Identification of consonants and vowels presented to left and right ears. *Quart. J. Exp. Psychol.* 19:59-63

161Smith, A. 1966. Speech and other functions after left (dominant) hemispherectomy. *J. Neurol. Neurosurg. Psychiat.* 29:467-71

162Smith, A., Burklund, C. W. 1966. Dominant hemispherectomy: Preliminary report on neurological sequelae. *Science* 153:1280-82

163Smith, T. S. 1971. A phonetic study of the function of the extrinsic tongue muscles. *UCLA Work. Pap. Phonetics* 18

164Sparks, R., Geschwind, N. 1968. Dichotic listening in man after section of neocortical commissures. *Cortex* 4:3-16

165Spear, M. H. 1971. *Organizational aspects of memory in temporal lobectomy patients.* PhD thesis. Univ. Maryland, College Park

166Sperry, R. W., Gazzaniga, M. S. 1967. Language following surgical disconnection of the hemispheres. See Ref. 129, 108-21

167Studdert-Kennedy, M., Shankweiler, D. 1970. Hemispheric specialization for speech perception. *J. Acoust. Soc. Am.* 48:579-94

168Studdert-Kennedy, M., Shankweiler, S. 1972. A continuum of cerebral dominance for speech perception. *Status Rep. Speech Res.* 31/32:23-40

169Trager, E. C. 1960. The field of neurolinguistics. *Stud. Ling.* 15:70-71

170Ueki, K. 1966. Hemispherectomy in the human with special reference to the preservation of function. *Progr. Brain Res.* 121:285-88

170aVan Buren, J., Borke, R. 1969. Alternations in speech and pulvinar. *Brain* 92:255-84

171Vaughan, H. G. 1969. The relationshp of brain activity to scalp recordings of event-related potentials. See Ref. 37, 45-94

172Vinken, P. J., Bruyn, G. W., Eds. 1969. *Handbook of Clinical Neurology.* Amsterdam: North -Holland

173Wada, J. 1949. A new method for the determination of the side of cerebral speech dominance: A preliminary report on the intracarotid injection of sodium amytal in man. *Med. Biol.* (Tokyo) 14:221-22

174Wada, J., Rasmussen, T. 1960. Intracarotid injection of sodium amytal for the lateralization of cerebral speech dominance. Experimental and clinical observations. *J. Neurosurg.* 17: 266-82

175Warrington, E. K. 1969. Constructional apraxia. See Ref. 172, 4:67-83

176Weeks, R. A. 1973. A speech perception paradox? The right-ear advantage and the lag effect. *Status Rep. Speech Res.* 33:29-35

177Weigl, E., Bierwisch, M. 1970. Neuropsychology and linguistics: Topics of common research. *Found. Lang.* 6:1-18

178Weingartner, H. 1968. Verbal learning in patients with temporal lobe lesions. *J. Verb. Learn. Verb. Behav.* 7:520-26

179Whitaker, H. A. 1970. Linguistic competence: Evidence from aphasia. *Glossa* 4:46-54

180Whitaker, H. A. 1971. *On the Representation of Language in the Human Brain.* Edmonton: Ling. Res.

181Whitaker, H. A. 1971. Neurolinguistics. In *A Survey of Linguistic Science,* ed. W. O. Dingwall, 136-251. College Park: Univ. Maryland

182Whitaker, H. A. 1972. Unsolicited nominalizations by aphasics: the plausibility of the lexicalist model. *Linguistics* 78:62-71

183Whitaker, H. A., McAdam, D. W. 1971. Localization of speech function in the normal brain. *Neurology* 21:327-28

184Whitaker, H. A., Noll, J. D. 1972. Some linguistic parameters of the token test. *Neuropsychologia* 10:395-404

185White, H. 1961. Cerebral hemispherectomy in the treatment of infantile hemiplegia.*Confin. Neurol.* 21:1-50

186Wood, C., Goff, W., Day, R. 1971. Hemisphere differences in auditory evoked potentials during phonemic and pitch discrimination. *Science* 173:1248-51

187X-ray diagnosis peers inside the brain. *New Scientist,* April 27, 1972

188Yamadori, A., Albert, M. L. 1973. Word category aphasia. *Cortex* 9:112-25

189Zemlin, W. R. 1968. *Speech and Hearing Science.* Englewood Cliffs: Prentice-Hall

Addenda

Dennis, M. and H. A. Whitaker, 1976. Language acquisition following hemidecortication: Linguistics superiority of the left over the right hemisphere. *Brain and Language* 3.404-433.

Ojemann, G. 1976. Subcortical language mechanisms. Studies in neurolinguistics, Vol. 1, ed. by H. Whitaker and H. A. Whitaker, 103-138. NY: Academic Press.

Whitaker, H. A. and G. Ojemann. 1977. Lateralization of higher cortical functions: A critique. Ann. N.Y. Acad. Sci. Vol. 299.459-473.

Zaidel, E. 1973. Linguistic competence and related functions in the right cerebral hemisphere of man following commissurotomy and hemispherectomy. Unpub. Ph.D. dissertation. Pasadena: California Institute of Technology.

Chapter Nine

Experimental Psycholinguistics[1]

Philip B. Gough and Randy L. Diehl

The beginnings of contemporary psycholinguistics can be traced to the publication of a paper entitled "Some psychological studies of grammar" in November, 1962. In that paper, George Miller brought the work of Noam Chomsky to the attention of the psychological world, and he reported the first modern psycholinguistic experiments. That is, he presented the results of the first experimental studies of sentences fertilized by transformational analysis of syntactic structure.

Experimental psychology had cohabited with linguistics before. Their expected offspring had even been named *psycholinguistics* (Osgood and Sebeok, 1954). But it remained a gleam in the eye; the union bore no significant issue.

What was missing was the sentence. Prior to Miller's paper, a number of experimental psychologists were investigating one or another aspect of language (cf. Gough and Jenkins, 1963). But their investigations dealt almost exclusively with the word: its meaning, its associations, its role in memory and perception. At least in retrospect, these studies seem to reflect the assumption that the word was the basic unit of language, that a sentence was no more than a sequence of words strung together by associations.

This assumption was apparently bolstered by the results of a handful of studies of statistical approximations to English (see Rubenstein and Aborn, 1960), which appeared to show that as the associative constraints between words in a string are increased, the string behaves more like a sentence in perception and memory.[2] It must have seemed reasonable to assume that could we but fathom the word and the association, we would capture the sentence as a corollary. To be sure, the subtleties of linguistic structure could be expected to introduce complications (cf. Mowrer, 1954), but their investigation could be postponed until the basic problems of the word and the association were solved.

Then came Chomsky and Miller. Chomsky's contribution was to show that the sentence is not just a matter of words and associations: the structure of the sentence contributes as much to its interpretation as its elements, and that structure cannot be reduced to associations. Therefore, understanding of the sentence could not be expected as a by-product of study of the word, and study of the sentence could not be shelved.

Miller showed that it need not be. The seminal studies out of his laboratory suggested how the structural descriptions of sentences provided by the new linguistic theory could be exploited in experimental studies of the sentence.

The first psycholinguistic experiments aimed at little more than demonstrating this point, at showing that linguistic description was relevant to the behavior of sentences in paradigmatic psychological experiments. Note that we refer to *experiments,* not *processes.* The choice is deliberate, for the experimental psychologist is, sad to say, typically more impressed by problems posed by data than with puzzles set by mechanism. He is seldom persuaded that something matters unless you can show him it has an effect on a familiar variable under familiar conditions. So the first psycholinguistic experiments sought to show that linguistic description provided variables that count for something in the psychologist's domain.

Transformational grammar ascribed to every sentence a number of properties which held promise: degree of grammaticality, surface structure, deep structure, transformational complexity. These became the objects of a succession of studies examining their effects on a variety of dependent variables.

Degree of grammaticality was shown to determine the ease with which sentences could be perceived in noise (Miller and Isard, 1963), repeated (Epstein, 1961), memorized (Marks and Miller, 1964), or paraphrased (Downey and Hakes, 1968). Surface structure was found to influence the perceived location of clicks intruding on a sentence (Fodor and Bever, 1965), and to predict where errors would be made in the course of committing a sentence to memory (Johnson, 1966). Deep structure was found to be related to the way sentences are remembered (Mehler, 1963) and to the ease with which they can be perceived through noise (Mehler and Carey, 1967). The perceived similarity of sentences was shown to be related to their transformational distance from one another (Clifton and Odom, 1966), and some evidence was obtained to support the hypothesis that the perceptual complexity of a sentence is determined by the number of transformations in its derivational history (e.g., Gough, 1965).

The principal achievement of these studies was to demonstrate (to the psychologist) the "psychological reality" of these variables, and hence the importance of transformational grammar to the psychology of language. The studies were not, as a rule, designed to reveal the mechanisms by which sentences are perceived, understood, or remembered. Still, taken as a whole, they seemed to present a coherent picture of sentence processing.

The evidence suggested that, at some point in processing, the surface structure of a sentence is actually perceived, and the deep structure at another. That is, it suggested that surface and deep structure were "real" perceptual entities, not just linguistic fictions. Furthermore, the evidence seemed consistent with the view that grammatical transformations correspond to real mental operations performed by a listener in understanding or comparing sentences, operations which might bridge surface and deep structure in the mind just as they do in the grammar.

It is not hard to see how these lines of thought could merge into a model of comprehension, a model whose form would bear a striking resemblance to that of a grammar as it was known in those days. That is, it is easy to imagine that a comprehension device might include a lexicon, a parsing component which would convert that surface structure to deep structure, and a semantic component to interpret the deep structure. The construction of the model lay ahead, but the foundation had been laid, and the prospects looked good.

The salad days came to an end in 1966, when Fodor, Garrett, and Bever began to publish a series of papers (Fodor and Garrett, 1966, 1967; Fodor, Garrett, and Bever, 1968; Bever, 1970) which directly challenged the emerging view. Reviewing the results of the earlier studies, Fodor and Garrett observed that they seemed to converge on what they dubbed the Derivational Theory of Complexity (DTC), the hypothesis that the perceptual complexity of a sentence is determined by the number of grammatical rules employed in its derivation. But they noted with misgiving that these studies had involved pitifully few linguistic structures and even fewer transformations, and in the majority the structural variables had been confounded with potentially significant variables like sentence length. (For example, passives had been shown to be more "complex" than actives in a variety of tasks; but passives are obviously longer and, in some sense, rarer than actives.) Moreover, Fodor and Garrett found occasional discrepant results.

For example, it had been found (by Savin and Perchonock, 1965) that the number of unrelated words which could be remembered along with a sentence went down as the transformational complexity of the sentence went up. But Bever, Fodor, Garrett, and Mehler (reported in Fodor and Garrett, 1966) found that moving a verb particle from its place beside the verb, as in

(1) John phoned up the girl

to the end of the sentence, as in

(2) John phoned the girl up

did not increase the number of words that could be remembered with the sentence (as it ought if the particle-movement transformation increased the complexity of the sentence.)

In a new experiment, Fodor and Garrett (1967) found that inserting a pair of adjectives into a doubly self-embedded sentence like

(3) the shot the soldier the mosquito bit fired missed

to yield

(4) the first shot the tired soldier the mosquito bit fired missed

did not increase the difficulty of paraphrasing the sentence, even though insertion of the adjectives added several transformations to the derivation of the sentence.

Such negative evidence, combined with the infirmity of the positive, reinforced the critics' impression of the implausibility of the fundamental notion of the DTC, that given any two sentences, the one which requires the greater number of transformations will, *ceteris paribus*, be the more complex. Given that transformations permute and (especially) delete elements of the base P-marker, the surface structure of a sentence is routinely more condensed, more compact, than the deep, and the more transformations, the more so. Fodor, Garrett, and Bever were not surprised, then, to find that linguistic analysis provides a number of cases in which derivational complexity does not coincide with apparent perceptual complexity. For example, it did not seem to Fodor and Garrett (1967) that phrases like

(5) the red house

are perceptually more complex than phrases like

(6) the house which is red

from which they are transformationally derived. Or for Bever (1970, p. 287) a sentence like

(7) It amazed Bill that John left the party angrily

is "obviously not more complex to understand" than a sentence like

(8) that John left the party angrily amazed Bill

even though the derivation of (7) requires an extraposition transformation which that of (8) does not.

Examples like these suggested to Fodor, Garrett, and Bever that a monotonic relationship between derivational complexity, far from being demonstrated, is not even a good bet.

These considerations led Fodor, Garrett, and Bever to reject the DTC, and thence to re-examine the relationship between models of performance and competence. They observed that there is no logical requirement that the rules of the grammar be represented explicitly in the comprehension device. What would seem to be a reasonable constraint is that the grammar and the comprehension device be equivalent as recognition routines; that is, the comprehension device must assign to any sentence which does not exceed its mortal and limited capacity the same structural description the grammar does.[3] Thus Fodor, Garrett, and Bever accepted the prior view that the comprehender must recover the deep structure of a sentence, but they rejected the idea that grammatical transformations are involved.

If deep structure is not recovered transformationally, then there must be other operations, other mechanisms, which will achieve the same result. What Fodor, Garrett, and Bever have proposed is that the comprehender is equipped with a set of heuristics or perceptual strategies which enable him, given an input string, to project possible deep structures for that string. By definition (or at least connotation), the strategy may lead to an erroneous hypothesis. But the candidate deep structure is then evaluated against the evidence provided by the input string. If it is not compatible with that evidence, it is rejected and other heuristics are consulted to yield new candidates; otherwise the candidate is accepted as the appropriate interpretation of the sentence.

In effect, then, the perceptual strategies amount to a set of clues which determine the comprehender's hunches as to what a sentence might mean. Given some superficial evidence, the homunculus makes a guess, and then checks it out against the remainder.

Obviously, this theory does not suffer from premature formalization. Indeed, it is more a promissory note than a theory. We could not begin to evaluate it in any rigorous way until we are told exactly what the heuristics are, exactly how they are applied (i.e., the manner of their selection and implementation), and exactly how their results are evaluated. Little has been said about the latter matters, but Fodor, Garrett, and Bever have given us glimpses of the first.

Fodor and Garrett (1967) noted that certain surface structure features are associated with certain deep structure configurations. For example, the presence of the relative pronoun in sentences like

(9) The man whom the dog bit died

is a surface manifestation of a deep structure sentence in which the second NP is the subject, and the first the object, of the simple transitive verb immediately following. Fodor and Garrett proposed that such information is available to the comprehender in the form of "heuristics for making fairly direct inductions of base structure configurations" (1967, p. 295). Thus the presence of the relative pronoun in (9) provides an explicit clue to its deep structure, a clue absent in

(10) The man the dog bit died,

and the former should be easier to understand. This prediction has been confirmed by Fodor and Garrett (1967), Hakes and Cairns (1970), and Hakes and Foss (1970).

A handful of such strategies have been proposed, ranging widely in specificity and precision, and hence in testability. What is probably the most nebulous was recently proposed by Bever (1970, p. 296): "A basic strategy for functional assignment [i.e., for determining basic grammatical relations] is to combine the lexical items in the most plausible way."[4] What has probably been the most heuristic heuristic is that incorporated in the Verb Complexity Hypothesis (VCH).

Fodor and Garrett (1967) suggested that a primary component of the comprehension device is one which consults the internal lexicon for the "base structure properties" of incoming items. That is, the lexicon must contain information as to the deep structure configurations its elements can enter into. On this hypothesis, the main verb of the sentence is apt to be a crucial element, for it is well-known (to linguists) that verbs vary considerably in the nature and number of base configurations they can enter. Some verbs (e.g., *discuss*) take only direct objects, some (e.g., *remark*) take only sentential complements, and some (e.g., *fade*) take no complements at all. If information of this sort were at the disposal of the comprehender, it would decidedly restrict the number of deep structure possibilities he might entertain. But other verbs (e.g., *believe*) can enter more than one configuration, and deciding among then should require additional processing. Therefore, the number of deep structure configurations which the verb permits should be an important determinant of comprehension difficulty, and that is the VCH.

To test this hypothesis, Fodor, Garrett, and Bever (1968) asked subjects to paraphrase doubly self-embedded sentences containing simple or complex verbs. They found that sentences containing only simple verbs, like

(11) The box the man the child met carried was empty

were paraphrased more accurately, and slightly (but not significantly) more rapidly, than the same sentences when they contained a complex verb, as in

(12) The box the man the child knew carried was empty.

They also found that anagrams of sentences containing only simple verbs were solved more readily than anagrams of those containing a complex. As the authors admit, it is not clear that "the anagram task illuminates specifically perceptual processes in sentence analysis," but they argue that this result "does appear to illustrate the centrality of the lexical character of the main verb in the integration of linguistic objects" (Fodor, Garrett, and Bever, 1968, p. 459).

More recently, however, Hakes (1971) found that while simple verbs facilitated paraphrase in one experiment, they did not in another. Moreover, in neither study did he find that verb complexity increased the latency of responding to a designated phoneme occurring shortly after the verb, an index which has proved sensitive to momentary variations in comprehension difficulty (as we shall see later).

The evidence for the VCH is thus equivocal. The evidence for the other strategies is scanty and often ambiguous. (For example, the facilitation of paraphrase of self-embedded sentences by the presence of the relative pronoun is predicted by the DTC as well as the strategy hypothesis.) But the strategy notion has been taken quite seriously. It has led its proponents not only to challenge the psychological reality of transformations, but to question that of surface structure as well (cf. Bever, Lackner, and Kirk, 1969). It has even led at least one of them to question the psychological relevance of grammar itself (Bever, 1970, pp. 346-348).

The fate of the strategy theory cannot be decided on the basis of available evidence. In fact, it is not clear that it could be decided on the basis of any evidence whatsoever until it is more fully elaborated and constrained. For one thing, Fodor, Garrett, and Bever "have presupposed as input to the sentence recognition process a representation of the sentence which marks at least a crude segmentation, including the identification of the main verb" (1968, p. 460). In the words of Bertrand Russell, they have here achieved by theft what they should have earned thru honest toil: to evaluate their model of the sentence recognition process it would seem fair to ask how this marvelous "preanalysis" is performed. For another thing, the formal properties of *strategies* and *heuristics* have not been suggested, let alone investigated. If grammatical transformations are so powerful as to make possible the generation of any language from an arbitrary base (Peters and Ritchie, 1968), one wonders what couldn't be accomplished with an armful of strategies.

The proponents of the strategy position have not yet convinced us that they offer a tenable model of sentence comprehension. But their negative conclusions clearly merit attention.

We would like to suggest that their rejection of grammatical transformations as part of a model of performance is premature. Their arguments, both experimental and intuitive, against the DTC are compelling. Clearly, any theory which claims that perceptual complexity is a simple function of derivational complexity has its back up against a wall. But the only kind of theory in which this is true is one in which a sentence is analyzed in one fell temporal swoop: that is, the full structural description of the sentence is assigned in a linear sequence of operations after the sentence is complete. And only in the abstraction of analysis-by-synthesis has anything like this been seriously contemplated.

It seems much more reasonable to assume that sentences are not understood all at once. To be sure, a full representation of the sentence must be achieved, and that can happen only when the sentence is complete. But much of the work could be (and introspection suggests it is) done well in advance of the final boundary. Thus given doubly self-embedded sentences like (3) and (4) above (which figure importantly in Fodor and Garrett's disenchantment with transformational complexity), the first two NPs of both sentences are almost certainly understood before the end of the sentence is reached, and no differential performance springing from their differential transformational complexity could be expected on a measure (like paraphrase) taken well after the sentence. And virtually all of the evidence which Fodor, Garrett, and Bever consider relevant to the question of the psychological reality of transformations springs from studies which employed such measures.

This problem could obviously be eliminated by testing immediately after the internal segment in question, or by comparing sentences involving transformations (like extraposition) whose domain is the full sentence. But here another problem arises. Suppose, for the moment, that transformations (that is, their inverses) were psychologically real. What they would operate on — what they would transform — would be surface structures, and they would only be applied when they received, as input a surface structure segment, which met their structural indices. It would follow that a transformation could not commence until the relevant surface structure had been assigned. What this would mean is that evidence for the operation of a transformation, in the form of differential performance attributable to differential transformational complexity, could only be obtained using sentences (or sentence fragments) equated for difficulty of surface structure assignment.

It is not obvious how this is to be accomplished, save in the special case of sentences with identical surface structures and different deep structures. But it is obvious that it has not been accomplished in previous psycholinguistic research, for that research has routinely compared sentences systematically unequated with respect to surface structure. That is, virtually every study of the effect of syntactic structure on comprehension has compared sentences matched in deep structure, but varying in transformations, and thus inevitably differing in surface structure. Whether or not these different surface structures, structures as different as those of (5) and (6), for example, are equally easy to assign is presumably an empirical (if difficult) question. But until it is answered, there is no way to separate the contribution of parsing and transformation to the difficulty of comprehending these sentences. Thus the available evidence is simply irrelevant to the question of the reality of grammatical transformations.

What these remarks are intended to show is that that question is entirely open. To answer it, we will need to know a great deal more about the comprehension of sentences. In particular, we will need to know much more about the course of comprehension during a sentence and what determines it; we will need to know more about how the representation of a sentence achieved by comprehension is converted into action; and we will need to know more about how that representation interacts with the comprehender's prior knowledge and beliefs.

Given these considerations, three recent developments in experimental psycholinguistics are of particular interest.

The phoneme-monitoring technique. The "traditional" methods employed in the study of comprehension (e.g., verification, paraphrase, recall) have in common the fact that they measure comprehension after it is complete. It seems probable that if we are to understand what goes on in the head of someone comprehending a sentence, we will have to look into his head while he is doing it. In this light, a technique developed by Foss seems to hold considerable promise.

In this technique, a subject is asked to monitor a spoken sentence for the occurrence of a given phoneme and to make a given response as quickly as possible, if and when he hears it. The latency of his response serves as the dependent variable.

The technique is based upon the assumption that the subject can process only a limited amount of information at any given moment. To the extent that he is preoccupied with one task, his performance on another will suffer. In the present instance, this means that to the extent that sentence comprehension is demanding his attention, his ability to respond to the phoneme will be reduced, and his reaction time will increase. Hence an increase in the latency of the phoneme-monitoring response is presumed to signal a momentary increase in comprehension difficulty at (or just before) that point in the sentence.

In the first application of this technique, Foss and Lynch (1969) demonstrated that phoneme-monitoring latency (PML) is greater near the end of self-embedded sentences than at the same point in right-branching sentences (while near the beginning there was no difference), a result which suggested the validity of the technique. In subsequent studies, Hakes and Cairns (1970) and Hakes and Foss (1970) were able to further corroborate the hypothesis of Fodor and Garrett (1967) that the presence of a relative pronoun in self-embedded sentences facilitates their comprehension, as evidenced by a lower PML just after that pronoun.

Foss (1969) has also shown that PML is sensitive to presumptive differences in word comprehension difficulty within sentences: he found that PML was greater just after relatively rare words (e.g., *itinerant*) than after relatively common ones (e.g., *travelling*). Curiously, Cairns and Foss (1971) found in another study that this effect holds true for adjectives, but not for nouns or verbs; the source of this interaction remains something of a mystery.

Most recently, Foss (1970) has found that PML increases just after ambiguous lexical items, a finding which suggests that the phoneme-monitoring technique may prove of great value in settling the currently knotty problem of how the comprehension device deals with sentential ambiguity (cf. Garrett, 1970).

A model of (post-comprehension) performance. The problem of when and how a sentence is understood is, in our view, the central problem of experimental psycholinguistics. Its solution, in the form of a machine which could understand sentences, would, at the least, earn its inventor an invaluable patent. But while a machine which could understand would be something to marvel at, a man who could do only that would not even make good company.

To reflect comprehension, a man must act. His comprehension of a sentence may be manifested in infinitely many ways. Psycholinguists have used only a few of these as indices of comprehension: their subjects are routinely asked to paraphrase a sentence, verify it, answer a question about it, or follow its directions. But even in these few cases, we know next to nothing about how the comprehender maps his representation of the sentence onto the behavioral index.

Clark (1974) has recently proposed a model of this process. The model is based on the assumption that each of the tasks used to measure comprehension (with the possible exception of paraphrase) is, at bottom, a task of comparison. That is, each task requires the subject to compare his mental representation of the sentence with a mental representation of other information. The nature of that information distinguishes one task from another: in verification, it may be external evidence (e.g., a picture) or internal evidence drawn from the subject's store of prior information (e.g., the fact that two is an even number); in questioning, it is the question itself, and so forth. But in each instance, the subject's response is based on a comparison of his representations of the sentence and the information demanded by the task.

Accordingly, Clark proposes that the several comprehension tasks are all accomplished by means of a serial process with four stages. In the first, a representation of the sentence is achieved (i.e., the sentence is understood); that representation is assumed to correspond to the deep structure of the sentence as it is assigned by linguistic analysis. (Clark refers to the latter as the *deep-structure assumption.*) In the second stage, the information demanded by the task is represented; that representation takes the same form as that of the sentence. In the third stage, the representations achieved in the first two are compared, and in the fourth, the appropriate response is executed.

The crux of the model lies in the third stage. Clark proposes that comparison proceeds in accordance with what he calls the *principle of congruence.* This principle states that comparison is based on identity; if the representations being compared are not congruent, then they must be made so. The operations which accomplish this take time: the more operations required, the more time required for comparison, and the longer the comprehension task will take.

Clark has shown that this model can be applied to a wide variety of tasks and sentences. For example, in a paradigmatic application of the model, Clark uses it to account for the well-documented facts that affirmative sentences are generally verified faster than negative and true faster than false, but that these variables interact, such that true affirmatives are verified faster than false, but true negatives slower than false (cf Trabasso, Rollins, and Shaughnessy, 1971).

Much of the strength of the model evidently springs from the deep structure assumption, for Clark is able to show that many results can easily be interpreted within the model only if the comprehender's representation of the sentence closely corresponds to that posited by the linguist as the underlying form of the sentence. For example, Clark (1969) shows that the ease with which subjects answer questions like (13) and (14)

(13) Who is best?
(14) Who is worst?

on the basis of comparative and equative sentences like (15) and (16)

(15) John is (not) better than Bill
(16) John is (not) as good as Bill

can be readily explained only if it is assumed that a subject's representation of one of the latter sentences actually contains two sentences (e.g., *John is good, Bill is good*) related by a degree function. This analysis is just that which has been proposed by a number of linguists for the underlying structure of these sentences.

Clark readily acknowledges that his model is incomplete in several important respects. The model assumes, for example, that in the first stage the deep structure representations of sentences are given, avoiding the question of how such representations are derived from surface structures or how the surface structures themselves are assigned. Similarly, the model fails to specify how the second-stage representations are generated.

These omissions may be overlooked for the present if we can decide what the first- and second-stage representations should look like in any given instance. Here an appeal to linguistic authority is surely the right move to make. But finding two or more linguists who can agree even on basics is becoming increasingly difficult. In other words, though the deep structure assumption is a useful constraint, it does not uniquely determine a sentence analysis, and this of course means that Clark's model has some unwanted slack.

What is perhaps more serious is the lack of constraint on the comparison process in the third stage. The principle of congruence states only that the representations being compared must be made identical (in some sense); it does not itself provide a means to that end. Accordingly, Clark and his colleagues have proposed a number of algorithms for achieving congruence in various experimental tasks. It is not surprising that a good fit between model and data can be obtained given the almost unlimited options available for fashioning these algorithms. Still, one could not help being impressed if significant features of the hypothesized comparison process remained invariant across tasks and sentence types. This, unfortunately, is not so, as the following illustrates.

Representations in the first and second stages typically have the form of an embedded string together with an embedding string. For example, the sentence

(17) A isn't above B

is assigned the representation

(18) FALSE (ABOVE (A,B))

where ABOVE (A,B) is the embedded string and FALSE (. . .) is the embedding string. Clark and Chase (1972, 1974) propose an algorithm for comparing sentence representations such as (18) with representations of pictures (which are assumed to have a similar, though not necessarily congruent, form). This algorithm operates on the embedded strings *before* operating on the embedding strings. In contrast, Clark (1974) presents a comparison algorithm for handling active and passive sentences in which the embedded strings are processed *after* the embedding strings. Evidently, the comparison process is highly flexible and unconstrained.

Even this problem would not be too disturbing if there existed a principled basis for selecting a comparison algorithm in any particular situation. What is needed, of course, is a theory of how the comprehender uses information about the first- and second-stage representations in order to devise a procedure to compare them. But such a theory is nowhere in sight. When one considers types of verification and question-answering tasks which require complex inferential steps, it becomes clear why the third-stage comparison process resists general explication. We seem to be faced with a search problem which may be no less complicated than that involved in, say, assigning a deep structure to a sentence in the first place.

These remarks are not intended to disparage Clark's model but rather to suggest some areas where major work remains to be done. Clark's use of linguistic analysis in experimental psycholinguistics is exemplary, and the happy articulation of the deep structure assumption with his model of comparison reflects favorably on both. If further research can constrain its parameters, his model will prove valuable even if it should do no more than enable us to isolate comprehension from tasks in which it is embedded.

Some results on the sentence in memory. Not all sentences vanish when we press the right button. At least some enter and alter our cognitive structures. (One obvious, if mysterious, instance is the sentence registered by the child which results in a change in his grammar.) Clearly a complete model of linguistic performance must specify how the information in a sentence arriving at the mind of a listener is integrated with the information awaiting it.

This problem is, in the end, little short of the psychological problem of knowledge, and psycholinguistics is not ready for it. But psycholinguists have been concerned with a pale imitation, the problem of how a sentence is represented in memory.

It has long been obvious that a sentence in memory does not take the form of an acoustic record: what we remember is the gist of what we hear. But to say this is not to solve the problem; it is to name it. The solution of the problem of the representation of the sentence will be an algorithm which will characterize the "gist" of any sentence.

It has occurred to a number of psycholinguists (e.g., Rohrman, 1968) that linguistic analysis might, once again, provide the answer. Since the deep structure of a sentence seems adequately to characterize the form of the sentence when it is comprehended, it seemed plausible to assume that it is also the form in which it is remembered. A number of studies have explored this possibility, with mixed results (cf. Clark and Card, 1969, and Paivio, 1971). The safest conclusion that could be drawn from these results is that the memory representation of a sentence must be at least as abstract as its deep structure.

Bransford, Barclay, and Franks (1972) have obtained convincing evidence that the memory representation of the sentence is beyond any hypothesis offered by current linguistic analysis. What they found was that when their subjects were exposed to either of two sentences like

(19) Three turtles rested on the floating log and a fish swam beneath it

or

(20) Three turtles rested on the floating log and a fish swam beneath them

they could not tell which they had heard a few minutes later. But if those subjects were exposed to either

(21) Three turtles rested beside the floating log and a fish swam beneath it

or

(22) Three turtles rested beside the floating log and a fish swam beneath them

they could readily distinguish these sentences after the same time interval. Thus, the memory representations of (19) and (20) must be identical, while those of (21) and (22) are not. But the structural description of (19) must differ from that of (20) in the same way that that of (21) differs from that of (22). Therefore, the memory representation of the sentence cannot be equated with any level of its linguistic analysis.

What appears to be remembered about a sentence are the inferences which the subject makes upon hearing it. Additional evidence for this claim comes from a study by Johnson, Bransford, and Solomon (1973). They presented passages of the following type to an experimental group.

(23) John was trying to fix the birdhouse. He was pounding the nail when his father came out to watch him and to help him do the work.

A control group received the same story frames, but with a verb change in each case, e.g.

(24) John was trying to fix the birdhouse. He was looking for the nail when his father came out to watch him and to help him do the work.

Plainly, (23) but not (24) allows an inference as to the instrument of the action. During a later recognition test, both groups were presented with a passage in which the instrument is made explicit:

(25) John was using the hammer to fix the birdhouse when his father came out to watch him and to help him do the work.

As expected, (25) was falsely recognized much more often by subjects who had previously heard (23) than by those who had heard (24).

Perhaps the most striking demonstration of this general kind was provided by McCarrell, Bransford, and Johnson (cited in Bransford and McCarrell, 1974). Two sets of sentences were embedded in short story frames and presented to subjects. One set consisted of sentences which were self-contained in the sense that no special assumptions were required in order to grasp them, e.g.

(26) The floor was dirty so Sally used the mop.

The other set was composed of sentences designed to elicit special assumptions by the subject, e.g.

(27) The floor was dirty because Sally used the mop.

Sentence (27), but not (26), makes sense if one assumes an additional fact about the situation being described, namely, that the mop was dirty. Subjects who had heard (27) later showed a greater tendency than those who heard (26) to recognize falsely the sentence

(28) The mop was dirty before Sally washed the floor.

The memory representation involved here clearly has little to do with the deep structure of the original sentence.

As compelling as these demonstrations are, they do not provide us with an explicit solution to the problem of linguistic memory. Showing that we remember what we infer from a passage may rule out a number of current theories, but it does not suggest how we might proceed to build the "correct" theory. This is simply because we do not understand the inferential capabilities of humans, and we will not until we begin to make sense of human knowledge. As we said earlier, we doubt that psycholinguistics is ready for that one.

A question that can be addressed is at what point does the inferential representation of a sentence develop in memory. The intriguing possibility that is the product of comprehension appears to be ruled out by results obtained by Charles Jenkins in our laboratory. Jenkins found that if a subject hears a sentence like (19) and is immediately asked either

(29) Did the fish swim under the log?

or

(30) Did the fish swim under the turtles?

he will answer "yes" more rapidly to (29) than (30) (while the opposite holds if he had heard (20)). We are led to assume, then, that the information that the fish swam under the turtles is not present in the comprehender's immediate representation of (19), but that it appears within minutes.

Obviously, this is not the end.

References

Bever, T.G. The Cognitive Basis for Linguistic Structures. In R. Hayes (Ed.), *Cognition and Language Development*. New York: Wiley, 1970. Pp. 277-360.

Bever, T.G. Lackner, J.R., and Kirk, R. The Underlying Structures of Sentences are the Primary Units of Immediate Speech Processing. *Perception and Psychophysics*, 1969, *5*, 225-234.

Bransford, J.D., Barclay, J.R., and Franks, J.J. Sentence Memory: A Constructive Versus Interpretive Approach. *Cognitive Psychology*, 1972, *3*, 193-209.

Bransford, J.D., and McCarrell, N.S. A Sketch of a Cognitive Approach to Comprehension: Some Thoughts About Understanding What it Means to Comprehend. In D.S. Palermo and W.B. Weimer (Eds.), *Cognition and the Symbolic Processes*. Hillsdale, New Jersey: Lawrence Erlbaum Associates; 1974. Pp. 189-229.

Cairns, H.S., and Foss, D.J. Falsification of the Hypothesis that Word Frequency is a Unified Variable in Sentence Processing. *Journal of Verbal Learning and Verbal Behavior*, 1971, *10*, 41-43.

Clark, H.H. Linguistic Processes in Deductive Reasoning. *Psychological Review*, 1969, *76*, 387- 404.

Clark, H.H. Answering the Question "Where is it?" *Journal of Verbal Learning and Verbal Behavior*, 1972, *11*, 265-277.

Clark, H.H. Semantics and Comprehension. In T.A. Sebeok (Ed.), *Current Trends in Linguistics*, Vol. 12: *Linguistics and Adjacent Arts and Sciences*. The Hague: Mouton, 1974, Pp. 1291-1428.

Clark, H.H., and Card, S.K. Role of Semantics in Remembering Comparative Sentences. *Journal of Experimental Psychology*, 1969, *82*, 545-553.

Clark, H.H., and Chase, W.G. On the Process of Comparing Sentences Against Pictures. *Cognitive Psychology*, 1972, *3*, 472-517.

Clark, H.H., and Chase, W.G. Perceptual Coding Strategies in the Verification of Descriptions. *Memory and Cognition*, 1974, *2*, 101-111.

Clifton, D., Jr., and Odom, P. Similarity Relations Among Certain English Sentence Constructions. *Psychol. Monogr.*, 1966, 80 (5), 1-35, Whole No. 613.

Coleman, E.B. Approximations to English: Some Comments on the Method. *American Journal of Psychology*, 1963, *76*, 239-247.

Downey, R.G., and Hakes, D.T. Some Psychological Effects of Violating Linguistic Rules. *Journal of Verbal Learning and Verbal Behavior*, 1968, *7*, 158-161.

Epstein, W. The Influence of Syntactical Structure on Learning. *American Journal of Psychology*, 1961, *74*, 80-85.

Fillenbaum, S. Psycholinguistics. *Annual Review of Psychology*, 1971, *22*, 251-308.

Fodor, J.A., and Bever, T.G. The Psychological Reality of Linguistic Segments. *Journal of Verbal Learning and Verbal Behavior*, 1965, *4*, 414-420.

Fodor, J.A., and Garrett, M. Some Reflections on Competence and Performance. In J. Lyons and R.J. Wales (Eds.), *Psycholinguistic Papers*. Edinburgh: University of Edinburgh Press, 1966. Pp. 135-154.

Fodor, J.A., and Garrett, M. Some Syntactic Determinants of Sentential Complexity. *Perception and Psychophysics*, 1967, *2*, 289-296.

Fodor, J.A., Garrett, M., and Bever, T.G. Some Syntactic Determinants of Sentential Complexity, 11: Verb Structure. *Perception and Psychophysics*, 1968, *3*, 453-461.

Foss, D.J. Decision Processes During Sentence Comprehension: Effects of Lexical Item Difficulty and Position Upon Decision Times. *Journal of Verbal Learning and Verbal Behavior*, 1969, *8*, 457-462.

Foss, D.J. Some Effects of Ambiguity Upon Sentence Comprehension. *Journal of Verbal Learning and Verbal Behavior*, 1970, *9*, 699-706.

Foss, D.J., and Lynch, R.H., Jr. Decision Processes During Sentence Comprehension: Effects of Surface Structure on Decision Times. *Perception and Psychophysics*, 1969, *5*, 145-148.

Franks, J.J., Thompson, J., and Bransford, J.D. The Acquisition of Abstract Ideas. Paper Presented at the Convention of the Midwestern Psychological Association, 1971.

Garrett, M. Does Ambiguity Complicate the Perception of Sentences? In G.B. Flores d'Arcais & W.J.M. Levelt (Eds.) *Advances in Psycholinguistics*. New York: American Elsevier, 1971.

Gough, P.B. Grammatical Transformations and Speed of Understanding. *Journal of Verbal Learning and Verbal Behavior*, 1965, *4*, 107-111.

Gough, P.B., and Jenkins, J.J. Verbal Learning and Psycholinguistics. In M. Marx (Ed.), *Theories in Contemporary Psychology*. New York: MacMillan, 1963. Pp. 456-474.

Hakes, D.T. Does Verb Structure Affect Sentence Comprehension? *Perception and Psychophysics*, 1971, *10*, 229-232.

Hakes, D.T., and Cairns, H.S. Sentence Comprehension and Relative Pronouns. *Perception and Psycholphysics*, 1970, *8*, 5-8.

Hakes, D.T., and Foss, D.J. Decision Processes During Sentence Comprehension: Effects of Surface Structure Reconsidered. *Perception and Psychophysics*, 1970, *8*, 413-416.

Johnson, M.K., Bransford, J.D., and Solomon, S. Memory for tacit Impressions of Sentences. *Journal of Experimental Psychology*, 1972, 98, 203-205.

Johnson, N.F. The Psychological Reality of Phrase-Structure Rules. *Journal of Verbal Learning and Verbal Behavior*, 1966, *4*, 469-475.

Marks, L.E., and Miller, G.A. The Role of Semantic and Syntactic Constraints in the Memorization of English Sentences. *Journal of Verbal Learning and Verbal Behavior*, 1964, *3*, 1-5.

Mehler, J. Some Effects of Grammatical Transformations on the Recall of English Sentences. *Journal of Verbal Learning and Verbal Behavior*, 1963, *2*, 250-262.

Mehler, J., and Carey, P. Role of Surface and Base Structure in the Perception of Sentences. *Journal of Verbal Learning and Verbal Behavior*, 1967, *6*, 335-338.

Miller, G.A. Some Psychological Studies of Grammar. *American Psychologist,* 1962, *17,* 748-762.

Miller, G.A., and Isard, S. Some Perceptual Consequences of Linguistic Rules. *Journal of Verbal Learning and Verbal Behavior,* 1963, *2,* 217-228.

Mowrer, O.H. The Psychologist Looks at Language. *American Psychologist,* 1954, *9,* 660-694.

Osgood, C.E., and Sebeok, T.A., (Eds.) *Psycholinguistics: A Survey of Theory and Research Problems.* Indiana University Publications in Anthropology and Linguistics, Mem. No. 10, 1954. Reprinted in Bloomington, Indiana: Indiana University Press, 1965.

Paivio, A. Imagery and Deep Structure in the Recall of English Nominalizations. *Journal of Verbal Learning and Verbal Behavior,* 1971, *10,* 1-12.

Peters, P.S., and Ritchie, R.W. A Note on the Universal Base Hypothesis. *Journal of Linguistics,* 1969, *5,* 150-152.

Rohrman, M.L. The role of Syntactic Structure in the Recall of English Nominalizations. *Journal of Verbal Learning and Verbal Behavior,* 1968, *7,* 904-912.

Rubenstein, H., and Aborn, M. Psycholinguistics. *Annual Review of Psychology,* 1960, *11,* 291-322.

Savin, H.B., and Perchonock, E. Grammatical Structure and the Immediate Recall of English Sentences. *Journal of Verbal Learning and Verbal Behavior,* 1965, *4,* 348-353.

Trabasso, T., Rollins, H., and Shaughnessy, E. Storage and Verification Stages in Processing Concepts. *Cognitive Psychology,* 1971, *2,* 239-289.

Notes

[1]This paper was facilitated by NSF-USDP Grant GU-1598 and NSF Grant GU-3285 to the University of Texas at Austin. The reader should be forewarned that it is an interpretation, not a review. For the latter, he would be well-advised to see Fillenbaum (1971).

[2]Coleman (1963) presents persuasive arguments that this conclusion puts the cart before the horse: sentences do not behave as sentences because they are the ultimate approximations to English; rather, approximations behave like sentences to the extent that they approximate sentences.

[3]Fodor and Garrett obviously use the term *structural description* in a restricted sense, for ordinarily it would be taken to include, not just the deep and surface structures, but all the intermediate ones as well (and this is tantamount to including transformations).

[4]One is tempted to go him one better with "perceptual strategy": given a sentence, understand it.

DISCUSSION

Peter W. Carey (Graduate Center, C.U.N.Y.): I thought your review of Fodor, Garrett and Bever (1968) was very judicious. I just want to add one more log to the fire. Isn't it likely that there are other differences confounded into the verb complexity hypothesis? For example, if the comparison is between *believe* and *borrow,* the latter being a straightforward transitive verb, isn't it likely that the cognitive complexity of *believe* is somehow as important as the fact that it has three syntactic slots that it can be compatible with? Thus, when they find that it is harder to form a grammatical sentence out of the anagram containing *believe* than the one containing *borrow,* they may simply be finding out something about the complexity of the meaning of *believe* as opposed to the meaning of *borrow.* Their data for the difference between *believe* and *borrow* may not have anything to do with supporting the verb complexity hypothesis *per se.*

One more comment. Don't you think that the views of H. Clark — especially with respect to deduction — are entirely too linguistic? Don't you think he should benefit from a close reading of Bransford *et al.* (In press)? This is the point of Janellan Huttenlocher and of Tom Bever.

Philip B. Gough (U. of Texas): The verb complexity hypothesis itself hasn't earned its wings yet; that is to say I don't know of any really convincing evidence for it. I should have quoted in my paper what is my favorite line in psycholinguistics used by Fodor, Garrett and Bever when they report the results of having failed to show an effect of verb complexity in a paraphrase task which one would suppose ought to be sensitive to differences in comprehensibility. They then turn to an anagram task which is at best tangentially related to how we comprehend sentences. Having found an effect there, they state: "while it is impossible to prove that the anagram task illuminates specifically perceptual processes in sentence analysis, it does appear to illustrate the centrality of the lexical character of the main verb in the integration of linguistic objects." (1968:459) This, I think, is one of the grandest edifices ever erected on quicksand!*

[*Note: in the written version of Professor Gough's presentation portions of this "favorite line" are indeed quoted (cf. p. 252) but *sans* comment; this part of the discussion has thus been retained. [W.O.D.]]

At any rate, verb complexity hasn't been found to work. Let me just give you one example. We have been exploring at Texas the use of a task with sentences which has been found by us and more prominently by Herb Rubenstein to be revealing about how we understand words. In Rubenstein's task and ours, the subject is asked to decide whether a string of letters is a word or not. We have been trying to apply the same technique to sentences giving people perfectly reasonable sentences and sentences which depart from full grammaticality in some way asking them to press a button indicating whether the sentence is grammatical or not. In that setting, we have then given subjects very simple sentences like *John believed Mary* versus *John hit Mary* and examined their reaction time to such pairs. If, given *believe* you open your mental Webster's, find that *believe* can enter into various configurations and then choose among them, surely it ought to take longer to understand *John believed Mary* than *John hit Mary* but it doesn't at least in that particular task.

As to your second point — I'm impressed with the Clark work simply because of the methodological reasons I indicated, i.e., it seems to indicate something about what we do after we understand a sentence, and I can imagine that getting us some place where we can go backwards with it.

Peter Menzel (Florida State University): You say that sentences are somehow integrated into the cognitive system shortly after they have been heard. It seems to me that that introduces what used to be called an uncontrolled variable into the Clark experiments. If the subject, while he's processing the sentence and listening for the possible occurrence of *p,* is also integrating the earlier sentence into his cognitive system — something that Clark hasn't controlled for because he isn't aware of it, this fact might throw out half of his results.

Philip B. Gough (U. of Texas): I hope I didn't say that a sentence is integrated into the cognitive structure very quickly after we hear it. All that I take to be facts about that topic are the following: (1) that very quickly after you have heard a sentence you don't remember the lexical content nor do you remember the syntactic form insofar as that is merely a stylistic variation (2) furthermore, you don't even remember what was in fact the semantic content of the sentence itself very shortly thereafter.

Chapter Ten

Developmental Psycholinguistics

Dan I. Slobin

Every normal human child constructs for himself the grammar of his native language.[1] It is the task of developmental psycholinguistics to describe and attempt to explain the intricate phenomena which lie beneath this simple statement. These underlying phenomena are essentially cognitive. In order for the child to construct a grammar: (1) he must be able to recognize the physical and social events which are encoded in language, and (2) he must be able to process, organize, and store linguistic information. That is, the cognitive prerequisites for the development of grammar relate to both the *meanings* and the *forms* of utterances. This paper represents a preliminary attempt to explore these cognitive prerequisites in the light of cross-linguistic comparison of the ontogenesis of grammar.[2]

The past decade in developmental psycholinguistics has brought a vast increase in our knowledge of how English-speaking children acquire their native language.[3] The present decade promises to place those findings in broader perspective. Developmental psycholinguists are beginning to reach out to other language communities, in order to study children acquiring other native languages and in order to make contact with the findings of foreign colleagues (see *Table*). At the same time we are beginning to relate our work to the psychology of perceptual and cognitive development (see papers in Hayes 1970). Developmental psycholinguistics is thus moving from particularism to universalism in two significant ways: from the particularism of English to the acquisition of language in general, and from the particularism of linguistic development to cognitive development in general. We are just beginning to sense the intimate relations between linguistic universals and cognitive universals, and are far from an adequate developmental theory of either.

The psychology of cognitive development promises an eventual universal theory of the growth of the mind (see, for example, papers in Mussen 1970). The psycholinguistic aspects of this theory will require detailed information on the acquisition of a variety of native languages. The value of cross-linguistic comparison, of course, is to avoid drawing conclusions about child language development which may, in fact, be limited to the acquisition of languages like English. The hope is to find similar developmental processes in different sorts of languages. At present, we have suggestive acquisition data on at least 30 languages from ten or so major language families (see *Table*). Although the data for most of these languages are still rather scanty, striking developmental uniformities can be discerned (Bowerman 1970; Braine 1971; Slobin 1970). To the extent that a universal course of linguistic development can be confirmed, a language-free acquisition model is called for (see Bever 1970a; and papers in Slobin 1971b). Such a model bases itself on the assumption that the child brings certain operating principles to bear on the task of learning to speak, regardless of the peculiarities of the particular language he is exposed to. In this paper I will present some first guesses as to the nature of some of these operating principles.

Table. Available Material on the Acquisition of 30 Different
Native Languages*

INDO-EUROPEAN FAMILY

    Romance Branch

Italian:	Frontali (1943-44); Parisi & Antinucci (1970)
Spanish:	Gili y Gaya (1960)
French:	Bloch (1921, 1924); Cohen (1925, 1933, 1962); Grégoire (1937, 1947); Guillaum (1927a, b); Sinclair-de-Zwart (1967)
Romanian:	Slama-Cazacu (1957, 1960, 1962)

Germanic Branch

English:	(See *footnote 3.*)
Dutch:	Kaper (1959)
German:	Ament (1899); Lindner (1882, 1885, 1898, 1906); Park (1970); Roeper (1972); Scupin & Scupin (1907); Stern & Stern (1907)
Danish:	Jespersen (1916); Rasmussen (1913, 1922)
Swedish:	Bolin & Bolin (1916, 1920)
Norwegian:	Börgstrom (1954)

Slavic Branch

Russian: Bogoyavlenskiy (1957); Dingwall & Tuniks (1973); El'konin (1958); Feofanov (1958); Gvozdev (1949); Imedadze (1960); Pavlova (1924); Popova (1958); Slobin (1966, 1968); Sokhin (1959); Zakharova (1958)

Polish: Kaczmarek (1953); Pfanhauser (1930); Shugar (1971); Skorupka (1949); Smoczynski (1955); Szuman (1968); Wawrawska (1939); Zarebina (1965)

Czech: Pačesová (1968)

Slovenian: Kolarič (1959)

Serbo-Croatian: Mikeš (1967); Mikeš & Vlahović (1966); Pavlovitch (1920)

Bulgarian: Gheorgov (1905, 1906, 1908); Manova-Tomova (1969)

Baltic Branch

Latvian: Rūķe-Draviņa (1959, 1963)

SEMITIC FAMILY

Hebrew: Bar-Adon (1971)

Arabic: Omar (1970)

CAUCASIAN (?)

Georgian: Imedadze (1960)

URALIC FAMILY

Hungarian: Balassa (1893); Endrei (1913); Kenyeres (1926, 1927); Mikeš (1967); Mikeš & Vlahović (1966); Simonyi (1906)

Finnish:	Argoff (forthcoming); Bowerman (1970)

TURKIC FAMILY

Turkish:	Slobin (in preparation)

KOREAN FAMILY

Korean:	Park (1969)

JAPANESE-RYUKYUAN FAMILY:

Japanese:	McNeill (1966); McNeill & McNeill (1968); Sanches (1968)

HAN CHINESE FAMILY

Mandarin:	Chao (1951)

BODO-NAGA-KACHIN FAMILY

Garo:	Burling (1959)

AUSTRONESIAN FAMILY

Samoan:	Kernan (1969); Talmy (1970)

EASTERN SUDANIC FAMILY

Luo:	Blount (1969)

MAYAN FAMILY:

TZELTAL:	Stross (1969)

[*This is not a complete list of all available material; for fuller bibilographical information see Slobin (1967, 1972) and Slama-Cazacu (1969). In addition to the languages listed above, I am aware of ongoing research on the acquisition of the following native languages: Kurdish, Persian, Armenian, Albanian, Ukrainian, Swahili, Koya, Tagalog, and Quechua. The language classification comes from Voegelin and Voegelin (1966).]

My major concern here is with the *order* of development of various grammatical devices and with the child's strategies for organizing language. This focus leaves aside the problems of how language *begins* in the child and why linguistic universals exist. That is, I take for granted the fact that all human children are able to learn language, and ask: Are there common orders of acquisition of different linguistic features across languages?

Language-Definitional Universals

In order to begin at this point, therefore, it is necessary to take as given what may be referred to as *language-definitional universals.* That is to say, children (and adults) everywhere have the same general definition of the form and function of language. Everywhere language consists of utterances performing a universal set of communicative functions (such as asserting, denying, requesting, ordering, and so forth), expressing a universal set of underlying semantic relations, and using a universal set of formal means (such as combinable units of meaning, made up of combinable units of sound, etc.). Furthermore, language—everywhere—is grammatical, in the sense that the meaning of a message is not fully determined by any combination of the meanings of its elements. In all language which I will consider—child and adult—there is a non-direct relation between the surface, acoustic form of messages and their underlying meanings. It is in no way surprising that children should define language in the same way as adults: indeed, they could not learn language if they did not share this definition. In fact, one could argue that human language could not be so defined if it were not so defined by children, because, in a profound sense, language is created anew by children in each generation. Language-definitional universals are what David McNeill calls *strong linguistic universals,* and I follow his proposition that such universals reflect "a specific linguistic ability and may not be a reflection of a cognitive ability at all" (1970: 74). While much argument has centered on the issue as to whether language-definitional universals are innate, I will avoid this issue here, and merely point to them as basic linguistic capacities which are prerequisites to the questions which I want to consider (cf. Bever's *basic linguistic capacities* (1970a)). We will meet the child at the point when he knows there are meaningful words which can be combined to produce meaningful utterances. And at this point we will pose the question advanced above: Are there common orders of acquisition of different linguistic features across languages?

Content And Form In Child Speech

The first and most obvious point that comes to mind is that language is used to express the child's cognitions of his environment—physical and social—and so a child cannot begin to use a given linguistic form meaningfully until he is able to understand what it means. It should be possible, then, to rank linguistic forms in terms of the psychological, or cognitive complexity of the notions they express. For example, no one would expect a child to be able to form conditionals before he could make assertions, to make statements about time before making statements about place, and so on. Is it possible, then, to trace out a universal course of linguistic development on the basis of what we know about the universal course of cognitive development? (Can one take Piaget as a handbook of psycholinguistic development?)

In fact, many such expectations (including those suggested above) are supported by data. The earliest grammatical markers to appear in child speech seem to express the most basic notions available to the child mind. For example, in languages which provide a vocative inflection, this is typically one of the earliest grammatical markers to emerge in child speech (Hungarian, Serbo-Croatian (Mikeš 1967; Mikeš and Vlahović 1966); Polish (Shugar 1971). One of the earliest semantic relations to be formally marked in child speech is that of verb-object. In order languages, like English, this relation is marked early by consistent word order. In languages which provide an inflection for marking the object of action (accusative), this is typically an extremely early inflection to emerge—often the first (Finnish (Argoff forthcoming), Latvian (Rūķe-Draviņa 1959, 1963), Russian (Gvozdev 1949; Imedadze 1960)). In Luo the first inflections are subject and object affixes on verbs (Blount 1969). In every language for which relevant data are available, there is an early form of negation in which a negative particle is affixed to a simple sentence. In languages as diverse as English, Arabic, Czech, Latvian, Japanese, and Samoan, early yes-no questions are formed by rising intonation.

Numerous findings such as these offer support for the notion that the first linguistic forms to appear in child speech will be those which express meanings consistent with the child's level of cognitive development. But striking surprises occur in some languages. For example, yes-no questions in adult Finnish are not formed by rising intonation, but by attachment of a question particle to the word questioned and movement of that word to the front of the sentence. And, strangely enough, Melissa Bowerman, in her recent dissertation on Finnish acquisition (1970), reports that little Finnish children simply do not ask yes-no questions—at least not in any formally marked way. And Margaret Omar, in a recent dissertation on the acquisition of Egyptian Arabic (1970), reports that the noun plural "is the most difficult and latest aspect of the language structure to be mastered; older children in this study erred in pluralizing even familiar nouns" (367). And older children, in her study, meant children as old as 15! The reason apparently lies in the extreme complexity of plural marking in Arabic. Briefly: there is a small class of regular plurals, but most nouns fall into a large number of fairly irregular classes in regard to plural formation. There is also a special dual form; a distinction between pluralizing *counted* and *collected* nouns (for example, *trees* as a group, or *trees* as a collection of individual trees); what is more, the numerals 3-10 take the noun in the plural, while numerals above 11 take the singular.

So although one can talk about order of acquisition in terms of semantic or cognitive complexity, there is clearly a point at which formal linguistic complexity also plays a role. I think we can learn a good deal from discovering just what constitutes formal linguistic complexity for the child. If we can order linguistic devices in terms of their acquisition complexity, we can begin to understand the strategies used by the child in arriving at the grammar of his language. To put it the other way, a definition of what is simple for a child to acquire is a definition of the child's first guess as to the nature of language. The child must successively modify such first guesses until he ends up with the conception of language shared by the adults in his community.

Studies of bilingual children yield valuable suggestions as to what sorts of formal devices may be simpler to acquire than others. If a given meaning receives expression at the same time in both languages of a bilingual child, this suggests that the formal devices in the two languages are similar in complexity. For example, Imedadze (1960), studying the linguistic development of her Russian-Georgian bilingual daughter, noted the simultaneous emergence of the genitive and the instrumental in both languages. She concludes that: "The ease of acquisition and the simultaneous appearance of these forms of the genitive and instrumental cases can only be attributed to the fact that these forms express the very same semantic relationships in analogous fashion (in Russian and Georgian)."

If a given semantic domain receives expression earlier in one of the two languages, a difference in formal complexity is suggested. A useful example comes from studies by Melanie Mikeš and Plemenka Vlahović of Serbo-Croatian—Hungarian bilingual children in Northern Yugoslavia (Mikeš 1967; Mikeš and Vlahović 1966). Well before they were two years of age, two bilingual girls were productively and appropriately using a variety of Hungarian case endings on nouns indicating such locative relations as illative, elative, sublative, and superessive—that is, in plain English, the children were using inflections to express the directional notions of *into, out of,* and *onto,* and the positional notion of *on top of.* At the same time they had barely begun to develop locative expressions in Serbo-Croatian, which requires a locative preposition before the noun along with some case inflection attached to the end of the noun.

Now, the fact that this cross-linguistic discrepancy occurs *within* a single child speaking both languages, rather than between two monolingual children, poses a central question in clear focus: When the child speaks Hungarian, she appropriately uses directional and positional locative inflections, and one is confident to credit her with the semantic intentions to express such notions as *into, onto,* and so forth. What are we to say of the same child, however, when she fails to grammatically signal such intentions with the corresponding prepositions when speaking Serbo-Croation? It seems clear to me that if, for example, she puts a doll into a drawer, saying, in Serbo-Croatian, *doll drawer,* we must credit her with the same semantic intention as when, describing the same situation in Hungarian, she adds an illative inflection to the word for *drawer.*

The point I am trying to make, of course, does not depend on the child's bilingualism. The example merely illuminates the general proposition that a child's underlying semantic intentions can contain more information than his surface utterance. The speech of very young children is nearly always interpretable in context, and the very young child is neither able nor feels constrained to express his total intention in a single utterance. Lois Bloom (1970) has made this point abundantly clear in her recent book describing early grammatical development in three American children. For example, a child said *Mommy sock* in two different situations: when mommy was putting a sock on her, and when she picked up mommy's sock. Bloom is confident in labelling the utterance in the first situation as *subject-object,* and the second as *genitive,* and I think she is right. Previous descriptions of children's grammar were too bound to surface characterizations of word distribution and failed to differentiate between the several meanings of homonymous utterances, such as *Mommy sock* (e.g., Braine 1963; Brown and Fraser 1963; Miller and Ervin 1964). More recent approaches to child language (and to linguistic theory) pay increasing attention to the semantic substratum of speech and to the functions of utterances (e.g. Bloom 1970; Blount 1969; Bowerman 1970; Brown 1970a, b; E. Clark 1970, 1971, 1972; H. Clark 1970; Cromer 1968; Ervin-Tripp 1970a, b, 1971; Kernan 1969; Parisi and Antinucci 1970; Schlesinger 1971; Slobin 1970; Talmy 1970).

To sum up thus far: Cognitive development and linguistic development do not run off in unison. The child must find linguistic means to express his intentions. The means can be easily accessible (as, for example, the Hungarian locative), or quite unaccessible (as, for example, the Finnish yes-no question or the Arabic noun plural). The problem is: What makes a given linguistic means of expression more or less accessible to the child?

In posing the question in these terms, I am assuming that there is a fairly autonomous development of intentions to express various semantic notions. This claim must be defended before answering the questions of relative accessibility of formal linguistic devices, for one may be tempted to pose the counter-argument that grammar plays a leading role in cognitive development.

The Primacy of Cognitive Development

Let us return to the Hungarian—Serbo-Croatian bilingual example, and agree that we will assess semantic intention on the basis of the use of utterances in clear contexts, and not on superficial linguistic marking of such intentions. We will probably find, on deeper investigation, that the child intends to express the same locative relations when speaking either language. (The only alternative to this approach would be to claim that the problem of expressing locatives in Serbo-Croatian is such a bother to him, that he avoids speaking of moving and placing objects when speaking Serbo-Croatian. I think this alternative can be safely rejected—though it is, of course, open to investigation.)

Why the precocious marking of locative expressions in Hungarian, then? One line of argument would be to say that the abundance of clear locative inflections in Hungarian drew the child's attention to the relevant notions, and that he learned them earlier than if he had been speaking only Serbo-Croatian. This is a sort of Whorfian notion of linguistic determinism on the grammatical level, and I think it will turn out to be false when all the data are in. It seems unlikely that the structure of a particular language would draw attention more clearly to the possibilities of putting in, taking out, and so on, than would a child's everyday experience. It is difficult to imagine children NOT talking about such things. And, in fact, the cross-linguistic data suggest that children begin to express basic locative notions by noun-noun and noun-verb combinations at the two-word stage in all languages. Two-word utterances in Serbo-Croatian, Bulgarian, Russian, English, Finnish, Hebrew, and Samoan all seem to express the notions of *in* and *into, on* and *onto,* and *from*—at first with no inflections or prepositions. This can be quite reliably assessed from context, as when a Russian child said the equivalent of *pot stove,* pointing to a pot on the stove; when Roger Brown's famous "Adam" said *put box* when putting something into a box; and so on. In addition, locative notions are expressed at early stages by prolocatives and demonstratives, such as the English *there, inner, on,* and the like, and their equivalents in Bulgarian (Gheorgov 1908), German (Leopold 1939; Park 1970), Finnish (Argoff forthcoming), and other languages.

Furthermore, the order of acquisition of locatives seems quite certainly to be based on a sequence of cognitive development which goes beyond language. For example, Parisi and Antinucci (1970), following the work of Piaget, suggest an order of acquisition of locatives based on the development of spatial notions from simple topological notions (expressed by terms like *in* and *on*), to locatives involving notions of dimensional or Euclidean space (like *in front of, below, beside*), to locatives expressing more complex spatial notions (like *along* and *through*). They present some preliminary evidence from Italian children supporting this order of acquisition, and all of the cross-linguistic work of which I am aware supports a sequence such as this.

If the order of acquisition of locative notions is an aspect of general cognitive development, it does not seem likely to me that the development of these notions is very amenable to linguistic manipulation. Although the general question is not at all closed, a good deal of work emanating from Piaget's research institute in Geneva suggests that the rate of cognitive development cannot be significantly altered by teaching the child the vocabulary needed in order to function at a higher level of cognitive development (Sinclair-de-Zwart 1967, 1969). On the basis of current findings and theory (Furth 1969; Piaget 1967, 1970), it seems to me that the pacesetter in linguistic growth is the child's cognitive growth, as opposed to an autonomous linguistic development which can then reflect back on cognition. As Piaget has put it: " . . . language is not enough to explain thought, because the structures that characterize thought have their roots in action and in sensorimotor mechanisms that are deeper than lingusitics" (1967:98).[4]

The argument that language is used to express only what the child already knows can be supported by another line of evidence, coming from an examination of linguistic development from both a *formal* and a *functional* point of view. Studies which have considered the supposed intended meanings of children's utterances support a far-reaching principle which could be phrased as follows: *New forms first express old functions, and new functions are first expressed by old forms.* It turns out that this is a familiar principle in the psychology of cognitive developement, and it is not surprising to find it in linguistic development as well. For example, Werner and Kaplan state (1963:60):

> . . . wherever functional shifts occur during development, the novel function is first executed through old, available forms; sooner or later, of course, there is a pressure towards the development of new forms which are of a more function-specific character, i.e., that will serve the new function better than the older forms.

Numerous examples could be offered from grammatical development in support of this principle. I will mention only a few.

We already have the locative example. The use of utterances in context indicates that locative relations are intended; when the appropriate new forms enter—be they prepositions, postpositions, inflections, or what have you—they will be new forms expressing old functions.

Roger Brown (1970b:120-121) has performed a detailed analysis of the emergence of inflections in the English of the three children who have been studied in great longitudinal detail at Harvard. He discovered that the first verb inflections to emerge marked just those functions already implicit in verb use at the previous stage, when all verbs were unmarked. At the beginning stage, when verbs occurred simply in their bare, uninflected form, Brown noted that they were used to express four kinds of meanings: (1) "naming an action or state . . . of temporary duration and true at the time of the utterance," or (2) referring to the immediate past, or (3) as a statement of the child's immediate wish or intention, or (4) as an imperative. The first verb markings to emerge were used to express just these functions: (1) the progressive -*ing*, (2) the past tense, and (3) catenative verbs (*gonna, wanna,* and *hafta*). The last function, the imperative, continues, of course, to be expressed by an uninflected verb in English, but Brown notes that *please*, as an imperative marker, entered at about the same time as these other verb markings. Brown also found that his three children understood the semantics of possession well before they attained the possessive inflection. In all of these cases, then, the appearance in child speech of a new formal device serves only to code a function which the child has already understood and expressed implicitly.

How does a child go about expressing a new meaning—that is, how does he find the linguistic means for newly-developed cognitive notions? Here we have the other half of the principle proposed above: *New functions are first expressed by old forms.* Richard Cromer (1968) found many examples of this principle in studying the development of temporal expression in English. For example, shortly before emergence of the perfect tense, his subjects attached *now* and *yet* to statements about the past, producing utterances which performed the same function as the perfect tense (for example, *I didn't make the bed yet; Now I closed it*). Such forms were soon replaced by the perfect (*I haven't made the bed; I've closed it*). Here it is clear that cognitive development has given rise to semantic intentions for which new means of expression must be forged. In fact, children's temporary, idiosyncratic linguistic .forms often are cues to the fact that the development of a new notion has engendered a search for new means of expression. Miller and Ervin-Tripp (forthcoming) note this explicitly in their longitudinal studies:

> In all cases [of idiosyncratic rules], it appears that the non-standard rules developed because the child's semantic development had outstripped his formal grammatical development.

Acquisition of the complexities of English auxiliaries and negatives provide many familiar examples, as when my three-year-old daughter said such things as *Anything is not to break—just glasses and plates* [= *Nothing is breakable except glasses and plates*], or, when recovering from an illness, *I must have getting weller and weller.*

The picture we have so far, then, is the following: In order to acquire language, the child must attend both to speech and to the contexts in which speech occurs—that is, he must be trying to understand what he hears, and be trying to express the intentions of which he is capable. This means that he must have both cognitive and linguistic discovery procedures available—in order to formulate internal structures which are capable of assimilating and relating both linguistic and non-linguistic data, and which are capable of realizing intentions as utterances. The emergence of new communicative intentions must bring with it the means to decode those intentions in the speech the child hears, and this makes it possible for him to discover new means for expressing those intentions. Cromer summarizes this argument cogently in his thesis (1968:218-219):

> . . . prior to the development of particular cognitive abilities, the child has been exposed to forms, structures, and words— some of these with a very high frequency—which he fails to acquire. For example, forms of the perfect tense are found in the mothers' utterances from the earliest protocols, and though the child has a span sufficient to produce these and has the elements to do so at his disposal [i.e. auxiliary *have* and past participles], he does not produce the perfect tense until after age 4:6. He has been barraged by a multitude of time words, but he does not use entire classes of these sometimes for years.

On the other hand, once certain cognitive abilities have developed, we begin to find that the child uses forms he had been previously using only in particular limited ways, to refer to and express new ideas. . . . Furthermore,

> once certain cognitive abilities have developed, we also find an active search for acquisition of new forms. Suddenly forms (and words!) which the child has been exposed to for years become a part of his own speech.

A Method for Revealing Language Acquisition Strategies

Given the primacy of cognitive development in setting the pace for the development of linguistic intentions, it follows that many linguistic forms cannot appear in the child's speech until he is capable of grasping their meaning. If the stages of cognitive development are universal— as I would like to believe—then a very strong developmental psycholinguistic universal can be set forward: *The rate and order of development of the semantic notions expressed by language are fairly constant across languages, regardless of the formal means of expression employed.* (Note that this proposition applies to semantic *intentions*, rather than the formal marking of intentions. Thus, for example, Brown's children would be credited with the four verb meanings, in this sense of intention, at the stage when all of their verbs were in the root, uninflected form.)

If this universal is true, and if communicative intentions can be reliably assessed from a combination of contexual and partial linguistic cues, then we have a powerful research tool for probing the information processing devices used and developed by children to understand speech and to construct grammars. What is needed is a taxonomy and coding scheme for pre-linguistic intentions. We are beginning to develop such a system at Berkeley, in the hope that it will be possible to establish a stable and universal sequence of pre-linguistic communicative intentions.[5] If this is the case, then one can measure the lag between the appearance of a communicative intention and the mastery of the conventional linguistic form which the child's native language offers for the realization of the intention. (See *footnote 6* for a criterion of mastery.) The lag between the first attempts to express a meaning and the acquisition of the relevant linguistic forms should vary from language to language, determined by the psycholinguistic complexity of the formal means used by a particular language to express the intention under consideration. With sufficient information on the sorts of formal devices which appear difficult to learn, we will be in a position to make a much clearer formulation of the capacities and strategies involved in language acquisition. It is necessary to compare formal devices used to express the same semantic intentions in order to insure that the children studied are at roughly the same level of cognitive development, and that the devices are used for similar purposes.

A Test Case: Development of Locative Expressions

In effect, this research tactic attempts to separate the bilingual child into two monolingual children who are following the same sequence of communicative intentions. A useful test case of the proposed method, therefore, begins with a re-examination of locative development in the Hungarian—Serbo-Croatian bilingual girls mentioned above. Our procedure will be to compare development of the formal means of locative expression in several languages; to propose a developmental universal based on inductive generalization of these findings; and to propose a psycholinguistic operating principle which may be a partial determinant of the general finding. The locative example will clarify the procedure.

You will recall that the development of Hungarian locative inflections was in advance of Serbo-Croatian locative prepositions. Why should the Hungarian locative expressions be easier for the child to acquire? In order to attempt an answer, it will be necessary to look briefly at the grammatical devices for locative expression in the two languages. Hungarian has an abundance of nominal inflections which express combinations of position and direction. For example, with the word *hajó* 'boat', there are forms such as *hajóban* 'located in the boat', *hajóból* 'moving out from inside of the boat', *hajótól* 'moving away from next to the boat', and so on. The inflections are all monosyllables, and systematically encode position, motion toward a position, and motion away from a position. They apply to all nouns (there is no grammatical gender in Hungarian). Serbo-Croatian, like English, has a number of prepositions which encode locations: the equivalents of *in, on, from,* and so on. And, like English, some of these prepositions encode direction (as English *to* and *from*), while some do not distinguish between direction and position (compare: *Put it in the box* and *It is in the box*). In addition, unlike English, Serbo-Croatian encodes the distinction between position and direction by means of noun inflections. The accusative is used when an ambiguous preposition like *u* 'in' is used directionally, and the locative case is used when such a preposition is used positionally (e.g. *kuća* 'house', *u kuću* 'into the house', *u kući* 'located in the house). The situation is even more complex in Serbo-Croatian, because of a variety of semi-arbitrary pairings of preposition with case. For example, *blizu* 'near', *do* 'as far as', and *iz* 'from/from out of' must take genitive nouns; *k* 'towards' takes the dative; *pri* 'at/near' takes the locative, etc. In both Serbo-Croatian and English, position vs. direction is sometimes uniquely signalled by one preposition or compound preposition (such as *towards, out of,* and so on), and sometimes one preposition fails to distinguish between the two senses (as *in* and *on*). Serbo-Croatian is more complex, however, in that every preposition governs a noun inflection. Sometimes this inflection is meaningful, distinguishing position from direction, and sometimes it is redundant. Furthermore, the particular phonological realization of a given inflection is determined by the gender and by the final sound of each particular noun.

Why, then, is the Hungarian locative acquired before the Serbo-Croatian locative in bilingual children? In the most general terms, it seems obvious that the Hungarian means of locative expression is simpler: the locative marker is always at the end of the noun only, always unambiguously and consistently indicates both position and direction to or from. The example demonstrates—at the very least—that a system which can be described by a small set of consistent and regular rules is easier to learn than one less consistent and regular—even by children under the age of two. But we can go beyond impressionistic statements such as these. The value of such cross-linguistic examples—I have proposed—is to teach us something about the ways in which children process speech.

The Hungarian locative is expressed by noun *suffixes.* This fact may facilitate acquisition, in that the end of a word seems to be perceptually salient. Little children will often imitate only the last part of a word, saying, for example, *raff* for *giraffe* in English, *sáyim* for *mixnasáyim* in Hebrew (Bar-Adon 1971), *ḥibb* for *cam-yḥíbb* in Arabic (Omar 1970), etc. Unstressed initial syllables, prefixes, and prepositions are very frequently omitted in child speech, as virtually all observers have noted. Furthermore, evidence from Czech, where all words receive initial stress, suggests that the ends of words are perceptually salient even if unstressed. Pačesová, reporting on a detailed longitudinal study of a Czech boy, presents numerous examples of omission of initial stressed syllables in Czech child speech. She notes that if "stress were to be the relevant factor in the abbreviating operation, the syllabic prepositions, being stressed in Czech, should have been early in appearance and, as for shortening, they should have been preserved, which is certainly not the case" (1968:205).

In regard to our bilingual example, this suggestion of differential perceptual salience could be checked carefully by having children imitate Hungarian and Serbo-Croatian sentences and note what is omitted. This check remains to be carried out, but other evidence supports the suggestion that part of the difference in ease of acquisition has to do with the pre- or post-nominal location of locative markers in the two languages. The prepositions are missing from the earliest stages of Serbo-Croatian monolingual child speech, and inflections begin to emerge before prepositions (Mikeš 1967; Mikeš and Vlahović 1966; Pavlovitch 1920). Inflections are word-final, and would be more perceptually salient on the above interpretation. The best support for this suggestion is the finding that Serbo-Croatian children begin to express the difference between position and direction by adding noun inflections rather than prepositions.

Additional evidence comes from cross-linguistic comparison. Russian, which is extremely similar to Serbo-Croatian, demonstrates the same pattern of prepositional and inflectional acquisition described above (Gvozdev 1949). The first locatives are noun-noun combinations, as in the example given earlier of *pot stove*. At the next level, the first inflections emerge, and the child distinguishes between position and direction by contrasting the locative case with the dative and accusative cases. At this stage the child is expressing the locative notions *in* and *into, on* and *onto*, and *towards*, using inflections and no prepositions. Later, when prepositions emerge, it is first just *these* prepositions which are used—performing the same functions as the earlier prepositionless utterances. Several months later a flood of prepositions comes—the equivalents of *under, behind, through, along,* and so on.

Rūķe-Draviņa (1959, 1963) presents the same picture in Latvian, with early inflectional marking of *in, on, to,* and *from,* and later emergence of prepositions. She notes that: "Endings, as case markers, generally occur earlier than the corresponding prepositions" (1963:141); and that prepositions are learned gradually, with difficulty, and are often omitted even after they emerge in Latvian child speech.

In English, too, prepositions tend to be omitted in early child speech, but the English-speaking child has no inflections available to use in the place of prepositions. When prepositions do emerge in English, the first ones are *on* and *in* (Brown 1970b), followed almost immediately by a large number of other prepositions (Brown unpublished data). It is as if the child had to develop to the point where he could attend to prepositions; he then uses them first for well-practiced locative notions, and quickly develops the means for expressing a wide range of such notions.

The suggestion of perceptual salience can be approached obliquely in English. Well before the acquisition of prepositions, English-speaking children are using locative verb particles like *on, off, down,* and so on. These tend to occur towards the ends of utterances in adult speech addressed to the child: *Put the shirt on, Take your shoes off,* and so on. Some of these particles are frequently present as one-word utterances (Braine 1963; Leopold 1939; Miller and Ervin 1964). The same is true of analogous German verbal particles, such as *ab, an, auf, mit,* and so on (Leopold 1939; Park 1970). By contrast, Slavic verbal particles of this sort are prefixed to the verb (the equivalents of *down-fall, off-take,* etc.). Grace Shugar (1971), in longitudinal studies of Polish child speech, reports that locative verbal prefixes of this sort emerge at the same time as prepositions in Polish—that is, relatively later than they do in English. For example, *od* 'off of/away from' emerges simultaneously as a verb prefix (e.g., *odjechał* 'rode away', *odpadł* 'fell down') and as a preposition (e.g., *od mamy* 'away from mama'). Since the Polish locative particles are placed before the verb, they are probably at the same level of perceptual saliency as prepositions.

Thus the argument is that if a language expresses locative notions by means of inflections and post-verbal particles (and, by extension, post-positions), acquisition of the verbal expression of locative notions will be facilitated. This can now be checked by comparison with other languages of this sort. Preliminary data on the acquisition of Turkish (my data), Finnish (Argoff forthcoming), and Korean (Park 1969)—all similar to Hungarian in this respect—suggest that this is the case. The argument can now be rephrased, by inductive generalization, as a suggested universal of grammatical development:

> *Universal: Post-verbal and post-nominal locative markers are acquired earlier than pre-verbal and pre-nominal locative markers.*[6]

This developmental universal is undoubtedly not limited to the expression of locatives. In fact, it seems to reflect a general early tendency on the part of the child to attend to the ends of words when scanning linguistic input in a search for cues to meaning. This is a sort of general heuristic or *operating principle* which the child brings to bear on the task of organizing and storing language. Phrased roughly, one can say that the following is one of the basic "self-instructions" for language acquisition:

OPERATING PRINCIPLE A: PAY ATTENTION TO THE ENDS OF WORDS.

We have seen this operating principle reflected in data on word imitation and in the acquisition of locative expressions. It is also evident in the acquisition of other inflectional systems. For example, accusative and dative inflections are very early acquisitions in inflected languages like Russian, Polish, Serbo-Croatian, Latvian, Finnish, Hungarian, and Turkish—where they are realized as noun suffixes. But these inflections are relatively late in the acquisition of German (Stern and Stern 1907), where they are realized as forms of pre-nominal articles. English articles are also lacking at early stages of development. It is not the semantic nature of articles which accounts for the omissions in German and English, because the Bulgarian article, which is a noun suffix, appears early in child speech (Gheorgov 1908). Apparently Operating Principle A is at work here as well, making it relatively difficult for the child to detect German inflections. The principle also accounts for the finding (Grégoire 1937) that the first negative element in early French speech is *pas*—the final member of the separated pair *ne . . . pas.*

All of these findings taken together suggest a general developmental universal, based on the supposition that Operating Principle A is one of the first operating principles employed in the ontogenesis of grammar:

Universal Al: For any given semantic notion, grammatical realizations in the form of suffixes or postpositions will be acquired earlier than realizations in the form of prefixes or prepositions.

In order for this universal to be manifested, a number of language-definitional universals must be taken for granted (e.g., that there are words, that the meaningful unit is smaller than the word, that sounds can express grammatical relations as well as make reference, and so on). In addition, the emergence of inflections requires at least one other basic operating principle:

OPERATING PRINCIPLE B: THE PHONOLOGICAL FORMS OF WORDS CAN BE SYSTEMATICALLY MODIFIED.

Numerous observers have reported a period of playful modification of words which precedes the emergence of inflections. Werner and Kaplan, reviewing the European diary literature, note (1963:155):

. . . there are some indications reported in the literature which suggest that long before the child grasps the role of form-changes as grammatical devices, he grasps the fact that forms of vocables may be modified to express some qualification of, or affective reaction to an event.

They cite many examples of playful reduplication, suffixing, and so forth. In languages which provide inflectional diminutive or affectionate forms, such inflections are among the first to emerge. Shugar (1971), for example, cites early Polish diminutives for names (e.g. *tatunia* (= *tata* 'father') and mamunia (= *mama*)) and for other words (e.g. *śliweczka* (= *śliwka* 'plum') and *jabłuszka* (= *jabłko* 'apple')). Pačesová (1968:216) gives remarkable examples from the early speech of a Czech boy who inserted extra syllables into adjectives in order to intensify their meanings. For example, the child had the following series for the adjective *veliký* 'big': [velikej]—[velika:nskej]—[velikana:nskej]—[velikanana:nskej]; and *malý* 'little' was changed to: [mali:]—[maliŋki:]—[malineŋki:]—[malilineŋki:]—[malulilineŋki:].

Children frequently experiment with the forms of words before they discover the meanings of particular formal changes. For example, Rūķe-Draviņa (1959) gives numerous examples of the early noncomprehending use of linguistic forms in Latvian:

The inflections $-a$ / $-e$ (nominative) and $-u$ / $-i$ (accusative) are used in free variation as alternative pronunciations of nouns at age 1:6, not being differentiated for the two case meanings until 1:8.

The plural ending is occasionally attached to nouns referring to singular objects before the acquisition of the pluralization rule.

Masculine and feminine adjectives are first used indiscriminately, ignoring the gender of the associated noun.

In all of these Latvian examples the form in adult speech is salient (according to Operating Principal A) and is fairly regular. A similar example is the English plural, which sometimes appears in early child speech as an alternative pronunciation of nouns.[7]

Operating Principles A and B present part of an explanation for the relative ease of acquisition of Hungarian locative inflections: the inflections are presumably perceptually salient, and the child is presumably prepared to manipulate the forms of word endings in his production. These principles both relate to ongoing speech processing—the deployment of attention in speech perception and the production of grammatical markers in speaking, although they also have implications for the kinds of linguistic rules which will be formed. Another set of determinants of ease of acquisition has to do more directly with rule organization factors—both simplicity and consistency of rules from a formal point of view, and semantic consistency. In the Hungarian system the locative marker is directly bound to the noun, while in the Serbo-Croatian system it is divided between a prenominal preposition and an inflection. In addition, the choice of formal markers for locative expression is semantically consistent and non-arbitrary in Hungarian, but is much less principled and orderly in Serbo-Croatian. A full answer to the question posed in our test case, therefore, will require operating principles for rule formation as well as for language processing. Principles of this sort will be advanced later in the paper, in connection with broader ranges of data. (See Operating Principles D and G, below). The test case has played its role in demonstrating the types of cognitive prerequisites to grammatical development which can be revealed by the method outlined above.

Broadly speaking, there are three classes of such prerequisites: (1) those related to the underlying semantics of utterances, (2) those related to the perception and production of speech under short-term constraints, and (3) those related to the organization and storage of linguistic rules.[8] The first class of prerequisites falls within the domain of the general psychology of cognitive development; the remaining prerequisites must be elaborated by developmental psycholinguistics. These are essentially *language processing variables* which can be conceptualized in terms of *operating principles* such as those proposed above. A number of such operating principles, and the predicted developmental universals which flow from them, will be proposed in the last section of this paper. Such operating principles guide the child in developing strategies for the production and interpretation of speech and for the construction of linguistic rule systems. The operating principles function within a framework of constraints on linguistic performance. These constraints must be considered before enumerating specific operating principles in more detail.

Constraints on Linguistic Performance

By and large, the language processing variables to be discussed below are determined by the fact that human language is produced and received in rapid temporal sequence. That is to say, because we communicate through the rapidly-fading, temporally-ordered auditory modality, we must have strategies for quickly programming and deciphering messages. The sorts of processing variables considered here are therefore closely linked to general perceptual and performance-programming principles. Some of them may well be special biological adaptations for language processing, or may have evolved in connection with language—but the issue of evolutionary origin need not be decided here.[9]

The constraints on linguistic performance are both short-term and long-term. The short-term have to do with the ongoing use of speech, and the long-term with the storage and organization of the linguistic system. Child and adult alike must operate under pressures of fading signal and fading auditory image; child and adult alike must have ready access to stored linguistic rules in programming and interpreting utterances. Although short-term sentence processing span increases with age, similar performance constraints are present in childhood and adulthood. Bever (1970a, b) has proposed that certain linguistic structures are not found in human language because they cannot be processed perceptually; it is likewise true that certain linguistic structures are not found in child language because they exceed the child's processing span. Because this span increases with age, it is evident that many universals of linguistic development are based on increasing temporal scope of processing operations. This is, of course, true of speech production as well as speech perception.

Processing span at first is quite literally limited to the number of terms which can occur in an utterance. Almost all investigators report a two-word (or two-morpheme) stage of development. During this period the child can typically express such relations as agent-verb, verb-object, and agent-object, but cannot unite all three terms into a single utterance. The advance from two-word to three-word utterances involves filling in a three-term sequence with fragments which earlier occurred as two-word utterances (cf. Brown 1970a; Bowerman 1970). That is, with maturation, the child reaches the point at which all of the sub-parts of an agent-verb-object sentence can be spoken in a single utterance. Adjective-noun combinations, which also occur earlier as two-word utterances, can be combined into three-word sentences as well, but this requires deletion of one of the other terms—generally the subject—producing verb-object strings with a nounphrase in object position. Thus the child can say, for example, *Mama drink coffee* and *Drink hot coffee,* but not *Mama drink hot coffee.*

At this early stage, then, output length limitations are quite severe—literally limited to words rather than to structures or to linguistic operations. Such limitations do not occur in adult speech, and this aspect of development seems purely to be based on maturation of a very simple sort of short-term processing capacity. At somewhat later stages, however, one finds the same sorts of processing limitations as in adult linguistic performance—but cut down to child scale. For example, both adults and children have difficulty dealing with material interposed between related parts of a sentence (cf. Operating Principle D, below). The only important age difference is in terms of how much material can be interposed without losing track of one's place in a sentence. For example, children may have difficulty in dealing with a doubly modified object noun between verb and particle—as in *He called the little old lady up*—whereas adults may tolerate a longer intervening string. But for both children and adults short-term limitations constrain the amount of material which can be interpolated before production or interpretation of utterances breaks down. In similar fashion, children are limited in the number of grammatical operations which can be performed in an utterance (Bellugi 1968), but this limitation does not differ in kind from limitations on adult linguistic performance.

I am proposing, therefore, that the short-term limitations under which children operate—beyond the very early limitations on absolute sentence length—are universal human limitations on sentence processing, and that they are based on general perceptual and information-processing principles. The nature of their development can be revealed by the general psychology of perceptual development.

Constraints on production and comprehension are intimately related—especially in child speech, where the forms the child uses in his own speech must be those he has been able to perceive in the speech of others. Thus the operating principles proposed below relate closely both to comprehension strategies (cf. Bever's *perceptual mapping rules*) and to the sorts of linguistic rules originally preferred by the child. To a great extent, the form of linguistic rules is determined by the short-term processing limitations, because the rules refer to a system which is represented in the auditory-acoustic modality, and because they must be called into play during rapid speech processing. In fact, at the beginning levels, it could be that there is little difference between short-term processing strategies and linguistic rules. That is to say, the child's knowledge of language—beyond the definitional knowledge proposed at the outset—is represented chiefly by the techniques he uses to interpret and produce sentences.[10]

Suggested Universals in the Ontogenesis of Grammar

In the remainder of the paper I propose some very specific language processing strategies. The approach is to define a set of presumably universal operating principles which every child brings to bear on the problem of language acquisition. From these operating principles, a number of more specific strategies can be derived, finally resulting in language-specific strategies for the acquisition of aspects of a given native language. Although the operating principles and universals have been arrived at through the same procedures spelled out in the locative test case reviewed above, the format in the following section is more terse, working down from broad operating principles to suggested developmental universals, summarizing data which support those universals (marked by ⊕ in the text below). The universals are hopefully phrased in such a way that they can be supported, modified, or abandoned in the light of future research.

Word Order

One of the earliest and most pervasive operating principles has to do with attention to order of elements in an utterance. It seems that a basic expectation which the child brings to the task of grammatical development is that the order of elements in an utterance can be related to underlying semantic relations.

OPERATING PRINCIPLE C: PAY ATTENTION TO THE ORDER OF WORDS AND MORPHEMES.

Universal C1: The standard order of functor morphemes in the input language is preserved in child speech.

⊕ No observers report deviant orders of bound morphemes. Burling (1959) found that post-verbal and post-nominal morpheme order was always correct in Garo, where long strings of ordered affixes occur. The same is true of Turkish, Finnish, and Hungarian child speech. The elements of the English auxiliary phrase always occur in their proper order (e.g., *has not been reading, will not be able to come,* etc.).

Universal C2: Word order in child speech reflects word order in the input language.

The phrasing of this universal is purposely vague, because the data are, as yet, imprecise. Earlier, limited data had suggested that children would adhere to fixed word order regardless of the degree of freedom of word order in the input language (Slobin 1968). More recent data (Bowerman 1970) indicate considerable individual differences between children in this regard.

⊕ Word order in child speech is typically reported as more consistent in languages with fixed word order (e.g., English, Samoan) as opposed to languages with relatively more freedom in this regard (e.g., German, Slavic languages, Finnish, Turkish). (But see Burling (1959) and Braine (1971) for examples of deviant word order in English child speech.)

⊕ American children tend to retain word order in sentence imitation (Brown and Fraser 1963; Fraser, Bellugi, and Brown 1963), whereas Polish children (Shugar 1971) and Russian children (Dingwall and Tuniks, 1973) frequently change word order in imitating sentences.

⊕ A Finnish child studied by Bowerman (1970) seemed to have acquired the dominant word orders of adult Finnish by the time his mean utterance length was 1.42 morphemes. Bowerman presents the following figures on the frequency of occurence of various orders of subject, verb, and object in the speech of the child and his mother (figures represent numbers of utterances in recorded natural conversation):

	Child	Mother
SV	44	47
VS	4	5
VO	4	16
OV	1	3
SVO	7	32
OSV	1	0
OVS	0	1
VSO	0	1
SOV	1	1

Universal C3: Sentences deviating from standard word order will be interpreted at early stages of development as if they were examples of standard word order.

⊕ Fraser, Bellugi, and Brown (1963) found that English-speaking pre-schoolers would interpret passive sentences as if the order of elements were subject-verb-object. For example, *the girl is pushed by the boy* is matched with a picture of a girl pushing a boy. In other words, children's interpretations conform to the order principle, but reverse meaning. Bever (1970a:298) has proposed as a general strategy of English sentence interpretation: "Any *Noun-Verb-Noun* (NVN) sequence within a potential internal unit in the surface structure corresponds to *actor-action-object.*" He presents extensive data in support of this strategy. McNeill (1970:124) proposes a similar strategy.

⊕ Conjoined sentences referring to two temporally ordered events are first given the interpretation that order of mention matches order of occurrence, even if the conjunction indicates otherwise (E. Clark 1971; Cromer 1968; Hatch 1969). (E.g., it is relatively more difficult for children to understand sentences of the form *Event 2 AFTER Event 1* and *BEFORE Event 2, Event 1* than sentences of the form *Event 1 BEFORE Event 2* and *AFTER Event 1, Event 2.*)

⊕ Universal C3 is apparently applicable even in inflected languages, which allow more flexibility of word order than English. Roeper (1972) investigated German children's attention to word order and inflection. The standard word order for German imperatives is verb - indirect object - direct object (V-IO-DO), with inflected articles indicating the roles of IO and DO. The inflections make it possible for adults to vary the order of the two nouns without losing sense or grammaticality. When offered V-DO-IO sentences for imitation, some children tended to switch articles, placing the dative article on the first noun and the accusative on the second. That is, children showed their command of the inflections *and* their reliance on word order: they interpreted the first noun after the verb as the indirect object, and inflected the article preceding that noun accordingly. Similarly, in a comprehension task, Roeper found that V-DO-IO sentences were frequently comprehended as if they were V-IO-DO. Thus in both imitation and comprehension many children tended to rely on word order over inflections as a guide to grammatical relations.[11]

⊕ C. Chomsky (1969) and Cromer (1970) have demonstrated that children have difficulty in correctly interpreting sentences of the type *John is easy to see,* where the surface subject corresponds to the object in deep structure. Children as old as six interpret the first noun in such sentences as subject.

Surface Preservation of Underlying Structure

Psycholinguistic research suggests another sort of operating principle which is tied to the fact that speech is produced and processed sequentially in a rapidly fading modality. In its most general form, this principle states that interruption or rearrangement of linguistic units places a strain on sentence processing—both in production and reception. In other words, there is a pressure to preserve the internal or underlying structure of linguistic units in their surface manifestations. A number of strategies can be related to this principle—both strategies for speech perception and strategies for the formation and use of rules of production.

OPERATING PRINCIPLE D: AVOID INTERRUPTION OR REARRANGE-MENT OF LINGUISTIC UNITS.

Universal D1: Structures requiring permutation of elements will first appear in nonpermuted form.

⊕ English yes-no questions first appear in non-inverted form (e.g., *I can go?*); inversion of subject and auxiliary is also absent in the first forms of wh-questions (e.g., *Where I can go?*) (Brown, Cazden, and Bellugi 1969; Klima and Bellugi 1966).

⊕ The first relative clauses in English appear in sentence-final position without inversion (e.g., *I know what is that*) (Menyuk 1969).

Universal D2: Whenever possible discontinuous morphemes will be reduced to, or replaced by continuous morphemes.

⊕ Slavic case inflections are first used to express the contrast between position and direction, in the absence of prepositions—i.e. the locative notion is, at first, not marked on both sides of the noun (as discussed above).

⊕ The first form of the English progressive is the verbal inflection -ing with no preverbal auxiliary (Brown 1970b; and many others).

⊕ The first form of French negation is pas, the final part of the discontinuous morpheme, ne . . .pas (Grégoire 1937).

⊕ The discontinuous Arabic negative /ma-. . .-š/ is acquired later than the prefixed negative /miš/ by Egyptian children, although both are equally frequent. Children under 3:6 have a general negation rule of /miš/ + S, even when incorrect by adult standards (e.g. /huwa miš rāh/ instead of /huwa ma-rāh-š/ 'he not went') Above 3:6, the discontinuous /ma-. . .-š/ is never substituted for /miš/, but the opposite substitution does occur (Omar 1970).

Universal D3: There is a tendency to preserve the structure of the sentence as a closed entity, reflected in a development from sentence-external placement of various linguistic forms to their movement within the sentence.

⊕ Early negative forms in English are attached to primitive sentences (*No do this*), later moving within the sentence (*I no do this* and, with auxiliary modal development, *I can't do this*) (Bellugi 1967; Klima and Bellugi 1966; Menyuk 1969; Snyder 1914).[12]

⊕ Finnish yes-no questions require attachment of a question particle to the word questioned, and movement of that word to the front of the sentence. Acquisition of this form of question is exceptionally late in Finnish children (Argoff forthcoming; Bowerman 1970). An earlier form of yes-no question in Finnish child speech consists of a sentence-final interrogative particle (S + *vai* or S + *yoko*) (Argoff forthcoming).

⊕ Sentence-final relative clauses (*I met a man who was sick*) are earlier to develop than embedded relative clauses (*The man who was sick went home*) (Brogan 1968; Menyuk 1969; Slobin and Welsh 1972).

Universal D4: The greater the separation between related parts of a sentence, the greater the tendency that the sentence will not be adequately processed (in imitation, comprehension, or production)[13]

⊕ Brogan (1968), in analyzing unpublished imitation data gathered by Carolyn Wardrip, found that sentences (1) and (2) were easy for preschoolers to imitate, while (3) posed considerable difficulty:

(1) He knows how to read because he goes to school.
(2) I saw the man who fell down.
(3) The man that fell down ran away.

Note that sentence length and number of embedded sentences do not account for these findings. What is difficult is not embedding, but *self-embedding*, as exemplified in (3). Similar findings are reported by Menyuk (1969), Slobin and Welsh (1972), and Smith (1970).

Clear Marking of Underlying Relations

Children scan adult sentences for cues to meaning, and are aided by overt morphological markers which are regular and perceptually salient. Such markers probably play a similar role in production, helping the child keep track of where he is in the transition from thought to utterance. With maturation and psycholinguistic development, the child develops an increasing ability to derive deep structure from minimal cues. Bever (1970a:350) has set forth "a view of sentence complexity according to which the more internal structure material that is implicit in the external structure, the harder the sentence, since the child must contribute more information to the sentence himself."

Children apparently prefer that grammatical functors be not only present wherever possible, but also that they be clearly marked acoustically. In fact, functors may be more clearly marked acoustically in child speech than in adult speech. Levina has noted that for Russian children

Clarity and accuracy of pronounciation appear first of all in the inflections. At the same time the word stem continues to sound inarticulate. . . .The work carried out by the child in connection with rudimentary distinctions of grammatical meanings . . .facilitates more articulate 'perception of the acoustic composition of words at this stage (quoted by Leont'yev 1965:101).

Rūķe-Draviņa (1963) notes that in Latvian child speech newly acquired conjunctions and other connecting words are stressed, even if unstressed in adult speech.

These considerations suggest the following operating principle:

OPERATING PRINCIPLE E: UNDERLYING SEMANTIC RELATIONS SHOULD BE MARKED OVERTLY AND CLEARLY.

Universal E1: A child will begin to mark a semantic notion earlier if its morphological realization is more salient perceptually (ceteris paribus).

⊕ The notions of *more salient perceptually* and *ceteris paribus,* of course, are in need of more precise definition. Operating Principle A and the discussion of locative expressions offer some support for Universal E1. (Cf. early acquisition of the Hungarian locative inflections, the Bulgarian *suffixed article -at/-ta/-to,* etc.)

⊕ The Hungarian—Serbo-Croatian bilingual children acquired the Serbo-Croatian accusative inflection *-u* earlier than the corresponding Hungarian inflection *-t,* using it on words of both languages.

⊕ The development of the passive is late in Indo-European languages, where it typically requires several morphological changes, as well as a change in word order in many languages. By contrast, the Arabic passive is learned early by Egyptian children (Omar 1970), where it is formed by a prefixed /it-/ on the past tense of the verb, with obligatory agent deletion and preposing of underlying patient. Although several factors are at play in this comparison, the marking of the passive by a single clear prefix is probably one of the reasons for its early acquisition in Arabic.

⊕ The following finding, reported by Shugar (1971) for Polish child language development, suggests a role for perceptual salience in inflectional development: "The following oppositions emerged: singular vs. plural in nouns, verbs, and pronouns; first vs. second person singular in verb endings; nominative vs. accusative case for feminine nouns; masculine vs. feminine gender both in pronouns and verb-endings. Most of the above differentiations seem to rest upon a new phonological acquisition: an acoustically clear differentiation of /a/ and /e/."

Universal E2: There is a preference not to mark a semantic category by ∅ ("zero morpheme"). If a category is sometimes marked by ∅ and sometimes by some overt phonological form, the latter will, at some stage, also replace the ∅.[14]

⊕ The Russian noun singular accusative is marked by ∅ for masculine non-human and neuter nouns. Such nouns are first marked with the acoustically salient feminine accusative *-u* by Russian children (Gvozdev 1949; Pavlova 1924; Slobin 1966, 1968; Zakharova 1958). The very same is true of Serbo-Croatian language development (Mikeš and Vlahović 1966; Pavlovitch 1920).

⊕ Gvozdev's (1949) Russian child used the masculine and feminine *-ov* for all plural genitive nouns, replacing the feminine plural genitive ∅.

⊕ Arabic nouns are given in the singular (∅) with numerals over 10; but Egyptian children tend to use plural noun forms with all numerals (Omar 1970).

Universal E3: If there are homonymous forms in an inflectional system, those forms will tend not to be the earliest inflections ac-

quired by the child; i.e., the child tends to select phonologically unique forms, when available, as the first realization of inflections.

⊕ The first noun instrumental inflection used by Russian children is the masculine and neuter -*om,* rather than the more frequent feminine -*oy* (Gvozdev 1949; Pavlova 1924; Slobin 1966, 1968; Zakharova 1958). The suffix -*om* has only one homonym (masculine and neuter locative adjective inflection), while -*oy* represents five homonymous inflections (singular adjective inflections for masculine nominative and feminine genitive, dative, instrumental, and prepositional cases)..

Universal E4: When a child first controls a full form of a linguistic entity which can undergo contraction or deletion, contractions or deletions of such entities tend to be absent.

⊕ Bellugi (1967) has noted the clear enunciation of *I will*—even in imitations of sentences containing *I'll*—at a developmental stage at which special attention is paid to the auxiliary system.
⊕ Slobin and Welsh (1972), in a longitudinal study of elicited imitation, found numerous examples in which their subject supplied elements in her imitation which had been optionally deleted in the model sentence (e.g., Model: *I see the man the boy hit.* Child: *I see a man who a boy hit.*)

Universal E5: It is easier to understand a complex sentence in which optionally deletable material appears in its full form.

⊕ This statement is a version of Bever's suggestion that "the child . . . has some difficulty with constructions that depend on active reconstruction of deleted internal structure" (1970a:351). Psycholinguistic research on adults, such as that carried out by Fodor, Garrett, and Bever (1968), has shown that multiply self-embedded clauses are very difficult for adults to understand (e.g., *The pen the author the editor liked used was new*). There are, presumably, too many interruptions to keep track of. Such sentences can be made significantly easier for adults to understand if each embedded clause is marked by a relative pronoun (e.g., *The pen which the author whom the editor liked used was new*) (Fodor and Garrett 1967; Hakes and Cairns 1970). The notion here is that one scans a sentence perceptually, searching for cues to underlying meaning, and that the relative pronoun facilitates a particular strategy for interpreting multiply embedded sentences—namely, that in a sequence of *noun - relative pronoun - noun -transitive verb*, the first noun is object and the second subject of the following verb.
Children, of course, cannot understand multiply self-embedded sen-

tences, but they can begin to understand sentences with one embedded clause. For example, Charles Welsh and I found that a two-year-old girl could imitate many sentences with embedded clauses marked by relative pronouns, and that her imitations showed that she understood the appropriate underlying relations (e.g., Model: *The man who I saw yesterday got wet.* Child: *I saw the man and he got wet.*). Note that her imitation has preserved meaning, showing that she was able to decode the structure, but that she has avoided interruptions in her version. She gives back the full forms of the two underlying sentences, supplying the deleted repetition of the subject: *I saw the man* and *He got wet.*[15] (This is further evidence for Operating Principle D.) At this stage of development, the child is unable to interpret sentences from which the relative pronoun has been deleted (e.g., Model: *The boy the book hit was crying.* Child: *boy the book was crying*). These structures were clearly beyond her competence at this level, and were treated as word lists. (Cf. the example given above under Universal E4, drawn from a later stage in the development of the same child. In that example the deleted relative pronoun is supplied by the child in her imitation, indicating her ability to interpret the deletion, along with the need to mark the relative clause overtly with the pronoun in her own production.) (Slobin and Welsh 1972).

⊕ Olds (1968) found that boys aged seven, nine, and eleven responded more quickly to instructions in which a relative pronoun was present (e.g., *The piece that your opponent moved may be moved two spaces)* than to the corresponding shorter sentences from which the pronoun had been deleted (e.g., *The piece your opponent moved may be moved two spaces*).

⊕ C. Chomsky (1969) and Olds (1968) found that children were less likely to misinterpret the verbs *ask* and *tell* when a pronoun indicated the underlying subject of an embedded sentence. For example, (1) and (2) were more difficult to interpret than (3) and (4):

(*1*) *Ask Laura what to feed the doll.*
(*2*) *Tell Laura what to feed the doll.*
(*3*) *Ask Laura what you should feed the doll.*
(*4*) *Tell Laura what she should feed the doll.*

Overregularization

Perhaps the most widely-noted aspect of child speech has been children's tendency to overregularize or overgeneralize. Virtually every observer has noted some examples of analogical formations, overextension of regular principles, etc., and a comprehensive list of examples cannot be attempted here. Rules applicable to larger classes are developed before rules relating to their subdivisions. There is a tendency to apply a linguistic rule to all relevant cases. In short:

OPERATING PRINCIPLE F: AVOID EXCEPTIONS.

Universal F1: The following stages of linguistic marking of a semantic notion are typically observed: (1) no marking, (2) appropriate marking in limited cases, (3) overgeneralization of marking (often accompanied by redundant marking), (4) full adult system.

⊕ A classic example is the development of the English past tense, as represented by the following schematic sequence of stages of strong and weak forms in past tense contexts: (1) *break, drop;* (2) *broke, drop;* (3) *breaked, dropped;* (4) *breakted, dropted;* (5) *broke, dropped* (Slobin 1971a).

⊕ Stage (3) can consist of substages of successive overgeneralizations, in which one form drives out another (cf. the discussion of *inflectional imperialism* in Slobin, 1968). For example, Russian children first use the masculine and neuter *-om* inflection for all singular noun instrumentals; then replace this with the feminine *-oy;* and only later sort out the two inflections (Zakharova 1958). Similarly, Russian children first use the feminine past tense for all verbs, regardless of the gender of subject noun; then use only the masculine for all verbs; followed by a period of mixed usage and eventual separate marking of verb past tense to agree with gender of subject noun (Popova 1958).

⊕ The Arabic plural has a number of irregularities and inconsistencies, as described earlier in this paper (a large number of irregular forms; a separate dual; singular nouns with numerals over 10; separate forms for - *counted* vs. *collected* senses of given nouns). The regular feminine plural suffix is widely overgeneralized, and "was strongly preferred for pluralizing nonsense nouns by children of all ages" (Omar 1970:375).

Universal F2: Rules applicable to larger classes are developed before rules relating to their subdivisions, and general rules are learned before rules for special cases.

⊕ Gvozdev's (1949) Russian child did not distinguish between mass and count nouns, requiring that every noun have a singular and a plural form. Thus he pluralized mass nouns (*bumagi* 'papers'), counted mass nouns (*odna sakhara* 'one sugar'), and invented singulars for plural nouns which have no singular forms in Russian (e.g., **lyut* as the singular for the collective noun *lyudi* 'people'). Similar phenomena have been frequently reported for English-speaking children.

⊕ Masculine animate nouns take a special accusative inflection in Russian. Subdivision of the noun class into the categories of animate and inanimate masculine for purposes of accusative inflection is typically late in

Russian children, who prefer to use a single accusative form for all nouns (Gvozdev 1949; Solov'yeva 1960).

⊕ C. Chomsky (1969) found late acquisition of the special rules involved in the use of the verbs *promise* and *ask* in English. *Promise* is a special case in that it violates the *Minimal Distance Principle* (Rosenbaum 1967) generally used to decide on the subject of an infinitival complement verb; e.g., in (1) the subject of the complement verb is *Bill,* but in (2), where *promise* appears, the subject is *John.*

(1) John wanted Bill to leave.
(2) John promised Bill to leave.

Promise CONSISTENTLY violated the Minimal Distance Principle, while *ask* is *INCONSISTENT*—cf. (3), where *Bill* is the subject of the verb in the complement, and (4), where *John* is the subject:

(3) John asked Bill to leave.
(4) John asked Bill what to do.

While *promise* is consistently exceptional, *ask* is inconsistent. Chomsky found that full comprehension of *promise* came at an earlier age than full comprehension of *ask*, suggesting that it is easier to learn a consistent exception than an inconsistent exception.

Semantic Motivation for Grammar

The overgeneralizations engendered by Operating Principle F are always constrained within semantic limits. The child applies an appropriate inflection or function word within a grammatical class, failing to observe a detailed subdivision of that class, but errors in choice of functor are always within the given functor class. There are numerous examples in the cross-linguistic data of the principle that rules relating to semantically defined classes take precedence over rules relating to formally defined classes, and that purely arbitrary rules are exceptionally difficult to master (cf. *footnote 4*). Simply stated:

OPERATING PRINCIPLE G: THE USE OF GRAMMATICAL MARKERS SHOULD MAKE SEMANTIC SENSE.

Universal G1: When selection of an appropriate inflection among a group of inflections performing the same semantic function is determined by arbitrary formal criteria (e.g., phonological shape of stem, number of syllables in stem, arbitrary gender of stem), the child initially tends to use a single form in all environments, ignoring formal selection restrictions.

⊕ The examples cited under Universals E2 and F1 also support Universal G1. For example, a common error in both Russian and Serbo-Croatian child speech is to use the frequent and perceptually salient feminine accusative -*u* on masculine and neuter nouns as well as feminine nouns. But, when it is used, the -*u* inflection is added only to nouns, and not to other parts of speech, and only to indicate the direct object of action or the goal of directed movement. Thus the proper inflection is picked to express semantic intention (accusative inflection), though the child does not yet follow the subselections within that class on the basis of gender and phonology. For each particular grammatical case category, the Slavic child apparently selects one salient case ending to express the semantics of that case in connection with all nouns. The underlying grammatical rule, therefore, is semantically appropriate, but only formally deficient.

⊕ In languages requiring agreement between adjective and noun, case and number agreement is acquired before gender agreement. In Russian, for example, the child uses a single adjective inflection for each case and number combination, but does not make gender distinctions (e.g., one singular nominative for all genders, one plural nominative, etc.) (Gvozdev 1949).

⊕ Mikeš and Vlahović (1966) report for Serbo-Croatian that case distinctions (and the singular-plural contrast are acquired before gender distinctions (both selection of gender-conditioned noun inflection and agreement between noun and modifier in gender). They note that children stop themselves before expressing proper gender much more frequently than for other grammatical decisions.

Universal G2: Errors in choice of functor are always within the given functor class and subcategory.

⊕ Gvozdev (1949) points out that although there are many confusions as to the proper suffix to employ within a given Russian case category, the child never uses one case instead of another. For example, although the Russian child uses an instrumental noun inflection which fails to agree with the noun in gender, he does not express the notion of the instrumental case by means of a dative inflection, a verb tense inflection, etc.

⊕ English-speaking children at first fail to appropriately subdivide prepositions according to their detailed semantic functions, but do not confuse prepositions with conjunctions or other parts of speech, and so forth. Miller and Ervin note, in summarizing their longitudinal study: "The children seldom used a suffix or function word with the wrong lexical class" (1964:26).

Universal G3: Semantically consistent grammatical rules are acquired early and without significant error.

⊕ A Samoan child studied by Kernan (1969) had learned to appropriately use the articles *le* + common noun and *'o* + proper noun/pronoun at the two-word stage. Thus a choice of articles based on a clear semantic feature—[± human]—was acquired at a very early stage of development.

⊕ Roger Brown (1970b) has found that the English progressive is the only inflection which never overgeneralizes in American child speech. That is, children never add the progressive to *state* verbs, saying things like *wanting, liking, needing, knowing, seeing,* or *hearing;* but they freely use the progressive with a large number of *process* verbs. Brown argues that there is a clear semantic distinction between verbs which take the progressive inflection and those which do not. Those not allowing the progressive all indicate involuntary *states,* while those allowing the progressive indicate *processes* which can be voluntary when predicated of people. This is the only subclassification of English words, for inflectional purposes, which is semantically principled. There is no principled basis for remembering, for example, that some verbs form irregular past tenses, or that some nouns have irregular plurals. These lists must be learned by rote, and the result is that such forms are overregularized in child speech. It is easier to apply a rule uniformly than to block it for unprincipled reasons, and so, long after they show their knowledge that one cannot say *I am knowing*, children persist in saying things like *I knowed* and *two sheeps*.

CONCLUSION

What has been sketched out on the preceding pages is only an outline of what some day may evolve into a model of the order of acquisition of linguistic structures. It has several major components, all of which must be elaborated. The first component, I have argued, is the development of semantic intentions, stemming from general cognitive development. The child, equipped with an inherent definition of the general structure and function of language, goes about finding means for the expression of those intentions by actively attempting to understand speech. That is to say, he must have preliminary internal structures for the assimilation of both linguistic and non-linguistic input. He scans linguistic input to discover meaning, guided by certain ideas about language, by general cognitive-perceptual strategies, and by processing limitations imposed by the constraints of operative memory. As in all of cognitive development, this acquisition process involves the assimilation of information to existing structures, and the accommodation of those structures to new input. The speech perception strategies engender the formation of rules for speech production. Inner linguistic structures change with age as computation and storage space increase, as increasing understanding of linguistic intention leads the child into realms of new formal complexity, and as internal structures are interrelated and re-organized in accordance with general principles of cognitive organization. All of these factors are cognitive prerequisites for the development of grammar. While we can disagree about the extent to which this process of developing grammars requires a richly detailed innate language faculty, there can be no doubt that the process requires a richly structured and active child mind.

Notes

[1] The growth of the ideas set forth in this paper has been greatly stimulated by discussion with many students and colleagues. It is a pleasure to acknowledge some of them here: H. David Argoff, Melissa F. Bowerman, Ursula Bellugi, Thomas G. Bever, Roger Brown, L. Dezső, Susan Ervin-Tripp, John Gumperz, Paul Kay, Jonas Langer, David McNeill, Melani Mikeš, Lubisa Radulović, Grace Wales Shugar, Peyton Todd, Plemenka Vlahović. Part of the work reflected here has been supported by the Language-Behavior Research Laboratory of the University of California at Berkeley, which is supported by PHS Research Grant No. 1 R01 MH 18188-02 from the National Institute of Mental Health. This support is gratefully acknowledged.

[2] For background on the methods and results of the Berkeley cross-cultural studies of language development see: Blout 1969; Ervin-Tripp 1969, 1971; Kernan 1969; Slobin 1967, 1969, 1970; Stross 1969; Talmy 1970.

[3] The research on English child language development carried out in the sixties is too vast to list in a bibliographical footnote. The interested reader can find broad bibliographical coverage and valuable comment in the following recent publications: Braine, 1971; Brown 1970a, b; Ferguson and Slobin 1972; Hayes 1970; McNeill 1970; Menyuk 1969; Slobin 1971b.

[4] A related argument for the primacy of cognitive development comes from linguistic analyses of Samoan child speech carried out by Talmy. In one of the first studies to apply a complex modern semantic theory to child language data, Talmy was repeatedly impressed by the children's early command of semantic rules. He notes (1970:12-13): ". . . it is clear. . .that the children make many grammatical errors—often in omitting functor words and affixes—and make few semantic errors—either in the assignment of correctly delimited ranges and correctly filled-in componentry to lexical items, or in applying these lexical items correctly to realworld events. . . . Apparently the developing child achieves a close approximation of the adult semantic map and its use before he does the same for the adult grammar. One might tentatively conclude that the human language-acquisition mechanisms are geared to a primacy and integrity in content-words and a secondariness in grammatical form, is sooner attuned to a control over organically-interrelated implicit components than to the expression of temporally-concatenated overt components, and is organized to manifest the expressively meaningful before the mechanical aspects of communication."

⁵The current version of our analysis is based on an enrichment of Fillmore's *case grammar* (1968). A similar approach is currently being followed by Martin Braine at Santa Barbara (personal communication). Francesco Antinucci and Dominico Parisi, at the Instituto di Psicologia in Rome, are developing what promises to be an extremely valuable model on the basis of generative semantics (personal communication).

⁶The notion of "earlier" is crucial to the understanding of such proposed developmental universals. There are two operational criteria of "earlier": (1) If both means of expression are available in a given language, one will appear in development at a younger age than the other. This can be ascertained in either longitudinal or cross-sectional studies. If A and B are linguistic devices taken to be ordered in psycholinguistic complexity, one would expect to find a given child using either A or both A and B, but not B alone. (2) If only one means of expression is available in a given language, the relevant variable is the time from first reliable *unmarked* intention to express the notion encoded by the linguistic form and the first reliable and appropriate use of that form. Only longitudinal study is applicable in this case. Brown (1970b) has proposed a useful criterion of reliable and appropriate mastery of a linguistic form. He suggests that one examine the contexts in a corpus of child speech in which a given grammatical form is obligatory, and set an acquisition criterion in terms of "output-where-required." He has found it useful to define mastery of grammatical morphemes as appropriate production in 90% of obligatory contexts. For purposes of cross-linguistic test of a universal, one would measure the lag between the intention to express the content encoded by A and B and the mastery of A or B in terms of Brown's 90% criterion. The lag between emergence of communicative intent and the acquisition of A should be shorter than the lag between the emergence of intent and the acquisition of B.

⁷It should be noted that there are considerable individual differences between children in their propensity to play with form when not expressing meaning. For example, of the two girls studied by Roger Brown, Eve had a period of free variation of singular and plural forms, whereas Sarah did not use the plural inflection until she could use it correctly. The problem of individual differences between children in their approaches to language acquisition has not been addressed frequently in developmental psycholinguistics, but is obviously of great importance—especially in light of the typically small samples required by longitudinal research methods. Wick Miller (1964) has made a valuable observation in this regard:

> There are individual differences in grammatical development. . . some children are more prone to invent their own grammatical patterns, patterns that have no relationship to adult patterns. The early grammatical rules for some are limited and quite regular, and for other children they are more variable and more difficult to define. Some children are quite willing to speak at almost any time, whether or not they have the appropriate grammatical structures at hand to express their thoughts, whereas others are more reserved in this regard, and will avoid talking at all, or will use a clumsy circumlocution. . . . I am inclined to think that the variations that are closely tied to formal features of language reflect innate individual differences.

⁸Cf. the distinction made by Braine (1971) in his recently-proposed "discovery-procedures" model of language acquisition between (1) concept learning, (2) the scanner, and (3) the memory component. The operating principles proposed here are aimed at specifying some of the properties to which the scanner is sensitive and some of the organizational features of the memory. In addition, Braine's model posits a preferential order or hierarchy among the properties noticed by the scanner. The property hierarchy (cf. Chomsky's *simplicity metric*) for a given language would result from the application of the operating principles (e.g., the suggested preference for word-final markers), as well as a possible preferential order of application of some operating principles.

[9]It may well be that human skills associated with auditory pattern perception, production and perception of rapid temporally-ordered auditory sequences, and so forth, originally evolved to subserve the function of linguistic communication. Once evolved, however, such skills can be applied to a broader range of functions. For example, music may owe its existence to skills originally evolved for linguistic purposes.

[10]Beyond these language-specific constraints, however, many linguistic universals are undoubtedly shaped by general constraints on the kinds of rules which the human mind can function with. I suspect that if other complex domains were formally described to the extent that language has been so described we would find similar constraints on the abstract structure of rules.

[11]The operation of language processing variables can also be discerned in the process of language change (cf. Bever and Langendoen, n.d.). For example, inflections are replaced by word order in the development of pidgin forms of a language, thus suggesting that order is a more basic device than inflections. It is also probably the case that all languages make use of word order as a basic linguistic means of signalling underlying relations, while the use of inflections is not universal.

[12]But Shugar (1971) reports early sentence-internal placement of a negative particle in Polish, and proposes: "It would seem that relative freedom of word position in sentences as well as experience with diminutive infixes might facilitate such re-arrangements within linguistic units like sentences in the Polish language."

[13]This is, in fact, not a developmental universal, but a statement of a general psycholinguistic performance constraint. As pointed out above, the only age difference is in severity of the constraint. Watt has phrased this universal in terms of a "theory of cumulative assignments" (1970:151): ". . . psycholinguistic parsing complexity increases with the amount of deep structure whose correct assignment is postponed; with the length of sentence over which the postponment must be carried; and with the complexity of misassignments whose rescission returns the processor to an earlier point in the sentence."

[14]It may be necessary to draw a distinction here between marked and unmarked categories (Greenberg 1966). Children do not insist on an inflectional marker for the nominative case in the Slavic languages, although such overgeneralization is technically possible. Little English-speaking children are content to leave the third person verb singular uninflected (a category which is generally unmarked in the world's languages), while they overgeneralize the plural (e.g., *sheeps*) and the past tense (e.g. *cutted*) to all possible cases.

[15]Note that this example also shows that the perception rules are not identical to the production rules. That is, the child can retrieve meaning from structures which she cannot yet produce.

References

Ament, W. 1899. Die Entwicklung von Sprechen und Denken beim Kinde. Leipzig: Ernst Wunderlich.

Argoff, H. D. Forthcoming doctoral dissertation on the acquisition of Finnish. Berkeley, U. of California, Dept. of Linguistics.

Balassa, J. 1893. A gyemerek nyelvének fejlődéséről. Nvelvtudománvi Közlemények 23.60-73, 129-144.

Bellugi, U. 1967. The acquisition of negation. Unpublished Ph.D. disseration. Cambridge: Harvard U.

Bellugi, U. 1968. Linguistic mechanisms underlying child speech. Proceedings of the conference on language and language behavior, ed. by H. Zale. New York: Appleton-Century-Crofts.

Bar-Adon, A. 1971. Primary syntactic stuctures in Hebrew child language. Child language: A book of readings, ed. by A. Bar-Adon and W. F. Leopold, 433-72. Englewood Cliffs, N.J.: Prentice-Hall.

Bever, T. G. 1970a. The congitive basis for linguistic structures. Cognition and the development of language, ed. by J. R. Hayes, 279-362. New York: Wiley.

Bever, T. G. 1970b. The influence of speech performance on linguistic structures. Advances in psycholinguistics, ed. by G. B. Flores d'Arcais and W. J. M. Levelt, 4-30. Amsterdam: North-Holland.

Bever, T. G., & D. T. Langendoen. The interaction of speech perception and grammatical structure in the evolution of language. Unpublish MS. n.d.

Bloch, O. 1921. Les premiers stades du language de l'enfant. J. Psychol. norm. pathol. 18.693-712.

Bloch, O. 1924. La phrase dans le langage d'un enfant. J. Psychol. norm. pathol. 21.18-43. [English translation: The sentence in child language. Studies of child language development, ed. by. C. A. Ferguson and D. I. Slobin. New York: Holt, Rinehart & Winston, 1972.]

Bloom, L. M. 1970. Language development: Form and function in emerging grammars. Cambridge, Mass.: MIT Press.

Blount, B. G. 1969. Acquisition of language by Luo children. Unpublished Ph.D. dissertation. Berkeley: U. of California. [Working Paper No. 19, Language-Behavior Res. Lab., Univer. of Calif., Berkeley.]

Bolin, I., & M. Bolin. 1916. De två första årens språkutveckling hos en svensk flicka. Svenskt arkiv för pedagogik 4.159-223.

Bolin, I., & M. Bolin. 1920. Psykologiska och språkliga iakttagelser rörande en svensk flicka. Svekst arkiv för pedagogik 8.1-55.

Bogoyavlenskiy, D. N. 1957. Psikhologiya usvoyeniya orfografii. Moscow: Akad. Pedag. Nauk RSFSR. [English translation of pp. 261-271: The acquisition of Russian inflections. Studies of child language development, ed. by C. A. Ferguson & D. I. Slobin. New York: Holt, Rinehart & Winston, 1972.]

Borgström, C. H. 1954. Språkanalyse som barnelek. Norsk Tidsskrift for Sprogvidenskap 17. 484-485. [English translation: Language analysis as a child's game. Studies of child language development, ed. by C. A. Ferguson & D. I. Slobin. New York: Holt, Rinehart & Winston, 1972.]

Bowerman, M. F. 1970. Learning to talk: A cross-linguistic study of early syntactic development, with special reference to Finnish. Unpublished Ph.D. dissertation. Cambridge: Harvard U.

Braine, M. D. S. 1963. The ontogeny of English phrase structure: The first phase. Lg. 39.1-13.

Braine, M. D. S. 1971. On two types of models of the internalization of grammars. The ontogenesis of grammar: A theoretical symposium, ed. by D. I. Slobin, 153-86. New York: Academic Press.

Braine, M. D. S. 1971. The acquisition of language in infant and child. The learning of language, ed. by C. Reed. New York: Appleton-Century-Crofts.

Brogan, P. A. 1968. The nesting constraint in child language. [Unpub. paper in series: Language, society and the child, Language-Behavior Res. Lab., Univer. of Calif., Berkeley.]

Brown, R. 1970a. Stage I. Semantic and grammatical relations. Mimeo, Harvard Univer. [Chapter for A first language, to be published by Harvard Univer. Press.]

Brown, R. 1970b. Stage II. Grammatical morphemes and the modulation of meaning. Mimeo, Harvard Univer. [Chapter for A first language, to be published by Harvard Univer. Press.]

Brown, R., C. Cazden, & U. Bellugi. 1969. The child's grammar from I to III. Minnesota symposium on child development. Vol. 2, ed. by J. P. Hill, 28-73. Minneapolis: Univer. Minn. Press.

Brown, R., & C. Fraser. 1963. The acquisition of syntax. Verbal behavior and learning: Problems and processes, ed. by C. N. Cofer & B. S. Musgrave, 158-97. New York: McGraw-Hill.

Burling, R. 1959. Language development of a Garo and English speaking child. Word 15. 45-68.

Chao, Y. R. 1951. The Cantian idiolect: An analysis of the Chinese spoken by a twenty-eight-months-old-child. Univer. of Calif. Publ. Semitic Philol. 11.27-44.

Cohen, M. 1925. Sur les langages successifs de l'enfant. Mélange Vendryes, 109-27. Paris.

Cohen, M. 1933. Observations sur les dernières persistances du langage enfantin. J. Psychol. pers. pathol. 30.390-399.

Cohen, M. (ed.) 1962. Études sur le langage de l'enfant. Paris: Scarabée.

Chomsky, C. 1969. the acquisition of syntax in children from 5 to 10. Cambridge, Mass: MIT Press.

Clark, E. 1970. How young children describe events in time. Advances in psycholinguistics, ed. by G. B. Flores d'Arcais & W. J. M. Levelt, 275-84. Amsterdam: North-Holland.

Clark, E. V. 1971. On the acquisition of the meaning of before and after. J. V. L. V. B.

Clark, E. V. 1972. How children describe time and order. Studies of child language development, ed. by C. A. Ferguson & D. I. Slobin. New York: Holt, Rinehart & Winston.

Clark H. H. 1970. The primitive nature of children's relational concepts. Cognition and the development of language, ed. by J. R. Hayes, 269-78. New York: Wiley.

Cromer, R. F. 1968. The development of temporal reference during the acquisition of language. Unpublished Ph.D. dissertation. Cambridge: Harvard U.

Cromer, R. F. 1970. 'Children are nice to understand': Surface structure clues for the recovery of a deep structure. Brit. J. Psychol. 6.397-408.

Dingwall, W. O., & G. Tuniks. 1973. Government and concord in Russian: A study in developmental psycholinguistics. Papers in linguistics in honor of Henry and Renée Kahane, ed. by B. Kachru, R. B. Lees, Y. Malkiel, & S. Saporta. Urbana: Univer. of Ill. Press.

El'konin, D. B. 1958. Razvitiye rechi v doshkol'nom vozraste. Moscow: Akad. Pedag. Nauk RSFSR. [English translation of pp. 34-61: General course of development in the child of the grammatical structure of the Russian language (according to A. N. Gvozdev). Studies of child language development, ed. by C. A. Ferguson & D. I. Slobin. New York: Holt, Rinehart & Winston, 1972.]

Endrei, G. 1913. Adelékok a gyermeknyelv fejlődéséhez. A gyermek 7 (8-9).

Ervin-Tripp, S. M. 1969. Summer workshops in sociolinguistics: Research on children's acquisition of communicative competence. Items 23.22-26.

Ervin-Tripp, S. 1970a. Discourse agreement: How children answer questions. Cognition and the development of language, ed. by J. R. Hayes, 79-107. New York: Wiley.

Ervin-Tripp, S. 1970b. Structure and process in language acquisition. Report of the twenty-first annual round table meeting on linguistics and language studies, ed. by J. E. Alatis, 312-44. Washington, D. C.: (Georgetown Univer. Press.)

Ervin-Tripp, S. 1971. An overview of theories of grammatical development. The ontogenesis of grammar: A theoretical symposium, ed. by D. I. Slobin, 189-212. New York: Academic Press.

Feofanov, M. P. 1958. Ob upotreblenii predlogov v detskoy rechi. Vopr. Psikhol., 4 (3). 118-124.

Fillmore, C. J. 1968. The case for case. Universals in linguistic theory, ed. by E. Bach & R. T. Harms, 1-90. New York: Holt, Rinehart & Winston.

Ferguson, C. A., & D. I. Slobin, (eds.) 1972. Studies of child language development. New York: Holt, Rinehart & Winston.

Fodor, J. A., & M. Garrett. 1967. Some syntactical determinants of sentential complexity. Percept. & Psychophys. 2.289-96.

Fodor, J. A., M. Garrett, & T. G. Bever. 1968. Some syntactic determinants of sentential complexity. II: Verb structure. Percept. & Psychophys. 3.453-461.

Fraser, C., U. Bellugi, & R. Brown. 1963. Control of grammar in imitation, comprehension, and production. J.V.L.V.B. 2.121-35.

Frontali, G. 1943-44. Lo sviluppo del linguaggio articolato nel bambino. Vox Romanica 7.214-43.

Furth, H. G. 1969. Piaget and knowledge: Theoretical foundations. Englewood Cliffs, N.J.: Prentice-Hall.

Gheorgov, I. A. 1905. Die ersten Anfänge des sprachlichen Ausdrucks für das Selbstbewusstsein bei Kindern. Arch. ges. Psychol. 5.329-404.

Gheorgov, I. A. 1906. Pripos k"m gramatichniya razvoy na detskiya govor. Godishnik Sofiyskiya univer. Sofia.

Gheorgov, I. A. 1908. Ein Beitrag zur grammatischen Entwicklung der Kindersprache. Arch. ges. Psychol. 11.242-432.

Gili Y., and S. Gaya. 1960. Funciones gramaticales en al habla enfantil. Publicaciones pedagógicas, Serie II, No. XXIV. Rio Piedras: Universidad de Puerto Rico.

Greenberg, J. H. 1966. Language universals. Current trends in linguistics, Vol. 3, ed. by T. A. Sebeok, 61-112. The Hague: Mouton.

Grégoire, A. 1937 & 1947. L'apprentissage du langage. Vol. 1, Les deux premières années. Vol. 2, La troisième année et les années suivantes. Paris: Droz; Paris/Liège: Droz.

Guillaume, P. 1927a. Les débuts de la phrase dans le langage de l'enfant. J. Psychol. norm. pathol. 24.1-25. [English translation: The first stages of sentence-formation in children's speech. Studies of child language development, ed. by C. A. Ferguson & D. I. Slobin. New York: Holt, Rinehart & Winston. 1972].

Guillaume, P. 1927b. Le développement des éléments formels dans le langage de l'enfant. J. Psychol. norm. pathol. 24.203-29. [English translation: The development of formal elements in the child's speech. Studies of child language development, ed. by C. A. Ferguson & D. I. Slobin. New York: Holt, Rinehart & Winston, 1972.]

Gvozdev, A. N. 1949. Formirovaniye u rebenka grammaticheskogo stroya russkogo yazyka. 2 parts. Moscow: Akad. Pedag. Nauk RSFSR.

Hakes, D. T. & H. S. Cairns. 1970. Sentence comprehension and relative pronouns. Percept. & Psychophys. 8.5-8.

Hatch, E. 1969. Four experimental studies in syntax of young children. Tech. Rept. 11, Southwest Regional Lab. for Educ. Res. and Develpm., Inglewood, Calif.

Imedadze, N. V. 1960. K psikhologicheskoy prirode rannego dvuyazichiya. Vopr. psikhol. 6 (1).60-68. [English translation: On the psychological nature of early bilingualism. Translation and Abstract Series, No. 5; Dept. of Psychol., Univer. of Calif., Berkeley.]

Hayes, J. R. (ed.) 1970. Cognition and the development of language. New York: Wiley.

Jespersen, O. 1916. Nutidssprog hos börn og voxne. Copenhagen/Christiana: Gyldendal. [2nd rev. ed.: Børnesprog: En bog for for ldre. Copenhagen/Christiana: Gyldendal, 1923.] [English translation in Language: Its nature, development, and origin, 101-88. London: Allen/New York: Holt, 1922.]

Kaczmarek, L. 1953. Kształtowanie sie mowy dziecka. Poznan: Towarzystvo Przyjaciół Nauk.

Kaper, W. 1959. Kindersprachforschung mit Hilfe des Kindes: Einige Erscheinungen der kindlichen Spracherwerbung erläutert im Lichte des vom Kinde gezeigten Interesses für Sprachliches. Groningen: J. B. Wolters.

Kenyeres, E. 1926. A gyermek első szavai és a szófajok föllépése. Budapest. (A Kisdednevelés kiadasa.)

Kenyeres, E. 1927. Les premiers mots de l'enfant et l'apparation des espècies des mots dans son langage. Arch. Psychol. 20.191-218.

Kernan, K. 1969. The acquisition of language by Samoan children. Unpublished Ph.D. dissertation. Berkeley: U. of California. [Working Paper No. 21, Language-Behavior Res. Lab., Univer. of Calif., Berkeley.]

Klima, E. S., & U. Bellugi. 1966. Syntactic regularities in the speech of children. Psycholinguistics papers: Proceedings of the 1966 Edinburgh conference, ed. by J. Lyons & R. J. Wales, 183-208. Edinburgh: Edinburgh Univer. Press.

Kolarič, R. 1959. Slovenski otroški govor. Godišnjak Filizofskog fakulteta u Novom Sadu. (Novi Sad, Yugoslavia)

Leopold, W. F. 1939, 1947, & 1949. Speech development of a bilingual child: A linguist's record. Vol. 1. Vocabulary growth in the first two years. Vol. 2. Sound-learning in the first two years. Vol. 3. Grammar and general problems in the first two years. Vol. 4. Diary from age 2. Evanston, Ill.: Northwestern Univer. Press.

Leont'yev, A. A. 1965. Slovo v rechevoy deyatel'nosti. Moscow: Nauka.

Lindner, G. 1882. Beobachtungen und Bemerkungen über die Entwickelung der Sprache des Kindes. Kosmos 6.321-342, 430-441.

Lindner, G. 1885. Zum Studium der Kindersprache. Kosmos 9.161-173, 241-259.

Lindner, G. 1898. Aus dem Naturgarten der Kindersprache: Ein Beitrag zur kindlichen Sprach- und Geistesentwickelung in den ersten vier Lebensjahren. Leipzig: Grieben.

Lindner, G. 1906. Neuere Forschungen und Anschauungen über die Sprache des Kindes. Z. pädag. Psychol. Pathol. Hygiene 7.337-92.

Manova-Tomova, V. 1969. Emotsii i govor u malkoto dete. Sofia: Narodna Prosveta.

McNeill, D. 1966. The creation of language by children. Psycholinguistics papers: Proceedings of the 1966 Edinburgh conference, ed. by J. Lyons & R. S. Wales, 99-115. Edinburgh: Edinburgh Univer. Press.

McNeill, D. 1970. The acquisition of language: The study of developmental psycholinguistics. New York: Harper & Row.

McNeill, D., & N. B. McNeill. 1968. What does a child mean when he says "no"? Proceedings of the conference on language and language behavior, ed. by E. Zale, 51-62. New York: Appleton-Century-Crofts.

Menyuk, P. 1969. Sentences children use. Cambridge, Mass.: MIT Press.

Mikeš, M. 1967. Acquisition des catégoires grammaticales dans le langage de l'enfant. Enfance 20.289-298.

Mikeš, M., & P. Vlahović. 1966. Razvoy gramatičkih Kategorija u dečjem govoru. Prilozi proučavanju jezika, II. Novi Sad, Yugoslavia.

Miller, W. 1964. The acquisition of grammatical rules by children. Papers read at annu. mtg. Ling. Soc. Amer., N.Y.C. [In Studies of child language development, ed. by C. A. Ferguson & D. I. Slobin. New York: Holt, Rinehart & Winston, 1972.]

Miller, W. R., & S. M. Ervin. 1964. The development of grammar in child language. The acquisition of language, ed. by U. Bellugi & R. Brown. Monogr. Soc. Res. Child Develpm. 29(1) 9-33.

Miller, W., & S. Ervin-Tripp. Forthcoming. Development of grammar in child language. New York: Holt, Rinehart & Winston.

Mussen, P. H. (ed.) 1970. Carmichael's manual of child psychology. 3rd ed. New York: Wiley.

Olds, H. F. 1968. An experimental study of syntactical factors influencing children's comprehension of certain complex relationships. Rept. No. 4, Harvard R & D Dept.

Omar, M. K. 1970. The acquisition of Egyptian Arabic as a native language. Unpublished Ph.D. dissertation. Washington, D.C.: Georgetown U. [To be published by Mouton.]

Pacěsová, J. 1968. The development of vocabulary in the child. Brno: Universita J. E. Purkyně.

Parisi, D., & F. Antinucci. 1970. Lexical competence. Advances in psycholinguistics, ed. by G. B. Flores d'Arcais & W. J. M. Levelt, 197-210. Amsterdam: North-Holland.

Park, Tschang-Zin. 1969. Language acquisition in a Korean child. Working Paper, Psychologisches Institut, Universität Münster, Germany.

Park, Tschang-Zin. 1970. The acquisition of German syntax. Working Paper, Psychologisches Institut, Universität Münster, Germany.

Pavlova, A. D. 1924. Dnevnik materi. Moscow.

Pavlovitch, M. 1920. Le langage enfantin: Acquisition du serbe et du francais par un enfant. serbe. Paris: Champion.

Pfanhauser, S. B. 1930. Rozwój mowy dziecka. Prace filol. 15.273-356.

Piaget, J. 1967. Six psychological studies. New York: Vintage Books.

Piaget, J. 1970. Piaget's theory. Carmichael's manual of child psychology. 3rd ed. Vol. 1, ed. by P. H. Mussen, 703-32. New York: Wiley.

Popova, M. I. 1958. Grammaticheskiye elementy yazyka v rechi detey preddoshkol'nogo vozrasta. Vopr. psikhol. 4(3).106-117. [English translation: Grammatical elements of language in the speech of pre-preschool children. Studies of child language development, ed. by C. A. Ferguson & D. I. Slobin. New York: Holt, Rinehart & Winston, 1972.]

Rasmussen, V. 1913. Barnets sjaelige udvikling in de første fire aar. Copenhagen/Christiana: Gyldendal. [English translation: Child psychology. Vol. 1. London: Gyldendal, 1920 / New York: Knopf, 1923.]

Rasmussen, V. 1922. Et barns dagbog. Copenhagen/Christiana: Gyldendal.

Roeper, T. 1972. Theoretical implications of word-order, topicalization, and inflections in German language acquisition. Studies of child language development, ed. by C. A. Ferguson & D. I. Slobin. New York: Holt Rinehart & Winston.

Rosenbaum, P. S. 1967. The grammar of English predicate complement constructions. Cambridge, Mass.: MIT Press.

Rūķe-Draviņa, V. 1959. Zur Entstehung der Flexion in der Kindersprache: Ein Beitrag auf der Grundlage des lettischen Sprachmaterials. Internatl J. Slavic Ling. & Poetics 1/2.201-222. [English translation: On the emergence of inflection in child language: A contribution based on Latvian speech data. Studies of child language development, ed. by C. A. Ferguson & D. I. Slobin. New York: Holt, Rinehart & Winston, 1972.]

Rūķe-Draviņa, V. 1963. Zur Sprachentwicklung bie Kleinkindern: Beitrag auf der Grundlage lettischen Sprachmaterials. 1. Syntax. Lund: Slaviska Institutionen vid Lunds Universitet.

Sanches, M. 1968. Features in the acquisition of Japanese grammar. Unpublished Ph.D. dissertation. Stanford: Stanford U.

Schlesinger, I. M. 1971. Production of utterances and language acquisition. The ontogenesis of grammar: A theoretical symposium, ed. by D. I. Slobin, 63-101. New York: Academic Press.

Scupin, E., & G. Scupin. 1907. Bubis erste Kindheit: Ein Tagebuch. Leipzig: Grieben.

Shugar, G. W. 1971. Personal communication re study of Polish acquisition.

Simonyi, S. 1906. Két gyermek nyelvéről. Magyar Nyelvőr 35.317-323.

Sinclair-de-Zwart, H. 1967. Langage et opérations: sous-systèmes linguistiques et óperations concretes. Paris: Dunod.

Sinclair-de-Zwart, H. 1969. Developmental psycholinguistics. Studies in cognitive development: Essays in honor of Jean Piaget, ed. by D. Elkind & J. H. Flavell, 315-36. New York: Oxford Univer. Press.

Skorupka, S. 1949. Obserwacye nad jezykiem dziecka. Sprawozdaniya z posiedzeń Komisji Językowej Towarzystwa Naukowego Warszawskiego. Vol. 3. Warsaw.

Slama-Cazacu, T. 1957. Relaţiile dintre gîndire şi limbaj in ontogeneză (3-7 ani). Bucharest: Ed. Acad. R. P. R.

Slama-Cazacu, T. 1960. Aspecte ale relaţiilor dintre gindire şi limbaj în însuşirea structurii gramaticale de către copilul antepreşcolar (2-3 ani). Rev. Psihol. 6(2). 43-63.

Slama-Cazacu, T. 1962. The oblique cases in the evolution of child language. Rev. de ling. 7 (1) .71-85. Revised version in Studies of child language development, ed. by C. A. Ferguson & D. I. Slobin. New York: Holt, Rinehart & Winston, 1972.

Slama-Cazucu, T. 1969. Studiile europene asupra limbajului copilului (1920-1968). IV: Bibliografie. Studii şi cercetăre lingvistice 20.479-508.

Slobin, D. I. 1966. The acquisition of Russian as a native language. The genesis of language: A psycholinguistic approach, ed. by F. Smith & G. A. Miller, 129-48. Cambridge, Mass.: MIT Press.

Slobin, D. I. (ed.) 1967. A field manual for cross-cultural study of the acquisition of communicative competence. Berkeley, Calif.: Univer. Calif. ASUC Bookstore.

Slobin, D. I. (ed.) 1968. Early grammatical development in several languages, with special attention to Soviet research. Working Paper No. 11, Language-Behavior Res. Lab., Univer. of Calif., Berkeley.

Slobin, D. I. 1969. Questions of language development in cross-cultural perspective. In Working Paper No. 14, Language-Behavior Res. Lab., Univer. of Calif.

Slobin, D. I. 1970. Universals of grammatical development in children. Advances in psycholinguistics, ed. by G. B. Flores d'Arcais & W. J. M. Levelt, 174-86. Amsterdam: North-Holland.

Slobin, D. I. 1971a. On the learning of morphological rules: A reply to Palermo and Eberhart. The ontogenesis of grammar: A theoretical symposium, ed. by D. I. Slobin, 215-23. New York: Academic Press.

Slobin, D. I. (ed.) 1971b. The ontogenesis of grammar: A theoretical symposium. New York: Academic Press.

Slobin, D. I. 1972. Leopold's bibliography of child language: Revised and updated. Bloomington: Ind. Univer. Press.

Slobin, D. I., & C. A. Welsh. 1972. Elicited imitation as a research tool in developmental psycholinguistics. Studies of child language development, ed. by C. A. Ferguson & D. I. Slobin. New York: Holt, Rinehart & Winston.

Smith, C. S. 1970. An experimental approach to children's linguistic competence. Cognition and the development of language, ed. by J. R. Hayes, 109-35. New York: Wiley.

Smoczyński, P. 1955. Przyswajanie prezez dziecko podstaw systemu jezykowego. Lódz:Lódzkie Towarzystwo Naukowe, Wydział 1, (No. 19).

Snyder, A. D. 1914. Notes on the talk of a two-and-a-half year old boy. Pedag. Seminary 21. 412-24.

Sokhin, F. A. 1959. O formirovanii yazykovykh obobshcheniy v protsesse rechevogo razvitiya. Vopr. Psikhol. 5(5) .112-123.

Solov'yeva, O. I. 1960. Metodika razvitiya rechi i obucheniya rodnomu yazyku v detskom sadu. Moscow: Uchpedgiz.

Stern. C., & W. Stern. 1907. Die Kindersprache: Eine psychologische und sprachtheoretische Untersuchung. Leipzig: Barth [4th, rev. ed., 1928]

Stross, B. 1969. Language acquisition by Tenejapa Tzeltal children. Unpublished Ph.D. dissertation. Berkeley: Univer. of Calif. [Working Paper No. 20, Language-Behavior Res. Lab., Univer. of Calif., Berkeley]

Szuman, S. (ed.) 1968. O rozwoju jezyka i myślenia dziecka. Warsaw. Państwowe Wydawnictwo Naukowe.

Talmy, L. 1970. Semantic-componentry and Samoan acquisition. Working Paper No. 35, Language-Behavior Res. Lab., Univer. of Calif., Berkeley.

Voegelin, C. F., & F. M. Voegelin. 1966. Index to languages of the world. Anthrop. Ling. 8 (6-7).

Watt, W. C. 1970. On two hypotheses concerning psycholinguistics. Cognition and the development of language, ed. by J. R. Hayes, 137-220. New York: Wiley.

Wawrowska, W. 1938. Badania psychologiczne nad rozwojem mowy dziecka (od 1,0—2,3 lat). Prace psychol. (Warsaw), 1.

Werner, H., & B. Kaplan. 1963. Symbol formation. New York: WIley.

Zakharova, A. V. 1958. Usvoyeniye dishkol' nikami padezhnykh form. Dokl. Akad. Pedag. Nauk RSFSR 2(3) .81-84. [English translation: Acquisition of forms of grammatical case by preschool children. Studies of child language development, ed. by C. A. Ferguson & D. I. Slobin. New York: Holt, Rinehart & Winston, 1972.]

Zarebina, M. 1965. Kształtowanie sie systemu jezykowego dziecka. Wrocław/Warszawa/Kraków.

DISCUSSION

UNIDENTIFIED DISCUSSANT: Whereas many features of the paper were very beautiful and very expressive of the development of children, I am a little bit disturbed by the concept of a child having a kind of knowledge and mechanically looking around for the forms that would best express this knowledge. It seems to me that what really occurs is that the child works through forms which he is constantly playing with so that form and meaning get completely integrated. I don't have the concept of a child in my experience having some meaning for which he must find the form with which to express it. Rather these are interrelated. You may just as well say that the child has a form and then looks around for some meaning to put in it. I think either of these concepts is quite wrong.

PETER W. CAREY (Graduate Center, C.U.N.Y.): I don't think that Professor Slobin is disagreeing with you at all. Perhaps what I could do, which might help some people, is to suggest the straw man that has actually had some vogue in the past that Professor Slobin is trying to knock down in this paper. I think that very basically Professor Slobin's point is that the development of language in the child is not independent of cognitive development and in some sense the sophistication of the level of linguistic development may not exceed the sophistication of the level of cognitive development. He is not claiming that there is not a constant interrelation between the two. The straw man that is being knocked down in this very important paper is that language development is unique and that there is nothing common between linguistic development and other kinds of cognitive development. In a way, the last phrase: *other kinds of cognitive development* gives away the point. Other people have not been willing in the past to grant that language development is subsumed under cognitive development. Thus Dr. Slobin's paper is addressed to Chomsky when in *Language and Mind* [N.Y.: Harcourt, Brace & World, 1968.] (Chapter III), he makes the statement that language development must be studied hand-in-hand with a new kind of psychology characterized by the sort of mentalism discussed by Katz in his article: *Mentalism in linguistics* [Lg. 40.124-137 (1964)] and that psychologists know nothing so far about this kind of mentalistic psychology that is necessary in lingusitics. This is an assertion which Professor Slobin is taking direct issue with and with which I also disagree. Chomsky is asserting that we must have a new kind of mentalistic psychology to go with linguistics and nothing that psychologists have done in the past is relevant. Professor Slobin is pointing out that Piaget and various other kinds of cognitive psychologists know a great deal which, when applied appropriately, can illuminate certain issues in the development of language.

The other point that can be viewed as a straw man which is being knocked down in this paper is the view of McNeill expressed in 1966 in his article in *The genesis of language* [Ed. by F. Smith and G. Miller, 15-84. Cambridge: The M.I.T. Press.] that language development is determined partly by specific, innate universals—specific to language. There was a controversy between McNeill who maintained this and Fodor who maintained that there was some specific cognitive proclivity which might be innate which would be more general, i.e., would apply to other things than language acquisition. I am sure that many of you are bewildered by these earlier positions. How could anyone be so unsophisticated as to assert that language development could occur in the absence of more general cognitive development? That position almost amounts to the claim that children don't talk about anything, they just talk. In answer, I can only say that there seems to be a general applicability of one of Slobin's universals viz. that at early stages of development, the presence of a negative element in a sentence is accompanied by decreased complexity of the rest of the sentence. Perhaps in the history of science this sort of principle works also so that when you talk about one thing, you tend to ignore the complexities of the rest of the issue.

JAMES R. HOLBROOK (Georgetown University): I would like to make a comment on the previous dialogue. I also agree that Professor Slobin did not mean that language and cognitive development were independent but was simply postulating that language development cannot go faster than cognitive development. This I think is something that it's hard to argue with. I would like to direct a question to Dr. Slobin. I hope that this will be taken as a legitimate criticism from an individual who personally feels a great debt to Dr. Slobin's work. This comment is brought on by the fact that I am impatiently awaiting the results of the experiment in Yugoslavia. I feel that the speculation on the reason for the different rates of acquisition of the locative forms in Hungarian and Serbo-Croatian is unjustified by Dr. Slobin in this paper—at least until the data from the monolingual speakers is available. It seems to me that one of the justifications for speculation in science is the absence or inaccessibility of data; here, I would feel, that the data on the acquisition of locative forms in Hungarian or Serbo-Croatian would be easily available. The investigators could easily have ascertained whether the locative forms had developed very early in Hungarian monolingual speakers. I question this only from the point of view of what I hope to be the general trend in linguistics—viz. the avoidance of unnecessary speculation.

E. SCHOLNICK (U. OF MARYLAND): I would like to talk as a cognitive, developmental psychologist for a moment and consider the queston as to why disparities between language and cognition might exist and what the problems might be this time for a theory of cognition—not for a theory of language. The problem involves the results of tests such as those suggested by Piaget. If you pour milk from a tall narrow glass into a wide low one, the child cannot understand that though the level of the milk changes, the amount of milk remains the same. It poses a contradiction when the child by the age of five develops a well-formed grammatical system—how could the child's inferential ability in the linguistic realm be so well developed while it remains so poorly developed in Piaget's test? That's the problem. If you want to claim that cognition develops before language but you measure the cognitive tasks by language, you get into the question of which does indeed come first.

PETER W. CAREY (Graduate Center, C.U.N.Y.): I agree that the paper raises interesting issues for cognition. The paper implies that studies of cognitive development have really left out of consideration the most important things. We don't know enough about the short-term memory development of children; we don't know what kind of strategies children must use in order to understand sentences—the philosophy of the notion: *understanding of a sentence* is something we will have to elucidate in the decades to come. If you want to maintain that a child of two can understand a lot of sentences, as obviously he can, then it is incumbant on any cognitive psychologist to say what cognitive mechanisms the child possesses by means of which to do that. The point that cognition is a sort of limiting factor for language development means that the linguist must pay attention to the cognitive psychologist but it also means that the linguist expects a great deal from the cognitive psychologist which he hasn't got yet.

The point about semantics being especially important in determining linguistic development raises the issue as to the precise definitions of cognition, semantics and syntax. Such precise definitions are called for so that semantics will not be a cover-term for things that are partially cognitive and partially syntactic. We need to keep the fields separate so that at least we can talk about one in terms of the other.

HARRY A. WHITAKER (U. of Rochester): I would like to add a couple of comments based on some facts that I know and relate them to a good number of things that I have no knowledge about whatsoever. It's not entirely accidental that the cooing and babbling stages in the child's development of a vocal repertoire have nothing to do with the acquisition of language. The reason is that the various language centers in the brain aren't hooked up to each other at the time when one finds children cooing and babbling. In fact, it's not unreasonable to maintain that the cooing and babbling stages are undifferentiated motor output having little if anything to do with cognitive skills.

As far as I know, a number of the Piagetian studies are based upon visual tasks. A number of the so-called conservation tests, if I'm not mistaken, are based on visual tasks; i.e., the child is asked to visually estimate the quantity of liquid as it is poured from two different containers. It's reasonably well-established in studies of adults as well as in a number of primates that visual pattern perception of this nature is dependent on the elaboration of structures in the parietal lobe. It also happens that the neurophysiological development of the pariental lobe is the latest in the brain; it probably doesn't occur until the age of three or four. If this is the case, then it is conceivable that some of Piaget's failure to get conservation in younger children is simply due to the anatomical fact that the structures aren't developed. It would be interesting to pursue this with some hard statistics and this is the area where I have no knowledge whatsoever. That is, we should try to correlate some of the knowledge we have about the maturation of the brain at different times with the degrees of cognitive skills. I suggest that this isn't going to solve all the really interesting questions but it may provide a background against which we could say, e.g., the reason why very young children don't do this is simply because the brain can't.

PETER W. CAREY (Graduate Center, C.U.N.Y.): I would like to just make one comment on babbling. Bever did an interesting undergraduate thesis in 1961 [Cf. T. G. Bever. Pre-linguistic behavior. Honors Thesis. Cambridge: Harvard U.] showing that the stages of babbling are very different from the stages of real language development and that there is a hiatus of about a month and a half at 11 months where babbling ceases and real language usage has not begun. Thus babbling may even be irrelevant in some sense for language development. The question concerning the motivation for babbling is, however, I think still an interesting one, one that really is, ultimately, within the domain of cognitive psychology. Lenneberg [Cf. E. Lenneberg *et al.* 1965. The vocalization of infants born to deaf and to hearing parents. Human Develop. 8.23-37.] has pointed out that babbling up until the age of 6 months is identical in deaf babies and in hearing babies.

Therefore, at least for babbling, there may be something to the notion that the motivation for it is built into the genetic pre-programming which would say that certain aspects of phonation do fulfill these universal, innate claims of people like McNeill. If it should turn out that babbling is totally irrelevant for real language development, then that would be interesting.

MARGARET K. OMAR (Foreign Service Institute): I did my dissertation on the acquisition of Egyptian Arabic (1970) and I closely followed Dr. Slobin's *Manual* in this. In regard to the relation of cognitive development to language development, in my study I purposely centered on lower-class children, village children who have a very limited environment, and I found that these children were quite late in developing many aspects of language which I would have expected to have come along earlier such as pluralization, colors and even tenses. I cross-checked this briefly with middle-class children in Cairo who enjoy much more adult attention and certainly have a broader environmental experience, and I found that their language development was positively correlated with this. I think that this must have a relationship.

The other thing I wanted to note is that in Arabic we have the very common occurrence of equational sentences which really look like a *noun + noun sentence*. Therefore a child who is producing what we would call a two-word insufficient sentence in English is in fact producing a full utterance in Arabic. I wonder if this leads to the fact that the Arabic-speaking child has much more flexibility of word-order in his two-word stage than children who have to worry about other things. Since he is never going to have to put a copula in there, there is nothing missing. I never found a strong word-order consistency in the two-word stage. From the very beginning they apparently realized that they were producing full utterances and therefore flexibility came along much faster.

Finally, in one of Dr. Slobin's operating principles, he mentions that "intonation and intensity of vocalization are of expressive significance". Having worked briefly with Vietnamese, I would like to put this out as a question. How do we suppose that a child who is learning a tone language is going to use intonation for expressive significance? He cannot vary the tones in his langauge. Does he go into the second tone register, does he refuse to express his emotions through language or does he in fact play with the tone system which I don't think he can do?

DAVID L. HORTON (U. of Maryland): I would like to make one general comment on the issue that seems to be raised continually in the discussion. It is a problem which we're all aware of and which is implicit in what everyone has said. It's a methodological problem. There is a very critical problem we have in dealing with children since we aren't children right now. It's been a long time ago and our long-term memories aren't so good. It is a problem which Jim Jenkins among others has characterized as the "can do, do do problem". It has to do with the way you pose a question. Perhaps some of you recall a study by Don Foss and Jim Jenkins [Cf. J. Jenkins *et al.* 1968. Phonolocical distinctive features as cues in learning. J. Exp. Psychol. 77.200-5] a few years ago on the voiced-voiceless paired-associate learning. Take a very simple task, a six pair paired-associate list with pairs such as [pa/ba] and normal college students can't learn such a list in ten trials. This is a very, very easy task with nonsense syllables or even more obtuse material. If you tell them to pay attention to what their mouths are doing, they learn it very fast in about three trials. I raise the question that in many of the investigations we have with children, we pose questions which may often be very well-motivated from our adult cognitive points of view but may not in any way capture the way the child functions. This especially shows up in naturalistic observations of very strange things children say that we won't predict but which we are all widely aware of. Such things as when a three year old child says: *Daddy highered the swing.* There are all sorts of implications in such examples, very complex reasoning processes which may not be captured by the kind of tasks we give them.

Chapter Eleven

Second Language Acquisition*

Stephen D. Krashen

This paper presents a model of adult second language performance that attempts to account for several perplexing phenomena, such as discrepancies in oral and written second language performance, differences between careful classroom speech and students' casual conversation, and the observation that certain students display a firm grasp of the structure of the target language yet seem unable to function in the language, while others do poorly on structure tests and appear to be able to communicate quite well.

It is proposed that adult second language learners concurrently develop two possibly independent systems for second language performance, one *acquired*, developed in ways similar to first language acquisition in children, and the other *learned*, developed consciously and most often in formal situations. The phenomena mentioned above, as well as certain experimental results, can be accounted for by positing a model in which adult linquistic production in second languages is made possible by the acquired system, with the learned system acting only as a monitor. The monitor, when conditions permit, inspects and often alters the output of the acquired system.

Language Acquisition and Language Learning

The technical term language *acquisition* is used here to refer to the way linguistic abilities are internalized "naturally", that is, without conscious focussing on linguistic form. It appears to require, minimally, participation in natural communication situations, and is the way children gain knowledge of first and second languages. Research in language acquisition has indicated that the acquired system may develop, through a process of "creative construction", in a series of stages common to all acquirers of a given language, resulting from the application of universal strategies (Brown, 1973; Slobin, this volume; Ervin-Tripp, 1973; Dulay and Burt, 1975). Each successive stage approximates more closely the adult native speaker's set of rules.

Language acquisition is a subconscious process. Language *learning*, on the other hand, is a conscious process, and is the result of either a formal language learning situation or a self-study program. Formal learning situations are characterized by the presence of feedback or error correction, absent in acquisition environments, and "rule isolation", the presentation of artificial linguistic environments that introduce just one new aspect of grammar at a time (Krashen and Seliger, 1975). [1]

The "switch" from acquisition to learning has been thought to appear at around puberty (Lenneberg, 1967). The model presented here, while maintaining the acquisition-learning distinction, modifies this view. While most language teaching systems presume that second language skills are best gained by adults via learning (Newmark, 1971, describes an interesting exception), there is some suggestive evidence that adults are able to acquire language to at least some extent.

Evidence for Language Acquisition in the Adult

One hint that adult acquisition is possible comes from an experiment conducted by Braine (1971), in which subjects attended to and repeated sentences in an artifical, meaningless language. After such exposure, it was found that many subjects were able to discriminate "grammatical" from "anomalous" sentences with a high degree of accuracy. This experiment was actually designed to test the hypothesis that a small percentage of anomalous strings in the input would not cause a serious learning deficit. While this hypothesis was supported, what is of interest to us is that many of the subjects who could perform the task of discriminating grammatical from ungrammatical sentences were unable to state the syntactic principles involved. Rather, they reported that they relied on whether a given sentence "sounded right". It is plausible that in these cases language acquisition and not language learning was occurring, stimulated by the fact that the linguistic environment was basically that of exposure to primary linguistic data and not the rule isolation and feedback that characterizes formal language learning.

Similarly, Wakefield, Doughtie, and Yom (1974) found that adults, after a brief exposure to a language previously unknown to them, were able to acquire knowledge of word and constituent boundaries. Experimental subjects, who had listened (without comprehension) to 27 minutes of Korean, and controls, who heard 27 minutes of another language (Chinese) were asked to judge which of two members of a pair of Korean sentences "sounded more natural": in one member of the pair a pause interrupted a word or constituent and in the other it did not. Experimental subjects performed significantly better than controls at this task, especially in the case of constituents, indicating that adults can at least partially acquire linguistic structure from just listening to a language.

Another indication of adult acquisition is "foreigner talk", the tendency of adults to adapt to the speech of second language speakers. Hatch (1975) has documented several cases of foreigner talk and notes that it occurs after fairly prolonged exposure to the input it mirrors, and that it matches the syntactic characteristics of the input quite well. In addition, its users do not necessarily have a "meta-awareness" of the rules they use in producing foreigner talk and do not always have competence in the first language of the second language speaker they are adapting to. While other explanations may be available for foreigner talk, it is possible that acquisition has taken place in such cases.

Further evidence that supports the hypothesis that adults can acquire are studies that report that adult foreign students in American universities are able to increase their proficiency in English by language use alone, without extra ESL classes (Upshur, 1968; Mason, 1971; see below for a detailed discussion of these studies in relation to the model presented here).

The most spectacular evidence for adult acquisition, however, comes from research that shows that under certain conditions, adult second language performers show a difficulty order for aspects of second language grammar that is very similar to that seen in younger acquirers, indicating some similarity in language processing between children and adults. The details of these studies, discussed below, provide direct evidence for the Monitor Model of adult second language performance.

When the Monitor Operates

Figure 1 illustrates the operation of the Monitor Model for syntax in adult second language production. Production is initiated by an acquired system. When conditions allow, the consciously learned system can intrude and alter the shape of the utterance, often before it is actually uttered.

Figure One

The Monitor Model for Adult Second Language Performance

learning (the Monitor)

acquisition ⟶ output

(the creative contruction
    process)

The existence of the Monitor in first language use was suggested by Labov (1970), who noted that under conditions in which monitoring would be difficult, earlier acquired dialects became evidenced in speech production. Labov suggested that maintenance of prestige forms that are learned later in life is done via conscious audio-monitoring, and these forms may fall away when conditions make monitoring difficult ("when the speaker is tired, distracted, or unable to hear himself"; Labov, 1970, p. 35). It is suggested here that similar principles apply to adult second language performance.

The model predicts that the nature of second language performance errors will depend on whether monitoring is in operation. Errors that result from performance based on the acquired system alone will be consistent across performers, regardless of first language or style of learning or syllabus used in the classroom, as acquisition is guided by universal principles. Errors that result from situations in which monitoring is possible will be more idiosyncratic, as they will reflect each learner's conscious mental representation of linguistic regularities in the target language. These predictions are borne out by the experimental data: we find the "natural order", the child's acquisition or difficulty order, just in those situations where monitoring appears to be most difficult. Bailey, Madden, and Krashen (1974) evaluated adult ESL performance for eight grammatical morphemes, and reported a difficulty order that was very similar to that seen in younger children acquiring English as a second language (Dulay and Burt, 1973; see also Krashen, Madden, and Bailey, 1975). The first language of the subjects did not seem to affect the results; Spanish and non-Spanish speakers performed nearly identically. The Bailey et. al. data was elicited using the field test version of the Bilingual Syntax Measure (Burt, Dulay, and Hernandez, 1973), which is a set of cartoons and an accompanying set of questions which the subject is asked. The way the BSM was administered in Bailey et. al., subjects did not have time to correct themselves.

Larsen-Freeman (1975a) also used the BSM for adult ESL performers and got similar results: the difficulty order she obtained was nearly identical to that found in Bailey et. al. and was not significantly different from that found in children acquiring English as a second language. Larsen-Freeman, however, also administered four other tests, tests that focused on artificial problem-solving rather than on just natural communication: Listening (choosing which of three spoken sentences correctly describes a picture), Reading (choosing which of three spoken sentences or sentence fragments is correct in the context of a story), Writing (filling in blank spaces in a story context) and Imitation. From Larsen-Freeman's description and personal communication it seems to be the case that these extra tests, with the possible exception of Imitation, all required more response time for the subject than did the BSM. Larsen-Freeman found that they gave less consistent and somewhat different rank orderings of the grammatical morphemes studied. There was less agreement between different first language groups and the orderings produced by the different tasks were not identical. This could mean that these tasks were tapping a non-linguistic problem-solving ability that is not necessarily utilized in natural conversation or in the performamce of such tasks as the BSM.[2]

Analysis of the behavior of individual morphemes in Larsen-Freeman's data provides furthur insight into the operation of the Monitor Model: items that are usually introduced early in the pedagogical sequence, that are conceptually "easy", but that are acquired late in children, such as the third person singular ending on verbs in the present tense and regular past morpheme, hold relatively low ranks in tests allowing little monitoring time, such as the BSM and Imitation tests. Such morphemes, however, rise in rank in "slower" tests, such as the Reading and Writing tests. Article usage, acquired relatively earlier but harder to "learn", shows an opposite pattern. The additional processing time might even hurt some subjects' article performance, in that those with little confidence in their acquired skills might change utterances that were initially correct (see discussion on Monitor "over-users" below). This data, from Larsen-Freeman 1975a and Larsen-Freeman's unpublished doctoral dissertation, which includes a re-administration of the same tests two months later, is illustrated in Table 1.

Similar findings have been reported by Krashen, Sferlazza, Feldman, and Fathman (1976), who found a "natural order" for adults on Fathman's SLOPE test, an oral production test involving 20 structures of English. Again, no difference was found between different first language groups, the adult rank order correlated significantly with Fathman's (1975) child second language order, and again, the conditions were such that little monitoring was likely to have occured. Also, no significant rank order difference was found between "formal" learners, those who had a great deal of ESL schooling and little "informal" exposure, and "informal" learners, those who had acquired nearly all their target language competence outside the classroom. This result is predicted by the Monitor Model: the formal learners did not access their consciously learned knowledge of English on the SLOPE test. A written version of the SLOPE with some of the same subjects revealed changes in the rank order. High accuracy prevented rank ordering in all cases, but there were obvious changes that were consistent with the model. As in Larsen-Freeman's data (Larsen-Freeman 1975a, 1975b; see Table 1), items that were apt to be presented early but that are in general acquired late show a shift up in rank in the written version: the third person singular ending on regular verbs in the present tense, for example, jumped in rank from 19/20 on the oral SLOPE to 8/20 on the written SLOPE.

Table One
Performance on Grammatical Morphemes in "Slow" and "Fast"
Conditions
(data from Larsen-Freeman, 1975b)
ranks:[a]

test	third person singular	regular past	article
BSM I	7	6	3
BSM II	8	10	4
Imitation I	7	6	2
Imitation II	7	9	3
Reading I	2	4	9
Reading II	2	3	8
Writing I	3	5	7
Writing II	6	3	7

a: out of a possible ten

Mean rank			
Fast Tests	7.2	7.7	3.0
Slow tests	3.4	3.7	7.7

Mode Rank			
Fast tests	7	5	3
Slow tests	2	3	7

Range of ranks			
Fast tests	7-8	6-10	2-4
Slow tests	2-6	3-5	7-9

"Fast" tests = BSM, Imitation
"Slow" tests = Reading, Writing

Individual Variation in the Use of the Monitor

Given the model described above, one might suppose that individual second language performers would vary with respect to the extent to which they utilize the Monitor in second language production. At one extreme end of the continuum, some performers might utilize conscious knowledge of the target language whenever possible. Extreme Monitor users might, in fact, be so concerned with editing their output to make it conform with their conscious rules that fluency would be seriously hampered. At the other end of the continuum, we may find those who almost never monitor their output.

These sorts of individuals do exist, and their case histories are revealing, both as to the theoretical question as to the operation of the Monitor Model, and with respect to the practical question of what role instruction should play in helping second language performers improve.

General Characteristics of Monitor Users

Before describing the extreme cases, we will first turn to some typical instances of Monitor utilization in adult second language performance. Several informal case studies will be presented to illustrate some general characteristics of Monitor users, namely:

1. Successful Monitor users edit their second language output when it does not interfere with communication.

2. This editing results in variable performance, that is, we see different types and amounts of errors under different conditions. Monitoring generally improves accuracy levels, and, as we have noted above, under edited conditions, where attention is on form, we no longer see the child's "natural" difficulty order.

3. Monitor users show an overt concern with "correct" language, and regard their unmonitored speech and writing as "careless."

Case Studies of Monitor Users

An interesting case study, illustrating some of the points mentioned above, is P, a fairly typical successful Monitor user studied by Krashen and Pon (1975). P, a native speaker of Chinese, was in her 40's when studied, and began to learn English sometime in her 20's, when she came to the United States. About five years before she was studied by Krashen and Pon, she enrolled in college, and graduated with an "A" average.

Krashen and Pon studied P's casual, everyday language production. Observers, native speakers of English (usually P's son), simply recorded her errors from utterances she produced in normal family living or in friendly conversational situations. Immediately after an utterance containing an error was recorded, it was presented to the subject. The data was gathered over a three week period and about 80 errors were tabulated.

Upon considering P's self-correction behavior, the investigators came to what was then an unexpected conclusion: "We were surprised to note . . . that our subject was able to correct nearly every error in the corpus (about 95%) when the errors were presented to her after their commission. In addition, in nearly every case she was able to describe the grammatical principle involved and violated. Another interesting finding was that for the most part the rules involved were simple, "first level" rules (e.g. omission of the third person singular ending, incorrect irregular past tense form, failure to make the verb agree with the subject in number (is/are), use of 'much' with countable nouns, etc.)."

The fact that the vast majority of P's errors were self-correctable suggested that "she had a conscious knowledge of the rules" but did not choose to apply this knowledge. Further evidence that this is the case "is our observation that the subject is able to write a virtually error-free English . . . In writing, and in careful speech, she utilizes her conscious linguistic knowledge of English, while in casual speech she may be too rushed or preoccupied with the message to adjust her output."

P thus illustrates the general characteristics of the successful Monitor user noted above. She is able to communicate well in both Monitor free and edited situations, applying the Monitor when it is appropriate to focus on form. Her performance is variable, in that she makes some errors in unmonitored speech, while her written output is quite close to the native speaker's norm. In a sense, she is able to achieve the illusion of the native speaker's syntactic level of performance by efficient, accurate, monitoring.

Cohen and Robbins (1976) describe two more cases like this in their in-depth study of learner characteristics. Ue-lin, like P, can self-correct successfully, and describes her errors as "careless". She reports that she likes to be corrected and has the practice of going over teacher's corrections on her written work. Her background includes formal training in English.

Eva, also described by Cohen and Robbins, is also a Monitor user. Eva made the following statement, which appears to indicate a conscious awareness of Monitor use:

". . . sometimes I would write something the way I speak. We say a word more or less in a careless way. But if I take my time, sometimes go over it, that would be much easier . . . Whenever I go over something or take my time, then the rules come to my mind."

This statement is easily translated into the vocabulary of the Monitor Model. "Sometimes I would write something the way I speak" reflects the use of the acquired system in language production when monitoring is not involved. Eva's comments about the "carelessness" of her spoken language, which are similar to Ue-lin's statement, simply reflect the fact that ordinary casual speech is usually un-monitored. "The rules come to her mind" when she focuses on the form of her utterance ("whenever I go over something"), rather than just on its function as communication.

Until the creative construction process has completed its mission in the adult second language performer, the use of Monitoring in edited language can certainly be an aid. The world often demands accurate language, even from second language users, in just those domains where Monitor use is most possible, in the written language, and a clear idea of linguistic rules can be a real asset for the performer. An overconcern with correctness, however, can be a problem. The over-user may be so concerned with form that he or she is unable to speak with any fluency at all.

The Over-User

Covitt and Stafford (1976) present an instructive case of a Monitor over-user: S, a Finnish speaker, who, like P, knows many of the rules of English, but who is often unable to communicate in speech. While her written English is quite accurate, Covitt and Stafford remark that "she speaks very little, because she tries to remember and use grammar rules before speaking". S's self-correction behavior reveals her lack of faith in her acquired knowledge of English: Covitt and Stafford report that she generally does not trust her intuitions about English syntax but relies on conscious rules. S describes her own situation as follows: "I feel bad . . . when I put words together and I don't know nothing about the grammar."

Birnbaum (1976) characterized the speech of Hector, another adult second language performer and ESL student who shows signs of over-use, as follows: "In a segment of conversation that lasted slightly less than fifteen minutes, there is not a single lengthly utterance that is not filled with pauses, false starts, repetitions, and other speech repairs . . . there are over 69 . . . instances of repair (not counting pauses)." We are not surprised to learn that Hector's written English, his class compositions "produced in a situation where extreme monitoring is possible—are among the best in his section".

Why are some people over-users? Does the overconcern with correctness revealed in second language performance extend to other non-linguistic domains? Birnbaum provides a clue, noting that "Hector's personality is an accurate predictor of his reliance on the monitor. He tends to be a quiet, intellectual, and somewhat introverted person . . .".

Let us look at certain personality changes that take place at the close of the "critical period for language acquisition" as a clue to the over-user. I have suggested elsewhere (Krashen, 1975) that the Monitor may owe it's source to Piaget's Formal Operations stage (Inhelder and Piaget, 1958). At around twelve, the adolescent is able to think in purely abstract terms for the first time, that is, he is able to relate abstract concepts to other abstractions, dealing with them as if they were concrete objects. This new ability may allow the adolescent to become more conscious of abstract grammatical rules.

Elkind (1970) has suggested that profound psychological changes that occur at this time may be related to this cognitive change. He suggests that formal operations permit the adolescent "to conceptualize the thought of other people". This may lead the adolescent to the false conclusion that other people are not only thinking about him but are focussing on just what he considers to be his inadequacies. He assumes that "others are as admiring or as critical of him as he is of himself". This leads to the feeling of self-consciousness and vulnerability that one often sees in adolescents. In the case of the over-user, this fear of making what one perceives to be an error may extend into the linguistic domain and may remain in the individual long after adolescence.

Under-users

At the other extreme are adult second language performers who do not seem to use a monitor to any extent, even when conditions encourage it. Such performers, like first language acquirers, appear to be uninfluenced by most error correction, and do not usually utilize conscious linguistic knowledge in second language performance.

In previous reports (Krashen, 1975; see also Krashen, in press), the case of Hung was discussed in this regard. Hung, described by Cohen and Robbins (1976), is, for the most part, unable to self-correct his own errors in written English, and does not have a conscious knowledge of the rules he breaks. When he does attempt to self-correct, he reports that he does so "by feel" ("It sounds just right."), reflecting reliance on his acquired competence. Hung reports that his English backround is nearly entirely "submersion". He came to the United States at ten and did not receive formal training in ESL. Also, he reports that he does not like "grammar."

Covitt and Stafford describe several cases of Monitor under-users, and make the interesting point that under-users may pay lip-service to the importance of linguistic rules, but in reality may hardly use them at all.

First consider the case of V, an ESL student who is described by Covitt and Stafford as "verbal and energetic." V values the study of grammar very highly. On a questionnaire administered by Covitt and Stafford, he wrote "Grammar is the key to every language." V thinks he uses conscious rules in performance—"When I know a grammar rule, I try to apply it"—but careful questioning by Covitt and Stafford revealed that V actually knows few rules and self-corrects "by feel." The following exchanges, taken from a conversation between V and one of the investigators, illustrate this:

Interviewer	*V*
(When you write a composition) . . do you think of grammar rules? Do you think "Should I have used the present tense here or would the present continuous be better or . . .	
	I don't refer that to the books and all that, you know. I just refer it to this uh, my judgment and . . sensing it if I'm writing it right or wrong. Because I really don't know . . what where exactly how . . the grammatical rules work out.
Do you correct yourself when you talk?	
	Yeah, I watch out for that very good.
How do you know you made a mistake?	
	. . . it doesn't sound right . . . sometimes what I said I feel it that it doesn't register the way I want it.
Do you think grammar rules are useful?	
	Useful? Yeah. When you want to write they are very very useful.
But you don't use them when you write.	
	Yeah, I know. I don't use them . . . I don't know how to use them!

Another case described by Covitt and Stafford is I, an Israeli woman who has studied English formally and who also values conscious rules highly but utilizes them very little in performance. She is described as being "very friendly . . . loves to talk to people, and is not embarassed to make mistakes". This outgoing, uninhibited personality type seems to be shared by V, discussed above, and is in constrast to the self-conscious, introverted personality of the over-user.

I remarks that even in written performance ". . . first of all I listen to myself as it sounds. I mean I write it and then I see if it sounds correct." Also, "I listen to things, I don't know the rules. Really, I don't know them." On the other hand, she feels that conscious rules are necessary to speak "correctly". Interestingly, however, she advises a non-rule approach to second language study: ". . . I think when you are a foreigner in a country and you need the language just to speak it daily, you need an audio-visual course, and not, not grammar."

While students like I and V may not directly profit from a rule-type approach to second language, they think they will, and this fact may be a factor in lesson planning.

Table 2 summarizes the sorts of individual variation discussed here. While this certainly is not an exhaustive listing of every kind of variation seen in adult second language classrooms, it covers some common types.

Table Two
Individual Variation in Monitor Use

Monitor user	spoken style	uses conscious rules?	personality type
optimal	− hesitant	yes	
over-user	+ hesitant	yes	self-conscious
under-user	− hesitant	no[1]	outgoing

1: may pay lip-service to value of rules (see text)

The Role of Formal and Informal Environments

The Monitor Model may also help to resolve some controversy in another area of second language research. The results of several studies support the hypothesis that "informal" linguistic environments are superior to "formal" environments (e.g. the classroom) in increasing adult second language proficiency, while other studies suggest that formal study is better.

Among the former group of studies is Upshur (1968), who compared three groups of ten adult ESL students enrolled in a special summer course for law students at the University of Michigan. The first group, who scored highest on an entrance test, attended seminars and classes during the ten week period that were conducted in English, but had no extra classes in ESL. The second group, who scored lower on the entrance test, also attended law classes and had one hour daily of ESL in addition. The third group scored lowest on the pre-test and had two hours of ESL daily in addition to the law classes. At the end of the summer, an alternate form of the pre-test was given. While all three groups showed some improvement, Upshur's statistical analysis revealed "no significant effects on language learning attributable to amount of language instruction," and concluded that "foreign language courses may at this time be less effective means for producing language learning than the use of language in other activities".

Upshur's conclusion appears to be consistent with his data. Krashen and Seliger (1975) suggest, however, that motivated second language students are able to provide themselves with the essential ingredients of formal instruction (rule isolation and error detection/correction) without going to class. Rule isolation can be done by recourse to a text or by asking informants about grammar, while feedback is available when helpful friends correct the learner.

Mason (1971) is also interpretable in these two ways. In this study, certain foreign students at the University of Hawaii were allowed to follow regular academic programs without extra ESL, despite the fact that their English placement scores indicated that they should be enrolled in English for foreign students classes. Post-tests given at the end of the semester showed no significant difference in increase in English proficiency between those excused from ESL and controls who took the required ESL classes. This data is again consistent with the hypothesis that informal environments are superior, but other explanations are available.

Carroll (1967) studied the second language proficiency of American college seniors majoring in foreign languages (French, German, Russian, and Spanish). 2,784 seniors, about 25 per cent of the total population of senior language majors that year, were given form A of the MLA Foreign Language Proficiency test in their chosen language. Carroll's major finding was that, on the average, foreign language majors performed rather poorly.[3] Of more interest here is the relation found between attainment and measures of time spent in different linguistic environments. A strong relationship was found between time spent abroad (in the country where the target language was spoken) and test performance, with those who reported a year abroad performing best. A significant relationship was also found between test performance and the extent to which the target language was used in the students' homes. (Native speakers of the language majored in were excluded from the study.) Those reporting frequent parental use of the language had higher scores than students who reported occasional use, and this latter group outperformed those whose parents did not or could not speak the language at home.

These two findings (time abroad and parental use) are consistent with the hypothesis that informal environments are better, but they could also fit the alternative hypothesis: use of the language at home may have increased motivation to study, and time spent abroad may have meant more formal study and/or more chances for self-study, as well as increased motivation to learn formally. The hypothesis that *formal* environments are superior receives some support from Carroll's study also. It was found that those who started foreign language study early (grade school) achieved better scores. Those who studied the target language in high school did better than those who started in college (German majors were an exception to this). This relationship was independent of that found between proficiency and time spent in informal environments. Carroll notes that "the simplest explanation of this finding is that attainment of skill in a foreign language is a function of the amount of time spent in its study." (p. 136). The following series of studies also argue for this alternative.

Krashen and Seliger (1976)[4] and Krashen, Seliger, and Hartnett (1974) claim that when the effects of "exposure" and formal instruction are compared, it is reliably the case that more instruction means higher proficiency, while more exposure does not necessarily mean more proficiency in ESL. Both studies compared instruction and exposure by matching pairs of foreign students for one of these variables and seeing whether the student who excelled on the other was more proficient in English.

The measure of the amount of formal instruction was simply the students' report of the number of years he or she had studied English in a school situation. No questions were asked concerning factors such as the methodology used, the presence or absence of a language laboratory, how often the class met, the amount of time the student devoted to his studies, or grades. In Krashen and Seliger (1976)[4] exposure was defined as the product of the number of years the student reported having spent in an English speaking country and how much English the student said he spoke every day (on a scale of one to ten). In Krashen et. al. (1974) students were asked to indicate years spent in an English speaking country and also to indicate how much English they spoke each day (on a scale of one to four). Subjects with the same number of years spent in the country where English was spoken and the same report of speaking were considered to have the same exposure score.

Student samples differed somewhat: in the first study, subjects were registered in an intensive, 20 hour per week institute designed to prepare foreign students for study in American colleges. In the second study, subjects were enrolled in a part-time extension program; these students were, on the average, older, and many were permanent residents or citizens of the United States. The measure of proficiency used in the first study was teacher ranking (which correlated significantly with local placement tests), and in the second study the Michigan Examination in Structure was used.

In the first study, six out of 14 pairs of students matched for years of formal study of English were consistent with the hypothesis that more exposure meant more proficiency; that is, in only six cases did the student with more exposure show a higher ranking than his partner with less. Similarly, in the second study, more exposure was associated with a higher score in only 10 out of 21 cases, which is consistent with the hypothesis that exposure has no consistent effect on second language proficiency. When students were matched for exposure scores, however, it appeared to be the case that more instruction did indeed mean more proficiency. In the first study, this was true in seven out of nine cases, and in the second study it was true in eight out of 11 cases, which in both studies was statistically significant (Wilcoxen matched pairs test).

Krashen, Jones, Zelinski, and Usprich (in press) arrived at similar results. Placement test scores for 116 students of ESL in an extension program were correlated with students' reports of years of formal study and years spent in an English speaking country. The results confirmed the conclusions of the studies described above: years of formal instruction reported was a better predictor of English proficiency than was time spent in an English speaking environment. While exposure (here simply the report of years spent in an informal environment with no estimation of how much the S used the language) was shown to have a significant effect, it accounted for very little of the variation in the test scores.

The last three studies described above provide explicit support for the formal study position. These three studies, however, share a feature that prevents them from being convincing counter-examples to the "informal" hypothesis: "Years spent in an English-speaking country" need not be equivalent to time spent in a meaningful informal linguistic environment. There is an important difference between the measures used in the Upshur, Mason, and Carroll studies and in the measure used in the Krashen et al. series. In the former group of studies, we can be fairly certain that the second language student was involved in real and sustained second language use situations. Upshur and Mason's subjects were university students who were taking courses taught in English. In addition, they were also probably taking part in the social life of their respective schools. Carroll's "year abroad" students were also highly likely to have been engaged in real communicative use of the language, as their primary purpose for going abroad, in most cases, was to have additional opportunities to converse with native speakers of the language they were studying. In the Krashen et al. series we have much less knowledge of just how much or what percentage of time was spent in real and sustained language use. In the first two of the three Krashen et al. studies, the exposure measure included a self-report of how much English the subject spoke each day, but as Krashen and Seliger (1976)[4] point out, this estimate may not have been true of the entire time the S spent in the second language environment: some may have spent a fair amount of time in the United States before attempting to use English regularly. In the third study of this series, only "years in an English speaking country" was considered. A significant number of subjects who did not use the language regularly may have affected the sample. Thus, the Upshur, Mason, and Carroll subjects appear to have been involved in an intensive, daily, and often demanding second language environment. The Krashen et al. subjects may have varied much more with respect to the amount of real communicative use they made of their second language.

While the characteristics of utilized primary linguistic data (termed "intake" in recent years) have not been determined in detail, mere "heard language" is probably insufficient input for the operation of a language acquisition device at any age. The difference between "heard language" and "intake" is emphasized in Friedlander, Jacobs, Davis, and Wetstone (1972), who examined the linguistic environment of a child who at 22 months was judged to be nearly as fluent in Spanish as she was in English. The child heard Spanish primarily from her father. This input, according to Friedlander et al., made up only 4 per cent of the child's total "heard language," but was 25 per cent of the language directed at the child. This confirms that the relevant primary linguistic data is that which the acquirer is actively involved with: the total linguistic environment is less important.

The results of the studies reviewed here can all be considered as consistent with the hypothesis that informal environments are superior. The Upshur, Mason, and Carroll studies provide direct evidence, while the Krashen et al. series may be interpreted as showing that acquisition from the informal environment requires regular and intensive language use. The "formal" hypothesis, however, also receives no real counter-evidence from any of the studies. The correlations between years of formal study and proficiency found by Krashen et. al. are reliable and are consistent with Carroll's interpretation of his data. The "self-study" re-interpretation of Upshur's and Mason's results, as well as Carroll's "year abroad" and "home use" data, remains a plausable, but difficult to test, explanation.

Contributions of Formal and Informal Environments According to the Monitor Model

The Monitor Model predicts that formal and informal environments contribute to second language competence in different ways, or rather, to difference aspects of second language competence.

It is not simply the case, however, that informal environments provide the necessary input for *acquisition*, while the classroom aids only in increasing *learned* competence. The re-interpretation of the Krashen et al. series as well as the Friedlander et al. data described above suggests, first of all, that informal environments must be intensive and involve the learner directly in order to be effective. One might then distinguish "exposure-type" informal environments and "intake-type" environments. Only the latter provide true input to the language acquisition device. Second, it seems plausible that the classroom can accomplish both learning and acquisition simultaneously. While classwork is directly aimed at increasing conscious linguistic knowledge of the target language, to the extent that the target language is used realistically, to that extent will acquisition occur. In other words, the classroom may serve as an "intake" informal environment as well as a formal linguistic environment.

Since acquired knowledge contributes to performance on all second language proficiency tests (since acquisition is presumably involved in initiating all L2 production), even those that allow monitoring (the majority), it is therefore no surprise that studies show increased achievement with contextualized drills (e.g. Jarvis and Hatfield, 1971; Oller and Obrecht, 1969). Similarly, reports of success with new language teaching systems that provide a great deal of active involvement of the student (e.g. Gattegno's Silent Way, Asher's Total Physical Response Method, Newmark's Mimimal Language Teaching System, and Winitz and Reed's Method; see Diller, 1975, for discussion) also confirm the hypothesis that acquisition and learning can proceed simultaneously.

Both of these points are illustrated and confirmed by recent data on proficiency and linguistic environment using the SLOPE test with adult learners/acquirers of English. The subject pool was the same as used in Krashen, Sferlazza, Feldman, and Fathman (1976), described above: sixty-six subjects were tested, with thirteen first language groups represented. Some had studied English intensively while others had encountered English only in informal environments. Table 3 shows the relationship between overall SLOPE scores and measures of exposure. Despite our findings that the SLOPE, as administered (oral version), is primarily an *acquisition* measure (it yielded a "natural" difficulty order and did not encourage conscious monitoring), no relationship was found between the measure of exposure and SLOPE scores.

Table Three
SLOPE Performance and Measures of Exposure and Formal Instruction

	years in English speaking country	years of formal English study
	r p	r p
SLOPE scores	.014 ns	.42 p $<$.001

(Partial correlations were used, as years in English speaking country and years of formal study were correlated, r = .24, p $<$.01. Ordinary correlations were computed, however, and were quite similar to those reported above; for SLOPE and exposure, r = .003, and for SLOPE and formal study, r = 40.)

These results confirm the suspicions voiced above about using "exposure-type" measures of informal linguistic environments, and underline the claim that active involvement is necessary for acquisition to take place. Thus, if the SLOPE is a test of acquired competence only, it must be concluded that the question asked in the Krashen et. al. series is a measure of time spent in "exposure-type" environments only, and this apparent counter-evidence to the "informal" hypothesis disappears. No studies in the literature, however, are counter to the hypothesis that an "intake-type" informal environment may be quite efficient in increasing adult second language proficiency.

The significant correlation in Table 3 between years of formal instruction and SLOPE scores supports the hypothesis that the classroom can be of value, and in fact generally *is* of some value, in language acquisition as well as language learning.

Thus, the Upshur, Mason, and Carroll studies are consistent with the hypothesis that intake informal environments can be quite beneficial for adult second language acquisition, and the distinction between intake and exposure type informal environments disallows the Krashen et. al. series as counterevidence to the "informal" hypothesis. The ineffectiveness of exposure type environments is confirmed by the lack of relationship between reports of time spent in the country where the target language was spoken and the results of an "acquisition" proficiency test. No studies provide counterevidence to a modified version of the "formal" hypothesis: formal environments are also beneficial. The need to decide between the original formulations of the two hypotheses is obviated by the Monitor Model, in which intake informal environments and formal instruction make different sorts of contributions to second language competence.

Table Four

Linguistic Environments Relevant to Second Language Proficiency in Adults (from Krashen, 1976)

	In the Classroom "intake" informal (language use)	formal	Outside the Classroom "intake" informal	"exposure" informal	formal (self-study)
acquisition	*		*	*	
learning		*			*

Table 4 summarizes the implications of the literature discussed in this section and SLOPE data in terms of the Monitor Model. Both formal and informal linguistic environments contribute to second language proficiency, but do so in different ways: an intensive intake informal environment can provide both the adult and the child with the necessary input for the operation of the language acquisition device. The classroom can contribute in two ways: as a formal linguistic environment, providing rule isolation and feedback for the development of the Monitor, and, to the extent language use is emphasized, simultaneously as a source of simplified input for language acquisition.

Summary

This survey has reviewed a number of issues in adult second language from the point of view of the "Monitor Model"' of adult second language performance. This model claims that adult second language performers can both *acquire* and *learn* linguistic rules, and that *learned* rules are only used as a Monitor. The Monitor is brought in to inspect and occasionally alter the output of the acquired system when the performer edits his language production. The Monitor Model helps to explain several phenomena: 1. Variation in error patterns: we see the child's difficulty order in adult performance on "Monitor-free" tests, where the emphasis is on communication, but not on measures that encourage a focus on form and that require extra processing time. 2. Individual variation in second language performance: some performers can be characterized as Monitor "over-users", some as "under-users", and others as "optimal" Monitor users. 3. The role of the classroom and the informal linguistic environment in developing second language proficiency: classrooms may serve both acquisition and learning (something many experienced teachers seem to know already), and informal environments are only effective when they provide real and sustained language use.

Notes

*An expanded version of a paper in *Personal Viewpoints on Aspects of ESL* edited by M. Burt, H. Dulay, and M. Finocchairo (Regents Publishing Company). Portions of this paper also appeared in the *TESOL Quarterly*, June, 1976, vol. 10. Reprinted by permission.

For valuable criticism and discussion, I thank Peg Griffen, Heidi Dulay, Marina Burt, Victor Lane, John Schumann, Rosario Gingras, Evelyn Hatch, Diane Larsen-Freeman, Tina Bennett, Nathalie Bailey, Carolyn Madden, Ann Fathman, and Jacquelyn Schachter. Any errors are, of course, my own.

[1]Optimal acquisition environments may also contain rule isolation, or simplified input. See Snow, 1972; Cazden, 1972; Wagner-Gough and Hatch, 1975.

[2]It is interesting to note that the Imitation test, which probably allowed the least monitoring of all the supplementary tasks, showed the most consistency in rank order across subjects, next to the BSM.

[3]The median score on the MLA corresponded to a Foreign Service Institute rating of 2 plus (out of five), which is between "limited working proficiency" and "minimum professional proficiency".

[4]This paper was written in 1973, and accepted for publication in early 1974.

References

Bailey, N., Madden, C., and Krashen, S. 1974. Is There a "Natural Sequence" in Adult Second Language Learning? Language Learning 24, 235-243.

Birnbaum, R. 1976. Transcription and Analysis of the Speech of an Adult Second Language Learner. Term Paper, Linguistics 525, University of Southern California.

Braine, M. 1971. On Two Types of Models of the Internalization of Grammars. In Slobin, D. (ed.) The Ontogenisis of Language, 153-186. New York: Academic Press.

Brown, R. 1973. A First Language. Cambridge Ma.: Harvard Press.

Burt, M., Dulay, H., and Hernandez, Ch. E. 1975. Bilingual Syntax Measure. New York: Harcourt Brace Jovanovich.

Carroll, J. 1967. Foreign Language Proficiency Levels Attained by Language Majors Near Graduation from College. Foreign Language Annals 1, 131-151.

Cazden, C. 1972. Child Language and Education. New York: Holt Rinehart and Winston.

Cohen, A. and Robbins, M. 1976. Toward Assessing Interlanguage Performance: The Relation ship Between Selected Errors, Learner's Characteristics, and Learner's Explanations. Language Learning (in press).

Covitt, G. and Stafford, C. 1976. An Investigation of the Monitor Theory. Presentation at the UCLA-USC Second Language Acquisition Forum, May 25, 1976, UCLA.

Diller, K. 1975. Some New Trends for Applied Linguistics and Foreign Language Teaching in the United States. TESOL Quarterly 9, 65-73.

Dulay, H. and Burt, M. 1972. Goofing: An Indicator of Children's Second Language Learning Strategies. Language Learning 22, 235-252.

Dulay, H. and Burt, M. 1973. Should we Teach Children Syntax? Language Learning 23, 245-258.

Dulay, H. and Burt, M. 1975. A New Approach to Discovering Universal Strategies of Child Second Language Acquisition. In Dato, D. (ed.) Developmental Psycholinguistics: Theory and Applications, 209-233. Georgetown University Roundtable on Languages and Linguistics 1975. Washington, D.C.: Georgetown University Press.

Elkind, D. 1970. Children and Adolescents: Interpretive Essays on Jean Piaget. New York: Oxford University Press.

Ervin-Tripp, S. 1973. Some Strategies for the First Two Years. In Dil, A. (ed.) Language Acquisition and Communicative Choice, 204-238. Stanford: University Press.

Fathman, A. 1975. Age, Language Background, and the Order of Acquisition of English Structures. In Burt, M. and Dulay, H. (eds.) New Directions in Second Language Learning, Teaching, and Bilingual Education: On TESOL '75. Washington: TESOL.

Friedlander, B., Jacobs, A., Davis, B., and Wetstone, M. 1972. Time-sampling Analysis of Infant's Natural Language Environments in the Home. Child Development 43, 730-740.

Hatch, E. 1975. Foreigner talk. Presentation to the UCLA-USC Second Language Acquisition Forum.

Inhelder, B. and Piaget, J. 1958. The Growth of Logical Thinking from Childhood to Adolescence. New York: Basic Books.

Jarvis, G. and Hatfield, W. 1971. The Practice Variable: An Experiment. Foreign Language Annals 4, 401-410.

Krashen, S. 1975. A Model of Adult Second Language Performance. Paper Presented at the Linguistic Society of America, December, 1975.

Krashen, S. 1976. Formal and Informal Linguistic Environments in Language Acquisition and Language Learning. TESOL Quarterly 10, 157-168.

Krashen, S. The Monitor Model for Adult Second Language Performance. In Burt, M., Dulay, H., and Finocchairo, M. (eds.), Personal Viewpoints on Aspects of ESL. New York: Regents Publishing Company. (in press).

Krashen, S., Seliger, H., and Hartnett, D. 1974. Two Studies in Adult Second Language Learning. Kritikon Litterarum 2/3, 220-228.

Krashen, S. and Seliger, H. 1975. The Essential Contributions of Formal Instruction in Adult Second Language Learning. TESOL Quarterly 9, 173-183.

Krashen, S. and Pon, P. 1975. An Error Analysis of an Advanced ESL Learner: The Importance of the Monitor. Working Papers on Bilingualism 7, 125-129.

Krashen, S., Madden, C., and Bailey, N. 1975. Theoretical Aspects of Grammatical Sequencing. In Burt, M. and Dulay, H. (eds.) New Directions in Second Language Learning, Teaching, and Bilingual Education 44-54. Washington, D.C.: TESOL.

Krashen, S. and Seliger, H. 1976. The Role of Formal and Informal Environments in Second Language Learning: A Pilot Study. International Journal of Psycholinguistics 15-21.

Krashen, S., Sferlazza, V., Feldman, L., and Fathman, A. 1976. Adult Performance on the SLOPE Test: More Evidence for a Natural Sequence in Adult Second Language Acquisition. Language Learning (in press).

Krashen, S., Jones, C., Zelinski, S., and Usprich, C. How Important is Instruction? English Language Teaching Journal (in press).

Labov, W. 1970. The Study of Nonstandard English. Urbana: National Council of Teachers of English.

Larsen-Freeman, D. 1975a. The Acquisition of Grammatical Morphemes by Adult ESL Students. TESOL Quarterly 9, 409-420.

Larsen-Freeman, D. 1975b. The Acquisition of Grammatical Morphemes by Adult ESL Students. Doctoral Dissertation, University of Michigan.

Lenneberg, E. 1967. Biological Foundations of Language. New York: Wiley.

Mason, C. 1971. The Relevance of Intensive Training in English as a Foreign Language for University Students. Language Learning 21, 197-204.

Newmark, L. 1971. A Minimal Language Teaching Program. In Pimsleur, P. and Quinn, T. (eds.) The Psychology of Second Language Learning 11-18. Cambridge: University Press.

Oller, J. and Obrecht, D. 1969. The Psycholinguistic Principle of Informational Sequence: An Experiment in Second Language Learning. International Review of Applied Linguistics 7, 117-123.

Slobin, D. 1973. Cognitive prerequisites for the development of grammar. In Ferguson, C. and Slobin, D. (eds.) Studies of Child Language Development 175-208. New York: Holt, Rinehart, and Winston.

Snow, C. 1972. Mother's Speech to Children Learning Language. Child Development 43, 549-565.

Upshur, J. 1968. Four Experiments on the Relation Between Foreign Language Teaching and Learning. Language Learning 18, 111-124.

Wagner-Gough, J. and Hatch, E. 1975. The Importance of Input Data in Second Language Acquisition Studies. Language Learning 25, 297-308.

Wakefield, J., Doughtie, E. and Yom, B. 1974. The identification of structural components of an unknown language. J. of Psychling. Res. 3.261-269.

Chapter Twelve

Sociolinguistics

William Labov

There are two distinct but overlapping concerns that motivate the study of research methods. One is the desire to find an approved and practical procedure for gathering, processing and reporting data. The other is the need to discover if such results are right or wrong: to find ways of estimating the degree of error, isolate the sources of error, and eliminate them. The first approach involves tests of *reliability*: to be sure that different investigators will produce the same data and the same analysis from a given input. The second approach is concerned more with *validity:* notions of right and wrong imply some connection with a measurable or predictable empirical basis, independent of the investigators or their school. Valid reports or theories must be shown to fit that secular reality.

American linguistic practice of the nineteen forties and fifties was largely concerned with the first kind of methodology: procedures for segmenting and classifying the input data (Bloch and Trager 1942; Pike 1947; Nida 1949; Harris 1951; Gleason 1955). These are the "discovery procedures" criticized by Chomsky (1957:59; 1964:968-75) as unrealistically ambitious and mechanically limited. If linguistics followed the model of the more advanced disciplines, the techniques for gathering data would form an art (art of X-ray crystallography; of quantitative analysis; of recording sound on magnetic tape) and theories derived informally would be proved valid or invalid by scientific method. But the term *valid,* is not current in linguistics, and the notion of validity presented here is rarely to be found in the writings of most linquists. It seems to have been rejected by Chao (1934) and more recently by Harris (1965), arguing that there is no uniquely correct analysis of linguistic data and implying the absence of any decisive evidence independent of the activity of the linguist.

This discussion will be chiefly concerned with the second aspect of methodology—the search for error and efforts to eliminate it—and a concept of the validity of linguistic theories will be needed. It is proposed that a valid linguistic analysis will fit the characteristics of the language used in every-day life when the linguist is not present. Just as impressionistic phonetics should be calibrated against the readings of various instruments, so the intuitions of the theorist should be matched against observations of the unreflecting speech of ordinary men.

There are two distinct areas of linguistic activity which we must examine: first, contact with some aspect of language to produce the data; and second, the processing of this data to produce a list, paradigm, rule or theory. The distinct methodological problem of the first, data-producing activity is to measure or control the effect of the investigator's activity on the data so that the final result will not be an artifact of the investigation. The fundamental problem of the second, analytical activity is to cope with the variation found in the data. No serious linguistic problem can arise if the data is invariant: if, for example, the attributive adjective always follows the noun, any scholar can report that fact. But if the adjective sometimes follows and sometimes precedes, a linguist may be called on to discover the conditions that govern that variation. The classical assumption is that the linguist will either (a) resolve such variation into regular rules (e.g., a sub-set of common adjectives will always precede, the rest follow), or (b) declare that the two possibilities are in free variation and the choice of one or the other MAKES NO DIFFERENCE to speakers of the language. Ways and means of so resolving variation form the principal techniques in which linguists are currently trained.

Within this framework, I will consider methodological problems and practices in four particular fields of linguistics: historical linguistics, field methods, and analysis in the structuralist tradition, generative grammar, and the study of language within the speech community.

1. Methods in Historical Linguistics

The basic fact that influences the methods of historical linguists is that they have no control over the selection of their data. Their texts are the results of historical accidents, and the art of the linguist is to make the best use of this fragmentary material. To insure reliable results in this study there are two main conditions for handling data:

(1) It must be referenced and available. The first step is to edit and publish the texts so that they can be consulted by colleagues. Analytical arguments must be supported by references to the sources consulted by the author.

(2) For all but the most recent periods of Western European languages, a scholar is expected to consult all of the relevant documents before drawing conclusions. It is implicitly assumed that arguments in historical linguistics are *exhaustive:* that a professional scholar has read all the available texts attributed to the writer or period he is describing. He cannot defend an omission by restricting the range of his claims after the fact.

In these two respects, historical linguistics contrasts sharply with other fields of linguistics. Because the data are limited, and many crucial arguments depend upon a few occurrences of a form, historical linguists are deeply concerned with possible sources of error. Through painful experience, it is now generally required that scholars consult the original documents on such points rather than rely on the work of other editors. The dissertation of Asta Kihlbom, reviewing fifteenth century English spellings, provided startling evidence for this policy. Kihlbom pointed out that "most of the printed editions of early letters have been published with a view to their historical, rather than philological interest" (1926:ix). These editors ignored the fact that the manuscripts of one signatory were often in different hands. She discovered that many of the Paston letters, the Shillingford letters, and other important documents were actually written by secretaries who may well have come from other dialect areas. These letters had been freely used by many scholars, including H. C. Wyld, as evidence for the pronunciation of English in the speech community of the man who signed the letter. They did not realize, as Kihlbom pointed out, that "people of very high social position, especially, seem very rarely to have written their letters themselves." In returning to the original manuscripts, Kihlbom was also able to re-check all the important phonetic spellings "as a safe-guard against incorrect readings and misprints." Since even great scholars have been led into error on such points, the historical linguist is quite critical in demanding data which is authenticated, complete, and correctly assigned to the proper speech community.

In analyzing the data so gathered, historical linguists have accumulated a great deal of experience with unexplained variation. Again, we find that perfectly regular correspondences require no special skill; it is the irregular ones that are challenging. The well-known success of historical linguistics in reducing this variation to invariant rule is usually illustrated by such striking discoveries as Verner's, Lachmann's, or Grassmann's Laws. The Neogrammarian hypothesis generalized this success to the claim that in phonology, the classical solution to variation can always be found; "*all words in which the sound subjected to the change appears in the same relationship are affected by the change without exception*" (Osthoff and Brugmann (1878) as translated in Lehmann 1967:204). The only problem is, of course, to find the relationship.

Many examples can be cited from the history of English and other languages which show such regular conditioning rules; but there are as many cases of unexplained variation that have not responded to the classical approach. For example, all words with Middle English $\bar{\varepsilon}$ appear in Modern English with the same vowel as words with Middle English $\bar{e}$ except *great, steak, yea, drain* and a number of those ending in $-r$. No explanation for these exceptions based on regular sound change has yet been put forward. For such cases, the explanation of *dialect mixture* or *dialect borrowing* is introduced even when there is no evidence for it other than the variation itself (Bloomfield 1933:362). This type of explanation has become much more difficult in the light of the massive evidence for lexical diffusion in the history of Chinese dialects developed by Wang and his associates (Cheng and Wang 1970; Chen and Hsieh 1971). Nevertheless, adherents of the Neo-grammarian tradition continue to assert that dialect mixture must have been responsible for any observed break-up of word classes.[1]

The Neo-grammarian hypothesis has so far survived such difficulties and remains as a valuable working principle, encouraging linguists to search for conditioning factors behind the superficial variation. It is thus best seen as a methodological strategy rather than a theory about language change. One serious disadvantage of the Neo-grammarian hypothesis, if taken seriously, is that it removes the possibility of connecting historical events with current observations of change in progress. Almost every observation of present-day changes reports fluctuations which are inconsistent with the Neo-grammarian account of sound change. Gauchat, for example, showed that a change such as the lenition of /l'/ in the Swiss French of Charmey proceeded through an intermediate stage where the middle generation sometimes used *l'* and sometimes *y* (1905). In Philadelphia and its environs, we find that the originally uniform class of short *a* words before *d* is everywhere broken into sub-sets such as *mad, bad, glad* with [ɛːə] and the rest with [æ]. Those who adhere to the hypothesis of the absolute regularity of sound change react to such cases by rejecting them as examples of regular sound change, and finally declaring that true sound change is too slow to be observed in progress (Hockett 1958:444). But the methodological losses in rejecting current observations as relevant to the interpretation of historical events are very great, since we have access to an unlimited amount of data on present-day changes and can study them with the sophisticated techniques of acoustic phonetics.

The value of such interaction of past and present data can be underlined by a statement of the *UNIFORMITARIAN PRINCIPLE:* that *the linguistic processes taking place around us are the same as those that have operated to produce the historical record.*[2] This principle is not directly opposed to the Neo-grammarian hypothesis, but rather to the defensive posture of Neo-grammarians in rejecting current evidence. Since the unsupported claim for dialect mixture removes the Neo-grammarian hypothesis from any possibility of disproof, it must be rejected on methodological grounds.

The mutual interpretation of past and present can be seen most clearly in the resolution of a classical controversy on the mechanism of the *Great Vowel Shift.* The traditional view of Jespersen and Wyld accepted the evidence of Hart and other sixteenth-century phoneticians on the route followed by the diphthongized high front vowel of *die* as it descended from [dɪ̵̯] to [da̵̯]. The intermediate form is said to have a midfront nucleus, [dɛ̵̯]. But Kökeritz, Dobson, Stockwell and others found it difficult to see how this word class could then have escaped merger with the class of *day* as it rose from [dæ̵̯] to [dɛ̵̯]. They argued (Stockwell 1966) that *die* must have been first centralized to something like [DI̵̯] and then fell to [dɨ̵̯]. The controversy and the historical evidence is summed up by Wolfe (1969) who finds little hard data to support the centralized route advocated by Stockwell.

Our current spectrographic studies of parallel changes in English dialects show that the apparent contradiction between theory and reported fact can be resolved by a more detailed view of phonological space. In these dialects, the new high diphthong /iy/ in *see* falls to the mid position characteristic of standard /ey/ in *say* as part of a chain shift, obeying the constraint that in chain shifts the lax nuclei of upgliding diphthongs generally fall. But the route by which they fall does not coincide with the route by which tense nuclei (as in *man* or *now*) are currently rising. In London Cockney, in the Outer Banks of North Carolina, in Atlanta, and in South Central Texas, we find /iy/ and /ey/ falling along a track with moderate second formant positions, while the tense nuclei rise with high second formants (in articulatory terms, with extreme fronting). We cannot assert that the sixteenth century vowels followed the same path, but we can say that there was no necessity for a merger of *die* and *day*, even if they both remained as front vowels. There are many present-day examples to show that a fronted [dɛ< ^{i}] could remain distinct from a less peripheral [dɛ> ^{i}]. Given the similarity in the sound shifts shown in widely separated dialects today, and the parallels between these current changes and the historical vowel shift, it seems quite probable that the routes followed by *die* and *day* in the sixteenth century are reflected in *Figure 1*.

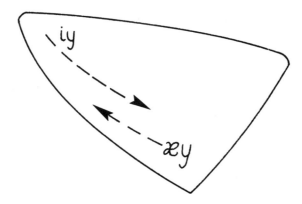

Figure 1. Shift of the vowels in English *die* and *day* without merger.

One of the classic unresolved dichotomies of historical linguistics is the opposition of the *Stammbaum* and *wave theories* of linguistic differentiation. Most reconstructions still neglect wave effects and proceed upon the older model because evidence to support the wave theory is largely fragmentary. But current studies of implicational phenomena in English dialects by Bailey (1970) and in Creoles by Bickerton (1971) have given us more detailed views of what wave effects may look like. In a two-dimensional matrix, one coordinate shows a range of linguistic environments, ordered in accordance with our general understanding of the relative weightings for the change involved. The other coordinate displays the array of individual speakers, communities, or dialects. Along the interface between the areas where the rule has applied and where it has not we observe a wave of variability. *Table 1* illustrates in a schematic way the wave pattern for the tensing and raising of short *a* which we are currently investigating in the middle Atlantic states. As we approach a rigorous demonstration of a dialect continuum in which all possible rule forms are realized at some point, the notion of a homogeneous speech community evolving independently becomes less and less plausible. On the other hand, we have the possibility of establishing empirically the existence of real speech communities by locating relative discontinuities in this temporal and spatial matrix.

		m _n	f θ _s	_d	_b	_ʃ	_g	v _z	p t _k	_l
Buffalo	(a)	+	+	+	+	+	+	+	+	+
.	(b)	+	+	+	+	+	+	+	+	±
.	(c)	+	+	+	+	+	+	+	±	−
NYC	(d)	+	+	+	+	+	+	±	−	−
Jackson	(e)	+	+	+	+	+	±	−	−	−
Ringoes	(f)	+	+	+	+	±	−	−	−	−
Mammouth Junction	(g)	+	+	+	±	−	−	−	−	−
Phila	(h)	+	+	±	−	−	−	−	−	−
Birdsboro	(i)	+	±	−	−	−	−	−	−	−
.	(j)	±	−	−	−	−	−	−	−	−
.	(k)	−	−	−	−	−	−	−	−	−

Table 1. Model of a wave pattern for raising of short *a* in middle Atlantic states.

2. Methods of the American Structuralist Tradition

It must be admitted that courses in *field methods* taught in American departments of linguistics are courses in analysis rather than training programs for the gathering of data. They do not in fact attempt to prepare the student for an encounter with language in actual use within the speech community. Instead, they anticipate the normal situation in which the linguist elicits data in a fact-to-face confrontation with a bilingual informant. No particular attention is given to the selection of informants: it is assumed that any one or two speakers of the language will do. Linguists have thus exploited the paradox which grows out of the Saussurian view of *langue:* that langue, the social aspect of language, is so general that it is in the possession of everyone. Granted the general success of this strategy, the question remains as to whether reliable and valid data can be elicited from any speaker under these formal conditions.

Though many linguists have an extraordinary gift for learning languages, they are not expected to make use of the data of ordinary conversation. The normal procedure is to transcribe texts of oral literature, to elicit translations and present minimal pairs. This is essentially normative data, delivered under the influence of conscious reflection. Hopefully, it is reliable. But to the extent that there is any disjunction between norms and behavior, it cannot be considered valid. The widest separation between norm and behavior is usually the result of overt prestige or stigma attached to particular forms. For example, speakers of Eastern *r*-less dialects consistently report themselves as using postvocalic *r* , which they rarely do in connected speech (Labov 1966a). Speakers in Norwich, England, habitually report themselves as using standard British vowel forms when they seldom do so in practice (Trudgill 1971). The self-report of most speakers is regularly shifted towards the norm that they aim at rather than the form that they use in actual speech, though this self-report may be reflected in their pronunciation of individual words. In retrospect, we find that some speakers have in fact reported their own usage accurately; but it is an unsolved psycholinguistic problem to isolate such speakers in advance from the population as a whole.

There are more subtle and systematic biases which are found in the formal elicitation of variables which have no overt social prestige or stigma. The *minimal pair or commutation test* has long been considered the most reliable approach to the sound system of a language, and has even been endorsed by Chomsky as one of the few behavioral tests which can reveal linguistic competence (1957:97). And it is unfortunately the case that a great deal of phonetic data has been discarded in the belief that only self-reports of sames and differents were relevant to linguistic analysis. A series of recent empirical investigations show that such confidence in this formal test was misplaced.

It was once believed by many that native speakers perceive only phonemic distinctions, and are incapable of distinguishing sub-phonemic differences. But subjective reaction tests to phonetic variants of several variables in New York City showed that perception of these forms is governed by recognition of their social stigma, not of their phonemic status. New Yorkers have no difficulty in hearing the difference between [l.ɔ ə] and [lo ə] for *law*. Conversely, speakers will make distinctions in minimal pair tests which they never observe in conversation if social prestige is involved. It is well known that many Americans will distinguish *latter* and *ladder*, *which* and *witch*, in their school pronunciation only. Despite these limitations, it has been generally believed that is a speaker FAILS to make a distinction in a minimal pair test that A FORTIORI he would not do so in ordinary speech. But in our current studies of sound change in progress we have located many cases where speakers violate this expectation. Younger speakers in Albuquerque make a small but consistent distinction between *fool* and *full, pool* and *pull* in connected speech, but fail to make or hear the distinction in minimal pair tests. Some speakers can produce distinctions in test situations, but still cannot perceive them. In our recent observations of sound change in Norwich, England, we find that younger speakers have a close approximation of *too* [tUᵘ˂] and *toe* [tU ᵘ˄], just perceptible to an outside phonetician. Keith, a thirteen-year-old boy, failed completely to hear the distinction in a randomized set reliably produced by his best friend, David. But Keith was able to PRODUCE the distinction: David had no trouble in identifying *too* and *toe* in a list read by Keith. David would have given a valid report to the structural linguist, Keith an invalid one.

Turning now to the analytical methods of structural linguistics, we find that the procedures in Pike (1947), Nida (1949) and Gleason (1955) are entirely devoted to the classical solution to problems of variation. The correct answers to training exercises are to discover the invariant conditioning rules that will eliminate variation or reduce it to free variation. Training of this sort has produced many valuable descriptions of little-known languages, as in the best of the University of California and Summer Institute of Linguistics grammars. But when the same methods were applied to well-known languages, it was quickly found that there was a great deal of unexplained variation left over, too gross to be plausibly assigned to free variation. The search for a homogeneous object of description led to the concept of the *idiolect* (Bloch 1948), which was ultimately reduced to the speech of one person in one context talking for a short period of time. The need for such a construct represents a serious defeat for the Saussurian concept of *langue* as a general possession of the entire population.

The classical dichotomy of invariant conditioning vs. free variation dominates the formal descriptions of the structuralist tradition. Since forms that are in free variation are effectively THE SAME in a linguistic sense, nothing further can be said about their occurrence. It is theoretically incoherent to say that one form occurs MORE OFTEN than another. But serious students of language often discover such relations of greater or lesser frequency which appear significant to them; they are then faced with the choice of discarding such data or reporting it informally. Any review of current journals which include descriptive reports will show that a great many choose the option of reporting informally. Thus Echeverría and Contreras report of Araucanian that:

The labial fricative /f/ varies from entirely voiceless to fully voiced, the voiceless allophones being the most frequent ones. Its articulation may be either bilabial or labiodental, the former being the most frequent. Thus there is free variation between [ɸʒɹɔ], [fʒɹɔ], [βʒɹɔ], and [vʒɹɔ]. (1965:133).

If the variation is free, the statements about frequency are plainly irrelevant; yet they are made. Linguists are also often confronted with conditioning factors which appear to them significant, yet not as precise as the solutions they were trained to find. The rules themselves are variable and therefore cannot be expressed formally. Nevertheless, we find Bucca and Lesser reporting of Kitsai *I* that:

It is in free variation with i. The free variation is less frequent in final position where i is more used; and in medial position before the consonantal groups ts, st, sk, sn, tjk, where I is predominant (1969:11).

This description of a constrained "free variation" is incoherent as it stands; what are we to make of the idea of a FREE variation which is allowed to occur less frequently in some environments? The authors obviously had something to say about the language and would not let the conventional analytical methods stand in their way. Similarly, Redden reports of Walapai that:

The dental and glottal fricatives are usually voiceless, except that /θ/ is very often voiced intervocally and between a voiced consonant and a vowel (1966:10).

These are not occasional examples; dozens more could be drawn from the same authors, and any issue of I.J.A.L. will show the same pattern.

The limitations of the traditional emic approach appear even more sharply when such data are used to make generalizations about the sound patterns of languages. In Sedlak's study of universal relations among vowels, we find the general statement:

A front rounded vowel implies a back rounded vowel at the same tongue height. (1969:31).

That is, the presence of *ü* implies *u*. But the data upon which this study was based is limited to phonemic reports, and one principle of phonemics is to disregard unnecessary phonetic detail; another is to avoid diacritics unless there are no standard letters left to register a distinction. Therefore a vowel pronounced [ü] and often transcribed as [ʉ] or [u<] will be phonemicized as /u/, unless there is another phoneme closer to [u]. Such practices make Sedlak's investigation somewhat circular, and effectively disguised counterexamples. There are in fact many English dialects which have [ü] in *boot* and *two* and no high back vowel. This is true of some Cockney speakers, and of large areas of North Carolina, as shown in our spectrographic studies. One independent demonstration of this fact is that many students at Duke University have no trouble in learning to pronounce French *tu* but cannot manage the vowel in *tout* at all.[3]

Faced with such examples of theoretical limitations and errors in generalization, we infer that it is necessary for linguists to draw back from the single-minded pursuit of the classical solution for the elimination of variation, and consider other possibilities.

3. Methods in Generative Grammar

The basic methodology of generative grammar depends upon the full exploitation of the Saussurian Paradox noted above. If *langue* is conceived as the social part of language, and in possession of every speaker (Saussure 1962:321), it should then be possible to obtain data from any one speaker— even from the theorist himself. On the other hand, any form of language that varies from speaker to speaker must be outside of *langue* by definition. Thus we have the *SAUSSURIAN PARADOX: that the social aspect of language can be studied by the theorist asking himself questions, while the individual aspect can only be studied by a social survey.* Chomsky has repeatedly stated that the intuitions of the linguist form the proper and predominant subject matter of the discipline. He writes of "the necessity for present-day linguistics to give priority to introspective evidence and to the linguistic intuition of native speakers" (1965:20), and in actual practice, generative grammarians have followed his injunction to abstract from all individual and social variation (1965:3). This methodological revolution has gained support on the positive side from the great success of generative grammar in discovering new facts about English syntax, developing new grammatical formulations, and uncovering deeper theoretical problems. On the negative side, it has been supported by the assertion that nothing is to be learned at this stage from "data flux"; that the speech of every-day life is degenerate data; and that we are not ready to study actual speech (performance) until we have laid a better foundation in the study of competence.

The intuitive data upon which generative grammar builds consists primarily of (1) judgments of grammaticality and ungrammaticality, (2) recognition of ambiguity, (3) recognition of synonymity, paraphrase, and relatedness of sentences. Early challenges to the reliability of such judgments, especially (1) were answered by Chomsky (1961) with the suggestion of a quantitative scale of acceptability. The term *acceptability* is now generally used to indicate the subjective response of native speakers, and *grammaticality* is reserved for a more abstract construct dependent upon a particular theory, not necessarily isomorphic to judgements of acceptability.

The quantitative scale suggested by Chomsky has not been generally used, but generative workers who rely upon their own intuitions have begun to introduce a number of intermediate levels. Thus Ross, discussing the shift of object NP and verb particles, gives data on his own intuitions in forms such as:

He figured out the answer.
?He figured out something.
?*He figured out Ann.
*He figured out it.   (1967:61).

The asterisk * then designates *completely unacceptable*; ?* indicates *barely acceptable, if at all*; ? indicates *not quite fully acceptable*; and the absence of any mark, *completely acceptable* (1967:40). This enrichment of the input data leads to more powerful afguments for the existence of a single rule underlying a number of different surface phenomena, especially when it can be shown that the profiles of acceptability match. But it also poses difficulties in generating such data by rule conditions limited to the usual "optional" and "obligatory" dichotomy. Ross therefore proposes an *output condition* which establishes the preferential order among eleven postverbal constituents (1967:63). Thus *?*He figured out Ann* is barely acceptable because proper names (number 3 in the series) should precede particles (number 4).

In addition to these three types of intuitive data, we also find (4) intuitions about immediate constituents (Chomsky 1961) and (5) similarity among constituents (Ross 1967:17). One can also note in recent discussions (6) intuitions about *markedness*, although it is doubtful if many linguists would class such intuitions as reliable. Even less substantial are frequent references to (7) intuitions about the correctness of linguistic theories. These appear most often in the claim that certain solutions are "counterintuitive".[4]

This enrichment of the intuitive data has not been accompanied by a methodological concern for the reduction of errors or a search for intersubjective agreement. Originally, Chomsky hoped that the area of agreement would be so large that disagreements would be insignificant. But in practice almost every paper in the generative framework includes judgments of acceptability that are questionable to some or most readers. Thus Postal marks as unacceptable the following sentences in the course of his discussion of coreferential subject deletion (1970:460):

*Discovery that their $_i$ daughters were pregnant worried some old ladies$_i$.

*Kissing was fun for some kids.

And as a particularly clear example of the constraint against backward pronominalization from indefinite NP's, he cites:

*The fact that he$_i$ lost disturbed each candidate$_i$.

On the other hand, Jackendoff cites as acceptable in a recent study of - *Quantifiers in English* (1968):

The three of the men that you met yesterday have not left.

Of the men, the three you met yesterday have not left yet.

In the same discussion of extraposition cited above, Ross notes:

Knock out the sentry is as natural as *Knock the sentry out;* whereas *Let out the sentry* is somewhat less natural than *Let the sentry out!* (1967:65)

The normal reaction to criticisms of such data is for the author to assert that he is dealing with his own dialect. In the case just quoted, Ross takes pains to point out that these are only his own judgments. And in *Remarks on nominalization,* Chomsky cites pairs such as *our election of John (to the presidency)* vs. *our election of John to be president* and adds:

Reactions to these sentences vary slightly: [these] represent my judgments. (1970:201)

He then proceeds "Given such data. . ." The data are not the disagreements, but his own judgments.

The term *idiolect* is rarely used; the author usually cites *my dialect* or *most dialects* without further discussion. The reader assumes in the first case that someone has disagreed with the author; in the second case that he has asked several friends and most of them agree with him. The underlying assumption is that these differences are representative of well-formed social dialects, a part of *langue*, and not idiosyncratic decisions. Following Chomsky's position that the proper subject of linguistics is intuitions of the native speaker, and the logic of Saussure, the grammarian takes it without question that all of his judgments represent *langue*. This view is so generally accepted that it is now rare to hear any objections to data when generative papers are delivered.

It is not clear that Chomsky originally thought that the field would develop in this way. In 1964 he noted that "consistency among speakers of similar backgrounds and consistency for a particular speaker on different occasions is relevant." (1964:939). This statement is not entirely consistent, however, with the well-known position of *Aspects* that linguistics should take as its object the competence of the ideal speaker-hearer in a homogeneous speech community (1965:3).

A methodological search for sources of error would focus first of all on the reliability of intuitive data produced by the theorist himself, an issue which Chomsky has not dealt with directly. Good practice in the more advanced sciences distrusts most of all the memory and impressions of the investigator himself. As valuable and insightful as the theorist's intuitions may be, no one can know the extent to which his desire to make things come out right will influence his judgment. The polemical tone of most linguistic arguments suggests that this is a serious problem in our field, and that it will be some time before linguists put as much effort into trying to prove themselves wrong as they should. If we compare generative grammar with historical linguistics we find that we have lost even more ground in this respect, since the basic data—intuitions of the theorist—are now quite inaccesible for others to check.

Another methodological problem appears when we consider the factors which may influence the selection of the data. Given the unlimited character of syntactic combinations, how does one make a systematic search of the evidence? There are undoubtedly unconscious factors which lead investigators to find examples which support their own arguments and not to find counter-examples. No one would suggest that syntactic investigation can be reduced to a mechanical searching procedure, but some view of the selectional apparatus would be helpful. It is interesting to note that some grammarians feel that more progress has been made in phonology (with a closed corpus) than in syntax (with an open-ended one).

In the past several years, there has been some concern with the reliability of intuitive judgments and some empirical research into syntactic dialects.

Spencer (1973) obtained judgments of acceptability on a four-point scale to sentences cited in articles of seven leading linguists, from 60 subjects including people outside the university as well as inside, naive and linguistically sophisticated. On 30 per cent of the sentences, most of the judges disagreed with the linguists, and no linguist did better than any other in this respect.

Large scale investigations of grammatical acceptability by Quirk and his associates (Quirk & Svartvik 1966, Greenbaum & Quirk 1970) show that we are dealing with a statistical phenomenon where it is rare to find 100 per cent agreement on any sentence. In this tradition, Greenbaum has been the most vigorous in the experimental investigation of such judgments, focusing on matters of central interest to current syntactic theory.

The elicitation of syntactic judgments has generated a large number of "dialects" in the literature. Two such dialects are established each time two speakers disagree on a syntactic judgment. These are often referred to as "randomly distributed" to indicate that there is no connection with any other linguistic or social fact. But the distribution of such dialects is far from random: they are the result of exchanges among linguists with opposing theoretical predispositions. Thus Linguist A supports his theory by finding sentence X acceptable; when Linguist B with a different view disagrees, A states that his theory only applies "to my dialect." This creates Dialect A and Dialect B.

Thus Grinder and Postal (1971) expressed a crucial disagreement with Chomsky's acceptance of "John didn't leave until midnight, but Bill did." They reported that nine out of ten people they asked agreed with them. A linguist from UCLA wrote to me that the great majority in a room full of students agreed with Chomsky. The crucial issue here was that generative semantics would derive this sentence from an unacceptable "*John didn't leave until midnight but Bill left until midnight," but at that time UCLA favored the interpretive approach of Chomsky, which did not reconstruct such an underlying stage. With this type of distribution in mind, it would be best to refer to such dialects as "idiosyncratic" rather than "random."

Elliott, Legum and Thompson located four idiosyncratic dialects in reactions to sentences with deleted subjects of *while* clauses:

(A) Sophia Loren was seen by the people while enjoying herself.
(B) The people saw Sophia Loren while enjoying themselves.
(C) Judy was seen by the people while enjoying themselves.
(D) The people saw Karen while enjoying herself.

The acceptability of D implies C which implies B which implies A, in the author's analysis. For some speakers there exists a constraint that the deleted NP must be identical with the surface subject; and for another, overlapping sub-set of speakers, there is a weaker constraint that deletion in the *while* clause operates only with passive main clauses, not active ones. The four possible combinations of these two alternative rule forms yielded four idiosyncratic dialects, arranged in an implicational series. Greenbaum found no significant pattern of response in an investigation that controlled the order of presentation of sentences, which is a major determinant of responses (1973). Legum, Elliott and Thompson (Legum 1975) then did an even more extensive study, with both timed and self-paced subjects, and obtained clear evidence of an implicational relation in the response patterns: if someone accepted D he was much more likely to accept C than someone who didn't, and so on. But these more careful studies did not produce consistant individual responses that would confirm the existence of idiosyncratic dialects: the implications are discussed as patterns in a general grammar.

These results fit in with other studies (Labov 1975:90-91) which lead one to infer that idiosyncratic dialects may not exist in any linguistically significant sense. However, it is impossible to assert that negative principle in any strong form. The search for evidence in favor of such dialects remains an attractive challenge for those who would like to show that stable linguistic systems are established independently of any pattern of social communication.

The most consistent and careful work in this area has been carried out by Carden, in a series of investigations of quantifier dialects (1970, 1972). Carden has found that individual interviews lead to more reliable and consistent results than questionnaires, since in face-to-face interaction the concept of grammaticality can be explained and exemplified, and the more obvious misunderstandings eliminated. He examined 125 cases where an informant was asked the same question in a second interview and found no change in 99; change in 20; and possible change in 6, where identical responses might have been coded differently (personal communication). This is a promising beginning, but we will have to obtain even higher degrees of reliability than this in order to establish the investigation of introspective judgments on a sound footing. This limiting reliability of .86 refers to a repetition of judgment on only one sentence form. If we ask for judgments on five tokens of the same type to establish a firm pattern, we would then be reduced to $(.86)^5$ or .47, which is not a very attractive figure.

Carden has also begun to relate the study of syntactic judgments to the study of inherent variability, going beyond the categorical framework that is limited to obligatory or optional rules, and so relating this approach to grammar to the analyses of observational methods considered in the next section (1973).

The question of validity has been raised many times in regard to generative grammar, but Chomsky has explicitly rejected any definition of validity which would depend upon correlating linguistic rules with behavioral or biological data (1965:9). In its present form, a generative grammar is one of many models that are descriptively adequate, selected by an internal evaluation measure. The competence/performance distinction serves to insulate generative grammar from the definition of validity advanced in our first section—that our theories must apply to the unreflecting language used by ordinary people in every-day life. But the insulation is perhaps only temporary, a matter of strategy, as Chomsky seems to imply. It is not accidental that among those working within the generative framework, phoneticians and biologically oriented linguists are the most dissatisfied with the competence/performance barrier (see the papers of Kim and Dingwall and Whitaker in this volume). There seems to be general agreement that a valid theory of language must eventually be based upon rules that speakers actually use.

Some of the early findings in the studies of the acquisition of language produced encouraging results in this respect. It was evident that children did form general rules at specific points in their development, suddenly overgeneralizing from the available data (Berko 1958; Bellugi 1967). But recent studies of adults' ability to use rules have produced surprisingly negative results (Zimmer 1969; Hsieh 1970) and led to serious questions about the validity of some of the most convincing linguistic analyses. Hsieh found that completely productive rules of Taiwanese tone sandhi were not used by native speakers when they were presented with new words that filled accidental gaps in phonotactic structure. At the same time, they consistently applied the sandhi rules to words they already knew. Findings such as these pose a serious challenge to the accepted view that the grammar of a language is isomorphic to the linguistic knowledge or competence of the native speaker.

4. Observation within the Speech Community

The most obvious fact about our linguistic knowledge to date is that very little is based upon actual speech. Texts, elicitations, and intuitions are freely utilized, but the unreflecting conversation of everyday life is rarely cited in linguistic arguments. It has been argued on several grounds that speech cannot serve as the input for linguistic analysis, and the dichotomy of langue-parole and competence/performance has been extended to language /speech. It is said that the data of speech is phonetically degenerate; that it is ungrammatical due to the interference of performance factors; and heterogeneous due to uncontrollable dialect mixture.

From a methodological viewpoint, such a conclusion is unfortunate. The amount of data which is excluded is very large, many times the order of magnitude of all other data available. If language is conceived as a social phenomenon, following Saussure's reasoning, its regularities have formed and evolved under the influence of a vast number of speech events. Given the fact that many speak, but few analyze, we would insist that any theory of language be consistent with the language used by ordinary people in the course of their daily business. It must also be consistent with texts, elicitations, and intuitions, but the correlation may be much less direct. As we have noted, most texts are fragmentary results of historical accidents; elicitations are normative data that reflect social prestige and stigma; and the intuitions of the theorist are inevitably influenced by his theoretical orientation. Texts, elicitations, and intuitions are most useful when we are studying the language of a superordinate population. For subordinate groups (children; lower classes; Creole speakers) the sources of error inherent in these data are greatly magnified. For a large body of data independent of the activity of the linguist we must draw upon the conversation of every-day life. There are, however, some real and some ideological obstacles to obtaining this data.

Technical difficulties in recording speech have been greatly reduced in recent years by the development of battery-operated tape recorders and condenser microphones. Equipment is now available which allows the linguist to approach the best studio recordings while working in the field. At the lower end of the spectrum of equipment, there are now cassette tape recorders with built-in microphones which can capture the whole range of frequencies important for speech analysis with only a moderate amount of distortion. Nevertheless, good recordings in the field will always demand great care and technical competence, which must be exercised at the same time that the linguist is dealing with the speech situation. And since the technical art involved is in a continual state of development, the investigator must be regularly searching the literature for new possibilities and testing equipment under a variety of field conditions. With proper equipment and precautions, it is now possible to obtain recordings of speech in the field that are more reliable than the same data transcribed in person by an expert phonetician.[7]

One obstacle to the study of speech is entirely illusory. There is no empirical basis for the often repeated assertion that ordinary speech is ungrammatical (Chomsky 1965:58). Analysis of a wide range of conversations shows that the great majority of sentences spoken are grammatical by any criterion, and all but a small percentage can be reduced to well-formed status by the application of simple and universal editing rules (Labov 1966b). The only significant concentration of ungrammatical sentences reported to date is in the speech of some highly educated participants at learned conferences.[8]

On the other hand, it is perfectly true that the language of every-day life is certainly not homogeneous. Heterogeneity is the rule, and we have reason to suspect that homogeneity, if it existed, would be dysfunctional (Weinreich, Labov and Herzog 1968). Every speaker shows a range of styles governed by the social context, and in some communities speakers switch with extraordinary facility to different dialects or languages. Furthermore, different social levels and ethnic groups within the same community differ sharply in their speech. This variability gives some observers the impression of an uncontrolled and chaotic oscillation. Some conclude that it is necessary to resolve the community into as many separate grammars as there are speakers and styles. But when the data is examined carefully we find that each individual fits into a regular pattern of social and stylistic stratification. This may be exemplified by Trudgill's recent work in Norwich with a sample of 60 speakers. *Table 2* shows *ing* index scores for five social groups in four contextual styles; the figures represent the percentage of the [In] variant in the alternation of unstressed [Iŋ] and [In].

Socio-economic Class		Style		
	Word list	Reading	Formal	Casual
Middle Middle Class	000	000	003	031
Lower Middle Class	000	010	015	042
Upper Working Class	005	015	074	087
Middle Working Class	023	044	088	095
Lower Working Class	029	066	098	100

Table 2. ing index scores by class and style in Norwich, England (from Trudgill 1971).

Such regular patterns of stylistic and social stratification are characteristic of established sociolinguistic variables, and will readily emerge whenever a population is systematically sampled. As few as five speakers in a cell, and five examples from each speaker, will yield such a regular array as *Table 2*, which matches the findings of Fischer (1958), Labov (1966a) and Labov, Cohen, Robins and Lewis (1968). These quantitative relationships do not require elaborate statistical analysis to be detected; we are dealing with a strongly determined pattern characteristic of linguistic behavior. Thus Shuy, Wolfram and Riley (1967) showed regular patterns of class and sex differentiation after examining a sub-sample of only 25 Detroit speakers, out of an original sample of 795. Wolfram (1969) then found detailed quantitative relations in the speech of 48 Negro subjects from the same sample, divided into four social classes and three age ranges (four in each cell). Only when the number of speakers in a cell drops below four or five, will we expect to find unaccountable irregularities in the matrix (Labov 1966a:IV).

The emergence of such regularities implies the presence of some constant factors operating in the structure and evolution of the language, but their relation to the grammars used by speakers is still not clear. The style shifting shown here is a response to the social stigma placed on the [In] variant; if the stylistic dimension could be quantified (as, e.g., the amount of attention available for monitoring speech), we might be able to predict these distributions from a simple function. The listener need only know that [Iŋ] is [+ prestige] and [In] is minus that feature.

It is possible to discover such patterns in a limited range of styles which does not include the *vernacular* or *casual speech*, where the minimum attention is paid to speech. The vernacular is used with peers and family members with whom the speaker shares the maximum amount of knowledge; the interview situation, in which an outsider asks questions and the subject gives answers, defines a context in which there is less shared knowledge and more than the minimum attention to speech is necessary. The main body of connected speech within the interview may then be called *careful speech* or *formal speech* irrespective of its specific features, and we must assume that a more casual style is available to the speaker.[9] Given the formality of the interview situation, it is a simple matter to elicit a range of more formal styles with reading, word lists, and minimal pairs. Important findings on class and sex differentiation were reported by Shuy, Wolfram and Riley (1967) who did not succeed in isolating casual speech. The work of Levine and Crockett (1966) and Anshen (1969) in Hillsboro, N.C. was confined to an even more formal stylistic range, but data emerged which confirmed a number of important sociolinguistic principles: e.g., the steeper style shift of women, and the tendency of the second highest status group to show the highest slope of style shifting.

Nevertheless, the vernacular is the style which carries the greatest interest for the study of linguistic structure and linguistic change. It reflects the rule systems learned in pre-adolescent years, unmodified by the superposed rules acquired in later life. Vernacular rules are more consistant than the rules used in formal styles; word classes are more intact; and the vernacular is free of hypercorrection which can blur linguistic patterns in both directions. If we are to make theoretically sound distinctions between obligatory and variable rules, we must base our observations on the most consistent type of speech.[10] Furthermore, we find that the vernacular shows the most advanced forms in the course of new change in progress, well below the level of conscious attention, and a study of on-going change must be based on vernacular data.

Given this orientation towards the interview situation and the vernacular, we are faced with the *OBSERVER'S PARADOX: we want to observe how people talk when they are not being observed.* One solution can be rejected immediately: secret recordings without permission of the speakers are unethical, unwise, and unsuitable for obtaining the large body of well-recorded data that we require. Other solutions to the Observer's Paradox are necessarily the main focus of sociolinguistic methods.

One approach to this problem uses techniques which involve the subject in the topic to the extent that the constraints of the interview situation are overridden by the intensity of the emotions generated (Labov 1966a:IV). A second is to rely upon data generated in the margins of the interview situation, where the formal constraints are assumed not to apply. More effective methods go beyond the individual interview and deal with whole families and natural peer groups; here the vernacular is generated in normal interaction between peers and family members, and the effect of observation is reduced proportionately (Gumperz 1964; Labov, Cohen, Robins and Lewis 1968). In addition, various types of rapid and anonymous observation may be carried out in public places to observe the vernacular in use outside of the interview situation. A rapid survey of the use of postvocalic *r* in New York City department stores (Labov 1966a:III) has been followed by a number of such studies which have converged upon the general principles of stylistic and social stratification and added further detail. Surveys of this kind, limited only by the ingenuity of the investigator, will necessarily lack some crucial demographic information and produce less data than interviews. But they allow us to estimate the degree of error in approaching a description of the vernacular, since the sources of error are complementary with those of various interview methods. The most we can hope for is a systematic reduction of the observational effects: all of our techniques approach the vernacular asymptotically, and their over-all divergence gives us some idea of how far we are from a solution to the Observer's Paradox.

The analytic problems of dealing with variation are confronted directly by those studying language within the speech community. The first task is the definition of the linguistic variable, distinguishing constant elements from those which show inherent variation. A wrong definition or assumption about the variable will blur the quantitative relations by including items that are not affected by the rule at all. The case of *ing* will illustrate the point. The usual first approach is to see this variable as an alternation of two forms of the suffix *-ing*, failing to observe that *nothing* and *something* are affected in the same way as *walking* and *riding*. It quickly becomes clear that we are dealing with a phonological process that affects unstressed *-ing*, though it may show some grammatical conditioning. In some dialects, gerundives are distinguished from verbs with the progressive. Other dialects do not apply the rule to proper nouns like *Flushing* or *Manning*, where no grammatical boundary precedes the *-ing*; in others, such forms are affected. In its most general form, the variable includes all cases of unstressed *-ing*. But the degree of stress is also important; in Atlanta, *everything* and *anything* are excluded, no doubt because of the slight stress produced by the alternating stress pattern.

The *linguistic variable* is a heuristic concept, useful in making observations and gathering data. But we must find a place for such inherent variation within our current conception of a grammar as a set of rules for relating meaningful elements to sound patterns. The first step is to assign to each rule a quantity ϕ ranging from 0 to 1, representing the proportion of cases in which the rule applies out of all those cases in which it might have applied. For obligatory rules, $\phi = 1$, and for optional (or *variable) rules*, $(0 < \phi < 1)$ 1. For *ing*, the general rule might read:

(1) $g \rightarrow <\phi> / \begin{bmatrix} I \\ -str \end{bmatrix} \quad n \underline{\qquad} [-seg]$

where angled brackets around the rule output indicate a variable rule. The social and stylistic stratification of this rule represents the effect of an external environment. We can best show these effects by making ϕ a function of style and class; as suggested by the data of *Table 2*, a linear function.

(1a) $\phi^{(1)}$ = a (Class) + b (Style) + c

But as noted above such formulations are untestable and cannot be developed further as long as the dimension of style remains unquantified.

The crucial question involved in formalizing inherent variation in language involves variable constraints upon the rule: linguistic environments in which the rule operates more or less often. These form the largest body of examples of informal reporting of variability in structuralist descriptions. Thus we might formalize the complex statement of Bucca and Lesser about Kitsai   as:

$$
(2) \quad \begin{bmatrix} V \\ back \\ +high \end{bmatrix} \rightarrow <-\text{tense}> / - \left\{ \begin{array}{l} <+\text{seg}> \\ \begin{bmatrix} +obs \\ +cor \\ +ant \end{bmatrix} \quad <+obs> \end{array} \right\}
$$

The angled brackets around elements of the environment indicate variable constraints, which favor the application of the rule. This first approximation would then show that the high front vowel is variably lax, more often if another segment follows directly (and it is not in final position), and more often if it is followed by a second obstruent after an apical obstruent.

To draw upon a more carefully analyzed example from English, we can write a general rule for the simplification of clusters ending in -*t, d* which will apply to all dialects.

$$
(3) \quad t, d \rightarrow <\phi> / [+\text{cons}] <\phi> \underline{\quad\quad} \#\# \quad <-\text{syl}>
$$

This formulation states that a coronal anterior stop will be variably deleted at the end of a word after another consonant more often if there is no morpheme boundary between it and the preceding consonant, and more often if the next word does not begin with a vowel. This captures the general finding that in all dialects, the -*t* in *fist* will be deleted more often than the -*ed* in *missed,* and the -*t* in *just now* more often than in -*t* in *just a minute.*

The direction of these environments is constant for all dialects, but their relative weighting is not. Thus in rule (3) no indication of such weighting is given. But for young speakers of the Black English vernacular, the

phonological constraint <-syl>is predominant, and the effect of the morpheme boundary is relatively slight so that the rule applies to *missed me*
more often than to *just a minute,* and for older speakers of Black English,
and for most white dialects, the grammatical constraint is predominant, and
the rule applies to *missed me* less often than *just a minute.* We thus observe
a linguistic change taking place in the grammars of Black speakers as they
grow older (Labov, Cohen, Robins and Lewis 1968).

The re-weighting of variable constraints appears to be an important
mechanism of linquistic change. In the study of the centralization of /ay/
and /aw/ on Martha's Vineyard (Labov 1963) such a re-weighting of environments could be observed in the original impressionistic transcriptions.
For intermediate generations, every distinctive feature of the following consonants influenced in varying degrees the centralization of the nucleus of a
preceding /ay/ or /aw/. But as the change went to completion in the young-
est generation, one constraint dominated all the others: centralization occurs before voiceless consonants, uncentralized nuclei otherwise. Recent
spectrographic studies of the same data confirm this process of re-weighting
(Labov 1970a). These instrumental studies also show that the recent history
of the raising of short /a/ in New York City involves a re-weighting in
which the effect of a following nasal consonant shifts from the least important to the most important constraint upon the rule. Other examples of such
re-weighting are given by Bailey in his discussion of formal means of build
ing rate into a theory of linguistic description (1970).

Given the fact that variable constraints can be observed in linguistic behavior, and given formal devices for incorporating them into linguistic
rules, there remain several serious theoretical problems before such rules
can be included in our conception of grammar of a language. First, these
regularities are observed in the *production* of language; but from the
hearer's point of view, they may seem insignificant. All that the hearer has
to know to interpret sentences correctly is that -*t, d* may be optionally
deleted; the frequency of deletion in a given environment is irrelevant to the
interpretation of any one sentence. Secondly, it is not clear how children
would learn such rules. What kind of social reinforcement or correction
would operate to produce this result?

The first question involves the issue as to whether or not speakers of a
language are sensitive to frequencies. There is some evidence from subjective reaction tests which shows that they are, suggesting that stigmatized features are not overtly perceived up to a certain frequency, and heard beyond
a certain frequency, as occurring all the time. But no experimental demonstration of such a capacity has yet been made. On the second question, we
can consider two possible mechanisms for learning variable rules. One is
that adults will correct a child when the frequency of a stigmatized form
rises above a certain value; if, for example, the child produces *dh* as [d] over
90% of the time, he may be heard and rebuked for talking "too rough."

The only people who *always* use stops for *th-* in the United States are foreigners, and only foreigners delete all the *-ed* signals. It is possible that even the roughest speaker is expected to produce a certain frequency of a grammatical form like *-ed* in order to demonstrate the fact that he knows the language and is a native speaker of English. A second possibility is that behavior within a given frequency range is learned directly from observation of others without the necessity for such correction: that is, *reproduce* variable behavior at the same frequency as that modeled in the environment. Such a process of "probability matching" has been observed in some animals and in human beings, although the mechanism is not yet understood (Sternberg 1963).

These suggestions are put forward more as an outline for future research than as arguments that variable rules are actually "used" by speakers of the language. We are no more able to decide that question than resolve any of the other issues of validity raised in sections: 1-3. But the plausibility of variable rules as integral elements of grammar increases as we observe the high degree of intersubjective agreement on these abstract relations.

If we have evidence that variable constraints exist, a formal notation for incorporating them in rule systems, and some conception of their possible place in a grammar of linguistic competence, it still does not follow that such relations must be studied and reported. It is a hopeless fallacy to assume that everything can be described, and it is unlikely that a very large part of human behavior will be reduced to systematic description. We can only select those aspects of behavior that will demonstrate important general principles, and the direct study of variation must hold out such promise if it is to exert any claim on our attention.

The example of *ing* cited above is a relatively simple one, with limited linguistic interest. The rule for *-t, d* deletion is of greater significance, especially when it appears that a further generalization of this rule stands as a universal statement which applies to the aspiration and deletion of Spanish *-s* and many other rules deleting final consonants.

$$(3\,a) \quad \begin{array}{c} [+\mathrm{cons}] \\ \#\# \end{array} \begin{array}{c} \\ \langle -\mathrm{syl}\rangle \end{array} \rightarrow \quad \langle \phi \rangle \quad / \quad \langle +\mathrm{cons} \rangle \ \langle \phi \rangle \quad \underline{\qquad}$$

In this general form the rule asserts that whenever a final consonant is variably deleted, the rule will operate more often if another consonant precedes, if it is an integral part of the word and not a separate morpheme, and if it is not followed by a word beginning with a vowel. Variable rules can thus point in the direction of universal statements, comparable to the findings of Greenberg on universal implications in the directions of linguistic change (1969).

An even richer set of variable constraints appears in the English rule for contraction and deletion of the copula (Labov 1969). The existence of parallel contraction and deletion rules, in a feeding relationship, was established by the observation that contraction and deletion of *is* are both favored by a number of indentical variable constraints. Both rules are favored, for example, by a preceding pronoun subject, a following progressive verb, and (otherwise) a following predicate adjective. One variable constraint operates in opposite directions for the two rules: a preceding vowel favors contraction, and a preceding consonant favors deletion. In somewhat simplified form, the two rules appear as:

(4a) CONTRACTION

$$\vartheta \rightarrow <\phi> / \begin{bmatrix} <+Pro> \\ <+syl> \end{bmatrix} \quad \#\# \quad \begin{bmatrix} \underline{\quad\quad} \\ +Tns \end{bmatrix} [+cons] \#\# \quad \begin{bmatrix} <+Prog> \\ <+Adj> \end{bmatrix}$$

(4b) DELETION

$$[+cons] \rightarrow <\phi> / \begin{bmatrix} <+Pro> \\ <-syl> \end{bmatrix} \quad \#\# \quad \begin{bmatrix} \underline{\quad\quad} \\ -nas \\ +cont \end{bmatrix} \#\# \quad \begin{bmatrix} <+Prog> \\ <+Adj> \end{bmatrix}$$

The fact that the phonological constraint is reversed fits in exactly with the phonological difference between the two rules. Contraction removes a vowel, and deletion removes a consonant; the opposing effect of a preceding vowel shows that the pressure in both cases is towards a CVC structure; for contraction, the most favored case is CV##VC## → CV##C##, and deletion occurs most often when CVC##C## → CVC##.

Variable constraints produce a profile of contraction and deletion of *is* in which the rule operates least before a following NP, next before an adjective phase, next before a progressive verb, and most of all before *gonna*. Independent studies of Wolfram in Detroit (1969) and Mitchell-Kernan in San Francisco (1969) produced the same patterns. The matching of such quantitative patterns leads to a higher degree of confidence in the analysis than the observation that contraction and deletion are optional in all areas. It therefore seems quite clear that contraction and deletion are phonological rules controlled by the same prosodic or grammatical conditions, with complementary effects.

The methods concerned so far involve arithmetic manipulation to study the effects of various environments by subdividing the data. Thus the effect of pronoun subjects vs. others on contraction must be registered by comparing cases that differ only on this variable. As the analysis becomes finer, this becomes more and more difficult, without increasing the size of the data without limit. In some analyses, linguists have attempted to compare three variables pairwise (Fasold 1972), but this will lead to misleading results if the distributions of the various factors are badly skewed. Some form of multivariate analysis is required in order to advance the study of variation beyond its initial stages.

A fundamental difficulty in applying standard multivariate techniques is that linguistic data have several unusual characteristics. First, we find that some cells, representing the intersection of various phonological and grammatical variables, are certain to be empty or very small. For example, the great majority of subject pronouns end in vowels; the cells indicating pronouns ending in consonants are practically empty (*it, that* and *what* are subject to a different, interfering mechanism of assibilation). Secondly, we find most internal linguistic features are independent and do not show the typical interaction that is characteristic of social variables such as class, sex and age. Standard analyses of variance are based upon the possibility of filling all cells of a matrix evenly and the necessity of analyzing extensive interaction.

The major advance in the analysis of variation was made by D. Sankoff and H. Cedergren, who revised the mathematical interpretation of variable rules in the light of probability theory (Cedergren & Sankoff 1974). The Sankoff-Cedergren analysis takes into account the special characteristics of linguistic data outlined above, and in a maximum likelihood program that calculates the individual contributions of each environment to the probability of the rule applying. These individual probabilities are inserted in a formula such as

$$P - 1 - (1 - p_0)(1 - p_1)(1 - p_2) . . (1 - p_n)$$

where P is the over-all probability of the rule applying, p_0 is an input probability, and p_1 . . . p_n are the values of particular factors in each of n mutually exclusive sets of environments. This is the "non-application" model, which shows the effect of various factors in restraining the rule's application. A unique value is obtained by setting one factor in each group equal to zero: this is the factor which has the minimum effect in restraining the rule—or in other words, favors the rule most.

Cedergren and Sankoff applied this method to the data for copula deletion for four groups of adolescent speakers of the Black English vernacular in the data of Labov (1969); they obtained the values shown in *Table 3*.

TABLE 3

EFFECTS OF VARIABLE CONSTRAINTS OF DELETION RULE

Preceding environment	Following environment			
	___NP	___PA-Loc	___Vb	___gn
Pro_____	1.0 (2)	2.3 (1)	0.6 (1)	0.1 (0)
[-cns]				
Other NP_____ [+cns]	21.9 (22)	24.0 (24)	5.3 (5)	0.8 (1)
[-cns]	14.0 (13)	6.0 (7)	1.9 (2)	0.2 (0)

When we insert these values into the rule in a particular case, we can check the validity of the rule by comparing the theoretical or predicted frequency with the observed frequency. Thus when we consider the case of deletion after a noun phrase subject ending in a vowel before following predicate adjectives or locatives, we obtain

$$P = 1 - (1 - .27)(1 - .00)(1 - .00)(1 - .13) = .365$$

The observed frequency of deletion in this case was six cases out of 16, or .375. The model would predict 5.9 cases as against the six cases observed: one could not fit the data much better.

The data do not always fit prediction as well as this. In such a case, the assumption of independence which lies behind the program must be abandoned; that is, the rule must be rewritten or dissolved into different subrules. Thus the Cedergren-Sankoff program provides us with the first empirical method of deciding when a linguistic rule is worth writing, and when it is not, based on the characteristics of the data itself.

One of the first demonstrations of the power of the variable rule program was Cedergren's study of the aspiration and deletion of /s/ in Panamanian Spanish (1973). She located a massive interaction between the grammatical category of determiner and stress through lack of prediction and fit. For example, 103 occurrences of unaspirated /s/ were predicted in careful speech for determiners before a following consonant, but only 51 out of

1238 tokens were found. This anomaly was found to be due to the interaction of determiner and stress: stress in determiners heavily favored retention of the /s/ before a vowel, but not at all before a consonant. Thus we would have to remove the special case of stressed determiners from the general rule and write it as a specific sub-rule. A consideration of the special semantic and syntactic role of stressed determiners indicates that they may indeed be considered a different grammatical category.

The Cedergren-Sankoff program also allows us to examine far more factors than we could normally handle with arithmetical methods. At the same time, the reliability of the results is related to the number of tokens involved. Guy (1975) applied the program to -*t,d* deletion for 18 Philadelphians. The familiar major effects (such as a following vowel vs. a following obstruent) were replicated in each individual even when very small bodies of data were studied. But the finer effects, such as the effect of a following glide vs. a following vowel, required larger bodies of data before uniform patterns emerged. Guy found that when the smaller of two cells contained more than 30 items, there were no cases of reversal of the expected distributions that emerged from the over-all pattern of the community. But when the data from an individual contained less than 30 in the given cell, one could expect a number of cases in which the expected values for the finer results were reversed or deviated strongly from the central tendency of the community.

In this case, it is obvious from our general knowledge of articulation that the effect of obstruent vs. vowel would be greater than glide vs. vowel. In general, the Cedergren-Sankoff program has opened up an avenue for the development of a higher-level theory which must account for the relative strengths of favoring and disfavoring environments. Thus the data of *Table 3* challenges us to explain why a following progressive favors deletion more than a following noun phrase. Recent re-analysis of the original data with the program has allowed us to make even finer sub-divisions, separating predicate adjectives from locatives, and confirms the suggestion (Stewart 1970) that these distributions show the effect of an earlier Creole history of the Black English vernacular.

Quantitative studies of sociolinguistic structure have now been developed to the point that they can support general conclusions on the mechanism of linguistic change. Inferences about language change can be made from an examination of social distribution. From three cases of on-going change in the vowel system of New York City (Labov 1966a), it was inferred that a curvilinear class distribution implied the existence of change in progress. On the other hand, completed changes normally showed linear distribution, with the maximum differentiation between the highest and lowest social groups, as a result of overt social correction. In Trudgill's study of Norwich (1971) we find confirmation of this general principle. One variable studied by Trudgill, the backing of short /e/ to [ʌ] before /l/, showed a curvilinear distribution as displayed in *Table 4.* The highest indices representing the greatest degree of centralization, are shown by the upper and middle working class for all styles, while the lower working class is parallel to the middle class groups. This situation is quite comparable to the New York City case of the raising of the vowels of *bad, ask, dance* and *law, off,* etc. *Table 5* shows that *e* was indeed a case of change in progress as shown by its distribution in apparent time. The highest frequencies are shown by younger speakers in all styles.

Class		Style		
	Word list	*Reading*	*Formal*	*Casual*
Middle Middle Class	003	000	001	002
Lower Middle Class	007	012	023	042
Upper Working Class	027	039	089	127
Middle Working Class	030	044	091	087
Lower Working Class	009	026	077	077

Table 4. e indices by class and style in Norwich, England (from Trudgill 1971).

Age		Style		
	Word list	*Reading*	*Formal*	*Casual*
10-19	059	070	139	173
20-29	021	034	071	100
30-39	025	031	059	067
40-49	015	026	055	088
50-59	006	013	035	046
60-69	005	018	055	058
70+	005	031	050	081

Table 5. e indices by age and style in Norwich, England (from Trudgill 1971).

A parallel case appeared in the study of Panamanian Spanish by Cedegren (1970).

One of five variables studied—the lenition of *ch*—showed a curvilinear distribution; the same variable was the only one to show evidence of change in progress by its distribution across age groups. We conclude that if a general linguistic variable does not match the distribution of established socioeconomic variables in the speech community, it probably represents a relatively early stage of an on-going change, not yet subject to social correction.

The convergence of these independent lines of investigation is encouraging. But it cannot be denied that there are also serious limitations to the observation of language in use. Most of the syntactic forms that we would like to study do not occur often enough in ordinary conversation to be subjected to quantitative analysis. In order to expand the range of data that can be studied by these methods, it will be necessary to enrich the data of natural conversation by setting up the conditions under which such forms are used. Some success has been achieved in this area with relative clauses, futures and perfects, but such efforts are only in their infancy. It will no doubt always be necessary to draw upon our intuitions in any study of complex structures, and the art of arguing from observational evidence to intuition and back again must be developed.

It seems clear that good linguistic work will draw upon several types of data and methods in approaching a given problem. Since different methods will have different sources of error, even a partial convergence in the results will lead to a higher degree of confidence than we can give to work with one kind of data and one way of dealing with it. It was encouraging for us to discover that the rules for contraction and deletion of the English copula fitted in with and depended on the English stress rules developed by Chomsky and Halle (1968). For contraction operates only upon words with schwa as their only vowel; this schwa is the result of the vowel reduction rule which is in turn dependent upon the stress rules. Wherever stress has been applied (as in *Yes, he is*), contraction in standard English and deletion in Black English are equally unacceptable. These facts thus give independent confirmation to the stress cycle in sentence-level phonology.

On the other hand, it seems likely that variable rules may be written for the kind of output constraints which Ross has suggested for extraposition from noun phrases and for particle shifting. Current suggestions for output constraints have no formal place within generative grammar; many of them seem to reflect the same kind of firm quantitative relations of greater and lesser frequency in the application of a rule that we have exemplified here in phonological rules. Our current studies of negative attraction and negative concord show an even more intimate relation between the quantitative study of speech forms and the abstract analysis of intuitive data (Labov 1972).

Elicitation of formal data from native speakers must obviously play a role in our first approach to languages, and minimal pair tests and commutation tests will always provide important data, especially as we begin to understand their limitations. Experimental techniques have not been dealt with here, since other papers in this series are more concerned with laboratory techniques. But the interplay between experiment and observation can be seen in many of the studies cited (Labov 1966a; Trudgill 1971; Labov, Cohen, Robins and Lewis 1968). I have also tried to indicate the ways in which historical studies can interact with synchronic descriptions, and especially how historical linguistics can profit from the investigation of changes now in progress.

Through the convergence of several techniques, we can hope to make further progress towards the common goal of finding right answers to hard questions about language. But the finding that emerges most clearly from a study of methods is that we all share a common failing as linguists: we try too hard to prove ourselves right. In this strenuous effort we inevitably overlook the errors concealed in our assumptions, built into our methods, and institutionalized in our formal apparatus. This discussion no doubt contains many instances of this general tendency, and argues too strongly from one point of view. A permanent concern with methodology means living with the deep suspicion that we have made a mistake at some crucial point in the investigation. If we fail to find any substance for that suspicion, after several decades of worrying, probing and testing, there remains the possibility that we have been right all along. If it should turn out that we have been right about the language that other people use, and not some artifact of our own, we may be reasonably satisfied with this result.

Notes

[1] After Chen and Hsieh presented their evidence of massive splitting of word classes in Middle Chinese dialects at the 1969 meeting of the Linguistic Society of America, several historical linguists rose to make the point that dialect mixture must have been responsible, since sound change affects all members of the word class equally.

[2] The term *uniformitarian* is borrowed from geology, where it refers to the now generally accepted principle of Hutton that processes now taking place around us—weathering, sedimentation, volcanism, etc.—are the same as those which operated to produce the geological record.

[3] I am indebted to Alexander Hull for this observation.

[4] Or as Ross notes, "it seems intuitively abhorrent to assert that [in *John is taller than Bill*] the single word Bill has the same status as a constituent as the whole sentence." (1967:42)

[5] It should be noted that all of these investigations have been carried out with a sample of friends and associates or else with student subjects. Carden's work is the striking exception to this tendency.

[6] The reason that *all the boys didn't leave* is a relatively rare construction is that there appears to be a weak form of negative attraction exercised by the quantifiers *every* and *all*. Unlike the indefinite *any*, these do not enter into the absolutely obligatory relation which makes **any boys didn't leave* completely unacceptable. We seem to be dealing with a variable constraint rather than a categorical one.

[7]Of course there are times when observations of the movements of the lips, teeth or tongue are helpful, and these are lost in acoustic recording. Video tape recording or film is a natural resource where such data become critical.

[8]Transcriptions of my own comments at such meetings are among the best illustrations of this point.

[9]The term *consultative,* introduced by Joos (1960), seems to convey most aptly the typical question-and-answer style of the interview.

[10]The regularity of *Table 3* and similar displays in Labov (1966a) is best characterized as the result of a fine-grained and predictable dialect mixture, which responds sensitively to contextual conditions. In writing grammars, we will have no difficulty in incorporating the whole range of behavior into a single rule. But the crucial question remains as to whether the vernacular end of the style spectrum shows a categorical or variable rule— or no rule at all. See Labov (1970) for some of the issues involved here.

Reference

Anshen, Frank. 1969. Speech variation among Negroes in a small Southern community. Unpublished Ph.D. dissertation. New York: N.Y.U.

Bailey, Charles-James N. 1970. Building rate into a dynamic theory of linguistic description. Working Papers in Linguistics (Hawaii) 2.9.161-233.

Bellugi, Ursula. 1967. The acquisition of negation. Unpublished Ph.D. dissertation. Cambridge: Harvard University.

Berko, Jean. 1958. The child's learning of English morphology. Word 14. 150-77. [Reprinted in *Child language,* ed. by A. BarAdon and W. F. Leopold, 153-67. Englewood Cliffs: Prentice-Hall, Inc., 1971.]

Bickerton, Derek. 1971. On the nature of the Creole continuum. Unpublished MS.

Bloch, Bernard. 1948. A set of postulates for phonemic analysis. Lg. 24.3-46.

Bloch, Bernard and G. Trager. 1942. Outline of linguistic analysis. Special Publication of the Linguistic Society of America. Baltimore: Waverly Press.

Bloomfield, L. 1933. Language. New York: Henry Holt. [Chapters 17-27 reprinted as *Language history*, ed. by H. Hoijer. New York: Holt, Rinehart and Winston, 1965.]

Bucca, Salvador and Alexander Lesser. 1969. Kitsai phonology and morphophonemics. I.J.A.L. 35.7-19.

Carden, Guy. 1970. A note on conflicting idiolects. Linguistic Inquiry 1.281-90.

Cedergren, Henrietta. 1970. Patterns of free variation: The language variable. Paper presented to Canadian Sociology and Anthropology Meeting.

Chao, Yuen-Ren. 1934. The non-uniqueness of phonemic solutions of phonetic systems. Bulletin of the Institute of History and Philology, Academica Sinica 4.363-97. [Reprinted in *Readings in linguistics,I*, ed. by Martin Joos, 38-54. Chicago: The U. of Chicago Press, 1957.]

Chen, Matthew and Hsin-I Hsieh. 1971. The time variable in phonological change. Journal of Linguistics 7.1-13.

Cheng, Chin-Chuan and William S-Y. Wang. 1970. Phonological change of Middle Chinese initials. University of California (Berkeley) Department of Linguistics Project on Linguistic Analysis, Second Series, 10.CW1-CW69.

Chomsky, Noam. 1957. Syntactic structures. The Hague: Mouton.

Chomsky, Noam. 1961. Some methodological remarks on generative grammar. Word 17.219-39.

Chomsky, Noam. 1964. The logical basis of linguistic theory. Proceedings of the Ninth International Congress of Linguists, ed. by H. Lunt, 914-1008. The Hague: Mouton.

Chomsky, Noam. 1965. Aspects of the theory of syntax. Cambridge: The MIT Press.

Chomsky, Noam. 1970. Remarks on nominalization. Readings in English transformational grammar, ed. by R. Jacobs and P. Rosenbaum, 184-221. Waltham: Ginn and Company.

Chomsky, Noam and Morris Halle. 1968. The sound pattern of English. New York: Harper and Row.

Echeverría, Max S. and Heles Contreras. 1965. Araucanian phonemics. I.J.A.L. 31.132-35.

Elliott, D., S. Legum and S. Thompson. 1969. Syntactic variation as linguistic data. Papers from the Fifth Regional Meeting, Chicago Linguistic Society, ed. by R. Binnick *et al.*, 52-59. Chicago: Department of Linguistics, University of Chicago.

Ferguson, C. F. 1971. 'Short *a*' in Philadelphia English. Stanford Occasional Papers in Linguistics 1.2-27.

Fischer, John L. 1958. Social influences on the choice of a linguistic variant. Word 14.47-56.

Gauchat, L. 1905. L'unité phonétique dans le patios d'une commune. Aus romanischen Sprachen und Literaturen: Festschrift Heinrich Morf, 175-232. Halle: Max Niemeyer.

Gleason, H. A. Jr. 1955. Workbook in descriptive linguistics. New York: Holt, Rinehart and Winston.

Greenberg, Joseph. 1969. Some methods of dynamic comparison in linguistics. Substance and structure of language, ed. by J. Puhvel, 147-204. Berkeley: U. of California Press.

Gumperz, J. 1964. Linguistic and social interaction in two communities. The ethnology of communication, ed. by J. Gumperz and D. Hymes, 137-53. Washington, D.C.: American Anthropological Association.

Harris, Zellig. 1951. Structural linguistics. Chicago: U. of Chicago Press.

Harris, Zellig. 1965. Transformational theory. Lg. 41.363-401.

Heringer, J. T. 1970. Research on quantifier-negative idiolects. Papers from the Sixth Regional Meeting, Chicago Linguistic Society, 287-96. Chicago: Chicago Linguistic Society.

Hockett, Charles F. 1958. A course in modern linguistics. New York: The MacMillan Company.

Hsieh, Hsin-I. 1970. Is phonology generative? University of California (Berkeley) Phonology Laboratory, Monthly Internal Memorandum, 17-38.

Jackendoff, Ray S. 1968. Quantifiers in English. Foundations of Language 4.422-42.

Joos, Martin. 1960. The isolation of styles. Georgetown Monograph Series on Languages and Linguistics 12.107-13.

Kihlbom, Asta. 1926. A contribution to the study of fifteenth century English. Uppsala: Lundequistska.

Labov, W. 1963. The social motivation of a sound change. Word 19.273-309. [Reprinted in *Readings for the history of the English language*, ed. by C. Scott and J. Erickson, 345-79. Boston: Allyn and Bacon.]

Labov, W. 1966a. The social stratification of English in New York City. Washington, D.C.: Center for Applied Linguistics.

Labov, W. 1966b. On the grammaticality of every-day speech. Presented at the 41st Annual Meeting of the Linguistic Society of America.

Labov, W. 1969. Contraction, deletion, and inherent variability of the English copula. Lg. 45. 715-62.

Labov, W. 1970. The study of language in its social context. Studium generale 23.30-87.

Labov, W. 1972. The internal evolution of linguistic rules. Historical linguistics and generative theory, ed. by R. Stockwell and R. Macaulay. Bloomington: Indiana U. Press.

Labov, W., P. Cohen, C. Robins and J. Lewis. 1968. A study of the non-standard English of Negro and Puerto Rican speakers in New York City. Cooperative Research Report 3288. Vols. I and II. New York: Columbia University. [Reprinted by U.S. Regional Survey, 3812 Walnut St., Eisenlohr Hall 202, Philadelphia, Pa. 19104.]

Levine, L. and H. J. Crockett Jr. 1966. Speech variation in a Piedmont community: Postvocalic r. Explorations in sociolinguistics, ed. by S. Lieberson, 76-98. Bloomington: Indiana U. Press.

Mitchell-Kernan, C. 1969. Language behavior in a Black urban community. University of California (Berkeley) Language-Behavior Laboratory Working Paper No. 23.

Nida, E. 1949. Morphology. [2nd Edition] Ann Arbor: University of Michigan Press.

Osthoff, H. and K. Brugmann. 1878. Preface to *Morphological investigations in the sphere of the Indo-European languages I*. [Translated by W. P. Lehmann.] A reader in nineteenth-century historical Indo-European linguistic, ed. by W. P. Lehmann, 197-209. Bloomington: Indiana U. Press.

Pike, K. 1947. Phonemics. Ann Arbor: University of Michigan Press.

Quirk, R. and J. Svartvik. 1966. Investigating linguistic acceptability. The Hague: Mouton.

Redden, J. E. 1966. Walapai I: Phonology. I.J.A.L. 32.1-16.

Ross, J.R. 1967. Constraints on variables in syntax. Unpublished Ph.D. dissertation. Cambridge: M.I.T.

Saussure, F. de. 1962. Cours de linguistique générale. Paris: Payot.

Sedlak, P. 1969. Typological considerations of vowel quality systems. Stanford University Working Papers on Language Universals 1.1-40a.

Shuy, R., W. Wolfram and W. K. Riley. 1967. A study of social dialects in Detroit. Final Report, Project 6-1347. Washington, D.C.: Office of Education.

Sternberg, S. 1963. Stochastic learning theory. Handbook of mathematical psychology, ed. by R. Luce *et al.*, 1-120. New York: J. Wiley and Sons, Inc.

Stockwell, R. P. 1966. Problems in the interpretation of the Great Vowel Shift. Unpublished Ph.D. dissertation. Edinburgh: Edinburgh University.

Trudgill, P. J. 1971. The social differentiation of English in Norwich. Unpublished Ph.D. dissertation. Edinburgh: Edinburgh University.

Wedge, G. and F. Ingemann. 1970. Tag questions, syntactic variables, and grammaticality. Papers from the Fifth Kansas Linguistics Conference, ed. by Frances Ingemann, 166-203. Lawrence: Department of linguistics, University of Kansas.

Weinreich, U., W. Labov and M. Herzog. 1968. Empirical foundations for a theory of language change. Directions for historical linguistics, ed. by W. P. Lehmann and Y. Malkiel, 97-195. Austin: University of Texas Press.

Wolfe, P. 1969. Linguistic change and the Great Vowel Shift in English. Unpublished Ph.D. dissertation. Los Angeles: U.C.L.A.

Wolfram, W. 1969. A sociolinguistic description of Detroit Negro speech. Washington, D.C.: Center for Applied Linguistics.

Zimmer, K. 1969. Psychological correlates of some Turkish morpheme structure rules. Lg. 45. 309-21.

Discussion

JAMES R. HOLBROOK (Georgetown U.): Professor Labov, in Hockett's *State of the art* The Hague: Mouton, 1968), Zellig Harris' philosophy is summarized as follows: "the Real Truth (at least about language) is not attainable, so we might as well have a good time sharing our occasional dim glimpses in its direction, and not worry too much about Ultimates" (34-5). I wonder if this is not the underlying philosophy of most linguists? Do I take it that you are giving us some hope of eventually arriving at at least some ultimates about the nature of language?

WILLIAM LABOV (U. of Pennsylvania): I wouldn't have any hesitation about answering yes. I think that Professor Kim's and Professor Dingwall and Whitaker's papers which you heard earlier and which reflect the state of phonetic science and neurophysiological science would certainly point in that direction. I wouldn't want to make any statments about the future of semantics which is at the other end of the scale. Hockett is an incredibly able and penetrating observer who has changed his view from one time to another; his whole history could be compared to that of Chomsky who has maintained a different attitude towards rightness and wrongness. There is a playfulness which I see in the work of some linguists of the period of the thirties and the forties which I don't think is so universal today. My background is that of an industrial chemist and there is no question about right and wrong in that field. If you cast enamel on a steel panel and you put it out at a forty-five degree angle to the sun and then return six months later to find it completely cracked, you can say what you want but you were wrong. You may not know why you were wrong, but you were clearly wrong when you formulated that material. Confrontation with the hard facts of the physical world is very helpful in changing, I think, the point of view which you quoted from Hockett.

THEODORE M. LIGHTNER (U. of Texas): I have a background in theoretical chemistry! I'm a bit confused. What I'm confused about is: where do you set the boundaries of linguistics? What do you consider linguistics to be? Is it a universal behavioral science in which one is interested in any type of behavior of a human being or is linguistics a more narrow field? What leads me to ask this question is your interest in getting people to discuss things and noticing how they change their styles of speech —something which everyone is aware of. But how does that play a role in linguistics?

One more thing. Let us say that people contract 22 13/16 percent of the time in a certain environment. How is that relevant for linguistics?

WILLIAM LABOV (U. of Pennsylvania): I don't have a passionate interest in defining linguistics. Plainly linguistics has to do with the structure and evolution of language. We are all aware of the fact that linguistics has been too much confined to sentence grammar. We also are aware of the difficulties of studying discourse analysis. One of the ways you study discourse analysis is by looking at discourse. How far you would want to extend the boundaries of linguistics into other forms of communication, I don't know. I have a narrower view than some people. I would say that the advantage of linguistics for understanding human behavior is that it is the most developed of the disciplines that study social behavior. If there is going to be someday a social science, I think that some of the principles that emerge from linguistics will help. I'm aware of the fact that Chomsky's orientation is that linguistics has the same relationship toward psychology which can't be denied.

On the question of numbers, I think it should be plain right away that the numbers game is quite irrelevant, that what we are looking for is the same thing that all linguists are looking for, viz., relations. There are times when people go to excess—I have myself—in looking at quantitative relationships which are finer than the system would seem to support. The fundamental postulate of linguistics is that some utterances are the same and that implies that there exists free variation among those utterances that are the same. I would say that one thing that follows from that is that nothing further can be said. What we observe is that relationships of *more or less than* are all that count. In the case of the copula the percentages, of course, mean nothing. All that is important is that the copula appears more often before a noun phrase, let's say, than before a verb, that it appears more often after a noun phrase subject than after a pronoun subject. Those relationships provide a profile which is very powerful evidence about sames and differences and tells us something about the course of linguistic evolution.

The questions you ask are pointed and I think they are addressed to good ends. There is always the danger of bringing in all sorts of irrelevant factors. The only possible justification for a piece of data is that it is relevant to some major theoretical question on the structure and evolution of language.

JOHN UNDERWOOD (Georgetown U.): If I understand correctly what you have been saying, you appear to imply that what we have come to regard as a sub-field of linguistics, viz. sociolinguistics is more validly linguistics than many other sub-fields are. This sheds new light on the question: is sociolinguistics really a valid sub-field of linguistics? Maybe the question is rather: are any of the other sub-fields valid? Is this in effect what you are saying.

WILLIAM LABOV (U. of Pennsylvania): I am even less interested in sub-disciplines and interdisciplinary fields. There are no theoretical questions of importance, as far as I can see, in sociolinguistics as an interdisciplinary field. Presumably it represents the intersection of all the problems of sociology and all the problems of linguistics which is a hopeless field. Thus I have tended to avoid that term. I think Wittgenstein's term: *the language in context* or *language in use* would be nice. The trouble is he didn't do so well with it. I am not claiming an exclusive position for any particular field of work. If you look at some of the papers that we have written or that Bailey has written, you will find that one combines the use of intuitive judgments which are present all along the line with observation, with experiment and more recently with good scholarship. All I am claiming is that the vernacular that people use when they are not thinking about language is somewhat more systematic and regular in its relation to language change and the history of the language than certain literary forms. When you find that intuitions have dissolved into fragmentary, idiosyncratic views then it is quite possible that help from observation may be useful. I don't see any future for linguistics that drops the contribution of Chomsky and generative grammar off to one side and goes off doing something else.

DON G. STUART (Georgetown U.): I'm an electrical engineer by the way! I met the fellow at lunch who said he was a linguist but he wasn't coming back for the afternoon session. You began by saying that you didn't believe that linguistics was a science but I think you made an extremely good case for the possibility of linguistics being a science. The objective, empirical character of the physical sciences rests upon condition-bound observations which can be replicated by all normal, right-thinking observers. It rests upon a possible consensus of humanity as to the facts. You certainly pointed out what it is that makes a continuity hypothesis possible in language, viz. the consensus that exists between normal, right-thinking, initiated observers of a given conventional system of a language. You can get the native speakers of a language—if you take a community as a whole—to arrive at some kind of consensus. It seems to me that this is all that is essentially needed to have an empirical, objective science. Of course, since we have to deal with a community-bound consensus, it may have less determinacy than we can hope for in the physical sciences.

Chapter Thirteen

A Biological Perspective on the Evolution of Language

Philip Lieberman

The traditional mode of discourse regarding the source or sources of language has been philosophic and has usually focussed on the "uniqueness" of human language and human speech. The philosophic mode of analysis primarily makes use of the methods of logical analysis and predates the methods of science; it is indeed, as Francis Bacon pointed out, disjoint with the "scientific method." Logical analysis, in itself, can never test a scientific theory, the predictions of the theory and the data are the relevant scientific issues. However, the central premise of traditional philosophic inquiries on the nature of language, the hypothetical "uniqueness" of human linguistic ability, still pervades even recent comparative studies, e.g., Lieberman (1968); Lieberman and Crelin (1971); Lenneberg (1967). Though these studies have a strong biological orientation and investigate the communications of humans and other animals in terms of biological mechanisms the orientation is influenced by the "uniqueness" hypothesis. The biological perspective that I shall discuss is implicit in these studies as well as other recent ethological, psychological, and biological studies but an explicit and direct discussion of the biological perspective on the evolution of human language and human speech will, I think, provide a useful framework for further study.

A biological perspective on the evolution of language and speech must necessarily start with Charles Darwin. Darwin's (1859) statements of the principle of Natural Selection, the value of small changes, and the role of preadaption are still the central concepts that explain the data of evolutionary change. One of the primary aspects of Darwin's work that is crucial to a biological perspective on language is that language is not a biological isolate. Human language is not a phenomenon that can be completely divorced from other aspects of human life and human behavior. The biological mechanisms that form the basis of language are probably involved in other aspects of behavior. Darwin was aware of the complexity of life and the interrelated nature of the factors that may play a role in the evolution of a particular species or even of a particular attribute of a species. His discussion of the principle of Natural Selection thus notes:

> Owing to this struggle for life, any variation, however slight and from whatever cause proceeding, if it be in any degree profitable for an individual of the species, in its infinitely complex relations

to other organic beings and to external nature, will tend to the preservation of that individual, and will generally be inherited by its offspring. The offspring, also will thus have a better chance of surviving, for of the many individuals of any species which are periodically born but a small number can survive. I have called this principle, by which each slight variation if useful is preserved, by the term of Natural Selection, (1859, p. 61).

Modern insights into the mechanisms of genetic regulation have supplemented rather than refuted Darwin's theories.

The theory that I shall advance for the evolution of human language is that it involved a sequence of small variations. Some of these variations immediately yielded slight advantages in communication. They were retained because communication is an important element in the survival of most species. Other variations may have been at first retained because they yielded other benefits, e.g., more efficient upright posture which, in turn, made for more effective tool use. In time these variations became useful for human speech. Many of the biological mechanisms that make human language possible may exist in other species where they are retained for other functions. Darwin first noted the role of preadaption in his discussion of the evolution of the lungs of air breathing animals from the swim bladders of fish. The lungs of the first Lungfish had not evolved for respiration. They rather were the result of a long process of gradual, small variations that had been retained to make for more efficient swimming. The result of these variations for a different "cause" were preadapted for respiration. Preadaption may have been an important factor in the evolution of human language and human speech as it was an important factor in the evolution of air breathing animals. It therefore makes sense to study the biological mechanisms that are involved in the communication systems of other animals even though these animals obviously don't have human language. The same or similar biological mechanisms may still structure their communication systems or other aspects of their behavior. Humans appear to be better adapted for language than any other living species, but the mechanisms that are the biological basis of language are to be found in other species. We have "unique" linguistic abilities in the same sense that kangaroos are adapted to hopping or dolphins to swimming. Though a kangaroo is specially adapted to a "unique" pattern of locomotion the muscles of its legs work in the same manner as those of less specialized mammals. A physiologist specializing in the study of the kangaroo thus would be able to use information derived from the study of the muscles of horses or mice. Dolphins again have some specialized respiratory mechanisms but the systems for the transfer of oxygen to the blood in their lungs involves more general biological principles.

Human Language and Human Cognition

There are two sources of data that are available for the scientific study of evolution. These two sources are complementary and they can be applied to the study of the evolution of human language in relation to human cognition. We can study the record of fossil evidence for signs of the development of artifacts and culture which necessarily reflect the presence of human cognition and language. By these means evidence for the development of tool-making techniques can, for example, be derived. We can also study the behavior of living animals like chimpanzees who are genetically close (Sarich, 1974) to humans. Chimpanzees are not humans but as Huxley (1863) perceptively guessed, they are probably close to the ancestral species from which modern hominids and pongids have evolved. The study of chimpanzee behavior thus provides a base line for the study of the evolution of what we like to think of as "human" qualities and the commonality of these attributes with the behavior of non-human primates.

The direct evidence of the culture of fossil hominids shows that ritual burials occurred at least 100,000 years ago (Bordes, 1972). Systems for numeration and perhaps orthography data back to at least 30,000 years (Marshack, 1972). "Simple" stone tools date back several million years. Stone tools that were produced by the Levalloisian, or "core and flake" technique date back to at least 300,000 years (Bordes, 1968). If one thinks of a "grammar" as a set of formal "rules" that describe the possible form of a complex pattern of behavior then it is possible to derive "grammars" that describe tool making. The tool-making grammar would have the same psychological status as a grammar of language. It would be a formal model of some aspect of human behavior. The concept of a formal model does not mean that we necessarily expect a neurologist to eventually find a neural structure that corresponds to each grammatical step or "rule", but that we expect the formal rules to account for part of the observed behavioral pattern. People may make errors as they make tools as they do when they speak. The grammar thus attempts to account for "well-formed" utterances or tools. The grammar that is necessary to describe the Levalloisian tool-making technique formally is equivalent to a transformational grammar (Lieberman, 1975). The grammar for this advanced stone tool-making process requires rules that have to take into account some of the previous steps that the tool-maker took as well as the immediate state of the tool. This requirement also differentiates transformational grammars for human language from other "simpler" grammars (Chomsky, 1964).

The psychological basis of advanced hominid tool-making techniques and the syntactic component of human language thus may derive from similar biological sources. Both "grammars" may have been present for at least 300,000 years. It is, in fact, impossible to teach present day humans how to make these complex stone tools without explaining the steps. Simple imitation will not suffice. Even with the aid of human language it takes many months to learn the Levalloisian tool-making techniques (Washburn, 1969). The study of the play activity of rhesus monkeys (Reynolds, 1972) suggests that simpler grammars (phrase structure grammars) that don't require the "memory" of a transformational grammar, may describe these activities. The many studies of sign language and symbol communication in chimpanzees, e.g., (Gardner and Gardner, 1968; Fouts, 1973; Premack, 1972) also indicate that non-human primates have at least some of the syntactic and cognitive aspects of human language. It is clear that on the syntactic and semantic levels of language the distinction between human and non-human is not "all or nothing."

Human Speech and Animal Communication

It is at present impossible to specifically identify and compare the neural mechanisms that are the biological correlates of syntactic and semantic ability in humans and non-humans. We have many insights on the neurological levels of syntactic and semantic ability in humans but we still lack the detailed knowledge of neural function that would permit us, for example, to dissect the brain of a chimpanzee and identify a structure that was the biological correlate of some aspect of the animal's syntactic or semantic ability. We are in a somewhat better position with respect to the animal's phonetic ability. The anatomical and physiological basis of human speech has been known since the time of Johannes Müller (1848). In recent years our knowledge of the physiology of speech production has become quantified (Fant, 1960; Stevens and House, 1955). The development of the "Source-Filter" theory of speech production and the use of digital computers allows us to determine many of the anatomical and physiologic constraints of vocal communication in various species. Neurophysiologic techniques that are not appropriate in the study of humans correspondingly have increased our knowledge of the neural structures that various non-human species use to perceive their vocal communications. These new techniques have yielded new insights on the evolution of vocal communication. They demonstrate that there is a biological "match" between the neural mechanisms that animals use to perceive the sounds that they use in communication, and the anatomy of the sound producing mechanisms of these animals. They further suggest the gradual elaboration of these matched mechanisms in various species and the concurrent evolution òf the total communication system or "language."

The Source-filter Theory of Speech Production

The source-filter theory of speech production was developed from the studies of the supralaryngeal vocal tract of the late 18th century. In 1779

Kratzenstein constructed a set of tubes that he supposed were similar to the shape of the human vocal tract during the production of the vowels of Russian. The Academy of Sciencies of St. Petersburg had offered its annual prize for explaining the physiological differences between the five vowels that occur in Russian. Kratzenstein (1780) used these tubes to filter the output of vibrating reeds and thereby "explained" the physiological differences that differentiated these vowels. In 1791 Von Kempelen demonstrated his speech synthesizing machine. The relationship between the sounds of speech and the supralaryngeal vocal tract is analagous to the pipes of an organ and musical notes. In a pipe organ the length and shape (whether the pipe is open at both ends or closed at one end) of each pipe determines the musical quality of the note produced by that pipe. The organ pipes act as acoustic filters that are interposed between the common source of sound that can excite any particular pipe and the listener's ear. When we play a pipe organ we connect different pipes to the source. The production of human speech involves changing the shape and length of a "plastic" pipe, the airways of the human supralaryngeal vocal tract, as we talk. It would, in principle, be possible to make a pipe organ that had a single plastic pipe whose shape would change through the action of electrically controlled motors that distended or contracted the pipe. If we constructed such a pipe organ we'd have a closer mechanical analog to the human supralaryngeal vocal tract.

During the production of human speech the shape of the supralaryngeal vocal tract continually changes. The supralaryngeal airway always acts as an acoustic filter, suppressing the transfer of sound energy at certain frequencies, letting maximum energy through at other frequencies. The frequencies at which local energy maxima may pass through the supralaryngeal air passages are called *formant* frequencies. The formant frequencies are determined by the damped resonances of the supralaryngeal vocal tract which acts as an acoustic filter. Vowels like [a], [i],[æ], [ʌ] etc., owe their phonetic quality to their different formant frequencies.

Electrophysiologic and Comparative Studies

Electrophysiological techniques that can not be used in experiments with humans have isolated neural mechanisms in animals that respond to signals that are of interest to the animals. These signals include the vocal calls of the animals in question. Even simple animals like crickets appear to have neural units that code information about the rhythmic elements of their mating songs (Hoy and Paul, 1973). Similar results have been obtained in the squirrel monkey (*Saimiri sciureus*). Wollberg and Newman (1972) recorded the electrical activity of single cells in the auditory cortex of awake monkeys during the presentation of recorded monkey vocalizations and other acoustic signals. The electrophysiological techniques of this experiment involved placing electrodes that could record the electrical discharges from 213 cells in the brains of different animals. Some cells responded to many of the calls that had complex acoustic properties. Other cells, however, responded to only a few calls. One cell responded with a high probability only to one specific signal, the "isolation peep" call of the monkey.

The experimental techniques that are necessary in these electrophysiological studies demand great care and great patience. Microelectrodes that can isolate the electrical signal from a single neuron must be prepared and accurately positioned. The electrical signals must be amplified and recorded. Most importantly, the experimenters must present the animals with a set of acoustic signals that explore the range of sounds they would encounter in their natural state. Demonstrating the presence of "neural mechanisms" matched to the constraints of the sound-producing systems of particular animals is therefore a difficult undertaking. The sound-producing possibilities and behavioral responses of most "higher" animals make comprehensive statements on the relationship between perception and production difficult. We can explore only part of the total system of signaling and behavior. However, "simpler" animals are useful in this respect because we can see the whole pattern of their behavior.

The behavioral experiments of Capranica (1965) and the electrophysiological experiments of Frishkopf and Goldstein (1963), for example, demonstrate that the auditory system of the bullfrog (*Rana catesbeiana*) has single units that are matched to the formant frequencies of the species-specific mating call. Bullfrogs are members of the class Amphibia. Frogs and toads compose the order Anura. They are the simplest living animals that produce sound by means of a laryngeal source and a supralaryngeal vocal tract (Stuart, 1958). The supralaryngeal vocal tract consists of a mouth, a pharynx, and a vocal sac that opens into the floor of the mouth in the male. Vocalizations are produced in the same manner as in primates; the vocal folds of the larynx open and close rapidly, emitting "puffs" of air into the supralaryngeal vocal tract, which acts as an acoustic filter. Frogs can make a number of different calls (Bogert, 1960), including mating calls, release calls, territorial calls that serve as warnings to intruding frogs, rain calls, distress calls, and warning calls. The different calls have distinct acoustic properties, and there are obvious differences in the manner in which frogs produce some calls. For example, the distress call is made with the frog's mouth wide open, whereas all other calls are made with the mouth closed. The articulatory distinctions that underlie the other calls are not as obvious. Capranica (1965) has, however, analyzed the acoustic properties of the bullfrog mating call in detail.

The mating call of the bullfrog consists of a series of croaks. The duration of a croak varies from 0.6 to 1.5 sec and the interval between croaks varies from 0.5 to 1.0 sec. The fundamental frequency of the bullfrog croak is about 100 Hz. The formant frequencies of the croak are about 0.2 and 1.4

kHz. Capranica generated synthetic frog croaks by means of a POVO speech synthesizer (Stevens et al., 1955), a fixed speech synthesizer designed to produce human vowels that serves equally well for the synthesis of bullfrog croaks. In a behavioral experiment Capranica showed that bullfrogs responded to synthesized croaks so long as there were energy concentrations at either or both of these frequencies. The presence of acoustic energy at other frequencies inhibited the bullfrogs' responses. (The bullfrogs' responses consisted of joining in a croak chorus).

Frishkopf and Goldstein (1963), in their electrophysiological study of the bullfrog's auditory system, found two types of auditory units. They found cells in units in the eighth cranial nerve of the anesthetized bullfrog that had maximum sensitivity to frequencies between 1.0 and 2.0 kHz and other units that had maximum sensitivity to frequencies between 0.2 and 0.7 kHz. However, the units that responded to the lower frequency range were inhibited by appropriate acoustic signals. Maximum response occurred when the two units responded to time-locked pulse trains at rates of 50 and 100 pulses per second that had energy concentrations at, or near, the formant frequencies of bullfrog mating calls. Adding acoustic energy between the two formant frequencies at 0.5 kHz inhibited the responses of the low-frequency single units.

The electrophysiological, behavioral, and acoustic data all complement each other. Bullfrogs have auditory mechanisms that are structured to specifically respond to the bullfrog mating call. Bullfrogs don't respond to any sort of acoustic signal as though it were a mating call; they respond to particular calls that have the acoustic properties of those that can be made only by male bullfrogs, and they have neural mechanisms structured in terms of the species-specific constraints of the bullfrog sound-producing mechanism. Capranica tested his bullfrogs with the mating calls of 34 other species of frog, and they responded only to bullfrog calls, ignoring all others. The croaks have to have energy concentrations equivalent to those that would be produced by both formant frequencies of the bullfrogs' supralaryngeal vocal tract. The stimuli furthermore have to have the appropriate fundamental frequency.

The bullfrog has one of the simplest forms of sound-making system that can be characterized by the source-filter theory of sound production. Its perceptual apparatus is demonstrably structured in terms of the constraints of its sound-producing apparatus and the acoustic parameters of the source-filter theory, the fundamental frequency and formant frequencies. The neural property detectors that appear to be involved in the perception of human speech are more complex insofar as human speech involves a greater variety of sounds.

The Evolution of Human Speech

The same sources of data that are useful for the evolution of syntactic and semantic ability are also relevant with regard to the evolution of human speech. We can, however, be somewhat less speculative concerning the evolution of speech since the biological bases are somewhat more accessible. It's obvious that humans talk, animals don't; why? People of many different cultures and different times have tried to answer this question. Before the general diffusion of the theory of evolution with Charles Darwin's (1859) *On the Origin of Species,* one explanation of the apparent "uniqueness" of human speech was that it was one of the endowments to *Homo sapiens* from a higher diety. The presence of human language and speech indeed has been taken as an outward sign that demonstrates the existence of the soul. Descartes claimed that the presence of speech in humans and its absence in apes showed that humans had a soul and that apes lacked a soul. La Mettrie (1749) took this argument so seriously that he proposed that apes be taught to talk. This demonstration if successful would then in La Mettrie's view make the ape, "a perfect little gentleman". Attempts to teach apes to talk have persisted until recent years but they have always been unsuccessful (Kellogg, 1968). The lack of success involves the source-filter theory of speech production. Although the source-filter theory of speech production was developed in the early years of the nineteenth century, many people still don't know how human speech is produced. The common view is that speech is produced by the larynx. Since the larynges of chimpanzees and humans are not that different, the usual view since the first anatomical studies of chimpanzees have been that they could speak if they had the neural mechanisms that would allow them to control their tongues, larynx, lips, etc. There are differences between the larynges of chimpanzees and humans (Kelemen, 1948, 1969) but they would affect the chimpanzee's ability to sing or his vocal quality rather than speech. Chimpanzees and other non-human primates do not have a supralaryngeal vocal tract that would allow them to produce the full range of sounds of human speech. The study of the differences between the human and non-human supralaryngeal vocal tract has provided new insights on both the development of speech in human infants and the probable evolution of human speech and its interrelation with human linguistic ability.

Acoustic Analysis of Primate Vocalization.

In Figure 1. a sound spectrogram of a vocalization that was made by a gorilla is presented. It's useful to start with this gorilla vocalization since it shows some of the general characteristics of non-human primate vocalizations. The spectrogram was made with the normal 300 Hz bandwidth analyzing filter on the Sound Spectrograph. The fundamental frequency of phonation of this gorilla vocalization is about 100 Hz which can be determined from the spacing of the vertical striations on the spectrogram. The dark bands on the spectrogram thus reflect the formant frequencies of the gorilla vocalization. Note that the formant frequencies occur at approximately 500, 1500, and 2400 Hz. The sound thus approximates the formant frequencies of the human vowel / ə / (Fant, 1960). The spectrogram in Figure 1. shows that the fundamental frequency of phonation is irregular and that breathy excitation also occurs but the transfer function of the gorilla's supralaryngeal vocal tract configuration remains that of the vowel [ə]. Acoustic analyses of the vocalizations of non-human primates show that they produce cries that can be differentiated in terms of phonetic features (Lieberman, 1968, 1975). Chimpanzee cries, for example, may be produced with: periodic or breathy phonation, high or low fundamental frequency, continuous or interruped phonation, and rising or falling formant transitions (Lieberman, 1975). Animals like gelada baboon may even be producing formant transitions that are analagous to those that occur in the human vowel sequences [æ] to [I]. The only sounds that are not evident in the acoustic analysis of the vocalizations of non-human primates are formant frequency patterns like those that specify the vowels [i], [u] or [a] or velar consonants like [g] and [k]. The acoustic analysis of the cries of human newborns also reveals similar deficits (Lieberman et. al., 1972).

Figure1. Sound spectrogram of a gorilla vocalization. Note the relatively steady formant frequencies which appear as horizontal "bars" in this wide-bandwidth spectrogram. The sound approximates the human vowel [ə]. The irregular vertical striations reflect the fundamental frequency of phonation which is irregular and "hoarse" sounding.

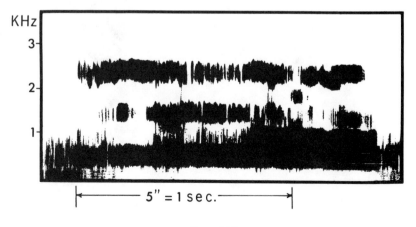

Gorilla

Computer modelling techniques that are the modern analogs of Von Kempelen's mechanical models have been used to establish the constraints that the anatomy of the supralaryngeal vocal tract may impose on the phonetic repertoires of these animals. In Figure 2 photographs of casts of the air passages of supralaryngeal vocal tracts of chimpanzee, human newborn, and human adult are shown together. The casts were made from cadavers following the technique described in Lieberman and Crelin (1971). In Figure 3 a midsagittal section of the chimpanzee from whom the supralaryngeal cast of Figure 2 was obtained is shown. Note the differences between the ape and adult newborn supralaryngeal vocal tract. The tongue in the chimpanzee is long and thin and forms the lower boundary of the oral cavity, whereas in humans it is thicker and shorter and forms both the lower boundary of the oral cavity and the anterior boundary of the pharynx. The larynx in the chimpanzee is sited higher than is the case in adult humans and opens almost directly into the oral cavity. The non-human pharynx lies behind the larynx and does not form part of the direct airway from the larynx to the lips.

Figure 2. Air passages of the supralaryngeal vocal tracts of human newborn, chimpanzee and adult human. The similarities between the human newborn and chimpanzee are apparent. Note the absence of the "bend" of the adult human vocal tract in these forms.

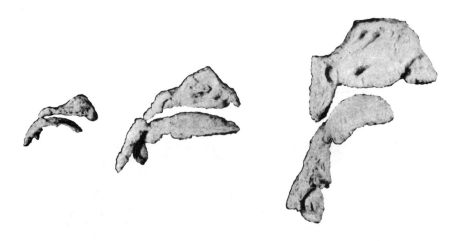

Figure 3. Midsagittal section of chimpanzee showing the supralaryngeal vocal tract. (after Lieberman, 1975)

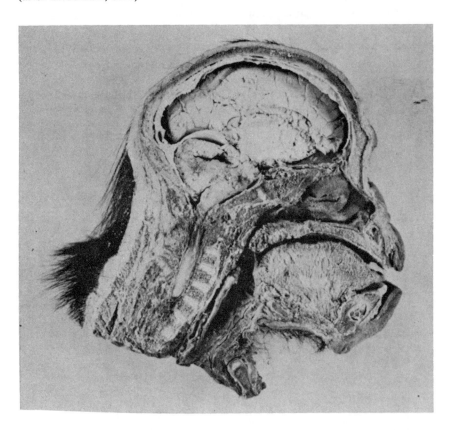

The supralaryngeal vocal tract of newborn humans is essentially the same as that of the adult chimpanzee. Since the transfer function of the supralaryngeal vocal tract is determined by the shape and size of the air passages, the total inventory of possible formant frequency patterns can be determined in principle, once we know the total range of vocal tract configurations. Cineradiographic data derived from newborn infants (Truby et. al., 1963) can be used to determine the total range of vocal tract configurations for newborns and pongids. In Figure 4 area functions that were used to control a distributed constant vocal tract analog are plotted. The area functions are the best approximations of the chimpanzee vocal tract for the vowels [i], [u], and [a]. These vowels are produced in human speech by shifting the body of the tongue up and down and frontwards and backwards. The pharynx is expanded in the sound [i] and the oral cavity constricted by shifting the tongue body forwards and upwards. The oral cavity is expanded and the pharynx contracted in the production of [a] by shifting the tongue downwards and backwards. The right angle bend of the adult human supralaryngeal vocal tract makes it possible to effect the abrupt 10 to 1 discontinuities in the area function of the supralaryngeal vocal tract that are necessary to produce these vowels. These vowels can only be produced by means of abrupt area function discontinuities (Stevens and House, 1955).

Figure 4. Area functions for the best approximations to the human vowels [i], [u] and [a] of a chimpanzee supralaryngeal vocal tract. The area functions were used to control a computer model of the supralaryngeal vocal tract that calculated the formant frequency patterns that particular vocal tract area functions would generate. This made it possible to determine the constraints of the chimpanzee vocal tract anatomy on vowel production. (after Lieberman et. al., 1972a)

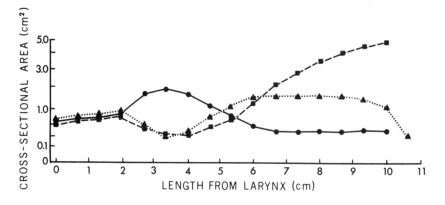

/i/ ●—●			/a/ ■--■			/u/ ▲····▲		
Formant	Freq.	Freq./1.7	Formant	Freq.	Freq./1.7	Formant	Freq.	Freq./1.7
1	610	360	1	1220	720	1	830	490
2	3400	2000	2	2550	1500	2	1800	1060
3	4420	2600	3	5070	2980	3	4080	2390

The supralaryngeal vocal tract of the chimpanzee lacks the right angle bend of the human vocal tract. It thus can not generate extreme discontinuities. The adult human supralaryngeal vocal tract is inherently a "two-tube" system that is well adapted for the production of the shapes that are necessary to produce these quantal vowels. The single tube vocal tract of the chimpanzee can be perturbed towards these shapes but it inherently can not produce abrupt midpoint discontinuities. The mechanical properties of the tissue of the tongue would prevent it from generating in a single tube system the abrupt area function changes that are necessary to produce these sounds. The calculated formant frequencies of the chimpanzee vocal tract perturbed towards these vowels show that the chimpanzee and newborn human infant supralaryngeal vocal tracts inherently can not produce these sounds. The absence of these sounds in the phonetic repertories of non-human primates and newborn infants thus can be ascribed to the constraints of their supralaryngeal vocal tracts, as well as to the possible lack of neural control of their vocal apparatus.

These limitations on the phonetic repertoires of non-human primates and newborn humans might, at first, seem trivial. There is, however, a selective advantage to having the sounds [i] and [u] in one's phonetic repertoire. Psychoacoustic studies (Peterson and Barney, 1952; Fairbanks and Grubb, 1961) show that these vowels are more correctly identified 5 to 30 percent of the time in controlled listening tests. Reconstructions of the supralaryngeal vocal tracts of fossil hominids like the La Chapelle-aux-Saints specimen of "classic" Neandertal man show that his vocal tract was probably similar to that of a huge human newborn infant (Lieberman and Crelin, 1971; Lieberman, 1973, 1975, 1976). The details of this reconstruction and similar reconstructions of the Australopithecine vocal tract are based on skeletal similarities that exist between the fossil skulls and those of human newborns and non-human primates. These reconstructions indicate that they probably had what I shall call a "standard plan" supralaryngeal airway. Victor Negus (1949) in his comprehensive and thorough comparative studies of the anatomy and physiology of the larynx really introduced this concept, though he did not use the words "standard plan". Negus noted that there is a supralaryngeal vocal tract that typically occurs in terrestrial mammals. The larynx is positioned high, close to the base of the skull and the tongue lies almost entirely within the oral cavity. The pharynx lies behind the entrance to the larynx. This supralaryngeal vocal tract, which is in a sense, the "standard plan" for the upper airways of the respiratory system, is typical of all normal non-human primates and newborn humans. The "single tube" non-human vocal tract (the chimpanzee vocal tract that we discussed is typical) is better adapted to breathing, swallowing and chewing than the adult human vocal tract. It is not as well adapted to vocal communication.

In Figure 5 the supralaryngeal oral and pharyngeal airways of modern *Homo sapiens* are shown together with the corresponding reconstructed airways of the La Chapelle-aux-Saints classic Neandertal fossil. This reconstructed vocal tract is essentially an enlarged version of the newborn human supralaryngeal vocal tract. When it is modelled it can not produce "useful" sounds like [i] and [u] (Lieberman and Crelin, 1971; Lieberman et. al., 1972a). In Figure 6 the reconstructed oral and pharyngeal airways of the Es Skhul V fossil are shown (Lieberman, 1973). The reconstructed supralaryngeal vocal tract of Skhul V is modern and would have allowed the production of any of the sounds of human speech including the vowels /i/ and /u/. Fossil hominids like Es Skhul V and classic Neandertal man lived during approximately the same period of time, about 70,000 to 40,000 years be-

Figure 5. The reconstructed supralaryngeal oral and pharyngeal airways of the La Chapelle-aux-Saints classic Neandertal fossil (right) compared with the corresponding airways of an adult human. Note the right angle bend in the human vocal tract. The pharynx exits behind the larynx in the Neandertal airway system. In the adult human vocal tract the larynx is positioned below the pharynx which forms part of the direct airway out from the larynx. The human vocal tract thus is a "two tube" system in which the pharynx and oral cavity can have radically different cross-sectional areas.

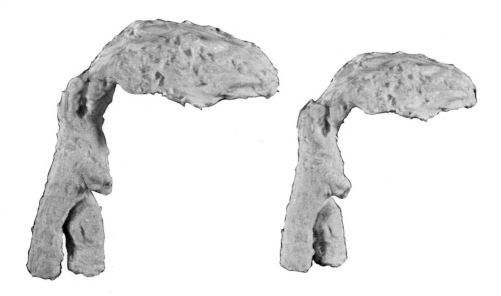

Figure 6. The reconstructed pharynx and oral cavity of the Es Skhul fossil (left) and an adult human (right). Note that the two systems are quite similar. The nasal cavities have been omitted in this figure.

fore the present. The remains that transmit whatever we know of their culture show that these hominids all had complex, similar cultures. There is evidence, for example, of ritual burials, care of the infirm and a complex stone tool tradition. It is apparent that all of these hominids must have been using some form of language. It is, for example, almost impossible to learn how to make the stone tools that these people made unless someone first explains the technique to you and carefully guides your first attempts. Communication was therefore an important element in the social life of these hominids. Quite obviously natural selection operated to favor the retention of hominids who had the anatomical adaptions that made "better" speech signals possible. The small, but effective, increase in phonetic efficiency that follows from the presence of sounds like [i] and [u] appears to have been a factor in the evolution of modern *Homo sapiens*. Language would obviously be possible if these sounds were absent, but hominid vocal communication would not be as effective. Studies of the possible phonetic abilities of fossil hominids thus provide a demonstration of the continuity of evolution with respect to language. Classic Neandertal man, for example, appears to have had advanced linguistic abilities that differed slightly from modern *Homo sapiens* in the direction of the more primitive vocal communications system that is typical of living non-human primates. Other hominids like the Broken Hill fossil may have had supralaryngeal vocal tracts that gave them phonetic repertoires that are intermediate between those of the "standard plan" vocal tract and the adult-like human vocal tract (Lieberman, 1975, 1976). The most conservative hypothesis that fits the data is that of gradual evolution of the human supralaryngeal vocal tract. Disputes concerning particular fossil's phonetic abilities (Lieberman and Crelin, 1971; Falk, 1975; Le May, 1975; Lieberman, 1976) can only involve the *stage* in hominid evolution at which phonetic ability comparable to that of modern *Homo sapiens* evolved. *Australopithecus africanus*, for example, has almost the same skull base as present day apes and probably had a virtually identical supralaryngeal vocal tract. Hominids *had* to evolve a specialized vocal tract that diverged from the "standard plan" supralaryngeal airways. Fossils like Broken Hill indicate that the process started at a point in time before the disappearance of Neandertal fossils like La Chapelle-aux-Saints. We can be certain that this is the case because there is not enough space between the foramen magnum and palate of the Broken Hill fossil for the high laryngeal position that characterizes the non-human supralaryngeal vocal tract (Lieberman, 1976). The Neandertal lineage may represent a population that retained the "older" non-human supralaryngeal vocal tract anatomy into a comparatively recent period. Even if late Neandertal populations had vocal tracts like adult humans there would have to be earlier hominids who represented intermediate stages between Australopithecines and forms like Broken Hill which is itself an intermediate stage with respect to fossils like Es Skhul V.

Neural Property Detectors in Humans

We've discussed the presence of neural mechanisms that are "matched" to the constraints of vocal communication in many non-human animals. Indirect evidence suggests that similar mechanisms exist in humans (Lieberman, 1970, 1976). Eimas, for example, has demonstrated that 1 to 4 month old human infants can perceive the distinctions of phonation onset that differentiate stop consonants like [b] versus [p] at the same 20 msec "categorical boundary" that adult human listeners use (Eimas, et. al., 1971). It is unlikely that the infants "learn" to make these distinctions; their behavior must reflect the presence of an "innate" perceptual mechanism. In other words, human beings are born with the neural mechanisms that are necessary for the perception of this phonetic distinction. Linguists have for many years supposed that human linguistic ability involves the presence of innate neural mechanisms. Chomsky (1968), for example, stresses the role of innate "competence" in his transformational theory. The evidence derived from the perception of speech is consistent with this view. Special neural mechanisms would account for the perception of speech and speech-like sounds by humans. The special neural mechanisms that are involved in speech perception, however, may not all be species-specific. Although the neural mechanisms that humans use to perceive speech may be more complex than similar mechanisms present in other species, it is apparent that many animals can also perceive and discriminate the sounds of human speech. Monkeys, for example, can be trained to perceive the formant transitions that differentiate the syllables [da] and [ba] (Sinnott, 1974) or the syllables [dae], [bae] and [gae] (Morse and Snowden, 1975). The ability to perceive human speech sounds is not even restricted to primates. Chinchillas (*Chinchilla laniger*) have been trained to discriminate the sounds [a] versus [i] (Burdick and Miller, 1975) and the stop sounds [d] and [t] (Kuhl and Miller, 1975). Chinchillas being rodents are among the "simplest" mammals yet they can discriminate some of the sounds of human speech. The neural mechanisms that are involved in the perception of speech thus probably have a long evolutionary history. Humans probably do have some "special" species-specific neural mechanisms that at least facilitate the perception of speech. It would be surprising if this were not so since even frogs have species-specific mechanisms that shape their responses to the acoustic signals that they produce. However, the species-specific perceptual mechanisms that underlie human speech communication must be related to analogous mechanisms that exist in other animals.

In conclusion, a biological perspective on the evolution of language seems to be a promising approach. It doesn't support the view that humans are the result of any "special" evolutionary "forces" but it may provide some insights on how we came to be and what we are.

References

Bogert, C. M. (1960) "The Influence of Sound on Behavior of Amphibians and Reptiles," in *Animal Sounds and Communication,* W. E. Lanyon and W. N. Tavolga eds., Amer. Instit. of Biological Sciences.

Bordes, F. (1968) *The Old Stone Age,* World University Library, McGraw-Hill.

Bordes, F. (1972) *A Tale of Two Caves,* Harper and Row.

Burdick, C. K. and Miller, J. D. (1975) Speech Perception by the Chinchilla: Discrimination of Sustained /a/ and /i/, *J. Acoust. Soc. Am., 58,* 415-427.

Capranica, R. R. (1965) *The Evoked Vocal Response of the bullfrog, MIT Press.*

Chomsky, N. (1965) *Aspects of the Theory of Syntax,* MIT Press.

Chomsky, N. (1968) *Language and Mind,* Harcourt Brace Javauovich.

Darwin, C. (1859) On the Origin of Species (facsimile edition), Antheneum.

Eimas, P. D., Siqueland, E. R., Jusczyk, P. and Vigorito, J. (1971) "Speech Perception in Infants," *Science, 171,* 303-306.

Falk, D. (1975) "Comparative Anatomy of the Larynx in Man and the Chimpanzee: Implications for Language in Neanderthal," *Amer. J. Physical Anthropology, 43,* 123-132.

Fant, G. (1960) *Acoustic Theory of Speech Production,* Mouton.

Fouts, R. S. (1973) Acquisition and testing of gestural signs in Four Young Chimpanzees, *Science, 180,* 978-980.

Frishkopf, L. S. and Goldstein, M. H. Jr. (1963) "Responses to Acoustic Stimuli from Single Units in the Eight Nerve of the Bullfrog, *J. Acoust. Soc. Am., 35,* 1219-1228.

Gardner, R. A. and B. T. Gardner (1969) Teaching Sign Language to a Chimpanzee, *Science, 165,* 664-672.

Hoy, R. R. and Paul, R. C. (1973) "Genetic Control of Song Specificity in Crickets," *Science, 180,* 82-83.

Huxley, T. H. (1863) *Evidence as to Man's Place in Nature,* Williams and Norgate.

Keleman, G. (1948) The Anatomical Basis of Phonation in the Chimpanzee, *J. Morphol. 82,* 229-256.

Kelemen, G. (1969) Anatomy of the Larynx and the Anatomical Basis of Vocal Performance, *Chimpanzee, 1,* 165-186.

Kellogg, W. N. (1968) Communication and Language in the Home Raised Chimpanzee, *Science, 162,* 423-427.

Kratzenstein, C. G. (1780) "Sur la naissance de la Formation des voyelles," *J. Phys. Chim. Hist. Nat. Arts, 21,* (1782) 358-381 (translated from *Acta Acad. Petrograd.* 1780)

Kuhl, Patricia K. and Miller, James D., (1975) "Speech Perception by the Chinchilla: Voiced-Voiceless Distinction in Alveolar Plosive Consonants," *Science, 190,* 69-72.

La Mettrie, J. O. (1747) *De l'homme Machine,* ed. A. Vartanian (critical edition 1960) Princeton University Press.

Le May, M. (1975) "The Language Capability of Neanderthal Man," *Am. J. Phys. Anthrop., 42,* 9-14.

Lenneberg, E. H. (1967) *Biological Foundations of Language,* Wiley.

Lieberman, P. (1968) Primate Vocalizations and Human Linguistic Ability, *J. Acoust. Soc. Am., 44,* 1574-1584.

Lieberman, P. (1970) "Towards a Unified Phonetic Theory" *Linguistic Inquiry, 1,* 307-322.

Lieberman, P. (1973) "On the Evolution of Human Language: A Unified View," *Cognition, 2,* 59-94.

Lieberman, Philip (1975) *On the Origins of Language: An Introduction to the Evolution of Human Speech,* MacMillan, N. Y.

Lieberman, P. (1976) Phonetic Features and Physiology: A Reappraisal, *J. of Phonetics, 4,* 91-112.

Lieberman, P. (1976) Interactive Models for Evolution: Neural Mechanisms, Anatomy and Behavior. *Proceedings of Conference on Origin and Evolution of Language and Speech.* New York Academy of Sciences.

Lieberman. P. (1976) Structural Harmony and Neandertal Speech: A reply to Le May. *Am. J. of Physical Anthropology.* 45. 493-496.

Lieberman, P. and Crelin, E. S. (1971) "On the Speech of Neanderthal Man," *Linguistic Inquiry, 2,* 203-222.

Lieberman, P., Harris, K. S., Wolff, P., and Russell, L. H. (1972) "Newborn Infant Cry and Nonhuman Primate Vocalizations," *J. Speech and Hearing Res., 14,* 718-727.

Lieberman, P., Crelin, E. S. and Klatt, D. H. (1972) "Phonetic Ability and Related Anatomy of the Newborn, Adult Human, Neanderthal Man, and the Chimpanzee," *Amer. Anthropologist, 74,* 287-307.

Marshack, A. (1972) *The Roots of Civilization. The Cognitive Beginnings of Man's First Art, Symbol, and Notation,* McGraw-Hill.

Morse, P. A. and Snowden, C. T. (1975) An Investigation of Categorical Speech Discrimination by Rhesus Monkeys, *Percept. Psychophys. 17,* 9-16.

Müller, J. (1848) *The Physiology of the Senses, Voice and Muscular Motion with the Mental Faculties, Trans. W. Baly, Walton and Maberly.*

Negus, V. E. *(1949) The Comparative Anatomy and Physiology of the Larynx,* Hafner.

Premack, D. (1972) Language in Chimpanzee? *Science, 172,* 808-822.

Reynolds, P. C. (1972) Play, Language and Human Evolution, Paper Presented at 1972 Meeting of the American Association for the Advancement of Science, Washington, D. C.

Sarich, V. M. (1974) Just How Old is the Hominid Line? *Yearbook of Physical Anthropology, 1973,* American Assoc. of Physical Anthropologists, Washington, D. C.

Sinnott, J. M. (1974) A Comparison of Speech Sound Discrimination in Humans and Monkeys, Ph.D. Dissertation, Univ. of Michigan, Ann Arbor, Mi. (78 pp.)

Stevens, K. N., Bastide, R. P. and Smith, C. P. (1955) "Electrical Synthesizer of Continuous Speech," *J. Acoust. Soc. Am., 27,* 207.

Stevens, K. N. and House, A. S. (1955) "Development of a Quantitiative Description of Vowel Articulation," *J. Acoust. Soc. Am., 27,* 484-493.

Stuart, R. R. (1958) *The Anatomy of the Bullfrog,* Denoyer-Geppert.

Truby, H. M., Bosma, J. F., and Lind, J. (1965) *Newborn Infant Cry,* Almquist and Wiksell.

Von Kempelen, W. R. (1791) *Mechanismus der menschlichen Sprache nebst der Beschreibung seiner sprechenden Maschine,* J. B. Degen.

Washburn, S. L. (1969) The Evolution of Human Behavior, in *The Uniqueness of Man,* ed. J. D. Roslansky, North-Holland.

Wollberg, Z. and Newman, J. D. (1972) "Auditory Cortex of Squirrel Monkey: Response Patterns of Single Cells to Species-Specific Vocalizations;" *Science, 175,* 212-214.

Topic Index

Abstractness, 10-11, 34-40
Algonquian, 52
  Delaware, 37
  Proto-Algonquian, 36-37
Alpha-convention, 4
Alternation condition, weak and strong,
  35, 40
Ambiguity properties, 87
Analogical change, 40-41, *see also*
    Linguistic change
Analysis-by-synthesis, 183
Animal communication, electrophysiologic
  studies, 381-383
Anywhere rules, 92
Aphasia
  bilingual, 207
  neurological and linguistic analysis of,
    212-217
  types of, 212-215
Arabic, Egyptian, 269, 272-273, 274, 280,
  291, 293, 296, 315
Araucanian, 347
Attention, 184-185
Australian languages, 47
Automata, hierarchy of, 86-87

Babbling, 175-176, 204, 314-315
Bartholomae's law, 52
Bilingualism, 273-274, 275-276, 279-281
Borrowing, 35
Brain function, manipulative studies of,
  218-236
Bulgarian, 269, 275, 283, 293

Canonical forms, constraints on, 38-40
Case grammar, 105-107, 301
Causal selection network (CSN), 99-102
Chinese, Mandarin, 270
Cinematography, ordinary and radio-
  graphic, 167-168
Closure properties, 87
Cognition, 275-278, 300, 311-312, 313-315
Commonsense algorithm (CSA) project,
  98-99
Competence/performance, 144-147,
  353-354
Computational linguistics, 97-134
Conditioning factors, grammatical *versus*
  non-grammmatical, 43-45
Congruence, principle of, 256-257
Consonant, long, 19-20
  production and perception of, 185-186
Context, 119-122, 274
Czech, 269, 281, 284

Danish, 268
Decidability, 87
Deep structure, 248
  assumption, 256
  constraints on, 92

Delaware, *see* Algonquian, Delaware
Derivational constraints, 92
Derivational theory of complexity (DTC),
  152, 248, 249, 253-255
Dichotic listening, 233-236
Distinctive features, 2, 186-188
Distinctiveness, 59
Dutch, 268

Electrical stimulation of the brain (ESB),
  226-228
Electromyography (EMG), 167, 170, 173,
  232-233
English, 6, 11-14, 34, 44, 46, 59, 60, 176, 177,
  179, 272, 275, 276-278, 281-282, 283,
  288, 289, 290, 291, 294-295, 296, 297,
  298, 299, 300
  Black, 42, 359-360
  Cockney, 48, 343
  Middle, 42, 341-342
Evaluation criterion, *see* Simplicity metric
Event-related potentials (ERP), speech pro-
  duction, 228-229
  speech recognition, 229-230
  visual processing, 230-231
Evolution, language, 377-395
  speech, 384 ff.
  theory, 377-378
Exceptions, 53-54
Experimental phonetics, *see* Phonetics,
  experimental
Experimentation, 151-154
Explanation, 180

False starts, 175, 202-203
Faroese, 48, 177-178
Feeding and bleeding relations, 41-42, 46,
  47-49, 50-51
Field methods, 345-346
Finnish, 7-8, 54, 176, 270, 272, 275, 282,
  283, 288-289, 291
Fixing belief, methods of, 135-136
Foreigner talk, 318-319
Formal contexts, 328-335
Formal operations stage, 325-326
Free variation, 346-347
French, 268, 283, 291

Garo, 270, 288
Generation, 122-124
Generative capacity, weak and strong, 87,
  89-90
Generative phonology, *see* Phonology,
  generative
Genitive, 273, 274
Georgian, 269, 273
German, 12, 20-21, 41-42, 59-60, 268, 275,
  282, 283, 289-290
  Swiss, 51
Germanic, 18, 54

Glottal features, 188
Grammars, 3-4
  hierarchy of, 85-87
Grammaticality, 355
  degree of, 151, 248
  versus acceptability, 349-353
Great Vowel Shift, 342-344
Grimm's law, 14, 18-19, 23, 28, 180

Hawaiian, 39
Heard language, 332
Hebrew, 52-53, 178-179, 269, 275, 280
Historical linguistics, 33-61
  methods in, 340-344
  nature of data in, 340-341
Hungarian, 269, 272, 273-274, 275, 279-281,
  283, 284-285, 288, 293

Individual differences, 301
Informal contexts, 328-335
Intake, 332
Instrumental, 273
Interruption, avoidance of, 290-292
Iranian, 52
Italian, 268

Japanese, 270, 272

Katz-Postal hypothesis, 65-66
Kitsai, 347-359
Korean, 270, 282

Language acquisition
  in adults, 318-319
  in children, *see* psycholinguistics,
    developmental
  rate and order, 271, 275, 276 ff., 301
  versus language learning, 317-318
Language and cognition, 379-380
Language functions, localization of, 208-212
Language pedagogy, *see* Second language
  acquisition
Laryngeals, 26
Latin, 24, 40-41, 53, 58
Latvian, 269, 272, 281, 283, 284, 292
Left-to-right iteration, 7-9
Levels of investigation, 147-149
Lexical representation, 75-76
Linguistic change, 33-61, 360, 365-366
Locative, 273-274, 275, 276, 279-282,
  284-285, 293
Logical form, 75-76
Luo, 270, 272

Maori, 38-40, 60-61
Marked *versus* unmarked rule order, *see*
  Feeding and bleeding relations
Mathematical linguistics, 83-95
Maximum opposition, 182
Memory, sentence, 152-154, 259-261

Metatheory, linguistic, 63-82
Methodology, 135-157, 339-354
Minimal pair test, 345-346, 367-368
Model, 142-143
Modeling, fallacies of, 150
Monitor model, individual variation,
  322-323
  second language production, 319-335
Montague grammar, 73-74
Motor theory of speech perception, 181-183

Natural selection, 377-378
Navaho, 58-59
Negation, 272, 277
Neighborhood convention, 6
Neogrammarian hypothesis, 341-342
Neural property detectors, 393
Neurolinguistics, 207-246
Neurophysiology, 162-164
Neurosurgical techniques
  commissurotomy, 220-224
  frontal lobectomy, 219-220
  hemispherectomy, 224-225
  temporal lobectomy, 218-219
Neutralization, absolute, 35
Norwegian, 268

Observer's paradox, 357-358
Open- and closed-loop models, 170-176,
  180, 181-183, 203
Operating principles, 283, 285, 287-299
Overregularization, 295-297

Paradigm conditions, 40-45, 53
Passive, 293
Perceptual strategies, 251-253
Pharmacological deactivation, 225-226
Philosophy of science, 135-157
Phoneme, 168-169, 171, 203
Phoneme-monitoring latency, 255-256
Phonetics, acoustic, 159-160, 161
  experimental, 159-205
  impressionistic, 159
  neurophysiological, 159-160, 161-189
Phonology, derivational *versus* inflectional,
  58
  generative, 1-32
Phrase-structure grammar, context-free, 90
  context-sensitive, 90
  formalization of, 85-87
  inadequacies of, 83-84, 87-88
Plural, 61, 272, 273, 284, 301
  loss of, 42, 43
Polish, 269, 272, 282, 284, 288, 293
Post-comprehension performance, Clark's
  model of, 256-259, 265-266
Preadaptation, 378
Pre- *versus* post-nominal marking, 281-285
Primate vocalizations, acoustic analysis,
  384-392

Processing span, 285-287, 302
Prosody, 176-177, 179, 204-205
Psycholinguistics, developmental, 11,
    125-126, 267-316, 354
    experimental, 151-154, 247-266

Question, yes-no, 272

Recoverability, 89
Reference, 124-125
Reliability, 339
Rhythm, 176-177, 203
Romanian, 268
Rule, detail, 9
    late phonetic, 1-2
    morpheme-structure, 1
    opacity, 46-54
    phonological, 1 ff.
    reordering, see Feeding and bleeding
        relations; Rule, opacity
    transparency, 50
    variable, 42-43, 59, 60, 358-365, 363-364
Russian, 2, 4, 10, 14-16, 19-20, 21, 269, 272,
    273, 275, 281, 283, 288, 293, 296-297,
    298, 341

Samoan, 270, 275, 288, 299
Sanskrit, 5-6, 16-17
Sausurrian paradox, 345, 346, 348-349
Scientific method, 136-139
Second language acquisition, 317-338
Semantics, 63-82, 271-274, 276-278,
    278-279, 297-299
    in computational linguistics, 97-134
    generative, 68-73
    interpretive, 67-68, 72-73
Sense selection network (SSN), 102-104,
    106-107, 108-123, 126-131
Sentence processing, see Psycholinguistics,
    experimental
Serbo-Croatian, 269, 272, 273-274, 275,
    279-281, 284-285, 293, 298
Sets, recursive, 86, 89-91
    recursively enumerable, 86, 90-92
    regular, 86
Simplicity metric, 3, 4, 11, 33-34, 35, 41,
    46-47, 60, 301
Sloppy-identity deletion, 75-76
Slovenian, 269
Socio-economic factors, 315
Sociolinguistics, 339-375
Source filter theory, 380-381
Spanish, 268
Speech encoding, unit of, 168-180
Speech production, anatomy and physi-
    ology, 232-233
    event-related potentials, 228-229
    models of, 168-180
    see also, Open- and closed-loop models

Speech recognition, 169, 180-181
Split brain, see Commissurotomy
Stammbaum theory, see Wave versus
    Stammbaum theory
Stress, 11-14
Stuttering, 175, 202, 203
Surface structure, 248
    constraints on, 92
Swedish, 268
Syllable, 169-180, 202-204
Syntax, 63-82, 97, 105-107, 126-128

Tape recorder, 355
Temporal compensation, 175
Theory, 139-142
    construction and validation, 161-162
Tool making, grammar, 379-380
Transderivational constraints, 92
Transformational rules, filtering function
    of, 89-91
Tubatulabal, 2-3, 6-7, 8-9, 177
Tunica, 176
Turkish, 270, 282, 283, 288
Tzeltal, 270

Ultra-sonics, 167
Underlying forms, 23-27
Underlying relations, 17-20
    clear marking of, 292-295
Uniformitarian principle, 342, 368
Universal base hypothesis, 91-93
Universals, developmental, 276, 278, 282,
    283, 285, 287-299
    language-definitional, 271, 283
    strong linguistic, 271

Validity, 339-340, 353-354, 373
Variation, 346-347, 355-367, 374
Verb complexity hypothesis (VCH), 252
Verb-object relation, 272
Vernacular, 356 ff.
Verner's law, 29, 180
Vocal tract musculature, 163-167
Vocative, 272
Voicing, 160, 187-188
Vowel, length, 20-21
    production and perception of, 185-186

Wada test, see Pharmalogical deactivation
Wave versus Stammbaum theory, 344
Word order, 288-290, 315
Word senses, 97 ff.
    see also, Sense selection network (SSN)
    senses of "take", 104, 108-119
Writing systems, syllabic, 168, 203-204